REPORT OF THE
NATIONAL LIBRARIES COMMITTEE

Presented to Parliament by the Secretary of State for Education and Science
by Command of Her Majesty
June 1969

LONDON
HER MAJESTY'S STATIONERY OFFICE
£1 8s. 0d. net

Cmnd. 4028

This report is also available
in a microfiche edition,
price 15s. 0d.

Note: The estimated cost of preparing and publishing the Report is £26,523 of which £4,523 represents the estimated cost of printing and publication.

SBN 10 140280 5

260334

LIST OF MEMBERS

Dr. F. S. DAINTON, F.R.S. (Chairman), Vice-Chancellor, University of Nottingham.

Professor Sir ROY ALLEN, C.B.E., F.B.A., Professor of Statistics, London School of Economics
  (December, 1967 to July, 1968).

Mr. J. G. N. BROWN, C.B.E., Publisher, Oxford University Press.

Mr. H. J. HABAKKUK, F.R.Hist.S., F.B.A., Principal, Jesus College, Oxford
  (from July, 1968).

Sir BERNARD MILLER, Chairman, John Lewis Partnership.

Professor D. TALBOT RICE, C.B.E., F.S.A., Vice-Principal and Watson Gordon Professor of Fine Art, University of Edinburgh.

SECRETARIAT

Dr. N. B. W. THOMPSON, Department of Education and Science.

Mr. G. A. C. JONES, Department of Education and Science.

Mr. N. W. STUART, Department of Education and Science
  (May, 1968, to July, 1968).

Mr. R. C. PULFORD, Department of Education and Science
  (from August, 1968).

iii

To the Right Honourable Edward Short, M.P., Secretary of State for Education and Science.

27th March 1969

Dear Secretary of State,

Just a little more than a year ago your predecessor charged us with the examination of the various National Libraries, and, in particular, to consider whether these institutions should be brought into a unified framework. We now send you our unanimous report.

There are literally thousands of libraries in the United Kingdom which attempt to meet the needs of a very wide range of users who may work in educational institutions, industry, commerce, and the professions, or who use the libraries for their private purposes. A library may be funded privately, or by local or national government; its collection may be comprehensive in a narrow subject field, or merely representative over many subjects, or a mixture of both; and it may operate as a lending or a reference library, or, rarely, as both. In addition, there are many information services which show almost as great variety of ownership, subject coverage and customer pattern as do the libraries.

We early took the view that the National Libraries must be seen in relation to these other parts of the national information system. Many of the services of the National Libraries complement those of other libraries and, in this respect, they form an essential part of the complete spectrum of library and information services. We also identified various aspects of library and information activity where there was a need to co-ordinate the efforts of many different libraries and institutions, in order that the substantial total resources involved would be used in the best possible ways. Here an organisation administering the National Libraries has a different, but no less important function to perform. Thirdly, the National Libraries should be the apex of the library system, representing the best in current practice and pioneering new developments, as well as covering all subjects and giving the best possible services to users of all types.

We have tried to measure the present needs of users, and to estimate their future requirements in the light of the presumed continuing enormous growth rate of publication, and the probably continuing differences in ways in which workers in the humanities, social sciences, and experimental sciences seek and use information in printed or other form. The identification of need has enabled us to specify the functions which a National Library and Information System should discharge, either alone or in association with other institutions, and finally we have recommended administrative arrangements which, if accepted, would go a considerable way to enabling these objectives to be achieved.

All our recommendations are listed at the end of the report in the order in which they appear in the text. Because they are very numerous and not all of equal importance we have provided a preface containing a summary of the major recommendations. We hope that this arrangement will be helpful to readers.

We have received a great deal of evidence from many sources, much of which will be published separately after the report is issued. We are most grateful to all who have submitted evidence and for the interest which has been shown

iv

in our work by learned and professional societies, universities and colleges, industrial organisations and many individuals. Several individuals and organisations whose names are included in the list in Appendix A have, at our request, made special enquiries or prepared papers which were of great value to our deliberations. Above all we especially appreciate the co-operation and help which have at all times been accorded to us by the staffs of the libraries covered by our terms of reference. They not only contributed to the preparation of the main evidence, but also carried out additional research to obtain the supplementary information which we requested.

We are sorry to have to record that owing to ill health Professor Sir Roy Allen had to resign from the committee in June, 1968. His place was filled by Mr. Habakkuk.

Yours sincerely,

(*Chairman*) FRED DAINTON

JOHN BROWN

H. J. HABAKKUK

BERNARD MILLER

D. TALBOT RICE

(*Secretary*) NOEL B. W. THOMPSON

(*Assistant Secretary*) G. A. C. JONES

(*Assistant Secretary*) R. C. PULFORD

TABLE OF CONTENTS

APPENDICES   *Page*

LIST OF FIGURES

x

LIST OF ABBREVIATIONS

ACSP	Advisory Council on Scientific Policy
ACSTI	Advisory Committee for Scientific and Technical Information
ASLIB	Formerly the Association of Special Libraries and Information Bureaux—now Aslib
BLA	British Library of Art
BLPES	British Library of Political and Economic Science
BM	British Museum
BML	British Museum Library
BNB	British National Bibliography
BNBC	British National Book Centre
BUCOP	British Union Catalogue of Periodicals
CSPC	Central Science and Patent Collections
DES	Department of Education and Science
DM	Department of Manuscripts
DOPBM	Department of Oriental Printed Books and Manuscripts
DPB	Department of Printed Books
DPD	Department of Prints and Drawings
EIU	Economist Intelligence Unit
LA	Library Association
LAC	Library Advisory Council
LPL	Lyon Playfair Library
MARC	Machine Readable Catalogue
MEDLARS	Medical Literature Analysis and Retrieval System
NCL	National Central Library
NCRLC	National Committee on Regional Library Co-operation
NLA	National Libraries Authority
NLLST	National Lending Library for Science and Technology
NRL	National Reference Library
NRLSI	National Reference Library of Science and Invention
OSTI	Office for Scientific and Technical Information
POL	Patent Office Library
SCL	Scottish Central Library
SML	Science Museum Library
SOAS	School of Oriental and African Studies, University of London
TIL	Formerly Technical Information Library of the Ministry of Aviation: now applied to the Reports Centre of the Ministry of Technology
UGC	University Grants Committee

SUMMARY OF THE PRINCIPAL RECOMMENDATIONS

The National Libraries Authority

In order that the services and operations of the principal national library institutions may be adequately co-ordinated and that they may develop in the most effective ways, the administration of the British Museum Library (BML) [including the National Reference Library of Science and Invention (NRLSI)], the National Central Library (NCL), the National Lending Library for Science and Technology (NLLST), and the British National Bibliography (BNB) should become the responsibility of a new statutory and independent public body, to be known as the National Libraries Authority (NLA). The property and stock of these institutions should, with certain exceptions, be vested in the Authority, which should also assume full administrative responsibilities for certain functions relating to research, bibliographic activities and translations, now carried out by the Office for Scientific and Technical Information (OSTI) and by Aslib.

The Science Museum Library (SML) should not be administered by the NLA, but should be integrated with the Lyon Playfair Library to form the central library for the Imperial College of Science and Technology.

With the creation of the National Libraries Authority, the BML should become the National Reference Library (NRL), and the NRLSI should become the Central Science and Patent Collections (CSPC), a separately administered unit within the Authority.

Management Structure

Management policies of the NLA should be the corporate responsibility of a Board composed of a Chairman, Secretary, up to three other full-time members and up to three part-time members, all of whom should be appointed by the Secretary of State for Education and Science.

One of the full-time members should be appointed in consultation with the Minister of Technology.

The appointment of the part-time members should reflect the need to establish and maintain channels of communication between the Authority and other library and information systems, and the special position of the NRL.

The part-time members should normally hold office for three years, renewable once only, and they should be paid for their services.

The Heads of the national library institutions should not be members of the Management Board, but should together constitute an Executive Committee, chaired by the Chairman of the Management Board.

Associated with the Executive Committee would be a structure of sub-committees on which appropriate Board members and senior executives would serve together.

Advisory Bodies

An advisory council should be associated with each major library unit or service. The Head of the unit concerned should be an *ex officio* member of the relevant advisory council; the remaining membership should reflect the use that is made of its services.

In addition to an advisory council, the National Reference Library (NRL), as successor to the present BML, should also have a body of trustees, which should include some Trustees of the British Museum.

The Trustees of the NRL would be invested with that material to be housed in the NRL which it is possible to identify as having been privately donated or bequeathed in the past in trust to the Trustees of the British Museum. The National Libraries Authority should determine the particular uses to which trust funds and material would be put, but the Trustees should ensure that the Authority's decisions in these matters would always be in accord with the terms of the original bequests.

The Trustees of the NRL should be represented on that library's advisory council up to two fifths of the Council's membership; they should also be responsible for submitting a list of names to the Secretary of State from which he would appoint one part-time member of the Management Board.

Finance

The principles of accountable management should be applied to all the Authority's operations. To facilitate this, all public finance for the Authority should be derived from a single source and the Management Board should be required to present the Authority's accounts in a form which indicates the full cost of each activity and service, including the real cost of accommodation.

The Management Board should be given the greatest possible freedom to deploy the Authority's resources in the most effective ways; in particular, it should be allowed to apply the profits from its activities and savings from its administration to the further development of its services.

National Policy for Library and Information Services

The Government should examine the feasibility of establishing machinery to provide it with advice on policy concerning the development and co-ordination of national information services—whether they are based on libraries or not—which are the direct or indirect responsibilities of Government departments.

Lending and Photocopying from the National Libraries

As an addition to the existing arrangements for lending from the national libraries, the BML—and, if necessary, the NRLSI—should lend under carefully controlled conditions when photocopying cannot provide a satisfactory solution and when material is not easily available from another library.

Legally deposited publications, material irreplaceable from any other source, or items of high intrinsic value should not be lent.

High priority should be given to improving and developing photocopying at the BML and its outhouses.

The loan stocks of the NCL should be transferred to Boston Spa.

A National Reports Centre at Boston Spa should be established to collect, process and supply report literature in all subjects.

Inter-library Lending

The highest priority should be given to bringing the union catalogues of the NCL up to date.

Financial assistance should be available to enable a few large libraries to work in particularly close association with the national inter-library lending service. The university libraries of Oxford and Cambridge are particularly well fitted for such a role.

Bibliographic Services

A National Bibliographic Service should be established which would initially combine and co-ordinate and then develop the bibliographic activities of the BML, the NCL, the NRLSI, the NLLST and the British National Bibliography.

The main unit of the service should be in central London.

The National Bibliographic Service should have the responsibility of co-ordinating the total national bibliographic effort in science and technology and of representing internationally British interests.

The responsibilities of OSTI in this field should be transferred to the National Bibliographic Service.

There should be a single centre to which loan and photocopy requests for all material in every subject should be addressed. This unit should be at Boston Spa and should house the union catalogues of the NCL as soon as the main centre of the National Bibliographic Service in London is fully operational.

Reference

The NRL should incorporate the library departments of the British Museum, including the Department of Prints and Drawings, but excluding the NRLSI, and should be organised in the main as a closed access library; that is, without providing for direct access by readers to the book stores.

It should continue to provide as complete coverage as possible in those subjects in the arts, humanities and social sciences where its present collections are uniquely good.

In others, adequate overall provision of foreign publications for research should be achieved through co-operation with other libraries, particularly by way of schemes for co-operative acquisition.

In science, the CSPC, being the successor to the NRLSI, should aim to provide a comprehensive collection of British and foreign patents, together with such technical literature as is needed to support the patent collection and to satisfy regional needs.

This library should continue to provide for some time ahead direct access by its readers to a substantial proportion of its stocks. However, because of the impact that automated information retrieval systems are likely to make on science libraries in the decades ahead, it is improbable that the initial arrangements within a new science reference library should continue unchanged for more than a small part of the expected life of a new building.

Science reference facilities in public and university libraries in all major industrial areas should be strengthened so as to be capable of meeting a high proportion of local requirements.

From library considerations alone, a site immediately adjacent to the British Museum is most suitable for the NRL. If, for other reasons, this is not possible, the NRL should be in central London, particularly convenient to the academic institutions in both Bloomsbury and Aldwych.

The CSPC should also be in central London, although they need not necessarily be on the same site as the NRL.

Because of the exceptionally high cost of storing library material in central London, lightly used material in both the NRL and the CSPC should be outhoused to one or more stores on low cost land.

Library Automation

The feasibility of applying automatic data processing to both the internal management operations and the services of the reference, lending, bibliographic and administrative divisions of the NLA should be studied in detail and without delay.

Research and Training

In order to improve the effectiveness of the existing services of the national libraries and to evolve new services as required, a wide range of research should be undertaken and sponsored by the NLA, for which adequate resources should be made available. In so doing, the Authority would assume many of the responsibilities for research now exercised by OSTI.

Consideration should be given to the creation of machinery to bring together the major national interests engaged in the development of information techniques so as to co-ordinate effectively the total research effort and to assist in the formulation of national policies.

The NLA should have an important responsibility for making its research and development widely known to librarians and others.

The contribution of the national libraries to professional training should be to supplement the existing arrangements, in collaboration with those now responsible for the training of librarians.

NOTE: The functional relationships between the Management Board, the Executive Committee, and the units and their Advisory Councils, which would comprise a National Libraries organisation are illustrated in Fig. 15 following page 134.

PART I

INTRODUCTION

CHAPTER ONE

THE COMMITTEE'S PROCEDURE

1. We were appointed by the Secretary of State for Education and Science in December 1967 with the following terms of reference:

" To examine the functions and organisation of the British Museum Library, the National Central Library, the National Lending Library for Science and Technology and the Science Museum Library in providing national library facilities; to consider whether in the interests of efficiency and economy such facilities should be brought into a unified framework; and to make recommendations."

Because the National Reference Library of Science and Invention is administered as part of the Department of Printed Books of the British Museum, our terms of reference cover this library also. It comprises the former Patent Office Library together with the science collections of the British Museum Library.

2. An invitation to professional organisations, and other interested bodies and individuals to submit written evidence was issued to the Press early in January 1968. We asked particularly for factual information concerning the adequacy and use of existing national library facilities, and for estimates of the pattern of future demands for these services. At the same time, the administration of each library covered by our terms of reference was asked to provide information about its aims, services, acquisition policies, stock, staff, expenditure and usage patterns; it was also invited to comment freely on any other matters relevant to our task. We also sought written evidence from all universities in the United Kingdom (including the individual colleges and institutes of London University), the professional library organisations, learned societies, certain Government departments, and numerous other bodies which we believed would be able to assist and advise us. They were requested, particularly, for information about the adequacy and suitability of the existing services of the national libraries in meeting present and future needs, and to suggest any necessary improvements. Subsequently, we asked a variety of industrial organisations about their information needs and the services required to satisfy them.

3. We also sought information on specific topics from appropriate organisations and individuals. This often entailed special research on their part and sometimes surveys were mounted to obtain the data which we required.

4. So that we might have up-to-date information about usage of the national libraries, arrangements were made, with the collaboration of the Trustees of the British Museum, for surveys of the readers at the British Museum Library and the National Reference Library of Science and Invention to be carried out by the Economist Intelligence Unit. The surveys of the British Museum Library were made in April and August 1968, and that of the National Reference Library of Science and Invention in July 1968. The staff of the other libraries in our terms of reference also carried out surveys at our request. Visitors to the

1

Science Museum Library were surveyed over a period in April 1968; the National Central Library analysed its loan requisitions at about the same time; and analyses of parts of the services of the National Lending Library for Science and Technology were made in June and December 1968. The results of all these surveys proved of immense value to us; they are published as appendices to this report.

5. We visited each of the libraries in the early stages of our work. During these visits, we were afforded all necessary facilities to study their operation and organisation, and to hold discussions with the staffs. Some months later we held separate discussions with the Trustees of the British Museum, the Trustees of the National Central Library, and representatives of the Department of Education and Science and the Ministry of Technology.

6. In May 1968, the Secretary visited the United States on the Committee's behalf, to study the organisation of the national and other libraries, and to review the latest developments in library technology. Among the institutions visited were the Library of Congress, the National Library of Medicine, the Clearing House for Federal Scientific and Technical Information, the Library of the US Patent Office, the National Advisory Commission on Libraries, the Institute of Library Research at the University of California, and the Massachusetts Institute of Technology. He also made a short visit to France, during which he obtained useful information and advice from the Director of the Bibliothèque Nationale. He also discussed the library needs of a national museum when he visited the Louvre.

7. The second Chapter in this report reviews library services in the context of the nation's information system. We then consider the present role of each of the national institutions covered by our terms of reference, dealing with such matters as administration, services, staffing and usage patterns. Relevant information about the national libraries of Scotland and Wales and the British National Bibliography is also included in this part of our report. In Part III, we examine the present-day requirements for national library services, and try to estimate how the pattern of demand may change in the years ahead. We then suggest those changes in the type, scale and organisation of existing institutions which may enable them to provide more effectively for the needs of users in the future. In this, we give particular attention to the discussion of the administrative arrangements necessary to establish a national libraries system, and to the possibilities afforded by the application of computers to its services.

8. A summary of our main recommendations is given at the beginning of the report, and a complete list, with relevant paragraph numbers, at the end. The appendices include the results of the surveys carried out at the principal national libraries, together with material which deals more fully with certain topics than was practicable in the main body of our report. The main collection of written evidence which we have received is being published separately.

PART TWO

LIBRARIES AND INFORMATION SERVICES IN BRITAIN TODAY

CHAPTER TWO

THE GENERAL SCENE

Introduction

9. The national library institutions mentioned in the Committee's terms of reference form part of a much larger and more widely distributed network of library facilities throughout the United Kingdom, which is principally concerned with providing information in the form of the printed word. Public expenditure on local and national libraries alone now exceeds £60m per year, and there are many library services whose costs are not included in this sum. Libraries form a large and important part of the nation's information services, the general aims of which are to collect and store whatever information is likely to be required, to provide access to it as speedily as necessary and to arrange its supply in the most useful form where it may be most effectively employed. These aims may be achieved in several ways, of which the following are typical examples:

    (i) by supplying a specified publication for reference, or loan, or as a photo copy;

    (ii) by providing facilities to enable an enquirer to embark on a search leading to the identification and acquisition of information in a field of knowledge in which he was initially ignorant of the source material;

    (iii) by compiling and publishing bibliographic aids, through which the existence of information is identified and by which its supply is made possible;

    (iv) by supplying either a complete answer to a specific enquiry, or information which will enable the enquirer to obtain an answer.

10. Not every information service carries out all of these functions and, indeed, the library and information network is composed of various types of institution, differing in size, purpose, administration and source of finance. The principal types are briefly described below.

The Public Libraries

11. The Public Libraries and Museums Act 1964, places a duty on local authorities to provide comprehensive and efficient public library services in the areas for which they have responsibility and it requires that the Secretary of State for Education and Science should superintend and promote the improvement of these services. The Act requires that the basic services of reference and lending, as far as they apply to books and periodicals, should, with minor exceptions, be free of charge, thus perpetuating a long-established principle. Charges may, however, be levied for the borrowing of other types of material, such as gramophone records, and for other services.

12. Because of the breadth of professional and leisure interests of the population served by the public libraries, the range of subjects covered by them

is very wide, although, as the UGC Committee on Libraries* (the Parry Committee) pointed out, local specialisms are by no means uncommon. Indeed, one of the consequences of the arrangements for inter-library co-operation, referred to in paragraphs 23 to 25, is that many public libraries are expected to cover specific subjects or other specialisms in depth, at least insofar as British monographs are concerned. However, with these exceptions, the public library has to cater for such a wide range of subjects that its stock is normally limited to the most heavily used material in each subject area; and, therefore, it falls to other libraries to collect the large volume of relatively lightly used and highly specialised publications. Even so, the largest public libraries have substantial holdings—for example, the central reference library in a large city may have 750,000 to one million volumes in its stock. The level of provision, as regards both the stock and the range of services, varies markedly in different parts of the country. For instance, the reference libraries provided by local authorities in central London are notably inferior to those of Liverpool, Manchester and Birmingham, partly because of the local government structure in London and partly because other types of library abound in the capital. In general, however, the smaller towns and the sparsely populated areas are less well provided for than the large centres of commerce and industry.

13. The bibliographic services of the public libraries are usually restricted to the use of the standard tools, supplemented to a certain extent by the libraries' own catalogues and published lists. However, a fairly recent development in a few of the larger industrial centres has been the establishment, mainly for local industry, of library-based referral and information services, aimed at providing more extensive bibliographic services, or at directing an enquirer to the most appropriate source of information.

University and College Libraries

14. The libraries of universities in Britain, unlike those in some Continental countries which serve a wide public, have as their predominant function at the present time the servicing of the teaching and research activities of their institutions. Their organisation, subject coverage, acquisitions policy and services tend to reflect these responsibilities almost exclusively. Nevertheless, there is a growing appreciation in universities and colleges of the potential contribution that they could make to the information requirements of the community as a whole. All university libraries are now associated with the national scheme for inter-library co-operation, and many with the regional systems. Many also provide—usually free of charge—some reference facilities to members of the public. This is not to say, however, that the general public may use university or college libraries as freely as the members of the institution. The facilities are often restricted to *bona fide* scholars and sometimes are only available if it has been shown that the material sought is unobtainable elsewhere. Lending facilities to individual members of the public are exceptional.

15. These variations in policy reflect the fact that each university library is administered as an integral part of the institution itself and is not controlled directly or indirectly, either by central or local government, or by any other outside body. The financing of a university's library facilities and the share of the total resources available for them are also internal matters for the institution

---

* University Grants Committee Report of the Committee on Libraries, HMSO, 1967.

itself to determine, although the bulk of the costs are met from public funds, supplied through the UGC in the same way as university finance generally. University libraries now account for over £7m of public funds annually, out of a library expenditure of about £12m on all higher education institutions taken together.

16. The size of university libraries is considerable, even in comparison with many public reference libraries—for example, the stock of one of the older provincial university libraries may exceed 750,000 volumes. Like the public libraries, university libraries are usually general collections and even those of the technological universities cover many disciplines, including some non-scientific subjects. However, one of the fundamental differences from public libraries is the type of material collected, which is very largely confined to what is relevant to university research and teaching. In many subjects most university libraries must have a great deal of material not held in the public libraries, particularly in their coverage of foreign publications, and some have substantial holdings which would be relevant to the research and possibly other interests of local industry and other sections of the community. To a lesser extent, this may also be true of the libraries of other higher education institutions, especially the larger colleges of further education and the new polytechnics.

Special Libraries and Information Centres

17. There is also a wide variety of libraries and information centres which concentrate on limited subject areas, or are restricted to certain types of publication. Their services may be directed to specific kinds of user and may involve the provision of specialised bibliographic or information facilities.

18. Many specialised information institutions are members of Aslib (previously known as the Association of Special Libraries and Information Bureaux). This body, which receives about £50,000 per year—that is, approximately one third of its total income—from public funds, facilitates the co-ordination and systematic use of sources of information covering both the arts and the sciences, by directing its members to sources of information; by providing certain bibliographic, translation and information services; by offering assistance and guidance in the setting up and running of libraries; and increasingly by carrying out user studies and other research. The recently published first part of a new edition of the Aslib Directory contains entries of nearly 3,000 specialised sources of information in science and technology alone, about half of which are special libraries. Few of these, however, have substantial resources or offer a wide range of services with exhaustive coverage of their specialisms.

19. These organisations fall into three main categories although the facilities offered by some entitle them to be included in more than one:

    (i) *Special Libraries*, which are associated with many professional institutions and learned societies, Government departments and research stations, the Industrial Research Associations, trade organisations and the larger commercial firms. Some special collections contain less than a hundred books and a handful of current periodicals. At the other extreme, however, a few of the great special libraries have incomparably the country's best collections in their subject fields.

5

Examples include the Chemical Society Library, the Library of the Royal Institute of British Architects, the British Library of Art at the Victoria and Albert Museum and, perhaps above all, the British Library of Political and Economic Science at the London School of Economics. The services offered by special libraries are geared to reference facilities, the loan of literature, and in many cases to the production of specialised bibliographies. The staff are frequently professional librarians.

(ii) *Documentation Centres*—such as the 11 Commonwealth Agricultural Bureaux—which process the literature in their fields. For this purpose subject specialists are usually employed.

(iii) *Information Centres*, which are principally associated with Government Departments or their research establishments, and with the Industrial Research Associations. They scan and evaluate the literature in their special subjects, and are thereby able to provide specific information either for general distribution to regular subscribers or to answer enquiries. Their staffs frequently contain more subject specialists than professional librarians.

20. Access to most of these sources of information tends to be restricted. Many are available as of right only to members and subscribers; others to research workers and qualified practitioners. Nevertheless, the organisations are usually willing to extend their services to all who have bona fide reasons for calling upon them. In particular, over 200 special libraries co-operate in the regional schemes for inter-library lending and over 700 contribute to the national systems.

Data Activities

21. In addition to special libraries and documentation or information centres, there are highly specialised information services which concentrate on the collection and processing of data. Three main types of service can be identified:

(i) *Data on materials and products for industry*. These are usually compiled by independent publishers, although some research and trade associations also offer this type of service.

(ii) *Design Data for Engineers*. Easily the most widely-based service of this type is that organised with support from the Ministry of Technology by the professional engineering institutions around a common engineering scientific data unit. Other, less ambitious projects are associated with certain Industrial Research Associations.

(iii) *Critical Data for Scientists* are compiled by specialist teams in universities, colleges and research establishments, often as part of international projects. The National Engineering Laboratory's " International Steam Tables " is an example. The Office for Scientific and Technical Information (OSTI) has started several experimental data centres, covering, for example, crystallography, mass spectrometry, and the thermo-dynamic properties of gases, and the Natural Environment

6

and Social Science Research Councils are encouraging data collection activities in their own fields.

Industrial Information Services

22. Technical liaison and advisory services for industry are provided by some Government departments and research establishments, and by certain trade and research associations. In addition, the Ministry of Technology has set up a network of industrial liaison officers, operating mainly from technical colleges. This provides, through personal contact, information and advice for local firms—particularly the smaller ones—which are neither members of Aslib, nor of an industrial research association. A similar service for agriculture is provided by the Ministry of Agriculture's National Advisory Service.

Schemes for Inter-Library Co-operation

(a) Inter-library lending

23. Few, if any, libraries can hope to satisfy from their own stocks and resources alone all the requests which they receive for publications and information. Even to attempt this would cause proliferation of a vast quantity of lightly used material at very substantial cost. Therefore, adequate machinery must exist for supplying as quickly as is necessary, on loan or by photocopy, publications which are not immediately on hand. Consequently, formal and informal arrangements have been built up over a long period of time to facilitate inter-library lending. Direct lending between libraries occurs to a considerable extent, especially at local level. This is often the quickest way of obtaining an item requested, especially when there exists a published locating tool, such as the British Union Catalogue of Periodicals (BUCOP). In addition, a local co-operative scheme providing library-based referral and information services is frequently used to facilitate inter-library lending.

24. This machinery is supplemented by the Regional Library Systems. In England and Wales nine of these were set up between 1931 and 1936, whilst Scotland became a library region in 1939. All public libraries are members of the Regional Systems and, with certain special and university libraries participating in some regions, over 600 libraries are involved in England and Wales. Each region, with the exception of Yorkshire, has a clearing-house containing the union catalogue, which forms the principal means of locating loan requests received from the member libraries. Not all regions provide the same quality of service, however, mainly because the effectiveness of the union catalogues is very dependent on whether they are kept fully up-to-date. In Yorkshire, the Regional System operates by circulating requests between libraries through a network of zones and sub-zones, whilst in the North-West a somewhat similar procedure is used to supplement the union catalogue. On average 75 per cent of the requests received by the Regional Systems are met within their respective areas; this corresponds to nearly a quarter of a million items annually. When, however, a request cannot be met regionally, either the originating library or the regional headquarters applies to one of the national institutions described below. Although some libraries apply to the national sources without having first tried regionally, there is no doubt that the Regional Schemes filter off a substantial volume of requests, especially for relatively heavily used and freely available publications. This they do at an annual cost for England and Wales

of about £70,000,* excluding expenditure directly incurred by the participating libraries.

(b) *Regional acquisition schemes*

25. In recent years, the largest Regional Schemes have each attempted to cover within their own libraries a high proportion of British monographs, as listed in the British National Bibliography (BNB), and British serial publications. To an increasing extent, therefore, the regions are approaching self-sufficiency in respect of British material. However, because each smaller region could not be self-sufficient in this way, the National Committee on Regional Library Co-operation in 1959 initiated an inter-regional scheme for acquiring all British books published subsequently. In practice, between 95 per cent and 99 per cent of British publications have been bought under this arrangement since 1959. In addition to this, the Joint Fiction Reserve of the former Metropolitan Boroughs aims to cover by purchase all new novels listed in the BNB. Since 1962, a similar scheme has been operated jointly by the provincial regions.

The National Institutions

26. Supporting the complex structure of public, university and special libraries; the various information services; and the local and regional schemes of inter-library co-operation are a few great national libraries and related services. Of these, the most important are the Library of the British Museum— including the National Reference Library of Science and Invention—which is by far the greatest general reference collection in the United Kingdom and one of the finest in the World; the National Lending Library for Science and Technology, which specialises in supplying on loan and by photocopy literature in all the sciences; the National Central Library, the principal service of which is to augment the regional schemes of library co-operation in facilitating inter-library lending; the British National Bibliography, which produces bibliographic information on new British publications; and the Science Museum Library, which has one of the largest collections of scientific literature in the country and which contributes to the lending services provided by the National Lending Library for Science and Technology. In addition, there are three national institutions whose services are principally directed towards serving the needs of Scotland and Wales: The National Libraries of Scotland and Wales, which house the main reference collections in their respective countries, and the Scottish Central Library, which combines the functions of a regional library headquarters with some of the wider national responsibilities of the National Central Library. These are described in detail in the succeeding chapters.

---

* Evidence from the National Committee on Regional Library Co-operation.

CHAPTER THREE

THE BRITISH MUSEUM LIBRARY

Background

27. The British Museum Library (BML) forms part of an independent organisation set up under the British Museum Act 1753. This Act, together with most of the sections of subsequent Acts, was repealed by the British Museum Act 1963, which made new provision for the regulation of the Museum (and Library) collections. The National Reference Library of Science and Invention (NRLSI) forms part of the BML, but because of its importance as a library for scientific and technological reference it is described separately in Chapter 4. Except where otherwise stated references to the BML in this report should be taken to exclude the NRLSI.

28. The British Museum Act of 1963 altered the composition of the body of Trustees governing both the Museum and the Library, and provided for the appointment of twenty-five persons as follows:

   (i) one appointed by the Sovereign;

   (ii) fifteen appointed by the Prime Minister;

   (iii) four appointed by the Treasury on the nominations of the Presidents of the Royal Society, the Royal Academy, the British Academy and the Society of Antiquaries of London respectively; and

   (iv) five appointed by the Trustees of the British Museum.

29. The Director of the British Museum is appointed by the Trustees with the approval of the Prime Minister.

30. The Trustees are charged with the duties of keeping the collections and making them available for inspection, although under certain conditions they may lend or dispose of material in their custody.

Functions

31. The primary function of the library is to provide a national reference collection of books, contemporary and antique, British and foreign. The Copyright Act of 1911 provides that the library shall, as of right, receive within one month after publication a copy of every book published in the United Kingdom. The origins of legal deposit, however, preceded the founding of the BML and its continuous operation over several hundred years has contributed very largely to the library's becoming by far the largest general collection of British publications of all periods. The range of foreign books and periodicals is also exceptionally extensive by any standard, although rapid increases in the rate of world publication and in the cost of acquisitions have put a considerable strain on the library's resources in recent years. Apart from legal deposit under the Copyright Act, and purchase, much new material is acquired by exchange, gift or bequest.

32. Because the collections cover many subjects incomparably well and because of the very high standard of bibliographic services provided by the staff, it is natural that librarians and research workers from all over the world

9

should turn to the BML when other sources of information have failed. But it is these same qualities that also make the library an international centre of learning in which many scholars pursue long-term research. To quote the evidence which we have received from the Trustees, it is, therefore, " simultaneously a library of last resort and a library of first instance ", the function of which is " to meet the needs of those users of books whose efforts are directed at bringing to light unknown or forgotten facts, finding significance in hitherto neglected material and combining ideas in new ways ".

Sources of Finance

33. Analysis of the finance of the library is made exceptionally complex for two reasons. Firstly, because both public and private resources are involved; and secondly, because the existing arrangements often do not enable the library departments to be distinguished from the rest of the Museum.

34. Public funds for the Museum, including the library, are derived from the following three departmental votes:

(i) that of the Ministry of Public Building and Works, which covers maintenance, furniture, fuel, light, rental values and rates;

(ii) that of Her Majesty's Stationery Office, which pays for stationery, printing, and binding;

(iii) that of the Department of Education and Science, which goes towards salaries, general administration, a substantial part of the total purchases, technical expenses, and publications.

It is estimated that three quarters of the library's income is obtained from public funds. Finance from private sources comes from trust funds administered by the Trustees. These funds originate in the main from bequests to the British Museum. That from the estate of George Bernard Shaw is a particularly valuable and well-known example.

Services

35. The library is organised in four departments: Printed Books, Manuscripts, Oriental Printed Books and Manuscripts, and Prints and Drawings. A diagram representing the organisation of these departments, and showing their relationship to the Museum departments is shown at Figure 1.

(a) Department of Printed Books

36. This is by far the largest department and contains collections of printed material of all countries and of all periods. The Newspaper Library at Colindale forms part of this department. Because of shortage of space at Bloomsbury, parts of the collections are outhoused in temporary premises at Woolwich Arsenal.

37. The administration of the department is arranged in Processing, Public Service and Special Materials Divisions. The Processing Divisions are responsible for:

(i) the selection and processing of acquisitions obtained by copyright deposit, purchase, donation or international exchange. There is a separate acquisitions division for Slavonic and East European material;

10

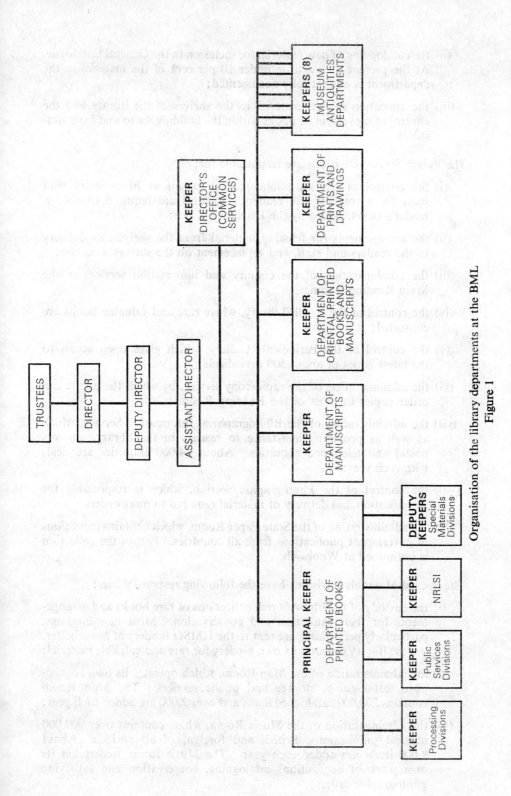

Organisation of the library departments at the BML

Figure 1

11

(ii) the cataloguing of new material for inclusion in the General Catalogue. At the present time a little under 10 per cent of the material in the department is not yet fully documented;

(iii) the allocation of new material to the shelves of the library and the control of movement of books within the building, or to and from out-stores.

The Public Service Divisions are responsible for:

(i) the control of the six public reading rooms at Bloomsbury with seats for a total of 680 readers. Readers are required to hold a reader's ticket, issued by the Director's Office;

(ii) the arrangements for fetching material from the shelves, its delivery to the readers and staff, and replacement on the shelves after use;

(iii) the administration of the enquiry and information services in the Main Reading Room;

(iv) the control of the North Library, where rare and valuable books are consulted;

(v) the control of the Periodicals Gallery, which gives open access to the latest issues of about 500 periodicals;

(vi) the administration of the rapid-copy service, by which the public can order copies in most of the Reading Rooms;

(vii) the administration of the Bibliographical Information Service, which as well as providing assistance to readers in the library, answers postal and telephone enquiries. About 14,000 enquiries are dealt with each year;

(viii) the control of the Photographic Section, which is responsible for identification and delivery of material required to meet orders;

(ix) the administration of the State Paper Room, which contains collections of government publications from all countries. Part of the collection is outhoused at Woolwich.

The Special Materials Divisions have the following responsibilities:

(i) the custody of the library's rich collections of rare books and arrangements for their exhibition and conservation. Most new bindings, particularly periodicals, are sent to the HMSO Bindery at Manchester, but the library operates its own bindery for rare and valuable material;

(ii) the administration of the Map Room, which operates its own acquisitions, cataloguing, storage and public services. The Map Room contains 200,000 catalogued items and over 2,000 are added each year;

(iii) the administration of the Music Room, which contains over 900,000 musical publications, British and foreign, of all periods. About 9,000 items are added each year. The Music Room undertakes its own work of acquisition, cataloguing, conservation and satisfying photographic orders;

(iv) the administration of the Philatelic Collection, which is one of the largest and richest in the world, and amounts to over 4 million items;

(v) the administration of the Newspaper Library at Colindale, which contains about 38,000 sets of British, Commonwealth and foreign newspapers; additions of individual newspapers amount to about 200,000 each year. A separate Newspaper Catalogue is maintained, and the library has its own photocopying unit on the premises.

(b) Department of Manuscripts

38. The function of this department is the collection of manuscripts and documents in European languages. The department holds some 75,000 volumes of manuscripts, 100,000 charters, 20,000 detached seal-impressions and casts, and smaller collections of other material. It is responsible for its own acquisition and cataloguing functions. The Manuscripts Students Room has accommodation for about 60 students. Other services to the public include photocopying, exhibitions, and dealing with enquiries.

(c) Department of Oriental Printed Books and Manuscripts

39. This department supplements the collections of the Department of Printed Books and the Department of Manuscripts by maintaining and developing collections of books and manuscripts in the languages of Asia and North Africa. It has a stock of about 250,000 printed books and 38,000 manuscripts. The department can acquire only a proportion of the large and rapidly expanding world publishing output in the relevant languages, but it tries to produce a balanced collection covering all subjects, with the exception of science. The selection of staff is naturally aimed at obtaining as wide a range of language expertise as possible. There is an Oriental Students Room with seats for about 30 readers. In addition to the reference collection, the department also provides photographic and photocopying facilities, and stages exhibitions (including loans to outside exhibitions). Because of the relative scarcity of subject and language experts in the disciplines covered by this department, the inquiry and information services provided by the staff are particularly appreciated by users of the department.

(d) Department of Prints and Drawings

40. This department contains a rich and balanced collection of Western Graphic art from the late Middle Ages to the present day. It produces its own illustrated and fully documented catalogues, and arranges exhibitions from its collections. There is a great demand for material from this department for exhibitions organised by outside bodies. Like the other departments, there is a Students Room and there are facilities for photographing items in the collections.

Stock

41. As there is no entirely satisfactory unit of stock measurement which can be applied to all types of material in the library departments, it is necessary to refer to the detailed statistics contained in the evidence of the Trustees of the British Museum (Appendix 1, Part 1, Section 3) to obtain an accurate assessment of the library's stock. However, the following figures give some idea of the holdings, excluding those of the NRLSI:

13

(i) The stock of the library extends to about 120 miles of shelving. In addition there are about 250 miles of microfilm which occupy a further half mile of shelving.

(ii) The number of units of stock, based on catalogue entries, is about 5½ million, but the number of volumes is considerably greater—about 7 million in the Department of Printed Books alone.

(iii) In 1967, additions to stock in the Department of Printed Books alone amounted to over 1¼ million items valued at nearly £700,000. Of this valuation, purchase and copyright deposit each accounted for only about one sixth whilst donations amounted to about one third. The international exchange arrangements, which enable the library to acquire foreign official publications in exchange for HMSO publications of comparable value were also a major factor, worth about one third of the total.

Staff

42. The staff of the British Museum is appointed by the Trustees with Treasury approval as to numbers, conditions of service and salaries. Such employment is treated as service in the civil service for superannuation purposes, and keeper and other civil service grades form the staff structure. Because of the difficulties in apportioning the substantial numbers of staff who provide common services for both Library and Museum departments, it has not proved possible to make a realistic estimate of the total staff needed to operate the library's services alone. These uncertainties apply mainly, however, to manual workers, security staff and some of the less skilled clerical grades. Of the staff engaged solely on the provision of the library's services in 1967/68, 90 were senior library staff including subject specialists, and 165 were other executive and higher clerical staff.

Costs of Services

43. Just as it is difficult to separate the library's income from that of the Museum as a whole, so is it also difficult to separate the cost of the library's services from those of the Museum. No separate costs for the library are available for building maintenance, furniture, fuel and light, rental values, rates, stationery, general administration, technical expenses or publications, but the total expenditure on these items for the Museum as a whole in 1967/68 was about £1½ million. It has not been possible to arrive at an overall figure, even including the Museum departments, for amortisation. Approximate estimates of the library costs for 1967/68 under those heads where costs can be isolated from those of the Museum are given below. They do not include the cost of the NRLSI, except where stated.

44. The cost of staffing the library departments, excluding staff engaged on common services with the Museum departments, was £672,000, comprising £526,000 for the Department of Printed Books, £74,000 for the Department of Manuscripts, £40,000 for the Department of Oriental Printed Books and Manuscripts, and £32,000 for the Department of Prints and Drawings. Acquisition costs for all library departments amounted to £136,000 financed from public funds, with an additional £127,000 from the Trustees' funds. The latter figure, however, was exceptionally high during that year. The cost of

14

printing and binding, including the NRLSI, was £300,000, and that of photographic services, including the NRLSI, £148,000 less £130,000 received from sales. The sum of these costs is about £1¼ million.

Usage Patterns

45. The Trustees' evidence reveals that the number of visits to the library departments (including the Newspaper Library at Colindale) was approximately 300,000 in 1967. The number of readers' admission tickets, including temporary tickets, on issue rose from about 20,000 in 1958 to 30,000 in 1967. Over the same period the number of volumes used by readers in the Department of Printed Books at Bloomsbury increased from 1·1 million to about 1·6 million.

46. To obtain more detailed information about the ways in which the library was used, this Committee, with the co-operation of the Trustees and the Director of the British Museum, commissioned the Economist Intelligence Unit to carry out surveys of the library in 1968. These comprised a survey conducted on six separate, randomly selected, days during the period 29th March to 2nd May, complemented by an analysis of the readers' application slips for the same period; and a further, smaller survey carried out on the 21st and 22nd of August. During the April survey, 4,839 questionnaires were issued and 3,777 returned (a response rate of 78 per cent) corresponding to about 250,000 visits per year. This figure is somewhat less than the 300,000 mentioned in paragraph 45. The difference is probably attributable to increased use during the summer months, which was confirmed by the August survey. During this latter survey a total of 1,469 visits was sampled over the two days, which on scaling up, shows an increase in use over the earlier survey period of about one fifth.

47. In most respects, however, where seasonal variations might be expected to be slight, the two surveys produced notably similar results. This close correspondence between two independent samples encourages confidence in the accuracy and validity of the data. The principal types of information obtained are summarised in the following paragraphs. The full survey reports prepared by the Economist Intelligence Unit are included in the appendices to this report.

(a) Users of the library

48. University staff and research students outnumbered all other users of the library, forming over two thirds of the total readership in April 1968. A further seventh were freelance writers or professional researchers. The evidence of the surveys, backed up by information submitted by the universities and other academic institutions, establishes that the library is used predominantly for academic research (Figure 12 (ii), page 89).

(b) Origins of readers

49. Two thirds of the readers using the library were found to be living in the London postal area. This proportion includes people not normally resident in London, but who were staying in London specially to enable them to visit the library. We have estimated that these temporary residents probably constitute about one sixth of the total readership; hence, about half of the total readers are permanent residents in the London postal area. The distribution of the remaining third of readers living outside London declined with increasing distance from London—well over half this group came from the Home Counties or S.E. England.

50. The April survey showed that visitors from abroad comprised about one third of the total readership, but about half of these were spending six months or longer at a British University or other higher academic institution. In August, however, the proportion of visitors from overseas increased to about half the sample of readers. Most of these additional overseas readers came from Europe, and particularly from two groups of countries—France, the Netherlands, Finland and Denmark; and Italy, Portugal and Spain. Analysis of the origins of the largest single group of users, students and academic staff, showed in April that over one third were from London University, compared with rather less than one third from all the other British Universities. In the latter group, Oxford and Cambridge were the largest users. In August, the proportion of readers from universities and institutions in London fell to a fifth of the academic category, and the proportion of readers from universities outside London fell even more sharply to a tenth of the academic readership. The proportions of readers from Oxford and Cambridge and other universities in south-east England were, however, unchanged.

(c) Types of material used

51. Information about the subject matter consulted came from two sources:

  (i) the subject headings indicated by readers filling in survey questionnaires, in which multiple ticking of subjects was permitted;

  (ii) the analysis of readers' application slips during the period of the main survey, in which each item was uniquely classified.

52. The April survey showed that one half of all readers used the library for historical study, one third for literature and more than a quarter for bibliography or general reference (Figure 11, page 73). Relatively little use was made of material in the following subject fields: children's books; mathematics; applied science and technology; biology, agriculture and geology; foreign law; medicine and pharmacology; and natural sciences. The analysis of the application slips showed a rather different subject breakdown, with literature in heaviest demand (24 per cent), and with theology, biography and history next, each with about 10 per cent. The differences between the two analyses may be due to the different standpoints from which each was made; but both surveys show that literary and historical studies predominate in the usage of the library. The August survey confirmed this subject usage.

53. An analysis was carried out to establish the extent of different kinds of inter-disciplinary studies amongst the April survey population of 3,059 visits. About a thousand of these visits involved some type of inter-disciplinary study, the most common being that spanning the humanities and social sciences, which comprised two thirds of all types. Types of inter-disciplinary study involving science on the one hand and other groups of subjects on the other comprised about one sixth of all inter-disciplinary studies and one-twentieth of all visits to the library during the survey period.

54. A little over a quarter of the application slips were for post 1950 publications (Figure 13 (ii), page 90), whilst nearly as high a proportion was for 19th century literature, and pre-19th century literature accounted for about 18 per cent. These figures do not, however, take into account the relative sizes of the stocks of materials of different periods. Information received from the Trustees

16

shows that, when allowance for this is made, the most intensively used stocks at Bloomsbury are pre-1700 literature and 20th century publications. The least intensively used stock was 19th century material.

(d) *Ways in which the library was used*

55. Less than one fifth of all visitors to the library expected their work to be completed in one day or less. On the other hand nearly a third of the users estimated that their work would take longer than three months to complete. The April survey establishes that over half the visitors use the library to carry out a relatively long, continuous piece of research. In August, this proportion was even higher, about two thirds.

56. Both surveys showed that well over half the readers tried to obtain their requirements in another library before going to the British Museum Library. This supports the Trustees' view that one of the most important functions of the BML is to serve as a library of last resort. Not surprisingly, the Department of Manuscripts differed from the other library departments in that only a quarter of its readers had tried other libraries. The surveys also established that about two thirds of the visitors to the library were principally seeking items that were known to them before their visit. Previously unknown items of literature were identified mainly by use of the BML catalogues and indexes (two fifths of all readers) and by consulting other reference books (one fifth of all readers).

57. Both the April and August surveys revealed that 6 per cent of all visitors intended to use departments of the Museum other than the four library departments on the same day as their visit, but only about half of these considered it essential for their work to do so (Figure 14, page 93). The surveys indicated that there were only six visits by members of the staff of the Museum departments to the reading rooms during the combined period of the surveys. The Trustees have emphasised to us, however, that the staff use the library collections in other ways—for example, by personal visits to the shelves and by requisitioning books. There are no statistics by which an estimate of the importance of the former can be obtained, but the Trustees have stated that in a full year about 2,700 books are issued to staff of the Museum departments. Of these, about three quarters are delivered by the Museum's internal messenger service, without the staff members who originate the requisitions having to visit the library.

(e) *Use of photographic services*

58. The Trustees of the British Museum have provided information about the growth of the library's photographic services. In the Department of Printed Books, the number of photographic orders has risen from about 3,000 in 1958 to over 20,000 (including rapid copy orders handed in at the reading rooms) in 1967 (Figure 2, page 18). During both user surveys an attempt was made to assess the potential use of the photographic services. A third of all readers indicated that they could have used photocopies instead of the original material which they consulted at the library. Of these, rather more than half could have supplied sufficient information to enable a photocopy to be made without their having to visit the library. Therefore, approximately one fifth of all visits to the BML could be expected to be satisfied by photocopy orders, if the user

17

were prepared to pay the price, though the survey shows that the average number of pages that would be required (about 60) would be high.

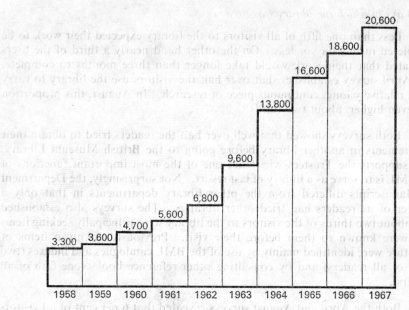

Photocopy orders handled by the Department of Printed Books (excluding the NRLSI) at the BML

Figure 2

The Library's Reputation for Scholarship

59. No chapter about the British Museum Library is complete without a reference to the specialist subject knowledge of the staff and their contribution to scholarship. Many of them have studied and published extensively in their particular fields and the expert assistance which they are, therefore, able to give to users of the library is especially valuable. Undoubtedly their international reputations have contributed greatly to the prestige of the BM as a whole, and have been instrumental in attracting many donations and bequests to the library.

18

CHAPTER FOUR

THE NATIONAL REFERENCE LIBRARY
OF SCIENCE AND INVENTION

Background

60. In 1885, the Patent Office Library (POL) was founded within the Board of Trade as a public reference library of the physical sciences and their associated technologies. The library was not restricted to meeting the patent needs of industry, but developed a general scientific collection. It continued to expand over the years until in 1951 the Advisory Council on Scientific Policy (ACSP) recommended that it should be developed as the NRLSI. In 1960 the British Museum was given responsibility for the POL on the basis that the BML's collections of scientific and technical literature, including copyright deposit material in these fields, should be available to the reconstituted library. In 1966, the NRLSI was formally incorporated into the BML's Department of Printed Books.

61. Because of shortage of accommodation in the Holborn premises of the old POL, the library is now organised in two divisions, one at Holborn and the other in Bayswater. The Holborn division, which has expanded into a nearby annexe, allows for direct access by readers to the material on the shelves (see paragraph 84) and contains what is essentially a development of the old POL collection. The Bayswater collections are almost entirely on closed access and consist largely of older material which is progressively being transferred from the BML. The present administration plans to incorporate in this division the main collections in the life sciences until it can unite all the NRLSI material in a new building.

Functions

62. The conclusions of a 1959 Treasury Working Party, reinforcing the recommendations of the ACSP in 1951, were that the new national reference library should aim to provide all literature of current value in every language embracing the whole of the natural sciences and their associated technologies, with special coverage in the field of invention. It was also suggested that the library should have a high proportion of its material on open access so that users could search for and find scientific and technical information very quickly.

Sources of Finance

63. Finance for the NRLSI is included in the votes of the British Museum, referred to in paragraph 34. Expenditure is met from the general sub-heads of the Museum votes although, exceptionally, the library has received for a five year period from 1964/65 a special additional annual grant from public funds of £45,000 in order to improve the coverage of the collections.

Services

(a) Coverage

64. The NRLSI hopes to acquire and make available all the current scientific and technical periodical literature published anywhere in the world. Some 20,000 current periodical titles are taken by the library, of which approximately

70 per cent are foreign language publications. In addition, the library is intending to assume responsibility for the 4,000 current scientific and technical titles among the government publications which are now collected in the State Paper Room of the BML. The library also contains 7,000 periodical titles which have been discontinued.

65. The NRLSI has comprehensive coverage of both British and foreign patent specifications, which are particularly well indexed.

66. The library also collects other types of material, including books, trade literature and research reports. As far as books are concerned, published British material is legally deposited; and the library is aiming to build up as comprehensive a collection as possible in the better known foreign languages.

(b) Operations

67. Just over half the NRLSI's total stock (including that housed in Bayswater) is available on open access, a pattern which is in marked contrast to the 1 per cent of total holdings on open access in the Bloomsbury sections of the Department of Printed Books.

68. Despite pressures on accommodation in Holborn, the NRLSI has developed a speedy photocopying service which is available to meet both postal and personal orders. Demands have doubled since 1963, and the library is now supplying about 160,000 photocopied items per annum. However, the limits to expansion have been reached if the present organisation of the library's material and services is to continue unchanged.

69. Also at Holborn is an established enquiry service, which in 1967 handled about 70,000 enquiries from remote users involving some consultation of records or literature (i.e. about five times the number of enquiries similarly dealt with in the Bloomsbury sections of the Department of Printed Books). Half the enquiries were primarily related to patents.

70. The library produces a number of publications designed to introduce new readers to its services, stock and organisations and to inform users of any changes.

Stock

71. The difficulty of arriving at any very meaningful figures for library stocks based on " units ", " items " or " volumes " applies particularly to the NRLSI. Estimates based on catalogue entries are especially misleading, since a single entry may relate to a monograph or to the complete back-run of a periodical amounting to many bound volumes. Estimates of " items " or " volumes " have similar limitations because of the 11 million patent items which occupy only 110,000 volumes. Perhaps the most useful figures for purposes of comparison are those based on shelving occupied. The NRLSI collections occupy about 20 miles of shelving, which is between one quarter and one fifth of that taken up by library material in the Bloomsbury sections of the Department of Printed Books. This figure relates to the library's books, pamphlets, trade literature and periodicals (including reports and abstracts). In addition there are over 500 stock units of other material, such as material in microform and maps.

72. The NRLSI acquired in 1967 over 500,000 registrable items of which almost 80 per cent were patent specifications. Excluding the patents, which are indexed but not catalogued, these represented about 11,000 new cataloguing units. Approximately 35 per cent of these were purchased, 25 per cent transferred from Bloomsbury, 25 per cent obtained through exchange and 15 per cent legally deposited. Donations accounted for a negligible proportion of the total acquisitions.

Staff

73. For reasons similar to those explained in Chapter 3, paragraph 42, it is extremely difficult to obtain a figure for the total number of staff employed in connection with the NRLSI. However, of those in 1967/68 engaged solely and directly on the provision of the library's services, 27 were senior library staff, including subject specialists, and 130 were other executive and higher clerical staff.

Costs of Services

74. Because of the way in which the statistics are compiled, it is often difficult to separate the costs of providing the NRLSI's services from those incurred in the BML as a whole. For example, the costs of printing, binding and photocopying of the NRLSI are included in the figures set out in Chapter 3, paragraph 44. However, it is known that for 1967/68 staff costs totalled £235,000, and £104,000 was spent on acquisition. As with the BML, we have not been able to estimate reliably the NRLSI's proportion of the total costs of maintenance, equipment, rates, amortisation, etc., of the British Museum as a whole.

Usage Patterns

75. In 1967 there were over 140,000 signatures in the visitors books at the Holborn division of the library. Since there are separate visitors books in the main library and in the adjoining annexe, some of these will be duplicate signatures relating to what were in fact single visits. The full extent of the duplication is not known, but on the basis of a sample check, the 140,000 signatures probably represent about 120,000 visits.

76. The user survey of the NRLSI, which we commissioned with the co-operation of the Trustees, was carried out by the Economist Intelligence Unit on six separate days randomly selected during two weeks in July 1968. The rate of response from users (over 75 per cent) was unusually high for the type of survey and yielded 1,158 completed questionnaires. Readers making repeat visits to the library on different days were not asked to answer new questionnaires in full, but repeat visits were recorded separately by allocating each reader a number at the time of his first visit and recording his subsequent visits against this number. The 1,158 readers sampled made 1,812 visits during the six days of the survey. Increasing this to take account of the survey response rate, we obtain a total of over 2,400 visits to the library. However, the average number of visits per week to the library for the first seven months of 1968 was just over 2,900. The comparatively low level of use during the survey period may indicate the effect of holidays on attendances at that time of year. Although it is difficult to know how this might affect the different categories of users, it

probably accounts for the negligible number of undergraduate users during the survey period.

(a) The Library users

77. The survey showed that by far the largest single group were patent workers, who accounted for almost half the total number of visits made. The second major group were research workers of various kinds, both from industry and from academic institutions. Analysis of the organisations from which the readers originated showed that about one third of the users represented industrial and commercial firms, and a further quarter firms of patent or trade mark agents. In marked contrast to the BML, only 11 per cent of the NRLSI readers were academic staff or post-graduate students.

(b) Origins of users

78. Three quarters of all readers worked in the London postal area, while almost a half worked within one mile of the library itself. Cross-correlations have revealed that nearly three quarters of patent workers worked within one mile of the library; that over half the research and development workers worked in the London postal area; and that almost three quarters of readers from universities or other academic institutions who specified their parent institution were from colleges in London. Only 2 per cent of all readers worked outside the South East of England, and they made only 1 per cent of the total number of visits (Figure 9 (ii), page 59).

79. In contrast with the BML, where well over half the readers who gave their place of work as being within two miles of the Museum said that they did so because they were working principally at the Museum itself, very few readers of the NRLSI work mainly in the library. Also in contrast with the BML is the negligible proportion of visitors from abroad (less than 1 per cent). However, of the 37 per cent of readers who said that they were seeking information in response to an enquiry originating outside London, one half said that the information was needed abroad, and about one third said the information was needed in South East England. The figure for enquiries originating abroad may reflect the high proportion of work carried out by London patent firms for overseas clients.

(c) The material used

80. The use that is made of the NRLSI by industry and commerce—either directly or through patent agents—is reflected in the material that is used. The EIU survey concludes that, " Interest in technological aspects exceeds that in scientific aspects by a ratio of at least 2 : 1 for most subjects". The subjects for which the library was most heavily used were manufacturing processes, mechanical engineering, polymer and other chemical industries, chemical science and electronics.

81. As far as patent literature was concerned, five sixths of the British specifications consulted by patent workers originated during the last 25 years, whilst a similar, if rather less pronounced predominance of recent material was found in the use of foreign patents. Of the items of non-patent literature consulted by all readers, about two thirds were periodicals. Ninety per cent

22

of these periodicals were published after 1950, a proportion which is in close agreement with the results of a recent survey of requisitions made on the NLLST (included in the Appendices to this report) and another* of inter-library lending requests for similar material.

82. An average of 40 patent items were used per visit by each patent worker, and about one third of the non-patent workers referred to some patent literature. Taken together, all readers consulted an average of nine non-patent items, although the average for non-patent workers as a group was more than twice that for patent workers.

(d) Methods of use of the library

83. The general pattern in the NRLSI is of short, relatively frequent visits. Seventy-seven per cent of the users stayed less than three hours, and the largest single group (41 per cent) stayed for one hour or less. In this respect also, the usage pattern of the NRLSI differs fundamentally from that of the BML, where the largest single group stayed for six hours (Figure 3, page 24). About threequarters of NRSLI readers said they visited the library at least once a month.

84. On average, patent workers came to the library more frequently and for shorter visits than non-patent workers, and the preponderance of patent workers among the library's users was no doubt partly responsible for the fact that only one fifth of all readers had tried another library before visiting the NRLSI. Like the BML, the catalogues, abstracts and indexes were heavily used by the NRLSI's readers, with less than a third of users stating that they had identified the material they were seeking by only looking on the shelves. However, in this largely open access library, the catalogues and indexes are not only a means by which unknown material can be identified, but they also serve to direct users to the part of the library where their known material is located.

(e) Photocopying

85. The user survey confirmed that visitors to the library are only the minority users of the rapidly growing photocopying service. Analysis of the completed questionnaires and of both postal and personal applications for photocopies revealed that about 70 per cent of all orders for photocopies were for postal delivery and that three quarters of the items photocopied were patent material. Most of the remainder consisted of extracts from periodicals. All photocopying orders taken together—and each class of material taken separately—showed for their place of origin a strong bias towards London and the South East. The EIU survey showed that about three quarters of all orders originated from these areas, although a survey carried out by the library staff two months later gave a figure of two thirds for orders from London and the South East.

---

* D. W. G. Clements, *Journal of Librarianship*, **1** (2), 107-118.

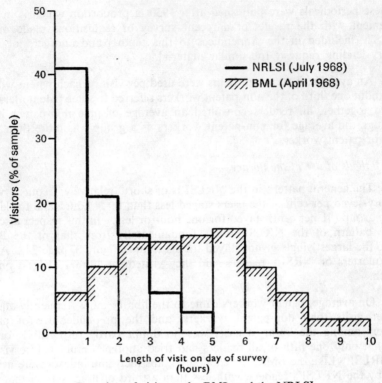

Duration of visits at the BML and the NRLSI

Figure 3

CHAPTER FIVE

THE NATIONAL LENDING LIBRARY FOR SCIENCE AND TECHNOLOGY

Background

86. In 1954, the Advisory Council on Scientific Policy recommended the creation of a national science lending library to take over and develop the postal lending service which the Science Museum Library was operating in South Kensington. The recommendation was influenced partly by the severe limitations of the South Kensington site and partly by the Science Museum Library's difficulty in combining successfully its growing postal lending operations with a public reference service and its lending services to local institutions.

87. Planning of the new library commenced in 1956 on the instructions of the Department of Scientific and Industrial Research (DSIR). It was intended that the new library should have adequate coverage of all scientific literature relevant to research and that it should give the quickest possible service, by having an organisation designed specifically for a lending function and by eliminating as far as possible waiting lists and delays due to binding. Surveys of the postal services led to the selection of a 60-acre site for the new library at Boston Spa in Yorkshire, from which virtually all parts of the United Kingdom can be reached by post within twenty-four hours. In August 1962 the National Lending Library for Science and Technology (NLLST) became fully operational.

88. When DSIR was split up in 1965 the responsibility for the new library was amongst those which passed to the Department of Education and Science, under the direct administration of which the NLLST still remains.

Functions

89. The main function of the library is to collect and make available the scientific literature of the world, and to promote its use. In 1967, it extended its activities to cover periodicals in the social sciences. The literature is made available chiefly through the library's loan and photocopying services, although there is also a reference reading room.

Sources of Finance

90. The library is financed partly through the DES vote and partly through the votes of other Government departments. The DES vote covers the costs of staffing, the purchase of literature and binding, the translating programme and miscellaneous items such as postage, telephone and Telex. The vote of the Ministry of Public Building and Works covers the costs of buildings, building maintenance, furniture, fuel and light and rates, whilst the Stationery Office vote bears the costs of stationery and packing materials, photographic equipment and related materials.

Services

(a) Loan procedures

91. The main purpose of the library is to supplement the internal resources of existing organisations by providing a rapid loan service. The use of the

NLLST has increased very rapidly during its seven years of operation and in 1968, loan requests exceeded 700,000, an increase of one fifth on the corresponding figure for 1967 (Figure 4). The list of approved borrowers at present numbers 3,100 industrial firms, research organisations, universities, colleges, hospitals and public libraries, but not individuals. Borrowers purchase pads of 50 loan request forms, priced at £4 to cover postage. The library aims to deal with all loan requests the day they are received, except Telex requests received late in the day, and despatches items by first-class letter post. The shelving of publications in alphabetical order without subject sub-divisions and the extensive use of mechanical handling techniques throughout the library contribute materially to the provision of an exceptionally rapid service. That the NLLST successfully meets a long-standing need and that its services are widely appreciated are abundantly clear from the many submissions which we have received.

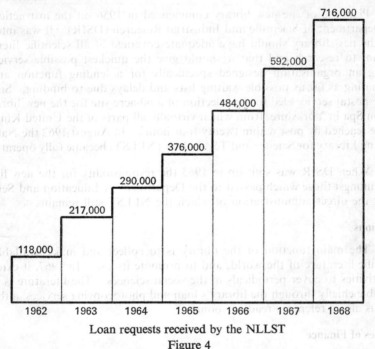

Loan requests received by the NLLST

Figure 4

92. Requests for publications not available at the NLLST are forwarded to the Science Museum Library or to the British Library of Political and Economic Science (BLPES), if those libraries are considered likely to satisfy them.

(b) Photocopying

93. The lending service is supplemented by a photocopying service which is available to both organisations and individuals. In 1968 63,000 requests were received, an increase of nearly half on the 1967 total (Figure 5, page 27). Requests are made on special pre-paid forms and the charge covers the photocopying production costs and postage. Government departments, however, use the service without charge. About 60 per cent of items are despatched on the day of receipt of the request. Orders are normally supplied either as full size electrostatic photocopy, or in microform.

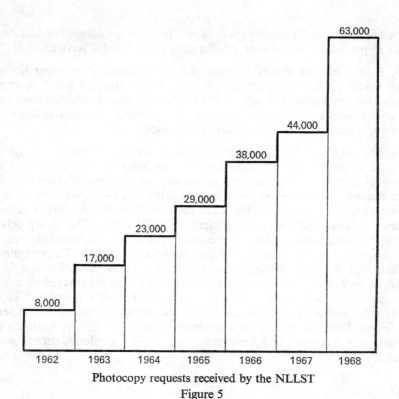

Photocopy requests received by the NLLST

Figure 5

(c) Reference

94. Visitors may requisition items from the library's stocks for perusal in the reading room, which contains on open access a selection of reference books, abstracts and other bibliographic tools. The photocopying service is also available to the users of the reading room during their visit. The present use of the reading room averages 7–8 people per day, four fifths of whom come from within 20 miles of the library.

(d) Other functions

95. Unlike other libraries, the NLLST does not produce a comprehensive record of its holdings. It relies on published bibliographies, abstracts and other indexing material to assist users in discovering references to a particular subject. It does, however, provide special facilities to organisations which prepare such bibliographic aids. It will, for example, assist abstracting organisations by arranging to circulate regularly to them the less frequently used journals in the appropriate subject areas.

96. Requests for technical information are also handled, mainly by referring the enquirer to the specialist organisation most likely to be able to assist him.

97. The library is responsible for operating the UK. MEDLARS service, which is an information retrieval service based on computer searching of the index of medical literature produced on magnetic tape by the National Library of Medicine in Bethesda, Maryland, U.S.A. The NLLST edits the enquiries it receives into a form suitable for computer searching which is then carried out

27

at the University of Newcastle-upon-Tyne. The average number of searches is about 35 per week. At present, no charge is made for this service.

98. Each week the library receives gifts of literature from other libraries which would occupy about 80 feet of shelf space. Material which is surplus to requirements is offered to other UK libraries. Much material in recent years has gone towards stocking the libraries of new universities and colleges. In addition, a small amount is used for foreign exchanges.

99. The NLLST makes special efforts to promote the use of the type of literature it collects by arranging courses, providing translation services and issuing publications. Regular courses on the use of scientific literature, and more recently on the use of social science literature, have been organised for academic and university library staff and for lecturers in library schools. Courses are also held for potential users of MEDLARS. The library collects available translations of Russian scientific literature and arranges for the translation of some Russian periodicals, books and articles. To promote the work in this field, the library issues the " NLL Translations Bulletin ". In addition, the NLLST attempts where possible to fill gaps not covered by existing scientific bibliographic tools. For example, it publishes a monthly " List of Books received from the USSR and Translated Books ", a quarterly " Index of Conference Proceedings ", a monthly bulletin entitled " British Research and Development Reports", and a comprehensive list of the titles of current serials which it receives.

Stock

100. The NLLST has about 36 miles of shelving and estimates that it will all be in use by 1971. The stock includes about 32,000 current serials, including medical and social science periodicals, and about the same number of discontinued titles. The book stock includes 95,000 English Language books, 45,000 Russian books, 30,000 in other languages and 32,000 overseas theses. Report literature and translated articles are kept mainly on microfilm (160 miles) or microfiches (150,000). The library's stock is growing rapidly and about 2,000 current serials, 31,000 books, 35,000 reports and 15,000 translated articles are added each year. The two latter items comprise an additional half mile of microfilm and 40,000 microfiches annually.

Staff

101. As the NLLST is part of the Department of Education and Science, the staff structure is based on civil service grades. Unlike the SML, however, the directing staff of the NLLST, almost without exception, are in the Scientific Grades. The following numbers of personnel are employed directly in providing the library's services:

senior staff including subject specialists	7
other executive and higher clerical staff	113

Costs of Services

102. It is difficult to estimate those costs of the library which are borne on the votes of the Ministry of Public Building and Works and HM Stationery Office.

The DES vote, however, carried the following major items of the library's expenditure for 1967/68:

Staff	..	..	..	..	..	..	£188,000
Direct purchase of literature		..	..	..	..	£225,000
Purchase of literature for exchange purposes		..		..	£9,000
Binding	..	..	..	..	..	..	£30,000
Translating programme	..	..	..	..	..	£175,000
Miscellaneous (postage, telephone, etc.)			..	..	£42,000

Receipts from the Translating Programme amounted to £126,000 and other receipts (mainly from loan forms) another £36,000. The net sum of these costs in 1967/68, therefore, slightly exceeded half a million pounds.

Usage Patterns

103. In order to augment the information previously supplied to us and to enable possible correlations to be tested, a survey of loan and photocopy issues was carried out by the library during the week commencing 9th December 1968. The survey sample was obtained by selecting for study every third item received in the packing bay for despatch. The sample consisted of 4,348 items, of which all except 120 were for users in the United Kingdom. When allowance for failures has been made, this figure corresponds almost exactly with the weekly average derived from the total requests received by the NLLST in 1968. Nevertheless, the issues during the survey week were 8 per cent below the weekly average for the preceding month, November. We understand, however, that a gradual decline in the usage of the NLLST is normal during December, and there is no reason to believe that the general pattern of usage revealed by the survey is seriously atypical. The principal types of information obtained from the survey are summarised in paragraphs (a) to (d). The full survey particulars are included in the appendices to this report.

(a) Users of the library

104. The greatest number of publications (about two fifths of the sample) were despatched to industrial users. The next largest group of users was the universities, with about one quarter of all the satisfied requests. No other category of users exceeded one tenth of the survey sample, although Government departments and educational users other than universities each accounted for 9 per cent. Government departments, however, made relatively greater use of the photocopying services by accounting for nearly half of all requests of this type. This is possibly related to the absence of charges. In general, demand for photocopies remains low—there were sixteen loans for each photocopy during the survey period.

(b) Origins of requests

105. Unlike the usage patterns of the SML and the NRLSI, the survey revealed no preponderance of local use of the NLLST. Over half the issues were made to London and the South East of England, about one tenth to the Midlands and a simialr proportion to the North West Counties (Figure 9 (i), page 59). These are all areas with great concentrations of industry. The high proportion of issues to London and the Home Counties (about two fifths of the

29

sample) indicates the value of the NLLST in supplementing the services provided by the scientific libraries in central London. Issues to universities in relation to the number of their academic staff show that a relatively high use of the library is made by the newer universities, Surrey, Sussex and Kent. Exceptionally low use was made of the NLLST by Oxford and Cambridge universities, probably because of their own outstandingly good sources of scientific literature.

(c) Types of material used

106. About nine tenths of all issues were serial publications, with books and reports making up the remainder. Over two thirds of the serial publications issued were in pure and applied science, about one sixth in medicine and about one twentieth in social science. Books and reports issues reflected a similar subject pattern. About half the items issued by the library were published in the last three years, nine tenths since 1950, and all but a twentieth since 1940. This pattern accurately follows that of the NRLSI and is markedly different from that of the SML. There was no significant difference between the distributions of date of publication for serials and for books. Among the specific categories of user, industrial organisations made a heavier than average demand for very recent material, but this was compensated by a relatively low demand for slightly older material.

(d) Use of photographic services

107. The survey shows that photocopying issues amounted to about 6 per cent of the total sample. It is understood from the NLLST that the demand for photocopying has been constant at about this proportion of annual demand for the last five years, although the volume of photocopying, like that of the library's other services, has increased rapidly (Figure 5, page 27).

(e) Survey of unsatisfied loan requests

108. During the week commencing 17th July 1968, the NLLST carried out a survey of its unsatisfied loan requests. The survey revealed that 87 per cent of the accepted requests were met from the NLLST stock and a further 4 per cent by the SML and the BLPES. Thus, the unsatisfied requests, which amounted to 1,052, represented less than one tenth of the total. About three fifths of the unsatisfied requests were for serials, about three tenths for books and the remainder for conference reports. Over half the serial failures were items which the library would consider for purchase in its review of serial holdings, about one eighth were items on order, and over a quarter were items about which insufficient information was given to enable an order to be placed. Of the unsatisfied requests for books, about one third were on order and almost a half were insufficiently described to make ordering possible. Nine tenths of the unsatisfied requests for conference reports did not give sufficient information to enable orders to be placed.

CHAPTER SIX

THE NATIONAL CENTRAL LIBRARY

Background

109. The library was founded in 1916 as the Central Library for Students. It was financed out of grants from the Carnegie United Kingdom Trust, and its primary purpose was to lend books to adult class students who had no other sources for borrowing. In 1927 the Kenyon Committee on Public Libraries* envisaged the library developing as the central clearing-house of an inter-library lending network embracing all the nation's library resources, and it suggested that this development should take place under the aegis of the British Museum. However, the Royal Commission on National Museums and Galleries subsequently recommended that the library should have independent status.

110. These several recommendations led in 1931 to the library's incorporation by Royal Charter as the National Central Library, which was to be the official clearing-house for inter-library lending. It was to provide a bibliographic service as well as continuing its original role in servicing adult classes. Under the Charter, the NCL is governed by a Board of eleven Trustees. Two of these are appointed by the Trustees of the British Museum, one by the Trustees of the British Museum (Natural History) and one by the Library Association. These four Trustees in turn appoint the remaining seven Trustees. The library is managed by an Executive Committee consisting of 25 members. The NCL Trustees appoint two of these, and most of the remainder are appointed by various library and adult education bodies. The Executive Committee elects its own Chairman and Vice-Chairman.

111. In 1966 the NCL moved to a new building in Store Street, about a quarter of a mile from the BML. These premises house the union catalogues (see paragraph 118), offices for the library's staff and about two-thirds of its book-stock. The remaining stock is outhoused at Woolwich.

Functions

112. As well as facilitating loans between libraries, the NCL contributes to inter-library co-operation by arranging the inter-change of duplicate and surplus library material both nationally and internationally. It also maintains and regularly publishes a catalogue giving the locations of new periodical titles held by British Libraries (BUCOP).

Sources of Finance

113. The major part of the NCL's income is now derived from a Government grant-in-aid for which the Department of Education and Science has responsibility. For 1967/68 this grant amounted to some 90 per cent of the library's estimated expenditure, the remaining 10 per cent being met mainly from voluntary contributions from public library authorities and other libraries.

---

* Report on Public Libraries in England and Wales, Cmnd. 2868, 1927.

Services

(a) Loan procedures

114. In arranging loans to other libraries, the NCL:

    (i) maintains union catalogues of the holdings of regional library systems and of individual libraries of all kinds which are willing to lend to other libraries through its auspices; and

    (ii) uses its own collection, which is composed of publications in demand but unlikely to be available elsewhere, together with material no longer needed by user libraries.

The library dealt with about 130,000 applications in 1967/68, an increase of one fifth over the 1964 figures. University and special libraries may apply directly to the NCL for loans, but in general public libraries apply first to their regional library systems, only passing to the NCL those requests which cannot be met regionally (see Chapter 2, paragraphs 23 and 24).

115. In meeting those requests which it cannot satisfy from its own stock, the NCL relies largely on the university libraries, the regional library systems, and on 391 special libraries which are known as " Outlier " libraries because they have formally agreed to lend through the NCL. Over 300 other special libraries lend occasionally through the NCL, and the library sometimes applies abroad for material not available for loan in Great Britain.

116. Most British libraries which lend through the NCL despatch the items for loan direct to the borrowing libraries. However, the NCL maintains a van to collect material from certain libraries in London. The NCL is, therefore, responsible for the despatch of these publications as well as those items lent from its own stock. This service is particularly valuable in the case of those special libraries within easy access from London with budgets too small to pay for special packing and postage facilities, since they could not otherwise afford to contribute to inter-library lending.

117. Most loan applications received at the NCL are for foreign and older British publications in the humanities and the social sciences. This is because:

    (i) many regional library systems are now virtually self-sufficient so far as recent British publications are concerned;

    (ii) the majority of loan requests relating to scientific and technical literature are sent to the NLLST, rather than to the NCL, since most can be satisfied quickly from the former's large stocks (see Chapter 5).

However, because of the high national demand for scientific and technical publications, and because the NCL is often tried after the NLLST has failed, over 25 per cent of NCL's loan applications are for this type of material.

118. When loan applications are received at the NCL, the staff refer to the 2,500,000 entries in the union catalogues (which include 450,000 entries for the NCL's own bookstock and a separate catalogue for Slavonic language material) in order to obtain a location for the material in question. Despite efforts to improve them, these catalogues have a number of serious limitations as locating tools:

(i) The holding library is not shown on entries lodged by regional library systems.

(ii) There are arrears of over one million items for inclusion in the catalogues, due very largely to staff shortages and the labour involved in making out catalogue card entries.

(iii) Many libraries are slow to notify the NCL of additions to, and deletions from, their stocks.

(iv) Some material included in the union catalogues proves not to be available for loan when requested.

119. If there is no entry in the union catalogues for a particular item, a bibliographic check is automatically carried out to verify the reference contained in the loan applications. The NCL itself has a very wide range of bibliographic aids, but in some cases a member of staff will go to the BML to consult other indexes and catalogues.

120. Where references in applications are correct and the union catalogues fail, the NCL staff has to rely on speculative searches of particular libraries which experience suggests as likely sources. This process is expensive and often slow in that it may occupy a great deal of specialists' time, but the expertise of the staff is reflected in that success is often ultimately achieved.

(b) Photocopying

121. The NCL also provides a photocopying service based largely on its own stocks and on the photocopying facilities at the BML. A request for a photocopy can often be met more quickly and probably at lower total cost than a request for the loan of the original material, particularly since, in dealing with many loan applications, the NCL staff has to embark upon protracted speculative searches for the loan of items which are known to be available for photocopying in the BML.

(c) The British Union Catalogue of Periodicals (BUCOP)

122. In 1962 the NCL assumed the responsibility for maintaining and publishing BUCOP, an index giving locations for British library holdings of periodicals which first appeared or changed titles after 1959. BUCOP is based on information supplied by some 450 libraries, and is published quarterly. Cumulated annual volumes are available, as well as separate cumulations covering scientific and technical titles only.

(d) The British National Book Centre (BNBC)

123. The BNBC is the name given to the NCL's exchange organisation. Since 1948 it has redistributed just under two million volumes and parts of books and periodicals—i.e. an average of 2,000 per week—among about 1,000 British libraries and, since 1960, has sent about 250,000 items to foreign libraries. In return, libraries overseas have sent the BNBC over 50,000 publiactions for distribution among British libraries, including the NCL. Although these flows are so different in size, the receiving libraries in Britain as well as overseas, find in this traffic a valuable means of augmenting their collections.

(e) Adult class book supply

124. The library continues the service originally provided by the Central Library for Students. Over 4,000 books were supplied for adult class use in 1967/68.

(f) Bibliography enquiry service

125. Apart from the bibliographic verification of loan applications described in paragraph 119, the NCL receives by post or telephone about 1,500 specific bibliographic enquiries per annum. Many of these require detailed reference to original material, and the NCL staff engaged on this work relies heavily upon its special privilege of direct access to the BML's bookstacks.

Stock

126. The NCL's own stock is estimated at about 450,000 volumes, which occupy over eight miles of shelving. Periodicals make up about 16 per cent of the stock; of the monographs, about 80 per cent are foreign publications and 85 per cent, by subject classification, are in the humanities and social sciences.

127. In 1967/68 the library acquired over 45,000 volumes, of which approximately one fifth was purchased. Gifts and exchange through the BNBC accounted in about equal numbers for the remainder. The total number of additions to stock has varied a great deal from year to year, and from 1963/64 has revealed no consistent trend. The number of volumes purchased annually has, however, shown a modest increase in recent years—from 8,216 volumes in 1963/64 to 9,498 in 1967/68.

Staff

128. Of those members of the staff directly concerned with library services, twenty-six are senior library staff, including subject specialists, and thirteen are other executive and higher clerical staff. Senior library staff have the same conditions of service as local authority librarians.

Costs of Services

129. The library's grant-in-aid from the Department of Education and Science for 1967/68 was £161,000. Its estimated expenditure for that year was £178,000.

130. Staff costs amounted in 1967/68 to over £110,000, and about £16,000 was spent on acquisitions and binding. The library recovers its postage and carriage costs and the costs (not including overheads or labour) of its photocopying services.

Statistics of Loan Applications and User Requirements

131. In 1964 the NCL carried out a six month survey of loan applications for the UGC Committee on Libraries. At our request, the library undertook a further survey of applications during March, 1968, and another of user requirements. The library's staff collated and analysed the survey data, as well as carrying out their normal duties. The succeeding paragraphs of this Chapter

34

draw extensively upon the results of the 1968 surveys and, for purposes of comparison, the 1964 survey.

(a) Success rates

132. During the 1968 survey period the NCL received nearly 11,000 applications, of which 78 per cent were satisfied (Figure 6 (ii)). This is very slightly less than the comparable figure in 1964, but the difference is almost certainly not significant.

133. Detailed analysis shows that the library is more successful in meeting requests for material in the social sciences and the humanities than in science and technology, and is markedly more successful at meeting requests for books than for periodicals. The success rates for scientific material and for periodical literature have declined by about 5 per cent and 10 per cent respectively since 1964. This is probably because the NCL is receiving proportionately fewer requests for the more easily traceable periodicals and scientific material as a result of an increasing reliance by user libraries on BUCOP as a locating tool for serials and rapidly increasing use of the NLLST.

134. As might be expected, the library is more successful in meeting requests for British publications (about 85 per cent success) than for American or foreign language publications (about 75 per cent and 65 per cent respectively).

(b) Sources of applications

135. Approximately 40 per cent of applications are made by university libraries and about 35 per cent by public libraries. There has been since 1964 a large increase in the proportion of loan applications from university libraries and an equivalent decrease in that of applications from public libraries. This probably reflects the increase in the number of universities and, particularly, the reliance of new universities on outside sources. During the same period, the coverage of British publications by the regional systems, of which all public libraries are members, has steadily improved.

136. About 3 per cent of applications are from " Outlier " special libraries, 15 per cent from other special libraries, and a further 6 per cent come from libraries abroad (Figure 6 (i)).

(c) Sources of loans

137. The NCL meets one fifth of all *satisfied* requests from its own stock. University libraries meet two fifths and public libraries and regional systems a further one fifth. The remainder is met almost equally from " Outlier " and other special libraries, with a small percentage met from foreign sources (Figure 6 (ii), page 36). The university libraries are now making a greater contribution to inter-library lending than in 1964, and the public libraries a smaller contribution. These changes are approximately in line with changes in the pattern of applications from these sources over the same period.

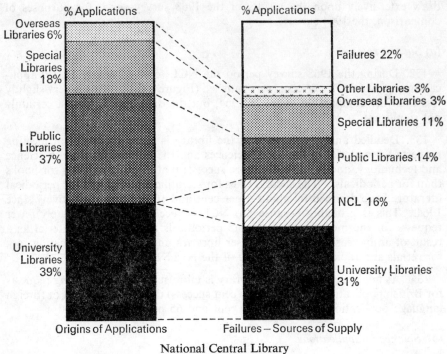

% Applications   % Applications

Overseas Libraries 6%
Special Libraries 18%
Public Libraries 37%
University Libraries 39%

Failures 22%
Other Libraries 3%
Overseas Libraries 3%
Special Libraries 11%
Public Libraries 14%
NCL 16%
University Libraries 31%

Origins of Applications   Failures – Sources of Supply

National Central Library

(i)   Figure 6   (ii)

(d) Search methods

138. Of those items supplied, about two thirds were obtained from the first location given in the union catalogues (including catalogued material from the NCL's stocks), one seventh was supplied from a second or subsequent location given in the catalogues, and a tenth as a result of speculative searches.

139. The library's efforts in recent years to improve the efficiency of the catalogues as locating tools have increased the proportion of all applications met from catalogue locations (including its own stocks) from about 60 per cent in 1964 to 66 per cent in 1968. The remaining applications required extensive bibliographic checking and speculative approaches, which were not always successful, as 22 per cent of all applications remained unsatisfied in the 1968 survey.

(e) User attitudes

140. The NCL surveyed 372 special, university and public libraries in order to obtain information about the characteristics of users, the reasons why requested items were wanted, and users' attitudes to delays in the supply of loan material.

141. Almost 70 per cent of the material requested by special library users and over 80 per cent of that by university library users were needed in connexion with formal or private research work. Requests by public library users were made for a much wider range of reasons, the largest single categories being " general interest " and " private research ".

36

142. In no type of library did more than half the users regard the material which they requested as " essential " or " very important to their work ", but the proportion was over 40 per cent for university libraries. Only 15 per cent of special library and public library users and 25 per cent of university library users thought that a delay of more than one month in the supply of loan material was intolerable. Half the public library users, almost half of those in special libraries, and one third of university library users were prepared to wait for varying periods in excess of two months. These figures may suggest that a loan service as offered by the NCL, mainly in the humanities and social sciences, does not need to be particularly rapid. Indeed, they could be interpreted as indicating that the speed of the existing services, under which the 1968 survey showed that nearly two thirds of all satisfied requests are met within two weeks and only a sixth take longer than four weeks, is satisfactory. However, about half the universities and many learned societies and individuals have indicated in evidence to us that, whilst requests may often not need to be satisfied within a matter of days, the delays associated with supplying urgently required material, together with a chance of total failure approaching one in four even after protracted efforts by the NCL staff, are causing considerable disquiet among the library's principal users.

CHAPTER SEVEN

THE SCIENCE MUSEUM LIBRARY

Background

143. The origins of the Science Museum Library (SML) go back to 1843 when the private collections of Sir Henry de la Beche became the nucleus of a library for the Officers of the Geological Survey and the Museum of Practical Geology. After the founding of the School of Mines in South Kensington in 1851, and aided by a variety of gifts from publishers, institutions and exhibitions, the library gradually developed general scientific coverage. In 1876, the collections were again augmented by the acquisition of the library which had been formed for the use of Inspectors of Schools. In 1883, when further reorganisation and amalgamation took place, the whole collection in South Kensington was renamed the Science Library.

144. After five changes of location in the old buildings of the South Kensington Museum, the library moved in 1908 to the building of the Royal College of Science, one of the constituent colleges of the Imperial College of Science and Technology. It is now, however, about to move to new, specially designed premises within the same building which will house the Lyon Playfair Library, the central library of Imperial College.

145. The SML is one of the nine departments of the Science Museum and, as such, is administered by a Keeper responsible to the Director of the Museum. Since the Science Museum as a whole is a responsibility of the Department of Education and Science, the Museum's Director is answerable for the library to the Secretary of State for Education and Science.

146. Associated with the Science Museum is an Advisory Council of 16 members appointed by and reporting to the Secretary of State for Education and Science. The Advisory Council, which at present includes in its membership the Rector and one of the Governing Body of Imperial College, meets normally about three times per year to consider library and other matters relating to the Science Museum.

Functions

147. The SML consists mainly of a large general science collection at postgraduate level. Its principal emphasis is on mathematical, physical, chemical and engineering sciences, although it also has substantial collections of literature in the biological and earth sciences. In recent years it has not attempted general coverage of publications in the less common foreign languages, although in its main specialism, the history of science and technology, it aims at complete world coverage of serials and of original primary monographs in all languages. The functions of the library are organised partly to help satisfy national needs for scientific literature and information and partly to serve the concentration of colleges and museums in South Kensington. Since the NLLST became operational in 1962, the SML has become more concerned with its local responsibilities, although the library is still open to the general public for reference and provides some national lending services in conjunction with the NLLST.

Sources of Finance

148. All the cost of maintaining the SML and of providing its library services is met from public funds. Salaries and general administrative expenses are accounted for by the Department of Education and Science, whilst building maintenance is the responsibility of the Ministry of Public Building and Works. The costs of purchases for the library, together with those for stationery and printing, are met out of the HM Stationery Office vote. Publications for the library are, however, also obtained through donations and exchange.

Services

(a) National responsibilities

149. In meeting its national responsibilities, the SML provides reference facilities, together with an information and bibliographic enquiry service, for the general public. The total number of visitors to the library's reading room has remained virtually constant at about 20,000 per year since 1963. This total includes all types of user, but a survey carried out on our behalf by the Keeper and his staff from 11th March to 6th April, 1968, showed that only about one third of the visitors sampled were not from the colleges and museums in South Kensington.

150. The library's information and bibliographic service handled nearly 5,000 enquiries during 1967/68, excluding help given to visitors in using the library's catalogues and services. About three quarters of them were phone enquiries, although one in eight involved a personal visit by the enquirer.

151. For many years the SML lent from its stock to Government establishments, universities, learned societies and certain approved libraries. However, in 1962 the NLLST took over from the SML the main responsibility for postal lending. Since then, the SML has restricted its national lending to those categories of stock not held by the NLLST. Loans of this type from the SML have remained at around 15,000 per year for several years, which, as the use of the NLLST grows, represents a declining proportion of the combined total of the two libraries' satisfied requests. At present the SML's contribution is slightly more than 2 per cent of the total.

152. The SML also operates a public photocopy service—including the production of microfiches—for literature held in the libraries of the four main South Kensington museums, viz. the Science Museum, the Victoria and Albert Museum, the Natural History Museum and the Institute of Geological Sciences. In 1967, photocopy requisitions received by the SML from the public totalled 20,400, of which 2,700 were forwarded from the NLLST. Over nine tenths of all orders were satisfactorily completed. In addition, the library photocopies without charge for Government departments and the staff of the local museums. The output of this service in 1967 was only slightly less than the volume of photocopy supplied to the public.

(b) Services to local institutions

153. In meeting local needs, the SML is both a working collection for the staff of the Science Museum, which has no departmental libraries, and an essential part of the library system of Imperial College, for which it provides

39

reference and lending facilities, information services and training courses. That the SML sees the servicing of Imperial College as one of its most important roles was made clear in its evidence to us; it is also reflected in the library's organisation and policies. In addition, however, it acts as a central photo-copying unit and a supplementary source of literature for the staff of the three other South Kensington museums.

Stock

154. The library's holdings fall into two main categories: (i) bound volumes of books, serials, patents and newspapers, and (ii) microforms. Figures supplied to us show that there are at present about seven and a half miles of shelving occupied by the library's 400,000 bound volumes, of which all except one third of a mile are closed stacks. The microform collection consists of 45,000 microcards, 28,000 microfiches and a few reels of microfilm.

155. At the end of 1967, the stock of the SML included 5,000 current periodical titles and a further 14,000 non-current serial titles. In recent years, the library has been growing at the rate of about 6,000 volumes per year, whilst the rate of acquisition of microforms has been accelerating rapidly, with 11,000 microfiches being added in 1967/68.

156. The policy governing the library's acquisition of new material is centred around meeting the essential and immediate needs of the Museum staff and Imperial College. The library attempts to maintain a comprehensive collection of monographs, trade literature, historical documents and journals to meet the professional needs of the staff in the various scientific and technological departments of the Science Museum. It is extremely difficult to make a clear distinction between material acquired primarily for the Museum and that for Imperial College, but the library's exceptionally good coverage of the history of science and technology is intended to satisfy one of the Museum's essential requirements. For Imperial College, the library undertakes the selective buying of monograph literature of postgraduate level and the most important journals. The College's emphasis on the physical, applied and engineering sciences is reflected in the library's acquisitions, the selection of which is made with the needs of staff, postgraduates and final-year undergraduates particularly in mind.

Staff

157. As the library is a department of the Science Museum, the whole of which is administered by the Department of Education and Science, keeper and other civil service grades form the staff structure of the SML. There are seven senior library staff, with a further 42 executive and higher clerical staff wholly engaged on library duties. The library and the museum departments have common secretarial and messenger services, whilst establishment work is either shared with the museum or carried out by the headquarters staff of the Department of Education and Science.

Costs of Services

158. During the financial year 1967/68 wages and salaries of staff wholly engaged on library duties amounted to £73,500, plus about £3,500 to cover the

library's share of the cost of staff from the common pool. The public photocopy service aims at being self-supporting and it is estimated that rather more than £2,000 was contributed directly through the purchase of photocopy requisition forms towards the wages of the staff engaged on photocopy work. The net staff costs were, therefore, approximately £75,000.

159. Acquisition costs for 1967/68 amounted to £24,200. In addition, the SML received by presentation or exchange material valued at around £11,500, less about £1,300 given by the SML in exchange. With binding costs of £16,300, salaries and the cost of acquisitions totalled £115,000.

160. Building maintenance and other running costs are as complicated and as difficult to assess as for the BML. The existing SML building is provided rent-free and is largely maintained by Imperial College, although furniture and shelving are the responsibility of the Ministry of Public Building and Works. The library's outstore at Woolwich, plus some accommodation in the Science Museum is also maintained by the Ministry. Office machinery and photocopying equipment, on the other hand, are provided by HM Stationery Office.

Usage Patterns

161. In 1967/68 there were about 20,200 visitors to the SML. Over a five year period, the number of visitors annually has varied little; the highest figure was 20,600 in 1963/64 and the lowest 19,500 in 1964/65. Requisitions for reference material on closed access have shown a tendency to decline slightly from rather more than 16,000 in 1963/64 to about 14,500 in 1967/68. A consistently high proportion of requests of this type was satisfied, however, with an average for the five year period of 92½ per cent. There are no comparable figures for consultations of the material on open access.

162. Loan requisitions satisfied during this period have shown no consistent trend; the annual figures have varied from a minimum of 21,192 in 1963/64 to a maximum of 24,933 in 1966/67. During 1967/68, slightly more than half the total was made in response to requisitions from users of the NLLST, with Imperial College accounting for over a quarter and the Science Museum about one sixth.

163. In 1967/68 the total output of photocopies was split approximately evenly between that carried out free of charge for Government departments and institutions and that provided for sale to the public. Since 1963/64, the total output of all types of photocopy has been increasing, with the 1967/68 figure of 186,000 pages or frames representing an increase of nearly a third over that for 1963/64.

164. The Keeper and his staff surveyed the use of the library from 11th March to 6th April 1968, a period which straddled term and vacation at Imperial College. The survey yielded 1,412 completed questionnaires, equivalent to a response rate of 78 per cent, which is a particularly satisfactory figure in view of the length of the survey period. When allowance is made for the response rate, it would appear that during the four weeks of the survey, the SML was rather more heavily used than a four-week average for 1967/68 of about 1,600 visitors might lead one to expect. The discrepancy was not marked, however, and is probably accounted for by normal seasonal fluctuations in the library's use.

(a) The library users

165. Three quarters of all readers during the survey period were staff or students of higher educational institutions, all but one twentieth of whom were from universities. Excepting Imperial College, London University contributed 7 per cent of the visitors, with an almost identical proportion coming from all other universities together. Outside these categories, the largest group consisted of research and development workers who made up one twelfth of the total. In contrast to the NRLSI, patent workers made only an insignificant use of the SML, and all industrial and commercial use accounted for only one sixteenth of the total.

166. The survey results give substantial support to the view expressed to us in several pieces of evidence that the major part of the SML's work is concentrated on meeting the needs of Imperial College. About 60 per cent of the library's visitors were associated with the College (Figure 7); half were postgraduate students and the rest were divided almost equally between staff and undergraduates. During the two weeks of the survey that were in term time, the proportion of readers from Imperial College reached two thirds of the total, but it fell to nearer one half during the vacation weeks. Analysis of the signatures in the visitors' book from 5th February to 27th April showed that on average two readers out of every three were from Imperial College. As this period is much longer than that of the survey, and as it is more correctly balanced between term and vacation, the higher proportion of use by Imperial College is probably the more typical. The loan statistics follow a similar pattern and, although the loan commitment of the SML remains predominantly national through its support of the NLLST, 60 per cent of all loan requests originating locally are from Imperial College, whose share amounted to over 6,000 loans in 1967–68.

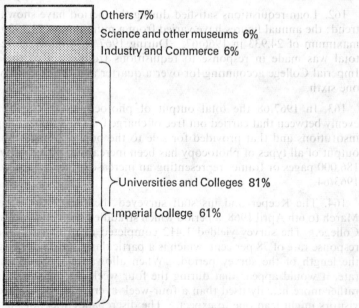

Occupations of readers at the SML

Figure 7

42

167. Whereas Imperial College is undoubtedly the SML's principal user, the library is not by any means the College's only source of literature. Not only has it a central library of its own, but there is also a system of departmental libraries, many of which have developed over a considerable period and are heavily used by both staff and students.

168. In addition to the readers from Imperial College, one reader in sixteen came from the institutes and museums of South Kensington. Of this latter group, three quarters were staff of the Science Museum itself. The survey almost certainly underestimated the use by the Science Museum staff, however, who, in having direct access to the closed stacks, did not always complete a questionnaire.

169. The geographical origins of the SML's users reflect the use of the library by the local colleges and institutions. Eighty-two per cent of the readers sampled travelled less than five miles to use the library, whereas only 2 per cent had come over 50 miles on the day of their visit. However, 8 per cent stated that their normal place of work was over 50 miles away, from which it may be surmised that a small but significant use of the SML is made by people temporarily resident in London, or by those who are combining a visit to the library with other activities locally.

(b) The material used

170. The most heavily used subject field was chemistry; nearly one in four readers specified that they were seeking literature in this subject. One reader in six consulted physics literature and one in six engineering publications. About one tenth of the readers surveyed mentioned biological science and a similar proportion mathematics. Other important subjects for which the SML is used include industrial chemistry, geology, the history of science and technology, and medical science.

171. Analysis of the reading room requisitions during the survey period shows that about three quarters were for serial publications and rather less than a quarter for books. This pattern is generally similar to those of the NRLSI and the NLLST, but the proportion of serial use is rather higher than at the NRLSI and slightly lower than at the NLLST. The date distribution of the material requisitioned shows a stronger bias towards older material than in the other two science libraries. Seventy-eight per cent of requisitions were for post-1950 publications and 85 per cent for post-1940 material. The use of the library for items of historical interest is emphasised by the 5 per cent of requisitions which were for nineteenth century material and the 1 per cent for earlier publications.

(c) Methods of use of the library

172. Like the NRLSI, the SML is used for short, relatively frequent visits. Three quarters of visitors stayed two hours or less and well over half for no more than one hour. Nearly one half of the library's users visited it at least once a week, reflecting the relatively frequent use of the SML by members of nearby Imperial College; others used the library much less frequently on average. Half the readers had tried another library before coming to the SML and of these two thirds had consulted a university or college library. It is

interesting, however, that a further one eighth had previously tried one of the national libraries—the BML, the NRLSI, the NLLST or the NCL.

173. Over half the readers were seeking only items for which they had precise references, although the catalogues and other bibliographic tools were heavily used. One in five readers answering said that they consulted only the material on open access. In view of the relatively small proportion of such material, this figure is particularly interesting. It is probably largely due to local visitors dropping into the SML to consult the current issues of periodicals.

174. The survey also showed that one in eight visitors used the SML only for study, and did not refer to the library's stocks. Three quarters of these were from Imperial College and almost all were undergraduates.

175. Nearly two thirds of the users who answered stated that they were wholly successful in obtaining what they required. When the proportion of those partly satisfied is added, rather more than three quarters of readers obtained some of the material for which they visited the library. In particular well over four fifths of those readers who had previously tried the BML, the NRLSI, the NLLST, or the NCL found that the SML had the items which they were seeking.

CHAPTER EIGHT

THE BRITISH NATIONAL BIBLIOGRAPHY

Background

176. In 1947, a committee of the Library Association was set up to consider the provision of centralised cataloguing and bibliographical services. This committee was ultimately superseded by the Committee on National Bibliography on which sat representatives from the British Museum, the Library Association, the Publishers Association, the Booksellers Association, the National Book League, the British Council, the Royal Society the Association of Special Libraries and Information Bureaux, the NCL, and the then UNESCO Co-ordinating Body for Libraries. This committee registered itself in July 1949 under the Industrial and Provident Societies Acts 1893–1928, as a non-profit making society, known as the Council of the British National Bibliography Limited (BNB).

Functions

177. The functions of the society at the time of its registration were defined as follows:

" to carry on the business of compiling, editing and publishing in appropriate bibliographic form lists of books pamphlets and other recorded material of whatever nature published in Great Britain, the Dominions and Colonies and/or foreign countries, together with such annotations or further information as may be desirable for the use of librarians, bibliographers and others ".

Sources of Finance

178. When BNB was set up in 1949, its assets were a capital of 15s., a guarantee for one year of £2,000 from the Library Association, and a promise of accommodation in the British Museum with access to books received in the Museum's Copyright Receipt Office. The work of the society has developed rapidly since 1949, and the income derived from its various services has enabled it to become financially self-supporting. Accommodation for the BNB was provided by the BM up to 1967 when the arrangement was discontinued because of the BM's acute space problems. The BNB is now mainly housed in new premises in Rathbone Street, W.1, but it also has some staff in accommodation at Ridgmount Street, W.C.1, and Bedford Square, W.C.1.

Services

(a) The British National Bibliography

179. The most important service is the production of the British National Bibliography itself, which is a record of most of the publications received by the BM under legal deposit. The number of entries has grown from about 13,000 in 1950 to nearly 27,000 in 1967. The Bibliography is published weekly, with cumulations monthly (alphabetical section only), quarterly, annually and every five years. When the BNB moved from the premises of the BM in 1967 it no longer had access to the books received in the BM's Copyright Receipt Office. An arrangement was, therefore, made with the

Copyright Libraries of Oxford, Cambridge, the National Library of Scotland and Trinity College, Dublin, to accommodate their agent on the BNB's premises, and to use the material deposited with him as the main basis for compiling the Bibliography. This arrangement has the advantage for the four Copyright Libraries concerned that they receive their books together with the necessary cataloguing data. But there is the disadvantage for the BNB that it has to retain staff at premises in Bedford Square close to the BM to carry out occasional checks of the items received by the Copyright Receipt Office, in order to ensure that items have not been missed. Production of the Bibliography would, therefore, be facilitated by a return to the former close association of the BNB with the BM's Copyright Receipt Office, on the same premises.

(b) The British Catalogue of Music

180. The BNB produces the British Catalogue of Music which is a record of music scores published in Britain received by the BM under legal deposit. It is issued at four-monthly intervals and is cumulated annually.

(c) The Printed Card Service

181. Printed catalogue cards from the weekly publication of the British National Bibliography are sold to individual libraries upon request. Depending on the rate of publication, which varies seasonally, orders for cards are met within two to seven days. Some 300 libraries regularly use the service and purchase about three million cards a year.

182. The service also provides the basic catalogues for six out of the ten Regional Bureaux, and reports monthly to these Bureaux the new books added to member libraries which use the printed card service. The service not only reduces the work of Regional Editors but eliminates the labour of reporting by the member libraries.

(d) The Shared Cataloguing Project of the Library of Congress

183. The project is designed to provide for the university and research libraries of the USA cataloguing information about all current books published anywhere in the world. The BNB supplies the Library of Congress with copies of catalogue entries in advance of publication.

(e) The Project for Machine-Readable Cataloguing Data (Project MARC)

184. The BNB is concerned with the preparation of an international format for a machine-readable catalogue record and keeps in close touch with the progress of a similar project at the Library of Congress, The objects of the BNB MARC Project, which is supported by funds from OSTI, are to develop computer-aided techniques for the production of the British National Bibliography, to provide a weekly service of bibliographic information on magnetic tapes for use in libraries generally, and to devise ways of exploiting the accumulation of cataloguing data in machine-readable form.

(f) The Fotolist Service

185. To cope with the volume of entries recorded in the British National Bibliography and to eliminate production delays caused through the limitations

of traditional type-setting, the BNB has, since 1960, used a special photographic technique, which is also made available to other bibliographic and indexing services.

(g) Other services

186. The staff of the BNB is in demand for consultation and advice on matters concerning bibliography, cataloguing and classification. Its members assisted, for example, in the preparation of the Revised Anglo-American Cataloguing Rules which require libraries to enter books under the form of author's name most likely to be looked for by the reader. The BNB has also been associated with the Publishers Association's proposals for Standard Book Numbering, by which each new book will be given a unique numerical identification. This scheme, in which the BNB will be an active participant, will greatly facilitate the introduction of computer methods to library management, stock control and bibliographic processing.

Staff

187. The BNB is controlled by a Managing Editor, and is organised in five departments: accounts, editorial, production, research and development, and secretarial and administration. In 1967 the total staff, excluding cleaners and messengers, was about 80.

Costs of Services

188. The BNB's annual accounts for the year ended 31st December 1967 show that staff costs amounted to about £90,000. The cost of printing and binding was about £22,000, and other direct production and distribution expenditure totalled £30,000. About £60,000 was spent on building maintenance, furniture and equipment, fuel and light, stationery, amortisation and general administration. All of these costs, totalling over £200,000, were covered by the income received by the BNB from subscriptions and revenue from its various services.

Use of the BNB Services

189. The School of Library Studies of the Queen's University, Belfast, has recently been studying the use of the BNB's services in the United Kingdom. The statistics in paragraphs 190 and 191 have been obtained as a result of this investigation.

(a) Current Booklist Services

190. In 1967, over 1,300 libraries were subscribers to the BNB's current booklist services. They comprised about nine tenths of the public libraries, over half the university and national libraries, half the college and school libraries and about one sixteenth of the special libraries. As would be expected libraries which did not subscribe, whether publicly maintained or in academic institutions, were almost all small units.

(b) Printed Card Service

191. Of the 300 libraries using the Printed Card Service in 1966, about three fifths were public libraries, and over a quarter college libraries. The

remainder consisted of a small number of university libraries and special libraries. About 80 per cent of all sales of BNB printed cards in the United Kingdom went to public libraries, although only about two fifths of all public libraries were subscribers to the service.

(c) Overseas Sales

192. The BNB's current booklists have a world-wide circulation among libraries of all kinds and thus serve a purpose of national importance by disseminating overseas complete information about books written and published in the United Kingdom. Overseas sales account for about 30 per cent of all sales of the Bibliography, and, in 1968, amounted to about 1,600 annual volumes, 1,200 quarterly cumulations and 1,400 weekly lists.

CHAPTER NINE

NATIONAL LIBRARIES OF SCOTLAND AND WALES

National Library of Scotland

(a) Background

193. The National Library of Scotland was established in Edinburgh as a reference library by the National Library of Scotland Act 1925. The Act transferred to a Board of Trustees the library founded by the Faculty of Advocates some 250 years earlier, and which had been since 1709 one of the six copyright libraries in the British Isles entitled to claim a copy of all UK publications. The Secretary of State for Scotland is an *ex officio* member of the Board of Trustees, and of the other 33 members, five are appointed by the Crown on the recommendation of the Secretary of State, twelve, including the Lord Advocate and the Lord Provosts of major cities, are *ex officio* members, five are representatives of the Faculty of Advocates, seven are representatives of other interests including the Scottish Universities, and five are co-opted by the Trustees.

194. Between 1925 and 1965 the library dealt directly with the Treasury for all matters affecting Government. In 1965 the Act of 1925 was amended by the Transfer of Functions (Cultural Institutions) Order 1965, and the functions formerly exercised by the Treasury were transferred to the Secretary of State for Scotland.

195. The Trustees are charged with the duties of maintaining the collections and making them available for inspection; they have the power to lend material, but this has only been exercised on rare occasions in respect of unique items sought by other institutions for exhibition purposes. The Trustees also have the power to dispose of material.

(b) Sources of finance

196. Public funds for the library are derived from the following departmental votes:

- (i) that of the Ministry of Public Building and Works, which covers maintenance, furniture, fuel, light, rates, etc.;
- (ii) that of HM Stationery Office, which covers stationery and printing;
- (iii) that of the Scottish Education Department, which covers salaries, general administrative expenses, purchases, and the subscription to the Copyright Agency.

The Trustees also administer a number of Trust funds, principally for the purchase of books and manuscripts.

(c) Services

197. The library is a major reference and research library for British and foreign literature, but specialises in material related to Scotland. The stock includes books, periodicals, newspapers, maps and musical scores in the Department of Printed Books, and manuscripts and drawings in the Department

of Manuscripts. Most of the manuscripts are records of life in Scotland. The material is organised on the closed access principle, and items are delivered to readers in the main reading room, which accommodates 100 readers. The Trustees' evidence to the Committee states that readers seldom wait more than 15 minutes for their material to arrive, and sometimes as little as five minutes.

198. Unlike the BML, the National Library of Scotland does not publish its general catalogue, which is maintained in card form, and contains almost a million entries. It is, however, engaged in the compilation of a series of catalogue lists designed to publicise the library's holdings of books before about 1800. These will include an up-to-date union list of books printed in Scotland before 1700, a list of the library's holdings of British books printed between 1641 and 1700, and another of foreign books before 1600 and eventually 1700.

199. The reference facilities are supported by a photocopying service providing full size copies or microforms.

(d) Stock

200. The stock is estimated to amount to about three million printed items and manuscripts, including about 3,700 current periodicals. Annual accessions amount to about 130,000 printed items.

(e) Staff

201. Keeper and other civil service grades form the staff structure, and there are about 24 senior library staff including subject specialists.

(f) Costs of services

202. The approximate cost of staffing the library in 1967/68 was £164,000, and general administrative expenses amounted to about £5,500. The annual expenditure from public funds on books for the collection has been £25,000 since 1964/65, and the subscription to the Copyright Agency in requisitioning legal deposit material was £3,000 in 1967/68. After allowing for income received, the sum of these costs is about £190,000.

203. Additional expenditure on the library borne on the votes of other Government departments amounted to about £54,000 in 1967/68. Of this, about £22,000 was spent on maintenance, furniture, fuel and light, rates, etc., and about £29,000 on stationery and printing.

(g) Usage

204. The evidence we have received suggests that the library is used extensively by Scottish scholars for its large collections of literature of the later 19th and 20th centuries, and for its collections related to Scottish interests. For some studies, however, the staff of the Scottish universities still rely on the much larger collections of manuscripts and foreign literature available only in the BML. The value of the library would be greatly enhanced if a complete catalogue were published and a reading room for current periodicals were available.

Scottish Central Library

(a) Background

205. In 1921 the Carnegie United Kingdom Trust established the Scottish Central Library (SCL) for the issue of books to full-time students and to adult education classes. By 1946 every county in Scotland was administering a county library service and, in consequence, the SCL discontinued the issue of books directly to individuals, becoming instead a clearing house for Scottish inter-library loans. A central book stock was, however, still maintained to supplement the union catalogues. The library is governed by a Board of Trustees, but for most purposes responsibility is exercised by an Executive Committee which consists of representatives of local authority associations, library associations and users.

(b) Functions

206. The library acts as the focal point for the co-ordination of library resources in Scotland, and arranges inter-library loans mainly between Scottish libraries.

(c) Sources of finance

207. The Carnegie United Kingdom Trust ceased payments to the SCL in 1955, when the Public Libraries (Scotland) Act gave local authorities power to contribute to the SCL. The Treasury and the local authority associations contributed equal amounts from 1955/56 to 1967/68. For 1968/69, in response to representations from the Executive Committee, the Treasury grant was increased to 75 per cent of estimated expenditure, leaving the local authorities to contribute the balance.

(d) Inter-library loan service

208. In 1967/68 the SCL dealt with over 25,000 requests for loans, of which about 85 per cent were satisfied. Loans were arranged mainly through the co-operating libraries but also to some extent from SCL's own stock of about 40,000 items. Included in the total of satisfied requests were about 2,000 items loaned to libraries in England and Wales in response to requests received from the NCL in London. The SCL borrowed about the same number of items through the NCL for Scottish libraries.

209. The SCL's union catalogue, at the end of 1967/68, contained over half a million entries of the holdings of Scottish libraries. In order to locate requested material, for which there are no entries in the union catalogue, the library circulates fortnightly to 85 Scottish libraries a list of wanted items. In 1967/68, almost two thirds of the items so listed were located.

(e) International book loans

210. The SCL is steadily developing arrangements for the exchange of books between Scottish libraries and libraries abroad. About 170 volumes were lent to foreign libraries in 1967/68, and over 100 were borrowed from abroad.

(f) Photocopying

211. The library's photocopying service supplied about 20,000 microfilm exposures and 2,000 prints in 1967/68, in addition to providing some xerographic copies of scarce books.

(g) Staff

212. The total staff of the library in March 1968 numbered 17.

(h) Costs of services

213. The Treasury (through the Scottish Education Department) and the local authorities each contributed £11,000 to the SCL's revenue in 1967/68. Other contributions and receipts from sales increased the total revenue to about £23,000. Expenditure included about £15,000 for salaries and superannuation, £1,700 for books and binding, £800 for printing and stationery, £250 for photographic material and equipment, and about £5,250 for furniture, rates, fuel and light, amortisation and general administration.

The National Library of Wales

(a) Background

214. The movement for the establishment of a Welsh national library dates back to 1873 when a large gathering at the National Eisteddfod proposed the formation of a national collection of books and manuscripts in connection with the University College of Wales at Aberystwyth, founded in the previous year. A Royal Charter was granted on 19th March 1907 and two years later various collections accumulated during the intervening years were brought together to form the National Library of Wales.

215. The Charter provided for the library to be governed through a President, a Vice-President, a Treasurer, a Court of Governors and a Council. Full control of the library and of its income is vested in the Court of Governors, which has about 150 members drawn from the principal cultural and administrative spheres of Welsh life. The Council is a smaller body, numbering about 35 persons drawn from the Court and having greater executive powers than the Court.

(b) Functions

216. The Charter records that the primary function of the library is to collect and preserve written and printed material in Welsh or any other Celtic language, or relating to Wales, the Welsh and the other Celtic people, or by Welsh authors. The secondary function is to build up a general library of all kinds of material to assist in further education, especially higher education, in Wales.

(c) Sources of finance

217. The library is maintained by a Government grant-in-aid administered through the Welsh Office. The grant covers salaries, general administration and purchases of material for the library. The library collections also benefit from donations made by the Society of the " Friends of the National Libraries ".

(d) Services

218. The library functions principally as a reference source, and is divided departmentally into Printed Books, Manuscripts and Records, and Prints, Drawings and Maps. From 1912, the Library became entitled under the Copyright Act of 1911 to free deposit, but with certain limitations to the right

of claim in the case of books not wholly or mainly of Welsh or other Celtic interest. It specialises, therefore, in books and manuscripts relating to Wales and the Celtic peoples, and publishes an annual register of such publications called the Bibliotheca Celtica.

219. The collections are for consultation in the library's own reading rooms, but under its Charter, the library is given the authority to maintain a department of duplicates to be lent for the purposes of instruction in connection with the educational institutions of Wales. Such loans are made through local libraries.

220. The National Library of Wales acts as one of the two regional library bureaux for Wales; the other is at Cardiff. All applications for books from libraries in Wales are first sent to the National Library or to the Cardiff bureau. If these libraries are unable to supply, the requests are forwarded to the NCL.

221. The library holds special collections of records relating to Wales including Welsh Probate Records up to 1857, and it also collects records of the Church of Wales. The manuscripts, maps and newspaper collections are mainly Welsh or of Welsh interest.

222. The photographic section undertakes the production of photostats, Xerox copies and microforms, and these services are available to help public libraries to build up, at reasonable cost, collections of documents relating to local history.

(e) Stock

223. The library contains about 2 million printed books including periodicals and newspapers, over 30,000 volumes of manuscripts and about 3½ million deeds and other documents.

(f) Staff

224. The staff structure is based upon civil service grades although the staff are not technically civil servants, and a contributory pension scheme operates. There are about eight senior library staff including subject specialists.

(g) Costs of Services

225. The cost of staffing the library in 1967/68 was about £143,000. General administrative expenses, which included maintenance of buildings and furniture, fuel and light, rates, stationery and printing, etc., amounted to a further £31,000. The library's own printing unit is largely self-supporting. The annual grant for Purchases of items for the collections has been £18,000 since 1964/65. After allowing for receipts, the total of these costs is about £190,000.

PART THREE

NATIONAL LIBRARY SERVICES FOR THE FUTURE

CHAPTER TEN

Introduction

226. For the nation's library services as a whole to fulfil the requirements of an ideal information service it would be necessary to achieve and maintain a complete collection of world literature in all subjects and to support it fully with up to date bibliographic aids. However, practical and economic considerations have so far prevented this ideal from being even remotely approached in many subjects. At present, there are large gaps in the total coverage which it is impossible to fill retrospectively and the current rate of acquisition of the national institutions and other libraries in many subjects is sufficient only to cover the most important publications. In the arts and the humanities and in some social sciences particularly the total material available in this country comprises only a fraction of the whole published output.

227. This situation is a reflection of the enormous and increasing problem of keeping pace with the output of world literature. The latest Unesco figures for world publishing show that in the four years 1960 to 1963 the total output increased by ten per cent to almost four hundred thousand monograph titles annually, even excluding all serial publications consisting of multiple parts. Asian countries, of which the most important is Japan, are now responsible for nearly a quarter of the titles published and with the rapid development of new nations in Africa and elsewhere the task and cost of collection are likely to become increasingly formidable as the rate of publishing accelerates. In science and technology the growth rate is particularly high and it has been estimated that the number of periodical titles is doubling about every fifteen years.*

228. These developments affect all aspects of library operation. The proliferation of publishers makes the collection of the material more difficult. The increasing quantity of material makes storage more expensive and the methods of rapid retrieval more complex. Selection of acquisitions, arrangements between co-operating libraries and bibliographic processing all become progressively larger and more complex tasks. It is certain that even to maintain the present level of partial coverage will become rapidly more costly as time progresses. It is also inevitable that the nation's library services will continue to have to compete with other national priorities for the substantial resources which they will require.

229. In some subject fields—particularly science, technology, economics and management studies—library and other information services will be so important to industry and commerce, and hence to the prosperity of the country, that the most comprehensive services will be widely regarded as necessary. But in some other disciplines, because a relatively low level of demand is associated with a vast quantity of potentially relevant material and also because it may not be possible to give as high a priority to services which are less directly

---

* D. J. des. Price, " Science Since Babylon", Yale UP, 1962, p. 96.

related to the nation's economic wellbeing, it will probably continue to be impracticable to provide comprehensive coverage or so elaborate a range of information services.

230. These unpalatable conclusions make it essential for libraries and information services of all types and in all subjects to work as efficiently as possible, in order that the best possible use of available resources is achieved, and it is particularly important that the services on which expenditure is greatest should achieve the maximum effectiveness at the minimum cost. This will obviously require close co-ordination of libraries and information services and the most effective management of services of all types.

231. Except in sharing a common aim to collect and make available information for which an existing or potential demand has been demonstrated, the many different library and information services do not at present form a well-ordered pattern of complementary and co-operating parts. Some units are large and have wide and deep coverage, but many more are very small, serving highly specialised needs. Some are supported entirely from private sources, others publicly financed and administered, and many more assisted in a variety of ways and to differing degrees from public funds, whilst still retaining their independent administration. With such a diversity of aims and services, unified administration is neither possible nor desirable but it is unfortunate that, with a few notable exceptions, there is little machinery for assisting the co-ordination of even national facilities in closely related subject areas, for avoiding wasteful duplication of effort, for ensuring adequate coverage of material and bibliographic services, and generally for making the best use of available resources of all kinds. Similarly, the lack of a national policy, relating the country's information needs to other national requirements has prevented the nation's library services from developing in accordance with a coherent and comprehensively considered plan.

232. Although the national library institutions are intended to complement other types of library by providing services which for economic or administrative reasons cannot be justified on a regional or local scale, there is remarkably little *formal* co-operation between the national and other libraries to identify users' needs and to co-ordinate activities. On the other hand, no responsibilities have been placed on the national institutions to foster co-operation between libraries, to encourage the universal acceptance of standards, or to stimulate interest and research in new developments. Even amongst the national institutions themselves, the variety of their administrative arrangements is not conducive to co-operation (Figure 8, page 56). Each institution enjoys either complete or a very considerable degree of independence from the others and from the other types of information service which it compliments. Where administrative links do occur, they have, usually, existed for a very considerable time and it is probably fortuitous if they continue to be appropriate to modern, rapidly changing conditions. There is, for instance, no formal machinery for consultation to prevent any unnecessary duplication of stock between the NRLSI and the NLLST, to link the NCL with the NLLST in subject areas where both have responsibilities, or to ensure that the bibliographic requirements of the BNB, the BML and NCL are co-ordinated to the advantage of all.

55

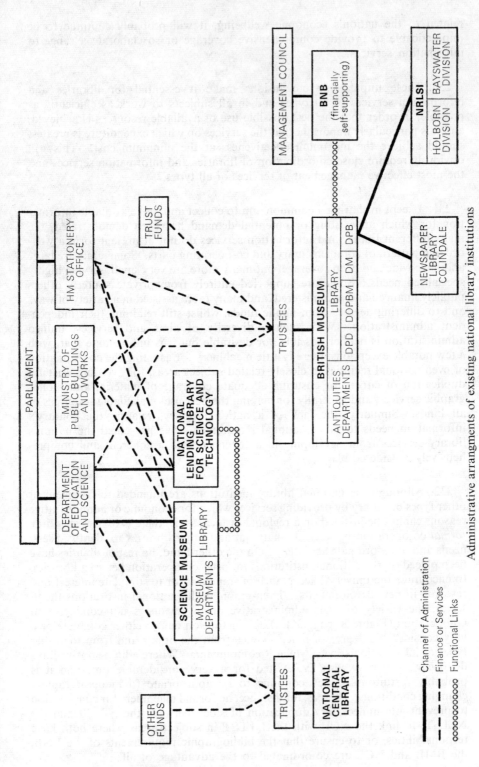

Figure 8 Administrative arrangements of existing national library institutions

56

233. In the following chapters we examine the activities and services of the national institutions to see how far they, together with other types of library and information service, could provide adequate coverage of material and sufficient variety of service to satisfy as economically as possible the needs of all types of user. While our terms of reference do not include the National Libraries of Scotland or Wales, we recognise that our recommendations for a national libraries organisation should cover the national library needs of all parts of the United Kingdom. We indicate where better channels of communication between users and those providing the services are desirable, where co-operation between libraries is necessary to obtain the best coverage at the minimum cost and where close administrative associations between institutions are necessary to eliminate unnecessary overlap and waste.

234. In Chapter 11 we consider how the development of lending and photocopying from the national libraries can meet the greatest proportion of requirements of users throughout the country which cannot be met from other sources. Subsequently, we examine present and future requirements for reference collections, in London and elsewhere. Because of the potential of computers and other forms of automation for enabling better services to be provided and economies to be achieved, we devote a separate chapter to the impact of technology on the national libraries. We then discuss the structure of national bibliographic services, which we consider are likely to be rapidly and profoundly influenced by the introduction of computers. If progress towards more comprehensive services is to be achieved without an unacceptable increase in cost, research and development of many different types will be essential. Chapter 16 deals with this topic and discusses how the results of a research programme can be made available as widely as possible to librarians and users alike. We have already indicated that co-operation between libraries and information services is necessary if scarce resources are to be most effectively used; in Chapter 15 we consider particularly the problems that will have to be solved to enable the national libraries to work as closely as is desirable with independently administered special libraries and information services. Probably the most important of all our recommendations concern the future administration of the national libraries and their organisation as part of the national network of library and information services. Chapter 17 contains an analysis of these crucial administrative and organisational problems and our recommendations for the establishment of a national libraries system. In the final chapter we attempt to assess some of the most important financial implications of our recommendations. Until further detailed studies can be carried out, these can in many instances be only very approximate. Consequently, we were initially reluctant to quantify them at all. We have, however, attempted to do so, firstly to indicate where the greatest scope lies for making better use of resources, and secondly to emphasise the cardinal importance of applying costing methods to the services of the national libraries.

CHAPTER ELEVEN

LENDING AND PHOTOCOPYING

Introduction

235. To fulfil a national role, the services of a library should ideally be capable of satisfying the requirements of all its potential users, irrespective of their distribution throughout the country. A lending library, such as the NCL or the NLLST, does this by making its stock available on loan, or as photocopy, to users anywhere in the United Kingdom (Figure 9 (i), page 59). Whilst the usage patterns of the two examples cited do not show an exact correlation between demands on their services and population distribution, it is, nevertheless, clear that their facilities are extensively used in most parts of Britain and that these libraries' locations do not appreciably affect the extent to which they are used or by whom. In contrast, a recent survey* has shown that the probability of a potential user exploiting the services of a public reference library is closely correlated with the accessibility of the library to him. It would appear from this that people will tend to use the more easily accessible sources of information in preference to more distant ones and may even be satisfied with incomplete information. The results of the surveys commissioned by us have verified that the same general pattern applies markedly to the use that is made of the reference services of both the NRLSI (Figure 9 (ii), page 59) and the SML and, to a lesser extent, even of those of the BML (Figure 10, page 73). However, these three libraries also cater to an increasing extent for the needs of remote users through their photocopying facilities (Figure 2, page 18). It is already abundantly evident that the extension of photocopying made possible by the widespread introduction a few years ago of electrostatic copying techniques has revealed a very substantial latent demand for these services which has by no means yet reached its peak. The extraordinarily rapid growth in the use of the BML's photocopy services doubtless prompted the Trustees to emphasise the importance of this development in their evidence to us. So long as it is possible for a remote user to obtain a precise reference to the material that he requires, it is likely to be cheaper to transmit the information to him by post, Telex or telephone—even allowing for the full cost of this service—than for him to travel to the information source—and this is especially the case for the highly paid professionals in industry, research establishments and universities who make up the majority of users of the national libraries. This is why we attach so much importance to the provision of satisfactory lending and photocopying facilities.

The Supply of Scientific Literature

(a) The existing arrangements

236. The scale of scientific and industrial research and development creates an exceptionally heavy demand for scientific literature, much of which is needed urgently. This high level of demand, together with the economic importance of scientific information, has contributed to the excellent bibliographic, abstracting and indexing services available in the sciences and technologies. The quality of the bibliographic coverage is also materially assisted by the fact

---

*D. W. G. Clements, *Journal of Documentation*, 23 (2), 131–146.

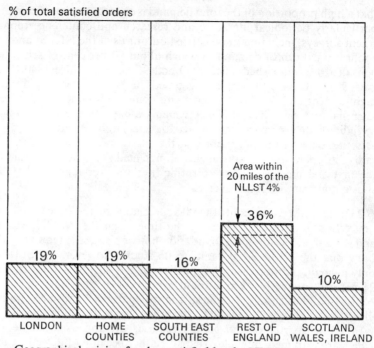

Geographical origin of orders satisfied by the NLLST

Figure 9 (i)

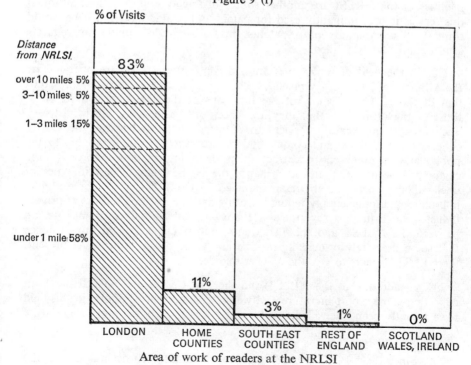

Area of work of readers at the NRLSI

Figure 9 (ii)

that a high proportion of the total demand is concentrated on recent publications, particularly periodical literature and research and conference reports. Three recent surveys, including those carried out for us at the NRLSI and the NLLST, confirm a pattern of demand in which about 90 per cent of scientific literature consulted was published since 1950 and 95 per cent since 1940 (Figure 13 (i), page 90). All these factors have enabled the NLLST very rapidly to become a highly successful means of satisfying loan and photocopying requests for scientific material. The evidence which we have received from many sources, including industrial concerns, universities, research institutions and professional societies, leaves us in no doubt that the speed and the very satisfactory success rate of its operations are universally appreciated and that this library has become the first and main source of scientific literature for remote users, including a substantial number from overseas.

237. The SML has contributed appreciably to the success of the NLLST, firstly by the transfer of stock at the time when the NLLST was established, and since then by supplying loans and photocopies at the request of the NLLST. Now that the NLLST has built up its stocks, however, the SML contributes only a small and decreasing proportion of the NLLST's total traffic—in 1967, $2\frac{1}{2}$ per cent of the loans and about 5 per cent of the photocopies. When the NLLST fails to supply a request, the originator may turn to the NCL, either directly or through a regional system. Despite the high success rate of the NLLST, a quarter of the NCL's requests are for scientific items, many of which are extremely difficult to satisfy, either because of defects or inadequacies in the reference, or because of the rarity of the material. The photocopy facilities of the NRLSI are another source of scientific information, although this service is predominantly used for patent and related material. We would think it unlikely that, except for patents, this library could supply many requests after the NLLST has failed.

238. In the field of report literature, the TIL Reports Centre operated by the Ministry of Technology provides a source of research reports additional to that of the NLLST. Many of the functions of the TIL Centre differ from those of the NLLST in that they are closely integrated with the Ministry of Technology's information services to industry and also because the Centre collects many defence and commercial reports not generally available to the public and is prepared to extract from them information tailored to the customers' needs. On the other hand, the NLLST covers certain types of unclassified reports not at present handled by the TIL Centre—for example, international atomic energy report literature and the research reports of private industry in Britain. Nevertheless, there are substantial areas of overlap between the NLLST and the TIL Centre and it appears from our evidence that some users rely principally on one and some on the other. At present, the NLLST appears to give the quicker service.

239. In addition to the NLLST and the TIL Centre, the NRLSI has been collecting some report literature and we understand that its efforts in this field have recently been intensified.

(b) *Future requirements*

240. Since the NLLST became effective, there has been general satisfaction with the arrangements for supplying scientific material to users throughout the

country. We have noted particularly, that, in less than seven years, the NLLST has become a most important source of information for industry throughout the country, and as such is undoubtedly making an important contribution to the country's economic wellbeing. Nevertheless, we have considered carefully whether there is a logical justification for having two large national scientific collections which at considerable cost substantially duplicate each other—the NLLST for lending and the NRLSI for reference. In Chapter 5 we have given figures for the direct costs of the NLLST's services, but these exclude the cost of accommodating staff and stock. Our reason is that such figures as are available for buildings for all the libraries covered by our terms of reference are so artificial as to be misleading, if used for assessing the cost of providing modern facilities of the standard required. In estimating a realistic cost for the different kinds of library service, we must, therefore, add to the actual cost of staff, materials, etc., a notional sum for accommodation based on realistic present-day costs. For the NLLST, we have assumed a figure of 22s. per year per square foot of working and storage space, to cover the first cost of building, amortisation, maintenance, rates, heating and similar expenditure. On this basis the total unit cost per loan issue would be approximately 23s. (Appendix D).

241. In their evidence, the Trustees of the British Museum have argued that the maintenance of two comprehensive scientific libraries is not only costly, but also unnecessary, and that a single collection of scientific and patent material in central London can meet the needs of all users, by providing simultaneously facilities for photocopying and for personal reference. We do not think that much weight should be given to the present relatively low demand for photocopies in comparison with loan requests. We believe that in time the present pattern of demand, conditioned as it is by the experience of many years when the supply of photocopies was both costly and slow, will change. The relative costs and advantages to both the user and to the supplying library of satisfying a request by loan or by photocopy have not been thoroughly investigated—and we hope that the DES will promote such a study as soon as practicable.

242. But the extent to which photocopies can replace loans is, in our opinion, secondary to whether a single collection can simultaneously perform a dual role when the total level of demand is high. The NRLSI has been designed on the open access principle to enable it to be used most effectively for browsing and general reference. On the other hand, the NLLST is organised very differently, in order to facilitate the rapid and certain location of publications for photocopying or despatch. Whereas the NRLSI at present successfully maintains a relatively small photocopy service, mainly used for patents, it is much more questionable whether it could handle sufficiently expeditiously, even with augmented facilities, the volume of demand of the present NRLSI and the NLLST together, When, in addition, it is appreciated that the use that is made of the existing photocopying and reference services of the NRLSI will almost certainly contine to grow substantially and that the loan and photocopying demands on the NLLST increased by 143,000 during 1968—the highest figure in that library's history of rapid growth (Figures 4 and 5, pages 26 and 27)—it is likely that at least a 20-fold expansion of the photocopying capacity of the NRLSI would be necessary in the next decade, if it were decided to handle the combined traffic there. Quite apart from the fact that the costs of accommodation

61

dwarf all others in the provision of library facilities in central London and that these costs are probably about five times their equivalents in Boston Spa, we are convinced that it is not practicable for a single collection to provide simultaneously for intensive use for reference purposes and also to handle most of the total national demand from remote users for borrowing or photocopying. We recommend, therefore, that the central London library of science and patent literature should aim primarily at meeting in the most effective way the *reference* needs which we shall discuss in Chapter 12. Apart from this, it should aim to complement the services of the NLLST by concentrating its photocopying resources in meeting the requirements of its personal visitors, and those of remote users for material—such as patents—which is not available from Boston Spa. The NLLST would, thus, continue to develop generally along its present lines, but placing greater emphasis on photocopying, if trends in demand indicated that this were desirable. In Chapter 12 we also report our conclusion that the SML should be fused with the Lyon Playfair Library of Imperial College. Nevertheless, we think that it should continue to make a small contribution to the national requirements, by helping to supply those publications which are not available from the other principal sources. Its assistance would mainly be required for a relatively small number of older scientific publications, particularly the literature of the history of science and technology. Similarly, the services at present provided by the NCL in assisting the location of rarely used material would still be necessary in the future, although the recent trend for this type of demand to diminish may be expected to continue.

(c) Facilities for report literature

243. Report literature comprises a wide variety of material, mainly in the sciences and technology, much of which is not generally available or covered by the usual types of abstracting and indexing publications. Its importance is that it provides the earliest information on current research and, in some instances, it may remain the only source of such information.

244. There are special problems associated with it. The term " report literature " is wide in scope and imprecise. This creates difficulties for those responsible for collection and indexing it and for potential users, particularly if requests for it have to be sent to a source different from that supplying other types of literature. The collection of reports is also often a formidable problem and this is especially true of reports which are not channelled through Government or international agencies. There is not only the difficulty of obtaining particular items when requested, but also that of checking whether arrangements for blanket cover are continuing to be fulfilled. And these problems are accentuated by the necessity of obtaining reports as soon as possible after they become available. Apart from speedy collection, report literature requires rapid bibliographic processing and a widely distributed announcement service.

245. The evidence which we have received shows that the present arrangements leave room for improvement. A substantial number of submissions indicated that the existing coverage is inadequate, but we do not know whether insufficient effort is being made to collect report literature from all sources and in every subject, or whether the principal defect is an inadequate bibliographic service. We stress, however, that without adequate announcement services and bibliographic processing, the effort put into collection is largely

wasted. We draw particular attention to the lack of co-ordination between the bibliographic activities of the TIL Centre and those of the NLLST, which partly duplicate each other without singly or together covering all reports to a sufficient standard. We recommend, therefore, that the efforts of these two agencies should be co-ordinated, so as to produce as economically as possible complete bibliographic coverage in such forms as are necessary to satisfy the requirements of all types of users—industrial or otherwise.

246. In the interests of economy we should also like to see the duplication of services for supplying reports which at present exists between the TIL Centre and the NLLST reduced to the minimum. In addition, we think it necessary in the interests of users that the responsibilities of each institution should be rationalised and clearly defined. But we do not think that this should be done by transferring to the TIL Centre part or the whole of the responsibilities for reports now exercised by the NLLST. It is not reasonable to expect an organisation provided to meet the requirements of one type of user alone to serve all others equally satisfactorily. The TIL Centre aims only to meet the requirements of industrial users, whereas the NLLST must serve also scientists and social scientists not in industry. In addition, we consider it essential that reports in all subjects should be collected and we note particularly the growing importance of reports in the social sciences.

247. The problems of collecting and processing report literature make it desirable to provide a special centre for it, but the difficulties of definition require such a centre to be located close to the main source of other types of loan and photocopy material and, above all, that requests for reports are sent by users to the same receiving point as are requests for other types of literature.

248. For all these reasons, we believe that the collection and handling of reports should be located at Boston Spa, but, since the purposes and needs of a reports centre are so different from those of the NLLST, the best solution, in our view, would be to establish as part of the national libraries organisation a National Reports Centre with the responsibilities to collect, catalogue and supply reports in all subjects. It would take over and develop facilities now available for reports at the NLLST, with which it would, however, work in the closest collaboration. The establishment of this national centre would obviously cost more than the NLLST at present spends on report literature, but, in providing an improved service, it would make possible economies in other libraries. The NRLSI and the BML, in particular, would leave to the Centre the task of collecting reports, because they could obtain from the Centre copies of any items needed for their reference collections. The development of a National Reports Centre at Boston Spa would make possible beneficial sharing of work with the TIL Centre at St. Mary Cray. For example, the Ministry of Technology could consider basing information specialists at Boston Spa where there would be immediately available unrivalled resources of scientific and related literature of all types, including reports, and comprehensive facilities for the production of hard copies or microforms. Even if this were not feasible, we believe that there would be no need for the TIL Centre to duplicate the effort of the National Reports Centre in collecting foreign reports and those not from Government agencies, since it could obtain from the National Centre copies of such items as might be required for the Ministry's technical information services.

The Supply of Literature for the Humanities and the Social Sciences

(a) The existing arrangements

249. The pattern of demand for literature in the humanities and the social sciences differs very considerably from that in the natural and applied sciences. Firstly, there is a much greater use of books rather than journal articles in these fields. The 1964 NCL survey showed that only 13 per cent of its requests in the humanities and 16 per cent in the social sciences were for periodicals, whereas, despite the existence of the NLLST, 45 per cent of its requests in science and technology were for periodicals and conference proceedings. A comparably detailed breakdown has not been produced from the 1968 NCL survey, but of the total sample—which was predominantly for humanities and social science material—80 per cent of the requests were for monographs.

250. Secondly, there is a much higher proportion of older material used. The latest NCL survey showed that substantially less than half the requests for books and under two thirds of those for periodicals were for post-1950 publications. One eighth of all requests were for material published earlier than 1900. Corroborative data may be found in the results of a recent survey of loan requests passing between libraries in certain selected areas*. Although an exact correlation between the results of this survey and the usage patterns of the services of the national institutions would not be expected, the survey data provide, nevertheless, a useful comparison between the dates of publication of material sought in different subject fields. Of loan requests in the sciences, 87 per cent were for items published since 1950. Corresponding figures for the social sciences were 81 per cent, including commerce, law and management, and 73 per cent excluding these subjects, and for the arts and humanities 48 per cent. In this respect, the pattern of demand for literature in the arts and humanities is very exceptional, whereas that in the social sciences conforms more nearly to the pattern for scientific material.

251. Thirdly, the bibliographic apparatus is much less comprehensive and co-ordinated than in science and technology. This is due, in part, to the relatively few workers engaged in the various branches of the social sciences and humanities compared with those in the natural and applied sciences; the difficulties in reaching internationally agreed terminologies in many fields; and the need for massive retrospective bibliographies. This makes national bibliographies in these fields less economic to produce and sell. Finally, in the social sciences particularly, there is a vast quantity of ephemera which forms the raw material for research and this is very intractable material for bibliographic control.

252. When social science literature is required from national sources, it may be supplied from or through the NCL, from the BML as a photocopy only, or from the NLLST if it is a periodical. The periodical service provided by the NLLST is relatively recent, as the ordering of social science serials not available in the library's science and technology collection began only in 1966. However, over three quarters of the NLLST's requests for this material are now being met from the library's stock, with a further $2\frac{1}{2}$ per cent from the British Library of Political and Economic Science. Although social science is only a small

---

* D. W. G. Clements, *Journal of Librarianship*, **1** (2), 107-118.

proportion of the NLLST's total traffic, the rate of supply as surveyed in December 1968 is equivalent to over 30,000 items per year. The 1968 NCL survey indicated that requests for social science books and periodicals comprised 21 per cent of the total sample. This suggests that the NCL is supplying through inter-library lending or from its own central stock more than 20,000 items per year. We have not been able to make an accurate estimate of the social science material supplied in response to postal ordering for photocopies at the BML, but we think that about 5,000 items per year may come from this source. Some of these, however, such as the backruns of newspapers, may be exceptionally substantial orders.

253. For the arts and humanities, the NCL is the major contributor in satisfying national demands for loans, although the BML photocopy service also makes a useful contribution. About one half of the NCL's requests are in the humanities and it appears to be satisfying about four fifths of these, equivalent to about 50,000 items per year. In 1967, the BML supplied over 7,000 photographic orders by post from the Bloomsbury section of the Department of Printed Books. It is difficult to assess this figure in terms of items of humanities literature, but it may be about 15,000.

(b) The possibility of developing a comprehensive central loan collection

254. Requests for loans in the humanities and the social sciences are less frequently satisfied than requests for scientific material handled by the NLLST. In addition, inter-library lending arranged through the NCL is all too often slow, a matter which has frequently been commented upon in the evidence which we have received. It is understandable, therefore, that many people have suggested either that the NLLST should be extended to cover all subjects and types of material, or that a separate lending library for the humanities and the social sciences, operating like the NLLST entirely on centralised stock, should be established. When discussing the lending arrangements for scientific literature, we argued that, because the bulk of the total demand was for very recent material, it was practicable for the NLLST to become effective very rapidly. We justified the expenditure in duplicating some of the stock available in other libraries by the exceptionally high level of demand for scientific publications and by the need for the speediest possible service. We believe that these same considerations should be taken into account when deciding whether to develop a central loan collection in the arts and the social sciences.

255. For periodicals in the social sciences—which the NLLST is already collecting—the pattern of demand makes it practicable to build up a useful collection fairly rapidly and the quantity of requests probably justifies at least some duplication of the stock of the reference collections. But we see no reason why use of the main reference stock should not satisfy the national demand for the very lightly used material.

256. It would take much longer for a national loan collection to acquire sufficient backruns to satisfy a correspondingly high proportion of the total demand for serial literature in the humanities, but it might be practicable in time. We do not propose it, however, because we believe the cost of acquisition alone—estimated by the NLLST at £35,000 per year—would be unjustifiably high, given the already large holdings in this field in the BML. Our proposals

for enabling the BML to meet sufficiently rapidly most of the national demand from remote users are discussed in subsequent sections, but we do not rule out some selective duplication at the NLLST of the titles in heaviest use.

257. As far as monographs are concerned, in both the humanities and the social sciences, there is very little prospect of developing retrospectively a central loan collection which could span the range of titles and dates of publication required to meet a high proportion of requests without extremely high levels of expenditure, which in our view could not be justified.

(c) The future of the NCL loan stock

258. Nevertheless, some controlled expansion of the NCL's bookstock could be beneficial to the overall efficiency of the service. Lending from a centralised stock is undoubtedly the quickest way of providing a lending service and the NCL is already able to meet one fifth of its requests in this way.

259. However, account must be taken of the cost. To the figures for the appropriate share of the NCL's direct costs should be added an estimate based on today's property values for accommodating staff and stock. We are advised that a realistic figure for the combined cost of buildings, maintenance, heating and rates for accommodation in Bloomsbury and other very central areas in London is unlikely to be less than £5 per square foot of floor space per year. On this basis, the cost of storing an average sized book will be about 5s. 0d. per year, even if the volume is not lent (Appendix D). When other factors are included, the realistic cost of sustaining the present rate of loans from a bookstock of the size of the NCL's in central London is about £10 per issue (Appendix D). As the controlling factor in this extremely high figure is the cost of accommodation—not labour or acquisition costs—there are obvious advantages in transferring the central loan stock to a low-cost site, if this can be done without seriously impairing the service. For example, we have estimated that the unit loan cost could be cut by more than half, if the loan service were transferred to Boston Spa (Appendix D). In addition, centralisation of all national loan stocks would, we believe, reduce the unit cost even further. It would also bring other advantages to the users, if a single entry point to all national lending arrangements were possible by establishing a national loan locating centre at Boston Spa. This proposition is discussed in more detail in Chapter 14, but consideration of all the relevant factors leads us to recommend an early transfer of the NCL's loan stocks to Boston Spa, where adequate land is available at low cost for the existing facilities and for future development.

260. Future expansion of a loan stock can, therefore, improve the speed and certainty of service to users, but only at substantial cost if the total level of demand is low. Even at Boston Spa, the cost per issue from the stock of the present NCL is likely to be several times the cost of issuing an item of scientific material, because of the higher demand for scientific publications. In determining acquisitions policy for future additions to the central stock, it is, therefore, important to consider whether:

(i) there is a case for the fastest possible service,

66

(ii) the intensity of demand is likely to be sufficiently high to produce an acceptably low unit cost of issue,

(iii) the material is not available more cheaply from another source.

Inter-Library Lending

261. The NCL's acquisition funds for their centralised stock are £27,000 for the current year, almost double the figure for 1967–68. The NCL has estimated, however, that, even if the annual acquisition expenditure were increased to £75,000, it would still expect to handle about 40 per cent of all requests through its co-operating libraries. Thus, if lending needs are to be met only in part from centralised resources, it will be necessary to continue to rely heavily on the national union catalogues and the stocks of other large libraries. Most of the cost of an inter-library loan is that of housing the union catalogues and the staff required to maintain and operate them. Estimates based on the 1967–68 scale of operations suggest that, if the union catalogues are housed in central London, the cost of identifying a library capable of making the loan would amount to over £2 10s. 0d. It would, however, be reduced to slightly more than half this sum if the catalogues were situated where accommodation costs were only one-fifth as great. These estimates do not include an allowance for costs incurred by libraries in supplying—or trying, but failing to supply—the item requested. These are very difficult to assess accurately, but they would add significantly to the figures quoted above.

262. Although inter-library lending is relatively inexpensive compared with meeting requests from a centralised stock when the level of demand is low, the present arrangements are failing to produce a satisfactory service to the users. There is no doubt that a service which cannot satisfy 22 per cent of requests (Figure 6 (ii), page 36) needs improving and the evidence which we have received shows that ultimate success—or failure—is too frequently accompanied by delays of months, rather than weeks. However, as the 1968 NCL reader survey indicated, there appears at present to be less insistence on the speediest possible service than obtains for scientific and technological material. The aim should, therefore, be to concentrate on reducing as far as possible the longest delays and to improve substantially on the proportion of requests satisfied within two weeks, which the 1968 survey showed to be less than two-thirds.

263. At the roots of the existing inter-library lending system, there are three fundamental weaknesses:

(i) the incompleteness of the union catalogues;

(ii) the unwillingness of co-operating libraries to lend items in heavy demand by their local users and their inadequate machinery for meeting any significant volume of loan requests rapidly;

(iii) the failure of the system taken as a whole to cover a sufficiently high proportion of the material requested.

Effective action to eliminate as far as possible each of these structural deficiencies could lead to a significant increase in the efficiency of the overall system and reduce to the minimum the need to pursue the time-consuming processes of speculative searches which, in the 1968 survey sample, had to be used for one-tenth of all items supplied.

(a) Union catalogues

264. The UGC report on libraries (paragraphs 107–109) has shown how far the incompleteness of the NCL's union catalogues has contributed to the overall delays in its services. This is partly because the union catalogues have, through lack of manpower, not been kept up to date and partly because some co-operating libraries for whatever reason have been unable to provide the NCL with records of their acquisitions and disposals in the most appropriate form or as quickly as desired. The very large arrears in entering details of items available for inter-library lending must seriously reduce the effectiveness of the union catalogues. Unless a substantial effort is devoted to correcting this situation there will be little hope of decreasing the present substantial proportion of cases in which resort has to be made to the slow, costly and relatively ineffectual speculative search. We, therefore, recommend that the highest priority should be given to this work on the union catalogues, if necessary at the expense of other activities. Even with the development of computerised cataloguing, which we believe offers the most hopeful long-term prospect for a rapid locating service, the satisfaction of the needs of users will depend on maintaining the primary locating tool as nearly up to date as possible.

(b) Co-operating libraries

265. One way of improving the effectiveness of the union catalogues, both before they are computerised and subsequently, would be to establish an inner circle of relatively few large co-operating libraries, which would work in close association with the NCL, by standardising their cataloguing techniques and by paying particular attention to rapid reporting on stock changes and availability for loan. Although the introduction of a system of this kind would lead to these libraries carrying a higher proportion of the total inter-library lending than at present, we do not think that this additional burden need prove too onerous. The implementation of our other recommendations would ensure that the loan material sought of these libraries would not, in general, be in heavy use by their own local users. Firstly, publications in heaviest demand would be bought for and available from the central loan stocks at Boston Spa. Secondly, the policy of aiming for regional self-sufficiency in post-1959 British publications will lead to an increasingly high proportion of requests for British material being met regionally. The main calls on the " inner circle " libraries would, therefore, be for foreign publications and older British material; and photocopying would enable some of these to be met without the originals having to leave the collections. So far as the additional responsibilities may call for more equipment and staff to be provided in some of the libraries, we think it reasonable that financial assistance should be available.

266. Among the libraries which are capable of undertaking such additional responsibilities, the university libraries at Oxford and Cambridge are particularly well-fitted. In size and general coverage they are second only to the BML, and their long-standing legal deposit privilege has enabled them to build up comprehensive collections of British publications. Recently both have shown an increasing awareness of the assistance which they could give to other libraries. We recommend, therefore, that the possibility of developing in the ways suggested above a close association between these two libraries and the national lending services should be explored.

267 Although we have not been able to estimate the cost of implementing this recommendation, we consider that the additional expenditure involved in providing financial assistance to the main supplying libraries should be considerably offset by the resultant savings in labour, particularly at the locating centre.

268. The use of Telex between the locating centre and the main sources of supply would, we believe, make a major contribution to improving the speed of service. The evidence which we have received from several universities emphasises the advantage of Telex in obtaining extremely rapid service from the NLLST. Indeed, a service which takes less than 24 hours from time of ordering by the user to receipt by him of the item requested is now easily attainable very cheaply, if Telex is used. We recommend, therefore, that its extensive and routine application to inter-library lending should be given detailed consideration.

(c) The contribution of the national reference collections

269. Improvements in the union catalogues and in the effectiveness of co-operating libraries can be expected to provide only a partial correction of the NCL's main weakness, which is that, even after long delays, users cannot be certain that their requests will be met. The high overall failure rate (Figure 6 (ii)), even more than delays, has tended to erode users' confidence in the inter-library lending service.

270. The greatest difficulty concerns the supply of foreign books; positive progress towards regional self-sufficiency in British publications makes the supply of British material progressively less difficult and this trend will obviously continue, and demand for older British books will, we envisage, be largely met by our recommendation concerning the Oxford and Cambridge university libraries. However, the rate of increase of world publishing has already made it impossible even for the BML to ensure that there is in this country a single copy of all worthwhile research material published abroad. The policy of the NCL in recent years has been to select for its own loan stocks a small fraction of the total output of foreign publications, in an attempt to fulfil loan demands which cannot be met elsewhere. On the one hand, the scale of its operations in this field has inevitably proved inadequate and, in terms of unit loan costs, extremely expensive; on the other hand, it seems certain that quantities of lightly used material held in the BML and other large libraries not part of the inter-library lending service have been duplicated by the NCL.

271. It is for these reasons that many people have suggested to us that the rigidity which at present exists between the national reference and lending stocks should be broken down and that there should be lending from the national reference collections under carefully controlled conditions.

272. We do not easily accept these arguments, however, as we recognise the danger that extensive lending could seriously impair the BML's—and the NRLSI's—reference functions. We greatly prefer the proposal put to us by the Trustees that the BML's contribution to satisfying the needs of remote users should be through the development of efficient and rapid photocopying facilities and we expect that the highest possible proportion of the demand would be met in this way. Despite the rapid growth in photocopying at the

69

BML, we are certain that there exists a large potential at present unsatisfied. Indeed, repeated references in our evidence to delays of many months in fulfilling photocopy orders make it evident to us that the widely-known inadequacies of the existing service are depressing the natural level of demand. In addition, demand is certain to accelerate as technological development makes possible better quality, speedier service and lower costs. Therefore, despite the severe space limitations imposed by the present building, we recommend that a high priority be given at once to developing the photocopy service at the BML and at its outhouses, and that adequate provision be made in any new buildings to be provided in the future.

273. Unfortunately, however, we do not see in photocopying the complete solution to providing an efficient and economical service to remote users. In the short term, the law of copyright is likely to restrict its development, particularly in respect of publications out of print, or when large extracts from books or multiple copies are required. It is clearly desirable that the supply of information should not be impeded by copyright restrictions, but the interests of authors and publishers must not be neglected. We recommend, therefore, that initiative should be taken by the Government to obtain as soon as possible a solution to this problem through an agreement which reconciles the interests of all concerned. But there are also other difficulties. In the humanities and the social sciences, where the items needed are likely to be monographs, rather than articles in periodicals, photocopying may prove so expensive as to be unacceptable to the user and wasteful of national resources. Even where only an extract is needed, the precise reference to it may not be known. It is, therefore, in our view inescapable that there will be a small residuum of the total national demand where the reference collections alone will have the material and photocopying will not be able to provide a satisfactory solution. This, subject to the exceptions mentioned in the next paragraph, should, we believe, be met by lending.

274. As the BML is the only library at which publishers are obliged to deposit without specific notice being given, it is the custodian of the definitive collection of British literature. We consider it most important that none of this material should be jeopardised in any way, especially by being lent. In addition, we would not expect material which could not be replaced in any form from any other source, or items of high intrinsic value, to be available on loan. Material in heavy demand would also not be lent; this should be duplicated in the national loan collections, if it were not available through the inter-library lending service. In general, therefore, the items which we are recommending should be borrowable from the national reference library are lightly used foreign books.

275. We accept that there is a remote possibility that an item of this type when on loan might occasionally be needed urgently for reference in the BML and we recommend, therefore, that the conditions of lending should provide for a speedy return in such circumstances. It would be reasonable, in our opinion, to stipulate that books should be loaned only for use in another library and for a short period of time.

276. By ensuring that the national reference collections are only used as a last resort for loans, by restricting the material which is loanable and by carefully

controlling its availability to the borrower, we believe that the BML's international reputation as one of the world's greatest reference sources will not be impaired. Limited use of its stock for lending would, however, make an important contribution to the national lending services for which there is no economic or practicable alternative.

Implications for Organisation

277. Our recommendations for improving the existing national facilities for lending are based upon the principle that only by utilising to the full the resources of the existing institutions will it be possible without prohibitively increased costs to provide a satisfactory service now or in the future. Even under present conditions, there is a need for closer co-operation between the existing library institutions and for a single entry point to the national lending services. With the implementation of our recommendations, more major libraries will contribute to the overall service than at present and a national locating centre, through which the largest possible proportion of loan or photocopy requests may be channelled to their most appropriate sources of supply, will be essential. In other respects also—for example, in determining acquisitions policies—our proposals will only be effective and economical if there is close co-operation between all the principal national libraries and related institutions. In particular, it will be necessary to establish a direct and intimate working relationship between those national libraries primarily concerned with lending and the national reference collections.

278. We do not believe that these changes can take place whilst the administrations of the institutions concerned remain independent of each other and whilst there exists no centralised body responsible for overall policy and for achieving the required degree of co-ordination between the different units and services.

CHAPTER TWELVE

REFERENCE FACILITIES

Introduction

279. In the previous chapter we have discussed the ways in which literature should be made available to distant users, either by lending or photocopying. Libraries primarily providing reference facilities must operate differently since their users travel to a central point to consult the literature they require. Consequently, the use made of a reference library by personal visitors is generally a function of its accessibility to them, and the users of a lending library are likely to be much more widely distributed geographically than those of a reference library. These factors make it difficult for reference facilities to assume a genuinely " national " role unless the collections are so outstanding either in size or quality as to offset for the user the inconvenience and expense of travelling large distances.

280. If the reference facilities are in central London these problems are minimised because:

    (i) London is the focal point of the national communications networks.

    (ii) Most of the national learned societies have their headquarters and hold most of their important meetings in London.

    (iii) The level of use of libraries and information sources in London is exceptionally high, firstly because of the high density of population and secondly because it is the seat of Government and the centre of commerce.

    (iv) Many specialised academic institutions which rely heavily on outstandingly good library facilities are in London.

The Arts and the Humanities

(a) The role of the BML

281. Although the BML surveys showed that its users are predominantly drawn from the south-east of England (Figure 10, page 73), the library has, nevertheless, established itself in a position of national and international importance unrivalled by any other reference library in the country. The evidence which we have received and the survey data both confirm that it attracts substantial numbers of readers from all over the world. Many of these, whether British or foreign, take up temporary residence in or near Bloomsbury primarily to be near the library, and it is probable that some of the overseas visitors attached to British universities have been influenced in coming here by the library's great wealth of research material in their specialist fields.

282. The predominant use of the library for studies in literature, history and biography revealed by the surveys reflects the library's particular strengths (Figure 11, page 73). In these subjects especially, it has built up over the years an incomparable collection from all periods, which includes many manuscripts and incunabula. For this reason the library, despite increasing inadequacy of space and growing pressure on staff and reader facilities, continues to fill a

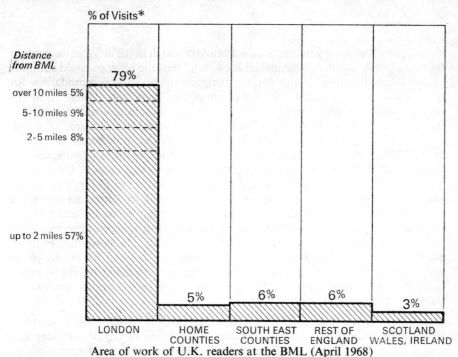

% of Visits*

Distance from BML

over 10 miles 5%

5-10 miles 9%

2-5 miles 8%

up to 2 miles 57%

79%

5%   6%   6%   3%

LONDON   HOME   SOUTH EAST   REST OF   SCOTLAND
          COUNTIES   COUNTIES   ENGLAND   WALES, IRELAND

Area of work of U.K. readers at the BML (April 1968)

N.B. The figure for readers working within 2 miles of the BML (and, hence, the percentage for London as a whole) includes many who normally work elsewhere in the country, but were working mainly at the BML at the time of the survey.

Figure 10

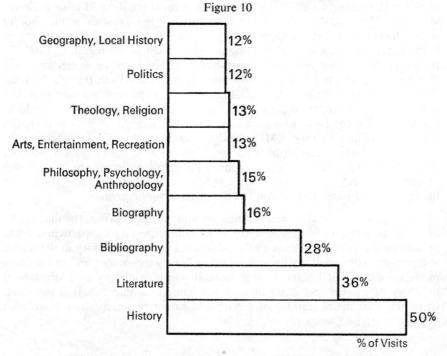

Geography, Local History	12%
Politics	12%
Theology, Religion	13%
Arts, Entertainment, Recreation	13%
Philosophy, Psychology, Anthropology	15%
Biography	16%
Bibliography	28%
Literature	36%
History	50%

% of Visits

Principal subjects studied by readers at the BML (April 1968)

Figure 11

*The percentages in figure 10 are calculated on the basis of the sample answering question 3 of the BML survey questionnaire.

unique role in satisfying the needs of academic research in the arts and humanities throughout the world. We consider it essential that the library should continue to fulfil this function in the future. Improvements in accommodation for readers and a more speedy service in supplying them with books from the central stocks and photocopies of library material should naturally result from the provision of a new building. These and other advances will almost certainly reveal a potential demand considerably in excess of that now being catered for in the BML. However, the rapid extension of photocopying and some lending under carefully controlled conditions, which we have discussed in Chapter 11, will undoubtedly enable many potential users to exploit the library's resources without making a personal visit. The development of better bibliographic aids and information services—together with a greater premium being placed on people's time—is a further factor which will tend to dissuade users from visiting the library personally if other methods of obtaining the required material exist. Accordingly, we doubt whether the demand for reader-places will grow in proportion to the increase in the total demand on the library's facilities and in time it may be overtaken in importance by other methods of transmitting information.

283. In addition to providing for a continuation of the BML's traditional role, the original plan of the Trustees for the development of the Bloomsbury site contained proposals for a public reference room, making 300 reader-places freely available to all. This would have the advantage of enabling some of the library's services to be made available without the need of a reader's ticket and of allowing demand to be filtered and directed to where it could most easily be satisfied. The public reading room envisaged by the Trustees would require some 20,000 square feet, which, on the basis of our assessment of current accommodation costs in central London, would cost in the region of £100,000 per year. We do not think that expenditure of this order, on functions which are the responsibilities of local authorities, is justified. Even though the local authority reference facilities in central London are at present less extensive than those in some of the larger provincial cities, we do not believe that it would be appropriate for the BML to extend its responsibility in this way. The design of the new building for the BML should, therefore, provide for such public reference facilities as cannot be made available, even in the long term, in other ways. In our view this points to the need for detailed discussions between the officers of the BML, local authorities and other bodies before a final decision on the size and type of provision for the general public is made.

284. Part of the BML's international reputation derives from the distinction of its senior staff, many of whom are noted authorities in their particular fields of academic research. Although the administration of the library in the future will require staff exceptionally well versed in library technology and in the most modern methods of library management, it will continue to need substantial numbers of subject specialists of high academic attainments. It is essential, therefore, that the conditions of service and career prospects should continue to be attractive to scholars.

(b) *The coverage of the BML*

285. Through the long-standing arrangements for legal deposit, the BML now has the most complete collection of British publications in the arts and humanities,

74

as in other non-scientific subjects. It should continue to aim at complete coverage of these publications. It has also extensive collections of foreign publications, but, like national reference libraries in other countries, it has not in the past achieved a uniform standard of coverage in all subjects. Although it has been repeatedly represented to us that the national reference library should try to collect every worthwhile piece of research material published throughout the world, it is erroneous to assume that by this means the library would become comprehensive in all subjects and in all languages, as we do not believe it to be a practical proposition for the BML to achieve retrospectively complete coverage. The national reference library should, in our view, largely continue its present policy of providing as complete coverage as possible in those subjects, like history and literature, where its collections are uniquely good. In others, where large special libraries are already catering for a substantial proportion of the national demand, we think the BML's future acquisition policies should take into account the existing patterns of usage, so that the resources of all these libraries are utilised most effectively. We have, therefore, given careful and detailed consideration to the means whereby the national reference library could work towards a common policy with others separately administered and we regard this subject as so important that we have devoted chapter 15 of the report to it.

(c) The Department of Prints and Drawings of the BM

286. In the BM Trustees' original plans for the development of the Bloomsbury site, the Department of Prints and Drawings (DPD) was to be incorporated in the new building with the other library departments (excluding the NRLSI). In the revised proposals, however, the NRLSI was to be united with the other sections of the Department of Printed Books on the new site and the DPD was to remain with the antiquities departments in the existing British Museum building. Under either of these arrangements the DPD would be sufficiently close to all the other departments for its precise siting to be of secondary importance. Irrespective of its siting, however, its administration and organisation should be associated with those departments with which it is most closely linked in terms of function and usage, if the maximum benefit to users is to result.

287. The DPD receives about 6,500 visitors per annum. If the results of the April survey are even approximately typical, by far the greatest proportion of these would have used the department in conjunction with a visit to the library. In our view, therefore, the DPD is most appropriately regarded as a library department, and should be included in any consideration of national reference library facilities.

(d) The British Library of Art at the Victoria and Albert Museum

288. In examining the national reference requirements for the arts and the humanities, we have considered the role of the British Library of Art (BLA), especially in relation to the major reference collections of the BML.

289. The BLA, administered by the Department of Education and Science as part of the Victoria and Albert Museum, is one of the largest special collections in the country and contains over 400,000 volumes, many of which are not available elsewhere. However, figures provided by the BLA, based on signatures

in its visitors' book have shown that well over 90 per cent of all users work in the south-east of England. This would suggest that there is considerable potential for extending the use of this unique library, if a satisfactory means can be found.

290. Some of the stock is not very closely related to the scope of the V & A Museum itself and might more usefully be kept elsewhere. It is also inevitable that there must be substantial duplication of its holdings at Bloomsbury, not all of which may be justified. There would, therefore, seem to be some scope for rationalising the stocks of the two libraries by eliminating wasteful duplication and by redistributing some material in the subjects of common interest.

291. For all these reasons, it appears possible that benefits to users and economies might result if the BLA were fully integrated within a national libraries organisation. But we cannot be certain that this would on balance be beneficial without more detailed comparisons of the patterns of use and the stocks of the BLA and the BML than we have been able to obtain. We recommend, therefore, that the future administration of the BLA should be the subject of further examination, by the Department of Education and Science, in association with a national libraries organisation.

The Social Sciences

292. The social sciences present particular problems for libraries. Academic research in these subjects is expanding very rapidly and the demands for literature are increasing commensurately. The social scientist is interested not only in published monographs, periodicals and reports, but also in a great quantity and variety of ephemeral material which is, nevertheless, important as primary material for research. These items are often difficult to identify and to acquire, and fine judgement is necessary in assessing which of them may be of interest to the social scientists of the future. Once acquired, the material presents formidable problems of documentation* if research workers are to have bibliographic access to it.

293. It has been put to us in evidence that the existing provision for the social sciences both in the national libraries and in the nation's libraries as a whole is inadequate, and that a great deal of primary research material which in a few years may be impossible to obtain is not now being acquired by any library.

(a) The role of the BML

294. The BML's collections in the social sciences are extensive, and almost certainly duplicate to a substantial extent the holdings of the British Library of Political and Economic Science (BLPES) at the London School of Economics. Because of this and their relative proximity, we have considered how far the two collections might be rationalised. However, analysis of the subjects in which readers said they were interested during the April survey of the BML has revealed that of the 40 per cent of readers seeking material in the social sciences over three quarters also used literature associated with other disciplines. It thus appears that the social science material most in demand in the BML is wanted in connection with its other holdings. Although we would hope that the principles that we have defined in paragraph 285 in regard to the BML's acquisition policies for material in the arts and humanities would also be

---

* J. E. Pemberton, *The Library World*, November, 1968. 136–140.

applied to social science publications, we emphasise that we do not recommend any major change of the library's acquisitions policy for the social sciences that would prejudice its utility in servicing this type of inter-disciplinary study.

(*b*) *The role of the BLPES and other social science libraries*

295. The BLPES is the largest special library in London and, probably, in the country. It contains over 800,000 volumes in the social sciences, and is widely regarded as the world's most outstanding library in its field. As the London School of Economics has said in its evidence to us, it is intended to serve not only as the working library of the School, but also as a national collection.

296. Several other universities and colleges, including some of those more recently established, are also developing extensive collections in the social sciences to serve their teaching and research requirements. Up to now, however, no attempts have been made by the BML, the BLPES and these other university libraries to collect in a systematic fashion primary research material, so at present there is certainly incomplete total coverage and possibly wasteful duplication of effort.

297. Clearly, there is an urgent need to tackle this immense problem co-operatively. One solution might be to share the responsibility between all the relevant institutions on a subject basis, but an alternative suggestion that has been made to us would be to establish a single national collection for all types of social science primary research material. We do not feel qualified to identify the most appropriate answer to this problem, but it should be the responsibility of a national library organisation to recognise situations of this sort as they arise and to take the steps necessary to find a solution. We recommend, therefore, that whatever organisation is to administer the national libraries should—probably in collaboration with the Social Science Research Council—initiate discussions with the BLPES and the other interested institutions, in order to establish the most practical and economic method of collecting and making available the primary literature necessary for research in the social sciences.

Science and Technology

298. Requirements for literature in science and technology are of two fundamentally different kinds. Industrial firms and research scientists need access to a wide range of recent publications from all over the world, whereas a great deal of older scientific material is primarily of interest to the historian of science. The distinction between these two categories is more directly dependent upon the age of the literature than upon its content. However, some publications, including the most widely read periodicals, continue to be consulted by the practising scientist for much longer than others; on the other hand, in some subjects where the advance of knowledge is particularly rapid, the literature becomes outdated very quickly.

299. In considering the national reference facilities for science and technology, we have been particularly concerned that the basic distinction between the requirements of the principal types of user should be identified and reflected in our recommendations.

(a) The role of the NRLSI in the field of patent literature

300. The user survey of the NRLSI referred to in Chapter 4 has demonstrated that the library is largely oriented towards the needs of industry and that the preponderant use of the library by industry is in connection with patent work. About half the total visits were by patent workers, and to this figure must be added the number of visits made by the one third of all non-patent workers who referred to patent literature. In addition, three quarters of all photocopy orders during the survey period were for patents. Over half the total number of visits, and three quarters of those made by patent-workers, were from people working within one mile of the Holborn Division. Evidently the patent collections are essential to, and are heavily used by the chartered patent agents in central London, who comprise half the total patent agents in the country. Since the patent agents with the largest volume of business tend to be based in London and many provincial patent agents subcontract their searches to London colleagues, it is clear that the NRLSI, directly and indirectly, has a most important national, as well as local, role in providing library services in conjunction with patent literature.

301. Although there are several provincial library collections of British patents, the NRLSI's dominance in the field of patent literature seems likely to continue in the future, particularly because of its unrivalled and comprehensive collection of foreign patents. Accordingly, we recommend no fundamental change in the responsibilities of the NRLSI for patent literature.

(b) The role of the NRLSI in providing non-patent literature

302. The position regarding non-patent literature is less straightforward. Some non-patent literature is required in connection with certain types of patent search (see Chapter 4). However, whilst there is reason to believe that the patent searches carried out for many industrial concerns in the provinces get subcontracted to central London agents who use the NRLSI, it is not clear that any other substantial requirements for scientific and technical literature in the provinces are met by the NRLSI.

303. Enquiries which we made of a representative cross-section of industrial firms in Great Britain have shown that even firms fully aware of the NRLSI's services usually rely on other national institutions—such as the NLLST and Aslib—when local resources fail to meet their general scientific literature and information requirements. This correlates closely with the results of the survey conducted at the NRLSI itself, which indicated that only 1 per cent of the total visits were made by people working outside the south-east region (Figure 9 (ii), page 59). In view of the general pattern of the use made of reference facilities to which we drew attention at the beginning of this Chapter, it would be expected that the library would not be extensively used by personal visitors from other parts of Great Britain.

304. Although a recent survey by the Confederation of British Industry suggests that, because the NRLSI's services are not very widely publicised at present, there may be a greater potential demand from industry in the provinces than the library is now supplying, there would have to be a very substantial increase in the use of the library for non-patent literature by personal visitors from provincial firms before it represented a significant proportion of the

total use made of the library or before it could be regarded as fulfilling a national role in this respect. On the contrary, the evidence points to a regional role for the NRLSI, as far as general scientific reference facilities are concerned.

305. We consider that the general reference requirements of industry and commerce are not at present being, and could not be met by a single library, wherever it might be situated. The alternative is a well developed system of regional scientific and technical reference facilities. Already in a few provincial centres of industry such facilities are of a fairly high standard, but the quality of the provision is not uniformly satisfactory. We recommend, therefore, that regional facilities, based principally upon public and university libraries, should be developed as follows:

(i) They should provide a good standard of general coverage, for the most part relating to recent serial publications.

(ii) They should include specialist provision reflecting the particular characteristics and requirements of local industry.

(iii) They should give convenient access to all the principal bibliographic aids, which will facilitate the use of the NLLST for lightly-used material not available locally.

We have noted that the results of a recent survey* showed that the best of four large regional reference libraries was able to meet all the requirements of 84 per cent of the readers sampled and supplied at least some of the material sought by 94 per cent. Although we would not wish to propose any precise figure, we believe that regional reference facilities serving major industrial areas should provide a level of service which approaches this standard. An appreciably better service than this, however, might well involve wasteful duplication of lightly-used material, requests for which could most economically be met, either by lending or photocopying from the central stocks of the NLLST.

(c) The photocopying service of the NRLSI

306. The analysis of photocopying at the NRLSI strengthens the argument that it has not developed a national role in terms of general scientific information. Over three quarters of all items photocopied were patent literature and the photocopying orders as a whole were mostly for the London area. From the survey data, we estimate that the NRLSI's annual volume of photocopying of non-patent items constituted only about 5 per cent of the national photocopying and lending demands for scientific literature satisfied by the NLLST and NRLSI together. This and the conclusions of the previous Chapter suggest that in future the photocopying services at the NRLSI should:

(i) continue to meet the demand for urgent orders for British patent specifications (non-urgent orders being met at the Patent Office itself);

(ii) continue to supply copies of foreign patents;

(iii) be responsible for meeting the demands of personal visitors to the library for photocopies;

---

* D. W. G. Clements, *Journal of Documentation*, **23** (2), 131-146.

(iv) satisfy the national requests forwarded to the library from the photo-copying and loan locating centre.

(d) The coverage of the NRLSI

307. The implications of the preceding paragraphs are that the coverage of the NRLSI should be adequate to satisfy the need for:

(i) a comprehensive collection of British and foreign patent literature;

(ii) such technical and trade literature as is associated with (i) above;

(iii) other technical and scientific literature which, with (ii), would satisfy a high proportion of the south-east regional reference needs in association with other libraries in the region;

(iv) such bibliographic, information and referral facilities as are justified by demands for (i), (ii) and (iii) above.

So far as non-patent literature is concerned, the survey does not suggest that a particularly extensive collection is needed by patent workers. Like other users of the library, they are primarily interested in the relatively recent publications. Although an analysis of the use of the library by title of publication and categories of user would have to be carried out over an extended period before the literature needs of users could be identified precisely, it is very probable that the great majority of the requirements under (ii) above would be met by the coverage provided to satisfy the general scientific reference requirements of the south-east region.

308. British publications would be acquired by legal deposit, the arrangements for which are described in paragraph 337 below. Indeed, by far the largest proportion of all legally deposited scientific material would probably be assigned to the NRLSI, rather than to the BML, although only those items likely to be in substantial demand would be retained in central London, the remainder being outhoused (paragraph 323). So far as foreign material is concerned, we recommend that the library should acquire by purchase or international exchange only those items for which there is likely to be a reasonable demand by patent workers generally or from other users in the south-east region. We stress that the considerable cost of acquiring and housing in central London very lightly used foreign publications, reports and other material would be wasteful, as they will be available from the comprehensive collection at Boston Spa.

309. Nearly 90 per cent of all non-patent items used in the library were published since 1950, and almost 95 per cent since 1940 (Figure 13 (i), page 90). Even when every allowance is made for the increased rate of publication in recent years, these and other figures show that the use that is made of scientific material falls off progressively as it becomes older. Hence, the demand for much of the stock of the library may be expected to become very light in the course of time. Because of the exceptionally high accommodation costs involved, we recommend that the NRLSI should not keep such lightly used material in central London. Legal deposit publications should obviously be preserved elsewhere within the reference division of the national libraries organisation, but the remainder could be transferred to other collections—whether or not administered as part

of the national organisation—where it might be more extensively used or economically retained.

(e) The role of the BML

310. The April survey of the BML showed that 7 per cent of readers sought information or literature in a scientific subject, although the overwhelming majority wanted material in non-scientific subjects as well. This is consistent with the view put to us by the British Museum that the library's science material is used very largely in connection with historical studies. We think it appropriate, therefore, that the BML should continue to hold and collect some scientific publications, but that this collection should differ in character from and be much smaller than that at the NRLSI. Some monographs and serials relating to the history of science—including legally deposited material—should be included in the BML's stocks, as would other scientific publications of relatively little interest to scientists, but likely to be of greater interest to historians and the other principal users of the library. We also envisage that the BML would acquire those items of the NRLSI's stock which, after they were no longer in demand by practising scientists, might continue to be of interest to historians.

(f) The role of the SML

311. The SML has emphasised to us its particular responsibilities to the Science Museum and to Imperial College. Even though there are no direct administrative links between the College and the library, the SML's acquisition policy is considerably influenced by the needs of the College staff and post-graduate students and there are arrangements for consulting Imperial College over the selection of material for purchase. Nevertheless, there is still substantial duplication of holdings and acquisitions between the SML and the College's many libraries, particularly the central Lyon Playfair library.

312. Although about 60 per cent of the readers of the SML are College members (Figure 7, page 42), the growth in recent years of Imperial College has not been reflected by a comparable increase in the use of the SML. Indeed, the College has pursued a policy of developing its own central and departmental libraries which, in our view, has tended to reduce its reliance on the SML. At least partly for this reason, the SML is overall relatively lightly used. For example, in 1967/68 the SML with a stock of 400,000 volumes had about 20,000 visitors compared with over 120,000 at the NRLSI which has about 600,000 volumes.

313. When, in the summer of 1969, the SML moves to a new building which it will share with the Lyon Playfair library, the use of its facilities by Imperial College will almost certainly increase substantially, because of the improved service and the much greater degree of open access in the new accommodation. But the situation will then be that two separately administered large libraries catering for essentially the same clientele and substantially duplicating each other's acquisitions will be immediately adjacent to, but not interconnecting with each other. This we consider to be wasteful and unnecessary.

314. One way of improving the utilisation of the SML would be to unite it with the NRLSI in the new accommodation in South Kensington. However, we are convinced that the new SML building would not be large enough both

to hold the combined stocks of the two libraries, even if all duplication were eliminated, and to provide sufficient space for readers. Furthermore, because of the high utilisation of the Imperial College site and, as we are informed, the exceptional difficulty of obtaining additional land in South Kensington, there is no scope for expanding the new library building beyond that originally planned. Quite apart from any fundamental objections to this solution, including the distance from the Patent Bar, we are, therefore, satisfied that it is physically impracticable.

315. We have sought instead a solution by which the resources of the SML would continue to meet primarily the needs of Imperial College and the South Kensington museums,whilst avoiding as far as practicable wasteful duplication of stock and facilities. In particular, we have examined the possibility of integrating the SML administratively with the Imperial College library system and we consider that it would have the following major advantages:

(i) The SML and the adjacent Lyon Playfair Library (LPL) would be operated as a single unit, with consequent savings in staffing, acquisitions and space.

(ii) The holdings of the SML and the LPL could be recorded in a single catalogue and the SML's mechanised indexing facilities could be fully exploited.

(iii) The development of a single major central library directly administered by Imperial College would simplify the College's library administration and would facilitate the co-ordination of its central and departmental library services in achieving the greatest efficiency and economy.

(iv) Following rationalisation of the stocks of the SML and the LPL, surplus material could be transferred elsewhere, filling gaps in other collections. It would clearly be desirable to ensure that the national libraries had first refusal of this material. At the same time, full account must be taken of the need to preserve and develop its strong specialist collection in the history of science and technology, particularly as it is essential to the work of the Museum staff. In this context, we would not exclude the possibility of transferring some material (apart from legal deposit material) to the SML from the national collections, such as the NRLSI.

We, therefore, recommend that the SML should not in future be administered by a national libraries organisation, but should be fully integrated with the Lyon Playfair Library of Imperial College.

316. It will, however, be necessary to guarantee that a combined library continues to meet the needs of the South Kensington museums, especially those of the Science Museum. In particular:

(i) The privileges and facilities at present available to the Science Museum staff should continue. To ensure this, the Museum should be represented on all the bodies controlling the administration and policy of the combined library system and its acquisitions policy should reflect these responsibilities.

82

(ii) The photocopying and other services at present provided for the other South Kensington museums should be maintained.

(iii) Adequate funds, administratively separate from those of Imperial College, should be made available for the continued development of the SML's special collection in the history of science and technology. Similar provision should also be made in respect of any other specialised material which is at present provided primarily for the use of the Science Museum staff.

(iv) Lending from the combined stocks through the national network should be on conditions at least as unrestricted as the present arrangements, and the SML's limited role in a national photocopying service should continue. We do not think that this would be an undue burden for the new library, especially as the SML's existing relatively small contribution would be further reduced if any of the stocks were transferred to national libraries, as we have suggested in paragraph 315 (iv), above.

In order to satisfy conditions (ii), (iii) and (iv) above, a special grant from national resources may be appropriate. However, integration of the SML with the LPL must lead to considerable economies which will undoubtedly produce a substantial net saving of national resources.

Outhousing Material from the BML and the NRLSI

317. The Trustees of the British Museum and several other important bodies have strongly urged in evidence to us that all the stocks of the BML and the NRLSI (in some cases, with the exception of the material outhoused at Colindale) should be kept together on a single library site in central London. Other bodies have recommended that, although the BML and NRLSI should remain physically separate, the complete collections of each library should be stored on their respective single sites. Most of this evidence has stressed that the value of the national reference collections would be enhanced if users could be certain that any item from the stocks of either library were immediately available to them from book-stacks on the same site as the reading rooms. It has been said that the present outhousing from both the BML and the NRLSI detracts from the usefulness of the libraries and that further outhousing would only aggravate the inconvenience to users. The attractions of this proposition are obvious, but practical considerations have led us to try to assess how high a priority should be afforded to its realisation.

(a) *The present situation*

318. At present two quite distinct types of outhousing policy are operated at the BML and NRLSI:

(i) Certain classes of publication, irrespective of the level of demand for them, have been outhoused from the BML to Colindale for a considerable time. The outhouse itself is purpose-built to store newspapers and periodicals, and there are facilities for readers and for photocopying.

(ii) More recently, lack of space in Bloomsbury and in Holborn has forced the administration to outhouse some of the least used material from

83

the BML in buildings vacated when Woolwich Arsenal closed. Scientific material in low demand from both the NRLSI and the BML is outhoused in Bayswater. Neither building was specially designed for the purpose and there are no facilities for readers at Woolwich, although these have recently been provided at Bayswater.

319. The Trustees, when urging the discontinuance of the Woolwich outhouse, pointed to the technical difficulties of selecting material on the basis of low demand and stated that in their opinion a policy based on this criterion is doomed to failure. The present methods by which material for storage at Woolwich is selected are admittedly unsophisticated, and it would be possible to improve them considerably if computerised methods of stock control were introduced. Despite this, however, the methods seem to have been fairly successful: although 7 per cent of the stock controlled by the Bloomsbury section of the BML is outhoused at Woolwich, the requisition slips examined in the April survey showed that the demand on the Woolwich stock was only 0·75 per cent of that at Bloomsbury. In view of the very small proportion (3 per cent) of the BML's readers who come considerable distances for visits lasting only a single day, the inconvenience resulting from this outhousing policy can be only slight. Indeed, we have received very little indication in our evidence of inconvenience resulting from outhousing at Woolwich. Similarly, there is very little factual evidence of inconvenience associated with the NRLSI's outhouse in Bayswater.

320. In contrast, the outhousing of newspapers and periodicals at Colindale has been subject to considerable criticism. At first sight it may be surprising that a purpose-built outhouse with its own reading room, much more easily accessible from Bloomsbury than is Woolwich, should be the source of a considerable measure of user dissatisfaction. However, the reason is, no doubt, that the selection of the material in Colindale is not determined by the level of users' demands, and it is evident that some of the material in Colindale is in relatively heavy demand, more so, perhaps, than a great deal of the material at Bloomsbury.

(b) *Financial considerations*

321. The main argument in favour of outhousing is the exceptionally high cost of land in central London. It has been estimated that to store a typical volume for one year in central London costs approximately 5s. 0d. (Appendix D). As the Trustees' original proposals for a new building to replace the existing BML included over 650,000 square feet of book storage space, the accommodation of stock alone would at present day costs amount to over £3m. per year (Appendix D). If, by outhousing, the total space requirements could be reduced even by a small proportion, there would be a considerable saving. For example, the annual savings which could result from replacing as little as five per cent of the central London storage space planned for the new library by an equivalent area on a low cost site would be approximately equal in value to the whole of the public funds which the BML (excluding the NRLSI) now receives for its acquisitions.

322. It is difficult to estimate the savings which could be achieved by a policy of outhousing based on level of demand. We do not know what proportion of the BML's stock is called upon less frequently than, say, once in five years,

84

ten years or twenty years. However, from statistics contained in the Trustees' evidence, it appears that, on average, each volume in the Department of Printed Books is used once in every seven years. There would seem, therefore, to be at least a *prima facie* case for supposing that a substantial proportion must be called upon no more frequently than once in ten years, and there is probably a significant fraction that is used very rarely indeed. It is salutary to realise that each time an item used only once in ten years is requisitioned, the storage costs alone amount to about £2 10s. 0d.

323. Similar considerations apply to the NRLSI. We have already recommended in paragraphs 307–309 above that the NRLSI, in fulfilling the functions which we have envisaged for it, should not attempt comprehensive coverage of the world's scientific literature and that the foreign material which it does acquire should not be retained when it is so old as to be very rarely consulted. In the case of older and lightly used British material, which would form part of the definitive collection of legally deposited publications, and possibly other material which, though lightly used, it was considered desirable to retain, outhousing would prove a satisfactory and relatively cheap alternative to keeping it in central London. An outhouse at Boston Spa would enable it to be quickly available for satisfying requests received by the location centre, or for facsimile transmission, if a circuit were established to link the various facilities at Boston Spa with those in central London.

(c) Future outhousing policy

324. In our discussion of outhousing we have tried to take into account the inconvenience to users as well as the potential savings in costs. However, we are of the opinion that there must be a substantial quantity of material in both the BML and the NRLSI which could be outhoused with very little inconvenience to users, and the level of this inconvenience could be reduced still further if the facilities for the prior reservation of books were better developed and were more widely used by readers before their visits. We recommend, therefore, the adoption of a deliberate policy of outhousing based on the following principles:

(i) The main criterion by which material suitable for outhousing is selected should be that of a low level of user demand.

(ii) The outhouse should be purpose-built and should, if at all possible, have facilities for readers.

(iii) Lightly-used material selected for outhousing should be stored in such a place that it can, if necessary, be transferred to the central reference point within 24 hours.

(iv) The proliferation of widely-scattered outhouses should be avoided.

325. We have examined the possibility of transferring to a central site the most heavily used material from Colindale. Although we appreciate that considerable inconvenience to users is caused by the present siting of the most heavily used newspapers, we are equally aware that newspapers take up a disproportionately large amount of storage space and that the economic advantages of keeping them outside central London are, therefore, very much greater even

than those of outhousing most other types of library material. Thus we recommend that the storage of newspapers and periodicals at Colindale should continue as at present, but that microform copies of the most heavily used items should be permanently available for consulation in the main BML, so that inconvenience to users may be minimised.

The Internal Organisation of the BML and the NRLSI

(a) The BML

326. The concept of a national reference library, as described by the BM Trustees, consists essentially of the provision of specialised reference facilities with their own reading rooms and associated services. Each of these would give direct access to specialist literature and would be backed up by the main book collection and the services of staff expert in the appropriate subject fields. We consider this idea to be basically sound, as it enables the library to adapt its services and organisation to the specialised information requirements of researchers in different disciplines, while retaining the unique advantages of its vast stocks and broad coverage for those following inter-disciplinary studies. However, in a time when the traditional borderlines between subjects are becoming progressively less sharp, and new methods of information handling are rapidly being developed, an organisation of the collections along the lines envisaged by the Trustees will need to be subject to continuing modification and development. Thus the design of the new building should allow for a greater degree of structural flexibility than would be necessary if the collections were largely to service a single main reading room as at present. We cannot emphasise too strongly our conviction that the new library building must incorporate above all else the possibility of being readily adapted for changing needs, changing services and rapid developments in library technology. In particular, the application of computers promises in the next few decades to transform the traditional methods of library management, organisation and services.

327. The Trustees' proposals involve storing about 5 per cent of the BML's total holdings on open access. It has been suggested to us in several pieces of evidence, however, that a much greater degree of open access is desirable in view of the benefits which many readers derive from browsing. We have considered the advantages of such facilities in a national reference library like the BML, but regard the following major disadvantages as decisive:

(i) In a library of such size, an extremely elaborate system of subject classification would be necessary and its complexities would probably hinder all but the most experienced library users.

(ii) The relatively large space requirements of open access storage, the need to protect much material by binding which would not otherwise be necessary, and the labour involved in the continuous process of selectively retiring material to closed access storage would all increase substantially the cost of maintaining the collections.

(iii) There would be major difficulties in preventing misplacing of items on the shelves and the mutilation and theft of books, all of which would seriously detract from the library's usefulness and jeopardise the integrity of the definitive collection of British literature of all ages.

86

In considering the problems of open access, we have been particularly assisted by two papers submitted to us in evidence. One of these, by Dr. F. W. Ratcliffe, Librarian of Manchester University Library, has been published.* The other, by Mr. E. B. Ceadel, Librarian of the Cambridge University Library, is reprinted in full in an Appendix to this report. We have accepted the implications of these two penetrating analyses and recommend, therefore, that only the most heavily and generally used titles—including standard reference works, indexes, abstracts and certain periodicals—should be directly accessible to readers, although we would expect the present policy of giving readers access to the closed stacks in exceptional circumstances to continue, and, possibly, be extended.

(b) The NRLSI

328. As the NRLSI is a smaller collection than the BML and as a high proportion of its users visit the library frequently, the disadvantages of open access are much less important in the case of this library. Indeed, it is clear from our evidence that the open access facilities at the Holborn division of the library are appreciated by many of the library's users—particularly by patent workers, who rely upon being able to make rapid searches through a large number of patent specifications and periodical journals. The present usage patterns of the NRLSI will almost certainly continue for some time ahead, and so we recommend that, despite the considerable savings of both space and expense that are possible through the use of closed access stacks, the library should provide open access to a substantial proportion of its stocks.

329. Nevertheless, economic considerations suggest that the proportion of material stored on closed access should be as high as posssible without causing serious inconvenience to users. We think that it would be reasonable for about 90 per cent of the material consulted to be on open access; analysis of non-patent items consulted by visitors to the NRLSI during the survey period (see paragraph 309) suggests that the application of this principle will involve the selective retirement of material to closed access stacks *on average* 20 years after its publication. No doubt a few of the library's visitors, however, will occasionally wish to make extensive searches of older literature which is not on open access. Like the BML, this library, too, might give readers access to the closed stacks in exceptional circumstances.

330. However, we consider that the need for an open access collection is transitory. Already plans are being considered by the Patent Office for making British specifications available on microform aperture cards, which would undoubtedly facilitate patent-searching and might lead many more organisations and patent agents to build up their own collections of British specifications. But this should only be the beginning: because of the particular characteristics of scientific information and the excellence of its bibliographic coverage, scientific information services may well become sufficiently thorough and selective as to make manual searching of all scientific literature unnecessary. The probable long-term changes in the pattern of use of the NRLSI, owing to the future development of more sophisticated information retrieval systems, make it unlikely that a new, open access, scientific reference library will continue unchanged for more than a fraction of the expected life of a new building. Thus

---

* F. W. Ratcliffe, Libri: 1968, **18**(2), 95–111.

the need for flexibility in design to which we have already drawn attention in the case of the BML will be even more important in the case of the NRLSI.

The Administration of the BML and the NRLSI

(a) The BML

331. The BML is at present administered as an integral part of the British Museum. However, the scale of the services provided by the antiquities departments of the Museum on the one hand and by the library departments on the other has grown to such an extent that the administrative requirements of each of these two sections are becoming increasingly specialised and demanding. Furthermore, the task of administering the library departments is likely to become even more onerous during the design and construction of the new building and the lengthy and complex process of transferring staff and stocks to it. We know, too, from the Trustees of the BM, that they envisage major developments for the antiquities departments, which will require considerable planning and effort to be put into effect. Thus it is probable that, to perpetuate the existing administrative unity, would inhibit the full development of the library's services which we regard as essential to the future wellbeing of the national libraries system and might also adversely affect the Trustees' reappraisal of the role of the antiquities departments.

332. In Chapter 11 we have recommended that the BML should in future participate extensively in the national photocopying services and should make a limited contribution towards meeting national loan requirements; in this Chapter we have stressed the need for the library to take account of the acquisition policies of other major national library collections; and in Chapter 14 we discuss the vital role of the BML in a national bibliographic service. All these considerations taken together quite clearly imply the need to associate the BML with other libraries and to link its administration with those of the NLLST, the NCL and a national bibliographic service.

333. On balance, therefore, although it will be desirable to maintain some links between the library and antiquities departments of the Museum, we recommend that the administrative responsibilities for the two sections should be completely separate and that the four library departments (Printed Books; Manuscripts; Oriental Printed Books and Manuscripts; and Prints and Drawings) should become the National Reference Library (NRL).

(b) The NRLSI

334. The NRLSI is at present administratively a section of the BML's Department of Printed Books. However, the existing functions and services of the library differ significantly from those of the remaining sections of the department, and our recommendations concerning the library's future role have tended to emphasise these differences. In particular:

(i) The usage patterns of the NRLSI are quite unlike those of the BML, in that most of its visitors make short, relatively frequent visits and require brief access to a large number of items.

(ii) The NRLSI is organised on an open access basis, and thus needs fundamentally different methods of stock control from the BML.

88

(iii) The NRLSI's users are drawn very largely from the patent profession, industry and commerce, whereas the BML's users are mainly university staff and post-graduate students (Figure 12 (i) and (ii)).

(iv) The users of the NRLSI are interested predominantly in recent publications, while at the BML the stock of 17th century material is used just as intensively as that of 20th century material (Figure 13 (i) and (ii), page 90).

(v) The NRLSI has not developed a substantial national role, except in the special field of patent literature.

(vi) When the current operation to rationalise the distribution of scientific publications between the two libraries is complete, the one administrative reason for linking the NRLSI with the BML will disappear.

(vii) In future, the NRLSI will need to be at least as closely linked with the NLLST as with the BML.

We consider, therefore, that the future development of the NRLSI is likely to have no more in common with the BML than with other units which together would comprise a national libraries organisation. Because we believe that the particular problems of the BML and the NRLSI would best be solved if the two libraries were more independent of each other than at present, we recommend that they should be administered as separate units within a national libraries system. The NRLSI should then become the Central Science and Patent Collections (CSPC).

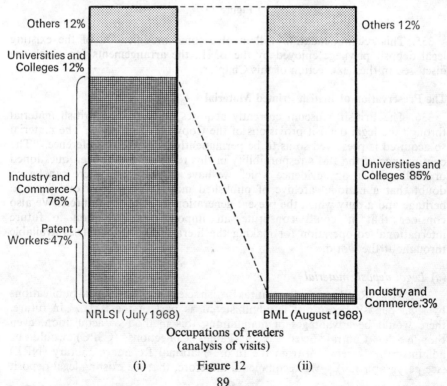

Others 12%

Universities and Colleges 12%

Industry and Commerce 76%

Patent Workers 47%

Others 12%

Universities and Colleges 85%

Industry and Commerce 3%

NRLSI (July 1968)   BML (August 1968)

Occupations of readers
(analysis of visits)

(i)   Figure 12   (ii)

89

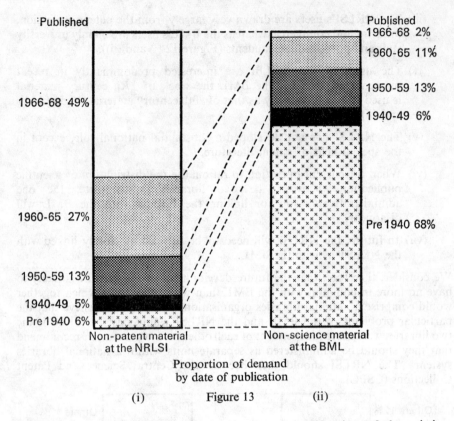

Published

1966-68 49%

1960-65 27%

1950-59 13%

1940-49 5%

Pre 1940 6%

Non-patent material
at the NRLSI

Published
1966-68 2%

1960-65 11%

1950-59 13%

1940-49 6%

Pre 1940 68%

Non-science material
at the BML

Proportion of demand
by date of publication

(i)   Figure 13   (ii)

335. This recommendation will involve some modification of the existing legal deposit privilege enjoyed by the BML, the arrangements for which are discussed in the next section of this Chapter.

The Preservation of British Printed Material

336. The British Museum currently acquires all published British material through the legal deposit provisions of the Copyright Act 1911. The material so acquired is preserved so as to be permanently available for reference. The continuance of the BM's responsibility in this respect has not been questioned or challenged in any evidence which we have received, and there can be no doubt that a national archive of published material is part of our national heritage and a duty which the present generation owes to the future. We also consider that it could constitute an important contribution to future international co-operation for making the literature of all countries available throughout the world.

(a) Legal deposit material

337. The NRLSI currently acquires British scientific and technical publications by legal deposit because it is administered as part of the BML. In future, there would be advantages in maintaining this method of acquisition, even though the Central Science and Patent Collections (CSPC) would be administratively separate from the future National Reference Library (NRL) (see paragraph 334). We recommend, therefore, that the existing legal deposit

provisions relating to the British Museum, which are the most feasible and economic way of ensuring that the national archive is as complete as possible, should be amended so as to require British publishers to deposit one copy of all their publications with a national libraries organisation. The organisation should have the duty of ensuring that the material is available for reference only, but should, we believe, be given discretion in determining which particular reference library under its administrative aegis should be responsible for storing it. This added degree of flexibility would, in our opinion, be wholly beneficial. For example, it would enable a national libraries organisation to transfer older and lightly used legal deposit material from the CSPC to a more suitable reference collection, such as the future NRL.

(b) *Other material*

338. We have already referred to the problems of collecting unpublished British material in the social sciences. Similar, though less serious, difficulties arise in other subject areas. We appreciate the importance of this material in supplementing the legally deposited national collection and, therefore, recommend that the reference section of a national libraries organisation should continue the BML's special responsibility of actively collecting and preserving important unpublished British material.

(c) *Problems of storage and preservation*

339. In recent years the rate of publication in this country has increased rapidly. An indication of this growth can be obtained from the increase in the number of entries in the BNB index, even though the index does not cover all classes of published material. During 1950 about 13,000 new entries appeared, and in 1967 the total was slightly more than double this figure. The growth rate in very recent years has shown a particularly rapid increase, and the 1967 figure was 24 per cent greater than that for 1963. The BM Trustees' evidence shows that the present rate of acquisition by the BML of legally deposited material amounts to about 40,000 monographs, 80,000 issues of periodicals and 140,000 newspapers per annum. Added to these figures should be an unknown, but certainly substantial, quantity of British material which is not published in the technical sense.

340. The storage of the accumulated legally deposited material will obviously become very much more expensive in years to come. The question arises, therefore, as to whether only a proportion of legally deposited material might be retained, but at the present time it seems unlikely that any very substantial savings could be achieved without seriously detracting from the value of the material to posterity. Nevertheless, we think that the possibility is worth studying in detail, most beneficially before new legislation is put in hand. This possibility apart, there would appear to be cogent economic arguments in favour of outhousing much legally deposited material and, where possible, retaining it in microform only.

341. Outhousing at least part of the legally deposited material should be possible in the future without causing serious inconvenience to users, since virtually complete collections of legal deposit material are available at five other reference libraries in Great Britain and Eire, and the British library regions are becoming increasingly self-sufficient in respect of recent British

91

publications. It would also have the particular advantage of enabling the material to be stored in a secure and controlled environment which would not normally be necessary for other material.

342. The reduction of part of the archive to microform might avoid some of the disadvantages associated with the permanent storage of recent publications. The advent of cheap papers produced from wood pulp and the increasing popularity of paperback publications pose serious problems of preservation, and we understand from the British Standards Institution that, without special and expensive treatment, much recent printed material may have a life-span of no more than 50 years before it disintegrates. Although relatively little is now known about the maximum life-span of microforms and photocopies, carefully produced copies should remain easily legible for at least 50 years and renewal by rephotographing is a simple and comparatively cheap process.

343. After consideration of the above issues, we recommend that the problems associated with the housing of the legally deposited material should be the subject of careful and continuing review by a national libraries organisation, and that the organisation should have the responsibility for ensuring that adequate research into methods of archival preservation is put in hand at the appropriate time. In order to assist the organisation in exercising its discretion in the handling of legally deposited material, we recommend that it should also be empowered to dispose of such material where it considers that a microform or photocopy is likely to be an acceptable substitute to users.

(d) Material in media other than the written word

344. We are aware of pressures, both in Parliament and elsewhere, to extend legal deposit to published material in other media, such as films and gramophone records. If the law of legal deposit had applied in these cases heretofore and if the British Museum had been responsible for receiving and preserving the material, many losses of now irreplaceable items would have been prevented. We consider that there would be major advantages if the preservation of all published material, irrespective of medium, could be ensured, although a national reference library is not necessarily the most suitable repository for all of it. We recommend, therefore, that the problems of preserving material published in media other than the written word should be regularly reappraised by the Secretary of State for Education and Science, in consultation with the national libraries organisation and other relevant bodies.

The Site for the National Reference Library

345. Much of the evidence which we have received concerns the future site for a new building to replace the BML, and of this a substantial proportion urges the advantages of keeping the present library departments of the British Museum close to the antiquities departments in Bloomsbury. This question, in particular, has aroused a great deal of controversy, and we have, therefore, examined carefully all the arguments which have been put to us.

(a) The needs of scholars using the BML

346. In their evidence the BM Trustees argue that academic researchers derive great benefit from the propinquity of the antiquities collections and the

library. In this they are supported by about two fifths of the universities throughout the country, and particularly by those with faculties of classics, archaeology, architecture, art history, ethnography, mediaeval and ancient languages, or oriental and African studies. However, our evidence also shows that a substantial proportion of university users does not consider it necessary that the library and the antiquities departments should be immediately adjacent to each other. Possibly because opinion is so divided on this issue, opposing views are strongly held, forcefully argued and often based on irreconcilable premises. In commissioning the BML usage surveys, therefore, we stressed that we wished to obtain as much factual information as possible relevant to this issue.

347. The results of the survey suggest that immediate access to the antiquities departments from the four library departments is important to only a very small minority of library users. Of the April survey sample, 6 per cent stated that they intended to use departments other than the four library departments on the same day as their visit. However, of these only half considered it essential to their work to do so (Figure 14). It is not obvious that all of these would be seriously inconvenienced by a relatively small physical separation of museum and library, particularly if a substantial proportion were engaged on protracted study which brought them to Bloomsbury frequently. Therefore, we examined the number of library users regarding the use of the antiquities departments as essential to their work who, having come a considerable distance, were spending only a single day in the British Museum before returning to their place of origin. The April survey showed that only half of one per cent of all visitors to the library were in this category, and this very small proportion

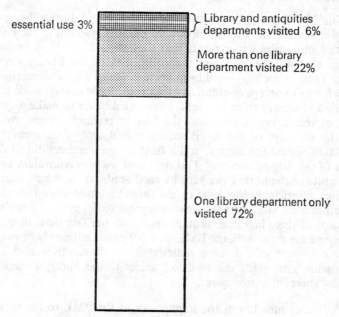

essential use 3%

Library and antiquities departments visited 6%

More than one library department visited 22%

One library department only visited 72%

Use of departments of the British Museum
by visitors to the BML

Figure 14

was confirmed almost identically in August. It would seem, therefore that little serious hardship would result on this account, so long as museum and library were within a reasonably short distance of each other.

348. There are cogent reasons, however, for ensuring that any new library is sited in central London. Students and staff of London University comprise the largest single group of visitors to the BML and of these nearly two thirds are from colleges and institutes in or near Bloomsbury and Aldwych. Proximity to the BML is a matter of day-to-day convenience for this numerically large group of users, who clearly depend very considerably on the facilities of the BML for their work. Indeed, as we mentioned at the beginning of this Chapter, it is almost certainly no coincidence that such a high proportion of the total use of the BML is concentrated close to its present site. There are, therefore, important advantages in ensuring that whatever site is ultimately chosen, it should not be appreciably less convenient to the central London academic institutions than is the existing one.

349. To the relatively small proportion of one-day visitors from afar (four per cent of the April survey sample) also it is important that a central London site is chosen for the new National Reference Library building—firstly, because with so little time available they need to be able to get quickly to the library from their arrival points, such as the main-line rail termini; secondly, because we are told that many of them find it useful to combine their visit to the BML with visits to one or more of the academic or professional institutions which are concentrated in Bloomsbury and other central areas.

(b) The needs of the museum staff

350. The BM Trustees in their written evidence and during discussion have impressed upon us their strong conviction that it is essential to the needs of the staff of the antiquities departments that they should be able to refer directly and easily to both the staff and the collections of the library departments. In this the Trustees are supported by many individuals and academic institutions. It is easy for us to accept qualitatively that some disadvantages will result from a separation of library from museum, but more difficult to make a quantitative estimate of the inconvenience and the loss to research which would result. During the six days of the April survey period, only four members of the museum staff visited the library, and a further two members did so during the two days of the August survey. This degree of usage is equivalent to only two or three visits to the library per year by each graduate member of the museum staff. This surprisingly low level of use probably reflects the fact that several of the antiquities departments have libraries sufficiently comprehensive to satisfy most of their literature requirements and the fact that, in the research fields of some museum staff, the BML may not contain the only or even the best specialist collection of reference material in London. It is also likely that some museum staff made use of direct access to the library's stacks without completing survey questionnaires.

351. A further measure of the importance of the BML to the museum staff is the number of books requisitioned by them from the library without making personal visits. In 1968 museum staff requisitioned a total of about 2,700 volumes, which represents a daily traffic of approximately 10 books in each

direction.   Separation of the library would, therefore, create some inconvenience on this account, but we do not believe that it would be difficult or very costly to arrange transport for these items over a relatively small intermediate distance.

352. Although we are aware that there is a danger of placing too much reliance on survey data in assessing the academic values and intangible benefits that proximity between library and museum confers, we have found no factual evidence to support the view that the union of the library and antiquities departments on the same site is an essential condition for the effective performance of the duties of the museum staff.

(c) *Material relevant to both museum and library*

353. The Trustees have argued that there are many items in the British Museum which are not easily classifiable as either library or museum material, and they have stressed, in particular, the position of the Department of Prints and Drawings.   However, we have already shown that, in terms of usage, the department is overwhelmingly associated with the other library departments, and we do not believe, therefore, that intolerable disadvantages to the museum would result from the DPD being administered and sited as part of the National Reference Library.

(d) *Staffing*

354. The Trustees have pointed out a further advantage of the present physical and administrative unity of the library and antiquities departments, in that it enables the two sections to share the services of expert staff who specialise in the less common subjects, such as Coptic.   Although we have recommended that the library and museum departments should be separately administered, we see no reason why it should not be possible to make some of the library staff available to assist the museum, and vice versa.   We recognise the importance to both institutions of co-operation of this kind in subject areas where neither library nor museum could justify a full-time appointment, but we do not think that it is critically dependent on the library and museum being on the same site, so long as they are fairly close to each other.

(e) *Difficulties of removal*

355. The Trustees rightly point out in their evidence that the removal and reorganisation of the library departments will be, at best, an immensely complex manoeuvre which will have to be spread over a considerable period of time. There is no doubt that, if the removal involved only crossing a street, the whole operation would be relatively simple, but that, if removal required transport over even a slightly increased distance, the operation would be very much more complicated and costly because motorised intermediate transport would be necessary.

356. Some evidence has suggested that the BML should remain on the existing site, but that the museum should be sited elsewhere.   This, involving as it would the transportation of extremely valuable and fragile exhibits in the antiquities collections, has been rejected by the Trustees on what we believe to be sound practical grounds.   Unless there are much more persuasive arguments than we are aware of, we do not think that this proposition needs further consideration.

(f) Administrative advantages of separation

357. The only argument of any substance which has been put to us in favour of separating the library and museum physically is that this would facilitate the integration of the library organisationally into a new administrative structure together with the other national libraries. We are not convinced by this argument—and, indeed, there may even be marginal administrative benefits to be derived from physical proximity during the period of transition. We therefore record our view that no benefits would result to library users in general from moving the library away from the museum departments. Other arguments are outside our terms of reference and our competence to judge.

(g) Conclusions

358. After considering the relevant issues carefully and at length, we are satisfied that, except for its being one possible solution to the inadequacies of the present building, physical separation of the library from the antiquities departments would not have advantages for the staff or visiting scholars of the British Museum, nor would it assist the realisation of our recommendations for a national libraries service. From library considerations alone, therefore, the Bloomsbury site is the most suitable for the NRL.

359. On the other hand, the overwhelming majority of the library's users do not need to make use of the antiquities departments and, therefore, if it were decided for other reasons to separate the library physically from the rest of the museum, they would not necessarily be inconvenienced. We consider it essential, however, that despite the high cost of land, a new building for the National Reference Library, if not adjacent to the BM, should certainly be in central London, because in our view this is by far the best location for serving users in all parts of Britain and visitors from overseas. We also believe that the site selected should be convenient particularly to those colleges and institutions in Bloomsbury and Aldwych with which the largest group of the BML's readers are associated.

360. For a small proportion of the library's visitors and for some of the staff in the antiquities departments, any physical separation of library from museum would result in some inconvenience. The extent of this inconvenience would obviously vary according to individual circumstances and would depend on the particular site chosen for the new library. Almost certainly, the number of people seriously inconvenienced by moving the library to a site satisfying the conditions indicated in the previous paragraph would be very small. Whether the total disadvantage should be tolerated, however, would need to be judged against the weight of arguments which, being unconnected with the organisation of the national libraries' services, are outside our competence and terms of reference.

The Site for the Central Science and Patent Collections

361. The majority of the evidence urging the importance of keeping the library and antiquities departments sited together has also stressed the advantages of uniting the NRLSI with the main BML. As we have suggested in paragraph 357, we do not think that the administrative separation of the two libraries which we have recommended necessarily precludes physical proximity, and we have not, therefore, been influenced by this in arriving at our conclusions.

(a) Inter-disciplinary studies

362. Much of the evidence which we have received from individual academics and academic institutions emphasises the importance of what has been called ' the idea of the unity of knowledge '. There is a growing appreciation of the interdependence of fields of study previously regarded as totally distinct, and this suggests that there are advantages in combining under one roof all the resources of knowledge in different subjects. We have found it difficult to obtain any very precise information about the extent and growth of inter-disciplinary studies, partly because the term means different things to different people. However, so far as the siting of the NLRSI is concerned, the most important types of inter-disciplinary studies are those including the humanities or the social sciences on the one hand and the sciences on the other, and the BML surveys have yielded some information about these. The April survey showed that 70 visitors to the BML were interested in both the sciences and the humanities, 31 in both the sciences and the social sciences, and a further 80 in all three subjects areas. These three groups together comprise approximately six per cent of the total sample, and this figure agrees well with the very approximate estimates that we have been able to derive from other sources.

363. However, the use of scientific material in the BML is not necessarily a guide to the usage of that library in conjunction with the NRLSI. We have shown that the two libraries have very different types of users. The NRLSI is used virtually exclusively for industrial or commercial information and by scientists engaged on research or current studies. On the other hand, as the British Museum has told us, the type of scientific material required by readers at the BML ' reflects the use of the Bloomsbury Library for historical study of these subjects rather than for current research .' This being so, it may not be surprising that only two of the 2,248 readers at the BML sampled during the April survey period intended to refer to the NRLSI on the same day as their visit to Bloomsbury. While this clearly does not represent the total use of the two libraries for inter-disciplinary studies, it does suggest that such studies will have to be very much more extensive before they can constitute a compelling reason for uniting the collections. Particularly in view of the future role which we have recommended for the NRLSI, as the CSPC, it is difficult to imagine that serious inconvenience could result from the BML and NRLSI remaining on separate sites, so long as they continued to be reasonably accessible to visitors to either institution—say within half an hour's journey.

(b) The needs of patent workers

364. We have said that patent workers comprise the largest single group of the NRLSI's users (Figure 12 (i), page 89). Most London patent agents have their offices in the area around Patent Office and the Law Courts, and for them the present site of the library is undoubtedly very convenient. They would probably not find the necessity of making a somewhat longer journey to use the library intolerable, although the inconvenience would inevitably increase with the distance involved. So far as the Patent Court is concerned, we understand that occasionally articles or extracts are urgently required while a case is being heard, and for this purpose it would seem desirable that the CSPC should be sited no further from the Law Courts than could be reached by taxi within about quarter of an hour.

(c) Economic considerations

365. The Trustees of the British Museum have pointed out that uniting the NRLSI and the BML on the same site would, by enabling the two libraries to share certain facilities, produce economies. Although we accept the economic principles of this argument, the NRLSI would also be a large institution in its own right and we think it unlikely, therefore, that the potential savings will be so large as to have more than marginal influence on the siting of the library.

(d) Conclusions

366. A careful appraisal of the needs of users and the future role of the NRLSI, as the CSPC, suggests the following conclusions on the siting requirements of the library's new building:

(i) Even if inter-disciplinary studies expand rapidly in the future, we do not think that they will reach a level such as to constitute a compelling reason for the unification of the NRLSI with the other library sections of the British Museum.

(ii) On the other hand, there is also no compelling reason why the new CSPC should be sited in the immediate vicinity of the Patent Office.

(iii) However, inconvenience to the largest single group of users of the present library—i.e. patent workers—would increase with the distance of the new building from the existing one, and a site in central London is clearly necessary.

CHAPTER THIRTEEN

THE IMPACT OF TECHNOLOGY

The Prospect for Computers

367. There has been considerable discussion in recent years about the possibilities of applying automatic data processing, or ADP, to the operations of libraries and information services. Although ADP is strictly a collective term embracing mechanised methods as well as applications of electronic computers, it is often used in the context of the latter alone and computers are more likely to have relevance to the complex and large scale operations of a national libraries organisation.

368. Interest in and speculation about the uses of computers in libraries and information services have not, however, so far led to their introduction to any great extent in this country, although some interesting experiments are in progress. The greatest advances have been in connection with some specialised information services, especially in the United States. These have generally been applications where financial considerations have not predominated—for example, in space research and defence. Until very recently technical limitations have also seriously restricted the application of computers to really large information problems. Consequently, very few of the world's national libraries have any computerised services. Probably the most advanced example of a library-based service available to the public is the Medical Literature Analysis and Retrieval System (MEDLARS) of the National Library of Medicine in the USA, for which the British agent is the NLLST. Although MEDLARS became operational as recently as 1964, it is already technically obsolescent and a more advanced system is soon to be introduced. This, in itself, is an indication of the speed of technological development in computer technology.

369. There are prospects that in the next few years computers will be successfully applied to other important library services. These developments will be based on research recently completed or now in progress, of which we would particularly mention the outstandingly valuable work of the Library of Congress and, more recently, of the BNB in developing a format for a machine-readable catalogue (MARC project). Not only has the MARC format opened the door to computerised cataloguing in these two institutions, but, because of its general application, it is already well on the way to becoming an international standard. The MARC project exemplifies the efforts in detailed planning and in the development of suitable programmes, which together may take several years to complete, but which are the essential prerequisites of the computerisation of large and complex systems. The likelihood that great changes in the pattern of operation of large libraries are imminent is also indicated by the fact that the first costs of computers have been dropping substantially and steadily, a trend which may be expected to continue in the future. Further, the development of very large, relatively inexpensive " back-store " memories, employing large magnetic discs, offers the possibility of using a computer capable of searching rapidly a complete catalogue of the stock of a library as large as the BML.

370. The stage has now been reached when, for the first time, it will be possible to consider the application of computers to some of the most formidable tasks of the largest libraries in the world with a good prospect of finding it both technically feasible and economically sound.

The Immediate Scope for Computers in a British National Library

371. A distinction is commonly made between those library operations primarily concerned with organisation, stock control and management, on the one hand and bibliographic services on the other. Although it would be artificial and arbitrary to attempt to categorise all library activities into one or other group, it is, for all that, a useful distinction to make when computer applications are being considered.

(a) Bibliographic facilities

372. The evidence on the use of computers in libraries submitted to us has very largely concentrated on the bibliographic possibilities, rather than on library housekeeping. This is immediately understandable, because it is in this field that the computer has the most obvious scope in transforming the traditional role of the library and in meeting the increasing demands for better information —not only for science, technology and commerce, but also in the social sciences and the humanities. The emphasis on bibliographic needs is probably even more fundamental than this, because the key to a great many library operations, including much routine " housekeeping ", lies in the repeated use of parts of the basic bibliographic information contained in the full catalogue entry. This has already been recognised by the officers of the BML, who see the translation of their catalogue into machine-readable form as essential, not only to solve the ever-growing problem of maintaining the existing catalogue, but also to produce new and better bibliographic facilities previously unattainable by the traditional manual methods.

373. The direct benefits to the BML of a computerised catalogue are large and obvious. Further benefits would accrue from the application of the same basic information in other ways. For example, a central computer programmed to carry out the bibliographic services of the cataloguing division of the Department of Printed Books and the routine documentation of the BML's Copyright Receipt Office, could also be used to generate the BNB's card and list services. Already the BNB is well advanced towards automatic production techniques based upon magnetic tapes containing in MARC format information about new British publications. However, at the present time, there appears to us to be a possibility of the BNB and the BML establishing separate and mutually incompatible computer facilities which would result in considerable duplication of effort and capital expenditure. We, therefore, consider it urgent to investigate the possibility of developing a single computerised system for carrying out both applications.

374. This would not, however, be the largest possible application, even for a system based upon the limits of existing computer technology. The union catalogues of the NCL contain entries for items, a high proportion of which must also be recorded in the BML catalogue and some of which will be included in the BNB. We have already urged the need to take immediate steps to remedy

the arrears in the NCL's union catalogues as a first step towards improving inter-library lending. But, if the already stretched services of the NCL are not to break down in the course of the next few years under the continually increasing load of international book publishing and heavier demands on its inter-library lending services, computerisation will be essential. The conversion of the union catalogues alone into machine-readable form would be very costly, but if this could be achieved as part of a larger project which also embraced the computerisation of the services of the BNB and the BML, considerable economies should be effected.

375. The application of ADP to the CSPC could lead to the development of new bibliographic services of great economic importance to industry. In particular, computerised searches of the patent literature could within a few years result in considerable savings in time and cost over the existing manual search methods.

376. Although the NLLST has not, in general, kept catalogues of most of its holdings, we believe that it should extend its policy of providing bibliographic aids where existing coverage is inadequate. For example, in the case of translations and report literature, the application of computer methods and phototypesetting could lead to much more rapid announcement services and greater flexibility in meeting the requirements of different types of user throughout the country.

377. We also believe that it should be the responsibility of a national library organisation to co-ordinate and encourage the application of ADP to the bibliographic services now being carried out by professional bodies and research associations, so that, by ensuring the acceptance of common standards, it will be possible to develop as speedily as practicable full bibliographic coverage in machine-readable form. This in turn will permit the establishment of a common communication network linking computerised bibliographic facilities in many different subjects, which would thereby be immediately available to users everywhere.

378. Hitherto we have deliberately confined ourselves to discussing some applications of ADP which are already technically feasible. Even at the present early stage of development of computers, technical capabilities are adequate to store the information contained in the vast catalogues of the BML and the NCL, and to enable it to be electronically searched in a practicably short time. However, before it is possible to introduce very fast, selective and versatile bibliographic services based on a computerised catalogue of the stocks of the national libraries, there are formidable semantic and programming problems to be overcome and, above all, the enormous manual task of converting retrospectively the existing catalogues into machine-readable form. But we are very hopeful that all these problems can be overcome if there is determination to do so, and that it will be possible within a decade to achieve many if not all the possibilities which we have mentioned.

(b) *Library housekeeping*

379. Although the previous section has concentrated on the possible bibliographic applications of computers, some of those considered have relevance to the organisational and administrational procedures in the libraries

concerned. For example, it is difficult to distinguish the borderline between the bibliographic services of the NCL and the housekeeping procedures involved in the organisation of inter-library loans. On the other hand, there is a wide range of activities which are wholly or principally housekeeping. For example, the routine procedures involved in ordering, receiving and paying for the new acquisitions might be carried out most economically and speedily by a single computerised system for all the national reference and lending collections. In addition to effecting savings in time and staff effort, this would also assist in the close co-ordination of the acquisitions policies of the libraries concerned, the importance of which we have already stressed.

380. Acquisition policies for both reference and lending units will also be influenced by the content and comprehensiveness of the existing stock in particular subject areas and by the level of demand for particular types of material, or even of particular items. Especially in very large libraries, the difficulties of obtaining by manual means detailed and regular statistics of usage and of failures are very great, and yet such information is essential to efficient library operations. The selection of material for transfer to and from out-houses, decisions as to the suitability of particular items for loan, recording and control of loan circulation, the processing of photo-copying orders, and the regular preparation of statistics for costing and forward planning are a few examples of recurring procedures which could be made possible, or greatly simplified by computer techniques.

381. These, together with operational research and special surveys, would have a direct bearing upon the organisation of material resources and staff within each library unit, and more generally, on any organisation of national libraries which may be established. Indeed, only by making use of modern techniques of data handling will it be possible to formulate policies in response to and even in anticipation of developments in the patterns of users' requirements. Computer facilities for library housekeeping cannot of themselves, however, ensure that an efficient service is provided, but without them the most capable administration of such a complex organisation is bound to be limited in the degree of success which it can hope to achieve.

Library Technology in the Longer Term

382. The achievements of the applications mentioned in the preceding paragraphs will be only the beginning of the revolution in libraries and in the dissemination of information. It is not unduly fanciful to predict that within two or three decades the larger university and public libraries, research laboratories and industrial firms will be directly linked through their individual computer terminals not only to the computerised catalogue of our national libraries, but also to other types of information service in this country and abroad. By that time, if not before, the processes of searching and locating inter-library loans will be fully computerised and direct dialogue between interrogator and computer information source may well have become commonplace.

383. Beyond that period prediction is very uncertain, but since the first fifty years of the life of any new national library buildings will probably span five or more generations of computers, each one with greater capabilities than its predecessor, it is very likely that within this period computer storage capacity

will begin to be able to cope with the retention of full texts of the world's literature, to process it in response to particular queries and, if necessary, to display it remotely by facsimile transmission wherever it is needed. These facilities will develop first for scientific and commercial information, where linguistic problems are simplest to solve, where information has the greatest economic importance and above all where the pattern of usage makes retrospective translation into machine readable form least necessary. In many other subjects the book will continue to be indispensable as a research tool and a source of information, but libraries as we know them will be subject to continual and increasingly rapid change under the impact of new technologies.

Feasibility Study

384. From our studies of the potential for applying ADP to libraries and information systems at home and abroad, and from the advice that we have received from the Management Services Division of the Civil Service Department, the British Museum, the Ministry of Technology and others, we consider that developments in computer technology have now reached the stage when it is almost certain that ADP can make significant and economical contributions to the following types of activity of the national libraries:

(i) the improvement of existing services to users;

(ii) the development of new types of library and information service;

(iii) the internal management operations of a national library organisation and the library units associated with it.

Moreover, without the introduction of ADP, the increasing rate of production of printed information will ultimately defeat the purpose of the library as a source of easily accessible information.

385. Before it is possible to determine the type and scale of applications of computer methods to the national libraries, it will be necessary to study the associated problems in detail. Account will have to be taken not only of the technological possibilities, but also of likely patterns of demand for library services in the future, of the future administrative structure of the institutions concerned and above all, of economic considerations. Therefore, we have recommended that the feasibility of applying ADP to the operations and services of those units which will comprise the reference, lending, bibliographic and administrative divisions of a national libraries organisation should be studied without delay.

386. The successful application of computers to the principal facilities and operations of the national libraries is bound to have important implications for libraries and users throughout the country. To ensure the closest possible co-operation between the national libraries and other libraries and information services, wide consultation during the course of the feasibility study is essential.

387. We have already made known to the Government our recommendation that preparatory studies on the introduction of ADP should be initiated at once. It will probably take at least eighteen months to formulate proposals in a sufficiently detailed form to enable equipment to be ordered, and it will be several years longer before the systems are operational. During this period

some of the most serious problems of the existing national libraries to which we have already drawn attention will have become increasingly acute. We are also aware that some libraries and related services in different parts of Britain are already planning the introduction of ADP on a limited and local scale. Unless steps are taken without unnecessary delay to co-ordinate these activities to prevent duplication of effort and to ensure compatibility between computer systems, some of the economies which large scale ADP systems offer may not be realised. Lastly, we believe that the design of new library buildings, particularly that for the National Reference Library, must reflect the impact that ADP is likely to make on library organisation, staff and services in both the near and longer future. This will not be clear in sufficient detail until a feasibility study is well advanced. For all these reasons, therefore, it is in our opinion essential that a study is executed with great urgency and that its findings should produce speedy and positive action.

CHAPTER FOURTEEN

BIBLIOGRAPHIC FACILITIES

Introduction

388. In Chapters 11 and 12 we have stressed that the use made of library material is directly related to the ease with which potential users can obtain access to it and our recommendations for the national lending, photocopying and reference facilities have, therefore, been directed towards making the methods of disseminating information as effective as possible. However, these improvements will be of very limited value without equally efficient bibliographic facilities enabling readers to identify and locate useful information.

389. At present there is a great variety of bibliographic, abstracting and indexing services provided by the national libraries, professional and learned societies, research institutions, commercial associations, specialised publishers and others. Some are very broadly based, others highly specialised; some indicate the sources of indexed material, whereas others put their main emphasis on ensuring that the material processed covers comprehensively all that is relevant to the appropriate subject areas. Much of the evidence which we have received has suggested that many of the existing services are unco-ordinated, sometimes involving unnecessary duplication of effort and, in many subject areas, providing an inadequate guide to the literature.

Existing National Library Services

(a) The BML

390. By far the most comprehensive of the bibliographic services associated with the national libraries is the British Museum General Catalogue of Books: this is a 263 volume index arranged by author, which was published between 1959 and 1966. Although it does not cover the whole of the BML's collections and a considerable quantity of the library's material awaits bibliographic processing, the Catalogue, with 3,500,000 main entries, is one of the greatest bibliographic tools in existence. The BML also publishes a quinquennial subject index, several catalogues of incunabula, and the Catalogue of Printed Maps, Charts and Plans.

391. In the library itself are the catalogues which are essential to readers for requisitioning items from the stacks. The user surveys show that these catalogues are also extensively used as a bibliographic tool in identifying previously unknown items. They are not easy to keep fully up to date and the Trustees estimate that, because of pressures on staff time and the very high, but fluctuating, rate of acquisition by the library, about 10 per cent of total holdings have not yet been catalogued. There can be no doubt that this is a serious deficiency in a closed access library, since uncatalogued material is virtually inaccessible to readers.

392. The BML has produced a small number of select bibliographies available to users. Researchers with individual bibliographic requirements may seek the assistance of the library staff, but the pressure of work severely limits the extent of this service.

(b) The NRLSI

393. The NRLSI does not publish its general catalogues. Although it is largely an open access library, personal visitors refer a great deal to its catalogues and indexes, but we do not know how far these aids are consulted primarily to direct readers to the part of the library where the material they seek is located. The library also provides an enquiry service, which in 1967 handled about 70,000 requests for information, mainly from remote users. Half of the enquiries related primarily to patents.

(c) The NLLST

394. The NLLST differs from the other libraries in our terms of reference in that, as a matter of policy, it does not catalogue the bulk of its holdings. This is because it does not need a catalogue for locating required material in the library, and also because scientific literature is generally well covered by other bibliographic tools. However, where published aids are inadequate— for example in the fields of report and conference literature and of translations— the library has compiled and published its own lists, indexes and catalogues. The library also sponsors the regular translation of numerous Russian publications and will, in certain circumstances, supply other translations from Russian to meet individual requirements. About 70 per cent of the cost of these various translation services is recovered from receipts.

395. The library also handles requests for technical information, usually by referring the enquirer to the appropriate specialist source. As far as general scientific information is concerned, this service fulfils a similar function to that provided by the NRLSI, especially as the principal non-patent users of both libraries are industrial firms and both enquiry services primarily meet the needs of distant users.

(d) The NCL

396. The NCL makes a major contribution to the national bibliographic services through the publication of BUCOP. This undoubtedly facilitates the arrangement of loans directly between libraries and thus eliminates in many cases the need to forward loan requests to the NCL or NLLST. In addition to this published aid, the NCL maintains the national union catalogues essential to its own primary function as a clearing house and locating centre for inter-library loans. The inadequacies of these catalogues have already been described and we have proposed means whereby their effectiveness may be improved. The compilation of these catalogues has features in common with the production of the catalogues at the nearby BML.

397. Under its Charter, the NCL also has a duty to provide a bibliographic enquiry service. Not only does this service duplicate that of the BML, but, in answering bibliographic enquiries, the NCL staff frequently visit the BML in order to consult its stocks. There is no firm evidence to show why some distant enquirers prefer to use the NCL, rather than the BML itself. Whereas a few of the NCL's enquiries are connected with loan applications, many are not, and it has been suggested to us that the NCL staff engaged full-time on answering enquiries can provide a quicker service than the BML's subject specialists, whose time is greatly occupied with other duties.

Other Existing National Services

(a) The BNB

398. Probably the most important range of bibliographic services is provided by the BNB. In Chapter 8 we have detailed the principal functions of this organisation in publishing at frequent intervals indexes of new British publications and providing libraries with complete or specially selected sets of catalogue cards. Although the BNB is financially very successful and its services are widely used, we have received evidence pointing to some deficiencies in the existing arrangements. The Society of County Librarians suggests that delays in the appearance of entries in the BNB index and further delays in the supply of printed cards detract from the services' general usefulness to such an extent that some county libraries prefer not to rely on them. The delays are partly attributable to the rather cumbersome compilation techniques which the BNB has been forced to adopt since 1967 when it moved from the BML buildings and partly to the fact that some publishers are relatively slow to deposit material with the BML's Copyright Receipt Office.

399. The BNB's efforts in publishing its index involve a high degree of duplication of the cataloguing activities of the BML, which suggests that important economies might be effected. Indeed, the great majority of evidence which we have received concerning bibliographic facilities has urged that these activities of the BNB and the BML should be combined in a single operation. Although the BNB is an independent organisation governed by a Council on which many interests are represented, we do not think that this should prevent an arrangement by which the production of a published index of British publications and the cataloguing of the same material would be based on a joint operation.

400. In addition to its indexing and catalogue-card services, the BNB answers specific bibliographic enquiries. There are, therefore, three national institutions within a short distance of one another in central London independently providing facilities for answering bibliographic queries. Although each institution has its own specialities, there are no clear distinctions between the types of bibliographic enquiry which each answers.

(b) Indexes and abstracts in science and technology

401. Whereas the BNB's main services span all subject fields, there is a host of other published bibliographic aids and information services covering more specialised requirements, of which those in science and technology are by far the most numerous. The superiority of the bibliographic aids in the sciences and technology is due to many factors: firstly, the indexing and abstracting of scientific and technological literature are essential to the research activities of industry and commerce and, hence, there is substantial financial support for the compilation of bibliographic tools; secondly, the number of workers engaged in major scientific research fields is often greater than those in other types of research, where effort is more diffusely spread; and, thirdly, the use of scientific and technological material is concentrated on relatively recent publications, which enables the task of compiling a useful bibliography to be much less daunting and expensive than it would be in the humanities. The range of bibliographic aids in the sciences extends from very large works

covering many subject specialisms, such as " Chemical Abstracts " and " Index Medicus ", to much more specialised publications, like " Water Pollution Abstracts ".

402. In the field of report literature, the major British publication is the Ministry of Technology's " R and D Abstracts ", but this is partly duplicated and partly extended by the NLLST's " R and D Reports ". Because of this duplication and because together these two publications do not provide complete bibliographic coverage, we have recommended that the efforts of the two institutions should be directed to providing a co-ordinated, comprehensive service. In translation indexing, too, the NLLST's efforts are partially duplicated elsewhere: the library's " Translations Bulletin " indexes 120,000 translations known to have been produced in the UK, not all of which are in fact among its stocks; whereas Aslib maintains the Commonwealth Index of Translations, which lists 180,000 translations and their locations. Neither index is comprehensive, because it is often extremely difficult to obtain information about, and locations for, translations arranged privately or through special libraries to meet the *ad hoc* requirements of individual researchers. A user may ask Aslib for the location of a translation of a given foreign language publication and subsequently have to apply for it to the NLLST if it is said to be at Boston Spa; or he may apply in the first instance to Boston Spa, and, if it is not in stock, the NLLST may then pass the request to Aslib for an alternative location. Thus the existing situation almost certainly causes delays and inconvenience to users, and involves unnecessary duplication of effort in the compilation of the two indexes.

(c) *Scientific information and referral services*

403. Apart from indexes and abstracts, aids for the scientist and technologist include information and referral services such as those mentioned in Chapter 2. Although most of these are highly specialised, the referral services maintained by Aslib and the Ministry of Technology's Industrial Liaison Centres handle more general enquiries over a wide range of subjects and involve some duplication of the services of the NLLST and the NRLSI. All these services have developed independently and, if their expansion remains unco-ordinated, there is every reason to suppose that the extent of unnecessary duplication will increase in future. It is, therefore, desirable that these services should co-operate with one another in order to produce the maximum economy of effort coupled with the best possible service to users.

(d) *Bibliographic aids in the social sciences and humanities*

404. In the social sciences there are fewer available abstracts or indexes and together they provide very uneven coverage of literature. Researchers frequently have to rely on general annual or retrospective bibliographies, such as the " London Bibliography of the Social Sciences ", which is based on new catalogue entries at the BLPES. In the humanities there are still fewer published bibliographic aids and, beyond general catalogues of library holdings and the BNB index, most researchers have to rely very largely on their knowledge of their subjects. Detailed bibliographies in individual subject fields do not begin to cover the full range of humanistic areas of research.

405. In the social sciences and the humanities, therefore, the existing bibliographic facilities, even including the limited enquiry services of the BML, NCL and BNB, are far from adequate to meet existing requirements. These deficiencies are largely attributable to the fact that the level of demand cannot support the production of specialised bibliographies by the methods available. We have a great deal of sympathy with the view repeatedly urged in evidence to us that the national libraries system should be able to provide on request a much greater range of specialist aids in these subject areas. Although through the application of automatic data processing substantial improvements should be possible, the extent of the service available must be subject to economic considerations (see paragraph 411).

(e) Regional union catalogues

406. All the library regions, with the exception of Yorkshire, maintain union catalogues listing the holdings of all public libraries and some special and university libraries in the respective regions. These catalogues have three major functions:

(i) they enable the maximum proportion of loan requests originating in a particular region to be satisfied from resources within that region;

(ii) they provide a means for a continuing check on the effectiveness of individual regions' co-operative purchase schemes;

(iii) they facilitate loans between regions through the NCL, since the NCL's union catalogues include entries lodged by most of the regional library systems.

We have received no evidence to suggest any fundamental change in the functions of the regional union catalogues, and, provided that these are kept fully up to date, it should be able to continue to filter effectively loan demands which would otherwise be passed directly to the national lending libraries.

Future Developments—A National Bibliographic Service

(a) Concept and functions

407. Our appraisal of the existing bibliographic facilities has shown that there is very little co-ordination of effort in the compilation of bibliographic aids, even between the national libraries themselves. The BML and the NCL are each cataloguing independently a great deal of the same material; the BNB's main indexing activities are largely duplicated by the cataloguing departments in the BML; and the BML, NCL and BNB all provide essentially similar bibliographic enquiry services. The existing services also have major defects: the BML and NCL cataloguing efforts are not sufficient to cope with the scale of the respective tasks; the BNB's services are subject to delays; and the three bibliographic enquiry services together fail to meet the demand in the social sciences and the humanities not catered for by the published aids. We are concerned that wasteful duplication should be avoided and that existing deficiencies in the overall provision should be remedied as far as is economically practicable. Furthermore, the roles which we have recommended for the BML and the NRLSI in contributing to national photocopy and loan services

will only be fully realisable if the catalogues of their holdings are in the same form as catalogues in use at the national loan and photocopy locating centre.

408. Accordingly, we recommend the establishment within a national libraries organisation of a National Bibliographic Service in which all these bibliographic facilities would be combined. The main functions to be performed would be the compilation and publication of an index of all British publications, the production of catalogue entries, the answering of bibliographic enquiries, and the co-ordinating and bibliographic research functions which are defined below. The service should also continue and develop the BNB's catalogue card service, and further the BNB's contributions to international bibliographic development.

409. After the backlog of cataloguing arrears at the BML and NCL has been eliminated, the production of catalogue entries will involve the continuing tasks of cataloguing all new acquisitions by the national libraries and inserting new entries in the NCL's union catalogues, including BUCOP and the Slavonic union catalogues.

410. In the future, it should be the responsibility of the National Bibliographic Service to develop its facilities so as to meet as nearly as possible the individual bibliographic needs of all types of user. However, if these facilities are provided free of charge, the lack of financial constraints may lead to the cost exceeding the value of the information supplied, and thus we strongly recommend that this kind of work should in general be undertaken only where its cost is likely to be recovered or, in the case of a continuing service, where there are good prospects of its becoming self-supporting in a reasonable length of time. The National Bibliographic Service should also deal with particularly difficult problems passed to it by the loan locating centre.

411. The introduction of automatic data processing would revolutionise bibliographic and locating services. Although the manual task of translating the existing catalogues into machine-readable form would be very considerable, it would when completed, greatly ease the maintenance of the union catalogues and make possible the rapid compilation of selective bibliographic information. It also seems likely that, by the time the process of computerisation could be completed, " on-line " facilities would be available to some distant users through remote computer terminals.

(b) Legal deposit

412. The Copyright Act 1911 requires publishers to deposit at the British Museum one copy of all published material within one month following publication. Although most publishers deposit either before publication or very shortly afterwards, a sample check of books received at the BM's Copyright Receipt Office showed that 13 per cent were deposited more than a week after publication. Since the value of the BNB's services to libraries throughout the country is greatly dependent on how soon after publication a new title can be entered in the BNB lists, we believe that the existing provisions for legal deposit in the 1911 Copyright Act are inadequate for enabling a satisfactory national bibliographic service to be maintained. We, therefore, recommend that the 1911 Copyright Act should be amended to require publishers to effect legal deposit with a national libraries organisation on or before the date of publication.

(c) *Abstracting and indexing services for science and technology*

413. The literature of science and technology is vast in quantity, international in its scope and frequently highly specialised. The preparation of the associated bibliographic services reflects these characteristics by being decentralised and by relying extensively upon the contributions of subject specialists, often from more than one country. We recognise that this pattern of organisation should and will continue. Abstracting, particularly, needs the services of practising scientists who are in the closest possible touch with current research and we do not believe that centralisation of bibliographic effort on a national or international scale can meet this requirement.

414. But decentralisation brings its own problems. Co-ordination of the many independently administered services is necessary if waste is to be avoided, common bibliographic standards universally applied and coverage adequate. With the prospect of bibliographic services becoming computerised in the foreseeable future, these national and international problems become much more critical. Only if they can be solved will it be possible to use effectively the total international bibliographic effort, so as to create a network of compatible computerised services all directly accessible from users' terminals throughout the country.

415. We believe that a national library organisation must have the prime responsibility for ensuring that bibliographic coverage is in total sufficient, because only if this is so will its stocks be capable of being utilised by the widest clientèle. With the increasing use of ADP, the national libraries organisation will, on account of its own heavy commitment to computerising its operations, naturally take a leading role in developing bibliographic standards for machine-readable information systems. We are, therefore, convinced that the National Bibliographic Service is the most appropriate body to be given the responsibility for the co-ordination of the total national scientific bibliographic effort, and to represent internationally British interests in this field.

416. To carry out these duties effectively, the scientific section of the National Bibliographic Service will need sufficient staff and material resources:

(i) to extend the NLLST's attempts to fill gaps in the country's existing bibliographic services;

(ii) to carry out that bibliographic research which is necessary for the development of new techniques and of national and international bibliographic standards;

(iii) for sponsoring and assisting such work as is necessary for the co-ordination and development of important bibliographic services not administered by the national libraries organisation.

417. We consider that a corollary to these recommendations is that the responsibilities now exercised in this field by OSTI should be transferred to the National Bibliographic Service when it is established.

(d) *Translations*

418. The present extensive overlap between Aslib and the NLLST in the compilation of indexes of available translations and the inconvenience which

111

this causes to users points clearly to the need for a single reference point for those seeking the location of translations. We recommend, therefore, that the existing translation indexing functions of these two organisations should be combined as part of the National Bibliographic Service. We wish also to draw attention to the need to ensure that the index covers as comprehensively as possible the translations available, in order that the considerable costs of translating should not be wasted.

419. So far as the production of translations is concerned, the main needs arise in connection with research in the sciences and technology. An NLLST survey in 1966 revealed that 80 per cent of its users in the sciences had in the previous year needed to refer to an item available only in a foreign language. Of the sample, 30 per cent had needed to refer to literature in Russian, 30 per cent in German and 17 per cent in Japanese. But, whilst two-thirds of the scientists could read German, only a tenth could read Russian and just over 1 per cent any of the oriental languages. We know from our evidence that scientists not employed by large commercial organisations have considerable difficulty in arranging to have foreign language material translated, particularly from Japanese and, to a lesser extent, from Russian. We, therefore, recommend that the NLLST's Russian translation service should be maintained, and that a similar service should be available for translation from Japanese. However, as with bibliographic services, we consider it important that the translation facilities should be charged for on a properly costed basis.

(e) Scientific information services

420. Through the facilities available in Aslib and the Ministries of Technology and Agriculture, science and industry can draw upon far greater resources of highly specialised information than any one component unit of the national libraries system, or indeed the system as a whole, could possibly provide. This is largely due to the inherent limitations of libraries as sources of first-hand information when compared with specialised services in close touch with current research. This does not mean that the national libraries have no contribution to make to information services. The staffs of the NLLST and the NRLSI have great experience in the use of bibliographic tools of all types and knowledge which they have gained through day-to-day contact with the extensive resources of their collections. They are, therefore, in an excellent position to give bibliographic assistance, especially by directing technical enquiries to the specialised information services best equipped to deal with them. However, if undesirable duplication of effort is to be avoided, it will be essential that any information or referral services provided by the national science libraries should be developed in close co-ordination with each other and with other services provided by agencies outside the national libraries system.

(f) The location of the bibliographic services

421. In its cataloguing work and the compilation of the national bibliography, the National Bibliographic Service will have to rely heavily on access to the existing stocks and the new acquisitions of the future NRL and the CSPC. This will be particularly important during the process of converting present catalogues into machine-readable form. The service will also need to call upon the reference libraries' subject specialists, both in cataloguing and in

answering individual bibliographic enquiries, if the most economical use is made of the limited bibliographic expertise. We believe, therefore, that these facilities will in the main need to be centred near the national reference collections—that is, in central London.

422. However, this does not necessarily apply to all the bibliographic facilities to be provided within the national libraries system. Some of those in science and technology, such as the indexing of translations and report literature, might best be situated elsewhere, perhaps at Boston Spa, where it would be possible to have ready access to the most comprehensive collections of the relevant material.

(g) A loan locating centre

423. The determination of the best site for the national loan locating centre is a much more complex issue. While loan location work must inevitably have some links with other bibliographic services and, in some instances, will require the most expert bibliographic detective work, many of the activities of a loan locating centre are specialised and not directly dependent upon the types of general bibliographic services to be performed by the National Bibliographic Service. Hence, the necessity of ensuring the geographical proximity of some of the main bibliographic services to the principal reference collections does not necessarily apply in the case of the locating service.

424. One possibility would be to perpetuate the existing situation whereby those making loan applications through the national lending system have to choose to which of two agencies their requests should be directed. However, there is adequate evidence to show that the present situation causes confusion and delay, especially for material in the social sciences which is available through both the NCL and the NLLST. If this were to continue in future when lending and photocopying services draw upon several units of a national libraries system, as well as other co-operating libraries, the difficulties for librarians seeking loans would inevitably be considerably accentuated and additional delays would result. We recommend, therefore, that there should be one centre to which loan and photocopy requests in whatever subject should be addressed.

425. It is clearly desirable that this one centre should be where:

(i) the highest proportion of *urgent* loan and photocopy requests can be met on the spot; and

(ii) the highest proportion of *all* requests can be met locally.

We have already recommended that the central loan stock of the NCL should be transferred to Boston Spa. If this were done, approximately 75 per cent of all loan applications currently received at the NCL and the NLLST could be met from the combined stocks. Furthermore, on average the most urgent requests are likely to be for scientific items already housed at Boston Spa. A centre at Boston Spa would, therefore, simultaneously satisfy conditions (i) and (ii) above, and we recommend that all loan and photocopy applications should in future be sent there.

426. It is not, however, immediately clear that the union catalogues should be transferred for use there. If they were retained in London, all requests not

113

met from the stocks at Boston Spa would have to be transmitted to London. On present figures this would constitute a quarter of the total annual applications sent to the NCL and NLLST together, that is, over 200,000 per annum. Transmission on this scale by post or Telex would be expensive, and the use of postal services would involve at least a day's delay. This might not be unacceptable, but it would certainly constitute some disadvantage in view of the proportion of total requests involved. If some of the older material from the SML were transferred to Boston Spa and the central loan stocks in the humanities and social sciences were selectively expanded, the proportion of requests requiring transmission would probably decline slightly, but the number would remain substantial. Furthermore, we have shown in Appendix D that the real cost of an inter-library loan is much more expensive if the union catalogues are in London, rather than at Boston Spa. These are in our view weighty considerations.

427. However, in their written evidence and during discussion, the NCL Trustees have urged that the present inter-library loan service would be seriously impaired if the union catalogues were moved outside central London. In particular they have argued that:

    (i) the NCL relies heavily upon the intimate working relationship which it has built up over the years with the staff of special libraries in the south-east of England. This relationship is very important to the success of speculative searches; and co-operation is further encouraged by the provision of the collection service run from Store Street for the benefit of libraries without the means to provide their own packing and despatch facilities;

    (ii) the library needs physical access to the BML's stocks, in order to maintain its photocopy service and its bibliographic work in connection with both loan applications and individual enquiries.

428. It is certainly true that 34 per cent of the NCL's loan requests cannot at present be met from stock or through union catalogue locations, and in these cases the library resorts to speculative searches or to purchases for its central stock. However, we have already recognised the necessity of reducing the proportion of speculative searches if delays in meeting inter-library loans are to diminish to an acceptable level. This will be facilitated by a selective increase of the central loan stocks, by controlled lending from the BML and by calling upon the facilities of an " inner circle " of large co-operating libraries, which will, if necessary, receive financial support to enable them to meet these demands. Accordingly the dependence of the present NCL services on London-based facilities may be expected to become much less pronounced as time goes on, and particularly as the computerisation of the union catalogues makes positive locations of loan material an increasing probability.

429. Our recommendations concerning the developments of the national photocopy service and the establishment of the National Bibliographic Service will in time fundamentally affect the NCL's need to gain physical access to the BML's stocks. The bibliographic enquiries now catered for by the NCL will be handled by the National Bibliographic Service at its London headquarters, and we see no reason why an improved photocopy service at the BML should not itself handle speedily photocopy requests forwarded from the NCL.

114

Bibliographic problems arising from inaccurate or incomplete references in loan applications could best be sent to the main centre of the National Bibliographic Service for specialist attention. The number of applications to the NCL now requiring some kind of verification at the BML represents only about 1 per cent of all national loan applications. It should be possible to reduce even this very small proportion if the stock of bibliographic aids used in connection with the union catalogues were augmented. In any event, the traffic between the processing centre and London would be only about one twentieth of that necessary if the union catalogues remained in London.

430. The arguments that the NCL Trustees have put to us have some force in relation to the existing situation. However, when viewed against the wider background of our recommendations for the future services of the national libraries system, they are less relevant. We believe, therefore, that the union catalogues should remain in central London only until such time as the relative importance of the speculative search has substantially declined and the main centre of the National Bibliographic Service is well-established. Thereafter the balance of advantage will lie in uniting the full apparatus for the location of loans with the combined central loan stocks at Boston Spa.

431. Because the loan location service will have to work closely with the bibliographic facilities which we have previously described, we recommend that it should be administratively an integral part of the National Bibliographic Service.

CHAPTER FIFTEEN

CO-OPERATION BETWEEN LIBRARIES

Introduction

432. We have already identified several areas, such as inter-library lending and scientific information services, where close co-operation between the national libraries and other institutions will be necessary if their combined resources are to be fully used. This co-operation with other libraries can also be designed to obtain the additional and very important advantage of ensuring that the combined holdings are sufficient to meet much more nearly all known and foreseeable needs of a variety of users. In the following paragraphs we discuss certain aspects of this matter which merit particular attention at this stage.

Safeguards for Existing Collections

433. Although many valuable libraries have an assured future through their association with universities and official bodies of various kinds, we are aware that some collections of national importance have, for a variety of reasons, only very limited funds at their disposal. In future many of these are likely to find it increasingly difficult to maintain their services in the face of rising costs of labour, accommodation and publications. There is a serious and increasing danger, therefore, that important libraries may be broken up and dispersed. Because we conceive it to be a duty of a national libraries organisation to see that the library needs of scholars and researchers are met, it follows that it should be its responsibility to safeguard the future of existing, valuable collections. We recommend, therefore, that a national libraries administration should be empowered to offer financial or other support to such a library facing acute financial difficulties, in return for an undertaking that its stock and services would be available to meet national demands. In extreme cases, it might be necessary for a national libraries organisation to assume full administrative responsibility for a collection in order to prevent its dissolution.

A Policy for Future Acquisitions

434. A national libraries organisation should also be concerned to ensure as far as possible that the annual additions to the nation's total library resources are sufficient to meet present and future demand. Much of the evidence which we have received has, however, suggested that there are areas where the overall existing coverage in this country is unsatisfactory, and the Trustees of both the BM and the NCL have urged that their current purchase grants are inadequate. Understandably, therefore, considerable emphasis has been placed in evidence on the need to establish formal links between libraries with areas of common interest so that a co-ordinated policy of acquisition may be devised.

(a) *The problem*

435. We consider that a prima facie case for a scheme of co-operative acquisition exists whenever all the following conditions apply:

116

(i) where it is desirable that there should be an increased rate of acquisition in order to meet national demand;

(ii) where the level and distribution of demand is such that the financing of complete coverage by any one library cannot be justified; and

(iii) where financial limitations together with the volume of material make it essential to avoid the unnecessary duplication of acquisitions by interested libraries.

436. The acquisition of British publications presents few problems for the nation's libraries as a whole, firstly because of policies aiming at regional self-sufficiency, and partly because of the legal deposit provisions of the 1911 Copyright Act. However, single libraries or groups of libraries attempting even representative coverage of foreign publications face heavy costs and increasing difficulties of collection owing to the high and rapidly expanding rate of world publication.

437. In scientific subjects the level and pattern of demand makes it practicable for a single national library collection to meet a high proportion of all requests which cannot be met locally. In the humanities and social sciences, a relatively low level of demand spread over a vast quantity of widely distributed material rules out a similar solution. Improvement in the coverage of foreign literature in the humanities and the social sciences will, therefore, depend very greatly on co-operative schemes designed to avoid the duplication of lightly used publications.

(b) The present situation

438. There are now virtually no formal arrangements for co-operation in the acquisition of foreign material in the humanities and social sciences, either among the national libraries themselves or between them and other libraries of national importance. In 1959 the BML and SOAS agreed on an acquisitions scheme for Far Eastern material, but this recently broke down mainly because the staff of SOAS found it unacceptable not to be able to borrow material acquired under the scheme by the BML. At present, in this as in other subject areas, the situation is one in which major libraries, in the words of the BM Trustees, " are independently pursuing an illusory ideal of self-sufficiency on budgets which are quite inadequate to cover the whole field comprehensively ".

439. The BML aims to acquire any foreign material of research value within the limitations imposed by finance, staffing and space. However, in subject areas where other specialised libraries, such as the Library of the Institute of Advanced Legal Studies, are able to make much more extensive provision than the BML, it does not in practice attempt to acquire lightly used material. In other subjects the library has been forced by limitations on resources to aim at a representative rather than a comprehensive collection.

(c) Possible future developments

440. The acquisition policies of British libraries for foreign publications especially in the humanities and social sciences, are inadequately co-ordinated and this sometimes results in waste of resources and failure to satisfy total national research demands. In Chapter 12 we have discounted the possibility of the future National Reference Library itself attempting comprehensive coverage in all subject areas, and it would be still less feasible for any other

single library to do so. Already in some subjects, large special or academic libraries have built up the best collections of literature in this country and it would be wasteful if the National Reference Library were to attempt to duplicate either retrospectively or in the future these libraries' holdings of rarely-used material. The need to utilise as effectively as possible the resources available and to take account of the established patterns of usage point to the desirability of adopting a scheme or schemes of co-operative acquisition to govern the purchase of foreign publications likely to be in demand for research.

441. In considering possible patterns for the development of co-operative acquisition in this country, we have examined the schemes in operation in other countries, particularly the USA. The Farmington Plan in the USA is based on a large number of co-operating university and special libraries throughout the country, each of which is responsible for acquiring all foreign material likely to be of research value from allotted countries or in allotted subject fields. The scheme has achieved some degree of success, but has a number of major drawbacks:

    (i) Libraries have to meet their national responsibilities out of their own funds, and so Farmington Plan purchases are often the obvious targets for economies when financial restrictions are imposed on the libraries concerned.

    (ii) Some libraries place blanket orders for material and are consequently supplied with much that is highly unlikely to be of research value, thus wasting resources.

    (iii) Some others leave the selection of material to agents overseas, rather than to subject specialists, and thus fail to acquire much potentially valuable material.

    (iv) Some libraries in the scheme are not always prepared to make material acquired under the scheme available to other users.

We are not convinced that, even if these difficulties could be overcome, the Farmington Plan, or similar schemes in Western Europe, are suitable models for this country. They are based on a larger number of very big libraries than is to be found in Britain, and necessitate a complex system of central administration. More important, however, is the fact that each scheme requires the participating libraries to co-operate on virtually identical terms and is not readily susceptible of modification to take account of the differing needs of individual institutions and individual subject fields.

442. On balance we consider a more appropriate pattern for this country would be a series of agreements of limited scope, each involving co-operation between a national library, which would usually be the NRL, and at the most a small number of other libraries. Although, without much more detailed examination, we would not attempt to identify every type of library which might usefully participate in such schemes, co-operating libraries might include libraries of the national museums and the more important special libraries, particularly those, such as the BLPES, geographically close to the National Reference Library. We see no reason in principle why appropriate provincial collections should not also be included in such schemes, although libraries of adequate quality are relatively rarely found outside London and their geographical remoteness would hinder the rapid transfer of material to and from the National Reference Library.

443. Although we have stressed the importance of a flexible approach to the formation of the various co-operative acquisition schemes and we consider that a national libraries organisation should have discretion in negotiating the terms of particular schemes with the libraries concerned, experience in the USA and the breakdown of the recent BML–SOAS scheme, suggest a number of important factors which we recommend should be considered in the formulation of any future scheme:

(i) Policies of acquisition will need to be determined in consultation with panels of subject experts and users, rather than solely by librarians, if schemes are to succeed in satisfying user demands. Regular processes of consultation after the schemes' inception will provide a continuing check on their efficacy.

(ii) These panels will probably also be necessary in order to secure the best possible advice on the priority to be given to making good the deficiencies of existing collections, either by acquisition or redistribution or both.

(iii) A national libraries organisation should be able to make grants to co-operating libraries in recognition of their national responsibilities. This would avoid some of the drawbacks of the Farmington Plan and establish the organisation in an influential position in initiating or maintaining co-operative acquisition schemes.

(iv) There must be safeguards to ensure that the material acquired for the nation by any library not administered by a national libraries organisation will at all times be adequately protected; that it will be made available as freely as the holdings of the national reference library; and that it will not be lost to the nation through any change in the administration or location of the co-operating library. We regard these safeguards as particularly important in areas where the National Reference Library might have relinquished altogether to another institution its interest in the acquisition of lightly used material.

(v) If the needs of the users of co-operating libraries are to be met, we consider it essential that material acquired by the National Reference Library under a co-operative acquisition scheme should be available on loan to co-operating libraries, even though it may not be among those limited categories of material available for loan through the national inter-library lending service. However, the conditions governing arrangements of this kind must be such that the material is not jeopardised.

In short, each scheme will have to be a compromise based on the minimum safeguards necessary to secure the interests of the various libraries and groups of users concerned.

Other Kinds of Co-operation

444. It has been suggested to us in evidence that there may be advantages in amalgamating the existing stocks of the BML in some subject areas with those of appropriate special libraries to create more useful unified collections. We have considered this possibility carefully, with particular reference to the research

needs of SOAS and others engaged on Far Eastern studies, and we are most grateful for the assistance which we have received from Professor R. P. Dore, Professor W. Watson, Mr. K. B. Gardner and others.

445. In principle, whilst there may be circumstances which warrant a solution of this kind, we do not believe that it is likely to be justified if it involves fragmentation of the collections of the NRL. Furthermore, there would be substantial difficulties in ensuring that a combined collection of the kind suggested, even if jointly administered by a national libraries organisation and the specialist institution concerned, properly fulfilled a national reference function while continuing to satisfy the legitimate requirements of members of the specialist institution. However, we understand that plans are under discussion for the formation of a Central Medical Library in Edinburgh, where the extensive collections of recent material from the Medical Colleges, the University and the Scottish National Library can be gathered together. It is expected that the unification of this material in a single centre should lead to considerable economies. If the problems to which we have drawn attention can be overcome in Edinburgh, the principle might be successfully applied elsewhere.

446. Co-operation between libraries to their mutual benefit may also be feasible in ways other than those which have occurred to us. Accordingly, we recommend that a national libraries organisation should have the responsibility to identify situations where co-operative arrangements might prove particularly advantageous and to negotiate the most suitable form that co-operation might take in these circumstances.

National Libraries of Scotland and Wales

447. The Scottish and Welsh National Libraries and the BML currently operate an informal agreement not to compete with one another in the purchase of old library material primarily of interest to their respective countries. There is also an inter-library lending agreement between the NCL and the Scottish Central Library, and the loan traffic in each direction is about equal. We would not wish to recommend any changes in either of these schemes. However, we consider that there will also be major advantages for users in all parts of the UK if co-operation between the Scottish and Welsh libraries and the body responsible for administering the national libraries in England is extended to other fields, such as library research, bibliographic services and the development of common cataloguing standards. We recommend, therefore, that a national libraries organisation should have particular responsibilities for initiating discussions with the Scottish and Welsh National Libraries where it considers co-operation desirable and for maintaining any co-operative scheme to which it is a party either in its own name or through any of the units which it administers.

CHAPTER SIXTEEN

RESEARCH AND TRAINING

Introduction

448. In formulating some of our recommendations, we have occasionally referred to the need for research. For example, in Chapter 13, we drew attention to the need to study in detail the ways in which computers could be usefully applied to the activities of the national libraries, and in Chapter 12 we recommended that the methods of archival preservation should be thoroughly investigated. We have not, however, so far systematically reviewed the range of research which could be relevant to a national libraries organisation, nor have we discussed how such research could best be administered.

Library Research Today

(a) Research topics

449. The Library Association has supplied us with details of major library and information research in progress in Britain at Autumn 1968. The principal subjects can be seen from the following list of categories with most projects:

	No. of Projects
Information retrieval	33
Cataloguing/Classification	31
Bibliographic research (other than studies leading to the production of bibliographies themselves)	27
User studies	24
Library processes (other than cataloguing, etc.)	18

These five subject sub-divisions account for over half of the 250 projects in the Library Association's lists.

(b) Research organisations

450. The Library Association's data indicate the following principal types of organisation responsible for carrying out current research:

	No. of Projects
Research Institutions	
British Standards Institution .. 31⎫	
Aslib .. .. 14⎬	59
Other .. .. 14⎭	
Universities	53
Other Higher Education Institutions ..	30
Professional Institutions	
Library Bodies .. .. .. 19⎫	28
Other .. .. 9⎭	

121

National Libraries						
NLLST	..	..	..	..	7	
NCL					3	
BML	..	..	..	..	2	15
BNB	..	..			2	
SML	..	..	..	..	1	

Government Agencies
OSTI, DES, Library Advisory Councils   8

These categories account for nearly four fifths of all the projects; the remainder being attributed to individuals, most of whom are associated with universities through being registered for higher degrees.

(c) Funds for research

451. By far the largest single source of external funds for library research is the Office for Scientific and Technical Information (OSTI), through which a quarter of all library research projects listed by the Library Association are financed to the value of about £325,000 in 1968/69. As many of the projects supported by OSTI are large and relatively costly, at least half of the total national expenditure on library research would appear to be funded from this source. The importance of OSTI in sponsoring—rather than carrying out—library research is shown in the following list of the principal bodies supporting research in 1968:

	No. of Projects sponsored
OSTI ..	64
Library Association ..	4 plus 4 shared
BNB	3
Nuffield Fund for Research into Crippling Diseases	3

Many projects are, of course, financed by the organisation carrying out the work. In particular, these include a substantial number carried out in universities and library schools.

452. The predominant position of OSTI is a very recent development, as this agency has been in existence only since 1965. A substantial proportion of its funds is spent on investigation into computer applications and other forms of library mechanisation, but its research sponsorship programme reflects also the urgent need for operational research in libraries. OSTI has, in addition, been instrumental in providing support for research into reprographic techniques, particularly at Hatfield Technical College, where a National Reprographic Centre has been established. Other areas of library interest in which the support of OSTI has recently been evident include the development of documentation standards, and a variety of studies in specialised subject fields, including business studies, town and country planning and economics.

453. OSTI, more than any other body, has, by the size of its resources, the opportunity to direct and co-ordinate library research effort, but its responsibilities at present are limited to projects which have relevance and application to scientific and technical information. Even when full allowance is made for the fact that some OSTI projects primarily intended for application to scientific

libraries will also have wider relevance and that social science is included within OSTI's sphere of influence, a degree of inbalance, detrimental to library research in the humanities, remains.

Research Requirements of the National Libraries

454. The research data supplied by the Library Association show that the contribution of the national libraries, as a group, to the total national library research effort was small in 1968. A similar analysis of research during 1967 leads to a very similar conclusion. We are convinced that in the future a substantial increase in research effort will be essential to improve the effectiveness of the existing services, and to evolve and to provide at the most appropriate time new services in response to users' requirements. In the following sections we indicate the principal types of research in which a national libraries organisation ought to be engaged.

(a) Statistical data collection

455. We have previously commented upon the lack of data relating to stock, subject coverage and patterns of usage and we have emphasised the importance of this kind of information to the efficient organisation of library facilities and operation. Such is the inadequacy of existing arrangements that the routine collection and processing of data on a much greater scale than at present needs to be started at the earliest opportunity, even in advance of the introduction of computerised methods.

456. In addition to routine analyses, there will also be a requirement for occasional *ad hoc* investigations of limited duration. For example, at the present time there is an urgent need for basic information about users' preferences for photocopies or loans, in order to decide the optimum expenditure on periodical subscriptions and the capital investment for photocopying equipment. Statistical research is also a necessary prelude to the realisation of economies, to the rationalisation of acquisitions policies between the units of a national libraries system, and to the establishment of co-operative acquisition agreements between national libraries and other, independent libraries.

(b) Operational research

457. The application of modern management techniques throughout any national libraries organisation is in our view of paramount importance. It will be necessary to carry out research on the internal organisation and management of each national library unit and to build up an operational research unit for the national libraries. Some of the most urgent studies—for example, those relating directly to the designs of new library buildings—could be made by management consultants; but the continuing need for this type of activity in an organisation where users' needs may be expected to change in response to technological development, points to the desirability of building up and retaining specialised management expertise within the organisation itself.

(c) Forward planning

458. The borderline between planning and research is indistinct and it is, therefore, appropriate to discuss here studies relating to future developments

123

and in anticipation of new needs. Increasingly in private industry and in Government departments staff engaged on day-to-day administration do not find time for planning new developments. To avoid this situation arising in the national libraries we recommend that specific provision be made for forward planning.

(d) ADP and computer development

459. Many of the research functions which we have discussed above will depend substantially upon the use of computers and the national libraries computer system should be adequately staffed with programmers and systems analysts. In addition, the rapid development of ADP applications to which we have referred in Chapter 13 will require persons able to carry out the necessary detailed semantic studies and bibliographic research if developing technology is to be exploited. Just as a full feasibility study into the first applications of computers to a national libraries organisation is necessary (Chapter 13), so continuing studies and related research will also be required. In this case also, there are clear advantages in the work being carried out by people with intimate and continuing contact with the national library and information system, for this is undoubtedly the best way of ensuring that computer manufacturers are kept in touch with the requirements of a national libraries organisation, in particular, and possibly with more general library requirements as well.

(e) Technological research and development

460. The need to bring together specialists with a knowledge of library operations and technologists was, until very recently, almost entirely neglected, not only in this country, but also in the United States. As a result, technological advance has not been adequately oriented towards the requirements of library users or administrators. It is difficult to believe, for example, that manufacturers of reprographic equipment have so far given sufficient attention to satisfying library requirements; indeed, they are probably not yet aware of the full commercial potential of this market. We consider, therefore, that a national libraries organisation should pay particular attention to requirements which call for close collaboration between experts in library operation and equipment manufacturers.

461. Many of the problems that will arise will involve the development or adaptation of existing equipment to meet the special requirements of the national libraries. Possible examples might be improvements in photocopying equipment to suit library applications and the development of facsimile transmission links. Although some of the work involved would probably require research and development to be carried out by equipment manufacturers or in specialised research institutions, it would also be expected that certain types of technological development, if they are to be carried out at all, would need workshop and laboratory facilities within the national libraries organisation itself.

462. Archival preservation, whilst presenting problems to many types of organisation, has particularly important financial implications for a national libraries organisation, which has responsibilities for preserving legally deposited material. Any administration for the national libraries should, therefore, take

the initiative to ensure that adequate studies are carried out into the possibility of developing new and less costly methods of preservation.

463. Many other opportunities for profitable research on the part of a national libraries organisation can be envisaged. For instance, bookbinding costs at the BML alone last year amounted to a quarter of a million pounds. Because binding is still very largely a manual craft, labour costs have risen rapidly in recent years and this trend is likely to continue in the future. The possibility of finding a cheap, speedy, and largely mechanised alternative to binding newspapers and parts of periodicals by hand is obviously worthy of careful consideration. There must also be many other areas where relatively cheap research is justified by the large potential savings that could result. In many of these the national libraries would be by far the largest benefactors, but the results would have application to other libraries as well. It should not be overlooked, therefore, that research, if well organised and executed, could make possible savings of considerable magnitude in libraries of all types.

Implications and Recommendations

464. We consider that library research in the widest sense of the term will be of vital importance to a national libraries organisation from its inception. Whereas some research relevant to a national libraries organisation could with advantage be carried out in existing laboratories and institutions not administered by it, a considerable proportion of the total research effort will have to be so closely integrated with its day-to-day operations that substantial facilities for carrying out various types of research will have to be available within the organisation itself. This would provide an additional incentive and a sound basis for ensuring that the whole organisation were oriented towards improvement by keeping the senior administrative staff in close and frequent contact with research activity directly related to its problems. We also believe that the senior administrative and policy making body can best decide at any particular time the level of research effort necessary for the national libraries, and how it should be deployed and organised.

465. We, therefore, recommend that a national libraries organisation should have adequate resources to meet its research and planning. These resources should be entirely at the disposal of the organisation's administration to deploy in the ways it considers to be most useful. In particular, the national libraries organisation should establish such research facilities of its own as it considers necessary to support the operation and development of its services.

466. It should also be empowered to sponsor in other libraries or research institutions any relevant research which it is unable to carry out with its own facilities, or which it considers could most appropriately be executed elsewhere. Because we believe that a national libraries organisation should rapidly develop into if not the most important, then certainly one of the most active and influential library and information research institutions in Britain, we recommend that it should be encouraged to carry out or sponsor research projects of wide application to other library and information activities, so long as the research has some relevance to the efficient operation and potential development of national library services. In making this recommendation we are aware that a substantial proportion of current library and information research might come

into this category and that it implies that a national libraries organisation would increasingly assume many of the responsibilities now exercised by OSTI. We consider this development by no means undesirable, however, as it would mean that, for the first time, an institution having substantial responsibilities for undertaking library research would at the same time be exercising a co-ordinating function in respect of some of the related research being carried out elsewhere.

467. Throughout our report we have stressed the importance of co-ordinating the activities of a national libraries organisation with those of complementary services. We believe that this is especially important in the field of information research, which though it has great potential for increasing our national prosperity, is itself very costly. We, therefore, recommend that consideration should be given to the creation of machinery to bring together the major national interests engaged in the development of information techniques, so as to co-ordinate effectively the total research effort and assist in the formulation of national research policies.

Education and Training

468. If a national libraries organisation develops in the way we have envisaged, it will be exceptionally well fitted to contribute to the training of librarians and the education of users. In many specialist subjects—including library auto-mation, management techniques, statistical methods, bibliographic research, user studies and information retrieval—the national libraries will have expertise unrivalled in Britain and possibly elsewhere. We believe, therefore, that a national libraries organisation should accept as one of its important responsi-bilities the task of making the results of its research and development as widely known as possible to librarians and to others to whom the knowledge would be useful.

(a) Professional training for librarians

469. The contribution of the national libraries to professional training should be to supplement the existing arrangements in collaboration with those at present responsible for the training of librarians. The following activities are those which we consider most likely to be worthwhile:

(i) Short courses on specialist topics, such as those indicated in paragraph 468 above, could be of great value in helping practising librarians to keep abreast of modern developments. We also believe that courses could be usefully provided to enable the activities and services of the national libraries to be widely known. The success of new facilities and the impact of organisational changes may well depend upon how widely they are made known to librarians generally, and suitable short courses could make a useful contribution to achieving this end.

(ii) Conferences are widely acknowledged as being of considerable value in assisting the dissemination of the results of research of many kinds and in stimulating further developments. As we are expecting a national libraries organisation to take a leading role in library and information research, it would be in a unique position to organise conferences on library research and similar topics of national and international importance.

126

(iii) A national libraries service could arrange for undergraduate and non-graduate students of librarianship to be given a short period of practical training and experience in a national library, as an integral part of their library school or university courses. The numbers involved would make it impossible to give every student this opportunity, but it could at least be open to those intending eventually to make a career in a national library.

(iv) The national libraries service should wherever possible provide facilities for post-graduate students engaged upon research projects in library or information studies.

(b) Educational services for users

470. Some of the activities listed above—particularly short courses of the type now organised by the NLLST and the NRLSI for their users—could usefully be extended to cover more widely the activities and services of a national libraries organisation. We have evidence that the services of some of the existing institutions are not as widely known as they could be and we emphasise the importance of efficient publicity directed at all types of potential user. Courses, as well as other forms of publicity, would have a part to play in solving what is, in effect, yet another problem of the dissemination of information.

127

CHAPTER SEVENTEEN

MANAGEMENT AND ADMINISTRATION

Introduction

471. In previous chapters we have identified the library and information facilities which should be available nationally in order to supplement the services of the public, university and special libraries and of the existing information systems. In this chapter we consider how these national services can be administered most effectively and economically.

The Institutions Covered

472. We have recommended that most or all of the present functions of the following existing institutions should contribute to the services to be provided by the national libraries and information organisation:

    (i) The British Museum Library;

    (ii) The National Central Library;

    (iii) The National Lending Library for Science and Technology;

    (iv) The National Reference Library of Science and Invention;

    (v) The British National Bibliography.

In addition, we have recommended that some of the services or functions at present provided by the following institutions should be incorporated:

    (i) The Office for Scientific and Technical Information;

    (ii) Aslib.

473. We consider that the Science Museum Library, one of the libraries mentioned in our terms of reference, should not be administered by a national libraries organisation.

474. We have given careful consideration to the future administration of the British Library of Art at the Victoria and Albert Museum, and we recognise that there is a strong case for establishing close links between this library and the constituent parts of a national libraries organisation. However, until a sufficiently detailed study has been made of the stocks and patterns of use of this library in relation to those of the British Museum Library, we cannot be certain that benefits to users and economies would result if the British Library of Art were to be fully incorporated into a national libraries organisation, in the same way as the other institutions listed above. We have recommended, therefore, that the future administration of the library should be the subject of further and more detailed examination by the Department of Education and Science in association with a national libraries organisation.

475. We have also recognised that other libraries, or information organisations, will become associated with, but not administered directly by the management of the national libraries. Included in this category will be libraries involved in co-operative acquisition agreements, and institutions such as the Bodleian

Library at Oxford and the Cambridge University Library which we have recommended should be equipped and financially assisted to contribute further to the national inter-library lending arrangements.

Considerations Affecting the Pattern of Administration

476. Although the management of the national libraries has not been specifically discussed in the earlier chapters, some of our previous recommendations have implications for the administrative structure of a national libraries service. Usually they refer to specific services or library units, but taken together they emphasise the need for close links between the major components of a national library system, in respect of both policy and day-to-day administration. For example, the BML should be closely associated with the photocopying and lending organisation; similarly, the bibliographic services of the national library will involve co-operation between all the major units. In addition, BNB and some of Aslib's and OSTI's services need to be integrated into the new national framework at early stages in its existence. The view that we have taken of the potential uses of automatic data processing also points very clearly to a need for close co-operation and co-ordination of functions between the administration and the units providing the library and information services. Furthermore, we appreciate that the creation and development of costly new research facilities, which are essential if the new administration is to be sensitive to users' needs and responsive to technological advances, can only be justified if a sufficiently large and well-integrated organisation exists for their support.

477. We are, therefore, convinced that the future administrative structure of a national libraries service should be so designed as to ensure that the necessary degree of co-operation between the various library units can be established and maintained. This condition would not, we believe, be satisfied by any system based upon a federation of equal partners. Such a system is not likely to be appropriate where a close integration of existing institutions and services is envisaged, and particularly, where radical changes in organisation and facilities will have to be introduced speedily and effectively, as will be the case for the national libraries system. New services, such as those based on the National Bibliographic Service, should be developed; research should be initiated without delay; and wasteful duplication of both effort and facilities between some of the existing institutions should be eliminated. At the same time, any new national libraries organisation should take over the responsibilities for the design and construction of new libraries in London to replace the BML and the NRLSI, and will probably be responsible for commissioning what should be one of the largest computers in the country. Perhaps the most important of all its tasks will be to develop the principles of library management to meet the needs of the future.

478. Taken together, the tasks outlined above seem to us convincing arguments in favour of a strong central administration. In the early years particularly, there will be formidable problems of re-organisation to be tackled. But the need for effective and forward-looking management will continue, as it seems certain that information techniques will develop exceptionally rapidly and become increasingly complex. Therefore, we do not think that the administrative needs of the organisation can be successfully supplied by a

policy-making and management body consisting entirely of part-time members, nor do we think these responsibilities should be concentrated in the hands of one full-time professional. It seems much more appropriate that the supreme authority for the administration of the diverse national library and information services should be vested in a corporate body composed mainly of full-time members, so that a range of management skills may be brought to bear continually on the considerable problems which will be presented. Because of the importance of implementing policy decisions as quickly as possible, there will have to be good channels of communication and interaction between the administrative authority and those with executive responsibilities for the individual library units. Nevertheless, we think it important that policy-making should be clearly differentiated from the executive functions. Accordingly, the primary duty of the heads of the library units will be the executive management of the units themselves, although the policy-making body will undoubtedly draw extensively upon them for constructive proposals and professional advice in arriving at its decisions.

479. Our recommendations concerning inter-library lending, co-operative acquisition and national bibliographic services indicate the importance of establishing and maintaining very close links between national library-based services and other libraries and information systems. Furthermore, the development within the national libraries organisation of new techniques of library management and information handling will undoubtedly have applications elsewhere which, to be fully exploited, will need an environment in which the exchange of staff and the establishment of close working relationships between different types of library can be fostered. These considerations highlight the need for any administration of the national libraries to be outward-looking and to have the greatest freedom of action, particularly in recruiting staff and in determining conditions of service. A counter-argument has been put forward by the Library Association and others that a system of national libraries should be directly administered by central Government, in order that it should be favourably placed to attract adequate resources. We have carefully considered this, but we see no reason why the ability of a national libraries organisation to secure sufficient finance need be impaired by a form of administration detached from direct Government control. We recommend, therefore, that the management of the national libraries should be neither too closely associated with, nor of necessity influenced by, the organisational and administrative procedures of central Government.

480. Throughout the preceding chapters we have stressed that libraries should be regarded as centres for information in the form of the printed word, and that they operate most effectively only when continuous efforts are made to match the services which they provide with the developing requirements of the different types of users. We consider it to be most important, therefore, that the future organisation of the national libraries should include adequate machinery for representing the interests of users, which would enable the organisation to judge the effectiveness of its services. The essential contribution which users of the services can make is advisory in character and should not involve them in administrative responsibility.

481. We are particularly conscious that in the fields of scientific and technical information the establishment of an adequate library-based service, responsive

130

to changing requirements and to developments in information technology, is crucial to the economic wellbeing of the country, and we have some sympathy with the view strongly expressed in evidence which we received from the Confederation of British Industry that this constitutes a powerful argument in favour of the separate administration of national library services in these subject areas. Nevertheless, as we will explain later in this chapter, we think that the needs of industry can be fully met by a national library system covering all subjects. This would have the following advantages over a plurality of separately administered services, distinguished by their respective subject areas:

(i) Duplication of stocks and services would be avoided to an extent which would not otherwise be possible, because of the inescapable difficulties of defining subject boundaries.

(ii) The advantages, to which we have previously alluded, of integrating services by function, rather than by subject, would be attainable.

(iii) The simplification of entry points to the national libraries' services would be greatly facilitated.

(iv) The application to non-scientific services of the " spin-off " from developments in scientific and technical information services would be easier.

(v) Conversely, developments in non-scientific information handling—particularly in the social sciences—could be most easily exploited for the benefit of users of scientific and technical services.

(vi) Economies of scale would make it easier in a unified system to justify the introduction of new and costly facilities made possible by developments in information technology. It would also be cheaper to effect the improvements which we have recognised as being urgently necessary if existing services are to be adequately maintained.

(vii) The acceptance of desirable standards, both nationally and internationally, would be less difficult if the number of organisations involved were kept to a minimum.

(viii) The influence and, hence, the strength and effectiveness of a national libraries organisation would be directly affected by the size and economic importance of the total services provided.

The National Libraries Authority

482. In our view the conclusions embodied in Chapters 10 to 16, together with the principles of management outlined in the earlier paragraphs of this Chapter, point to the need for bringing into a unified administrative structure the institutions which will provide the services of the national libraries organisation. We recommend, therefore, that the existing administrative responsibilities for the five major units indicated in paragraph 472 above should be terminated and that they should become the responsibility of a new statutory body, to be known as the National Libraries Authority. In addition, this Authority should assume full administrative responsibilities for those functions and services of OSTI and Aslib which we have suggested should form part of

the national libraries organisation. The stock and the appropriate parts of the property of the four existing libraries should be vested in this Authority (with the exceptions indicated in paragraph 496 below) and the Authority should employ all the staff necessary to fulfil the functions which we have suggested as desirable.

483. We have already argued the advantages of facilitating the interchange of staff between a national libraries organisation and other parts of the library and information service. We believe that this would be best realised if the National Libraries Authority were constituted as an independent public body acting on behalf of the Crown. The employees would not, under this arrangement, be civil servants and the administration would be free of direct departmental control. The Authority would, however, be financed out of Government funds through the appropriate Minister, whom we consider should be the Secretary of State for Education and Science.

(a) The National Libraries Management Board

484. In considering the most suitable form of extra-departmental administration for the National Libraries Authority, we have given particular attention to the possibility of applying the principle of management by trustees, and studied the administrative structures of both the UGC and the Research Councils. However, we are not satisfied that any of these arrangements would meet the organisational requirements which we have discussed in paragraphs 476 to 481 above. We, therefore, reject these alternatives and recommend instead that the National Libraries Authority should be administered by a Board which, in exercising corporate responsibility for management policies, would have the following main characteristics:

(i) be composed substantially of full-time members,

(ii) be strong in management expertise,

(iii) have the greatest possible independence of central Government, commensurate with adequate supervision of public expenditure,

(iv) and have close links with other parts of the nation's library provision and information services.

485. Implicit in our thinking has been the idea that the Management Board should be organised in terms of function, rather than on the basis of the individual library units. We emphasise this point because the implementation of our recommendations will require the establishment of new and intimate functional relationships between the services provided by the component institutions—for example, lending and photocopying will involve not only the services now provided by the NLLST and the NCL, but also those of the NRLSI and the BML—as well as libraries outside the national organisation. We do not believe that functional reorganisation would work efficiently if the head of each library were also a member of the Management Board. The two roles are fundamentally different in character and we do not think it reasonable to expect individuals to combine them successfully. Nevertheless, we emphasise that we do not envisage that the position of the heads of the libraries should in any way decline in importance, nor that the role that we have suggested for them in paragraph 478 will be less demanding than that of the present senior officers.

486. To be effective, the Management Board should be as small as is compatible with the exercise of its considerable responsibilities. With this in mind, we believe that, at least initially, the Board should consist of a Chairman, Secretary and a maximum of three other full-time members, together with some part-time members, and we recommend that the Secretary of State for Education and Science should be responsible for making all these appointments

487. The Chairman's duties in conducting the formal meetings of the Board should constitute only a relatively minor part of his total commitments. We presume that he will also take a special interest in the co-ordination and the forward planning of all the services of the Authority, and this will require him to keep continually in view the development of all national library and information services. In addition, he will be the main personal communication link between the Authority and the Government by way of the Secretary of State. We suggest that he should also be the accounting officer and, as such, be responsible to the Secretary of State for the detailed disposition of the Authority's resources.

488. If the National Library Authority is to obtain adequate financial support in the future, careful attention will have to be paid to the effective formulation and presentation of proposals for the development and maintenance of its services. It is suggested, therefore, that the Secretary should have as one of his particular responsibilities the preparation of financial statements, annual reports and the documentation associated with the Authority's proposals for developing its facilities. To discharge these very important duties, he will have to work very closely with the Chairman and we consider that he should be a full member of the Board.

489. In a later section, we refer in some detail to the formidable problems of creating a unified staff structure. In the early years of the new Authority, particularly, we consider it most important that at least one full-time member of the Board should make this one of his specific and most important responsibilities. Even when this task is successfully accomplished, we believe that it is essential that staff and personnel matters should be capable of being adequately represented at Board level and that formal administrative machinery should be established for this purpose.

490. Other major functional responsibilities of the Board as a whole would include the formulation of the Authority's policy on reference, lending, photocopying and bibliographic services, research, co-operative acquisition and other joint activities with other libraries, scientific information services, external relations and publicity. We envisage that individual Board members would have particular responsibilities in ensuring the successful implementation of different aspects of the Authority's policies. However, the ways in which these functions, excluding those referred to in paragraphs 487, 488 and 489, are distributed should reflect the qualities and expertise of the different members of the Board.

491. Because of the importance which we attach to the Authority's scientific, technological and industrial services, and to ensuring that these are closely co-ordinated with the Ministry of Technology's information services to industry, we recommend that the Minister of Technology should be consulted over the appointment of one of the full-time members to the Board.

492. We appreciate that a management body composed of four or five full-time members can only draw upon limited expertise from within its own ranks. Whilst more specialised advice can be obtained from consultants and other types of adviser, we recognise the desirability of ensuring that an adequate breadth of experience is available to bear directly upon the processes of decision making. We, therefore, recommend that the Secretary of State should appoint to the Management Board up to three part-time members, who should be paid for their services. The part-time members would normally hold office for a period of three years, renewable once only. To avoid simultaneous vacancies for part-time members, we think that the first appointments might be for different periods and of up to five years in duration. We would expect the Secretary of State, in making these appointments, to take account of the need to establish and maintain channels of communication between the Authority and other library and infoimation systems and, for reasons given later, to recognise the special characteristics of the National Reference Library. We would hope that regular change in the composition of the part-time members would reflect developments in the Authority's services and modifications in the character of the Board's responsibilities.

(b) The Executive Committee

493. In paragraph 478 we argued that the policy-making and executive bodies within the National Libraries Authority should be clearly delineated, but that there should be a close working relationship between them. We believe that this can best be achieved by establishing an Executive Committee, composed of the heads of all the major service units in the Authority and chaired by the Chairman of the Management Board. Associated with these two primary bodies—the Management Board and the Executive Committee—would be built up a structure of standing and ad hoc sub-committees, on which the appropriate Board members and senior executives would serve together.

(c) Advisory Councils

494. In view of the emphasis we have given to the need to keep the administration of the National Libraries Authority in close touch with users' requirements, and with other parts of the library and information system of the country, we recommend that an Advisory Council should be associated with each major library unit or service under the Authority's control. The Director of the establishment concerned would be an ex officio member of the relevant Advisory Council; the remaining membership should in part reflect the use that is made of its services, although members should be appointed primarily on the basis of their personal qualities and experience. We recommend also that Management Board members should have a right of attendance. These Councils would provide a most important means by which the Authority's senior executives and the Board would be able to measure the success of the Authority's policies and the directions in which future developments would be needed.

(d) Trustees of the National Reference Library

495. At the NRL there would be special problems involving the acquisition and preservation of material which is primarily of intrinsic value. In this respect the NRL would differ from all the other units which we believe should

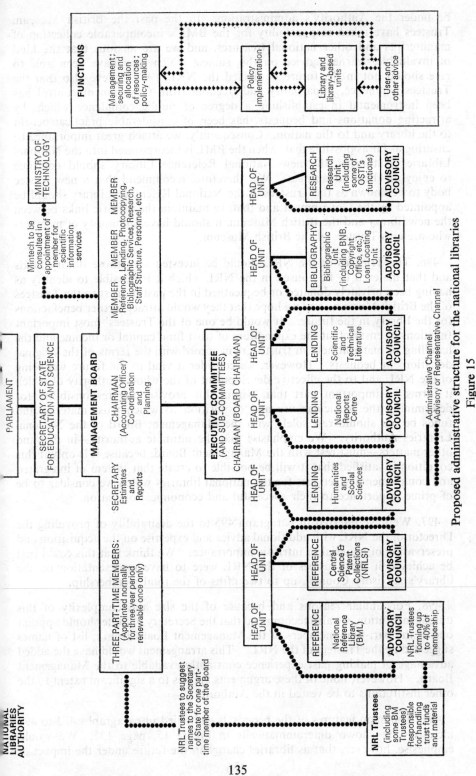

Proposed administrative structure for the national libraries

Figure 15

135

be under the Authority's administration. In the past the British Museum Trustees have taken responsibility for the BML's incomparable collection of manuscripts and other national treasures, and we are anxious that the kind of invaluable, learned advice on this subject which they have been able to give should not in the future be denied the NRL. We believe also that the Trustees' eminence, impartiality and freedom from Government control has been instrumental in establishing a degree of public confidence which, by attracting donations and bequests, has been of considerable practical benefit to the library and to the nation. Consequently, we attach great importance to ensuring as far as possible that, when the BML is incorporated into the National Libraries Authority, the new National Reference Library should continue to enjoy all these advantages. We, therefore, recommend that a new trustee body to be known as the Trustees of the National Reference Library should be appointed by the Government and that, to maintain the historic links between the new library and the British Museum, it should have a minority of members who are also Trustees of the British Museum.

496. The Trustees of the NRL should be invested with those library funds and that material to be housed in the NRL which it is possible to identify as having been privately donated or bequeathed in the past in trust to the Trustees of the British Museum, and we hope that they would attract further benefactions for the library in the future. It would be one of the Trustees' most important functions to ensure that the expenditure of trust fund capital or income and the handling of material held in trust were in accord with the terms of the original donations or bequests. However, we consider it vital to the future wellbeing of the NRL and to the effective development of the whole Authority of which it forms an important part that, within this proviso, the responsibility for determining the particular use and disposition to which trust material and funds be put should rest solely with the Management Board of the National Libraries Authority. We emphasise that the ultimate authority—in this and other matters—must rest with the Management Board, because it is only if this condition is satisfied that it will be possible to create that system of integrated and complementary services for the national libraries which we consider to be of prime importance to their successful and economical operation.

497. We have referred in paragraph 495 to the desirability of providing the Director of the NRL with additional advice and expertise on the acquisition and preservation of material of intrinsic importance. We think that this could best be achieved if the Trustees of the NRL were to have representation on the library's Advisory Council, up to two fifths of the total membership.

498. For similar reasons and because of the size and complexity of this unique institution, we also recommend that the Secretary of State should appoint one of the part-time members of the Management Board from a list of names suggested by the Trustees of the NRL. This arrangement would have the added advantage of making past experience constantly available to the Management Board. However, none of these arguments applies to a significant extent to the other institutions to be vested in the Authority.

499. The main features of the proposals embodied in paragraphs 482 to 498 inclusive are shown diagrammatically in Figure 15, page 135. We would emphasise, however, that as libraries change in the future under the impact of

136

technological development so must the administrative arrangements be allowed to evolve. Figure 15 should, therefore, not be regarded as a blueprint valid for all time.

Relations with Central Government

500. We have strongly argued earlier that the National Libraries Authority should have the maximum degree of autonomy in maintaining and developing its own services and facilities, and in Chapter 16 we have drawn particular attention to the need for adequate finance for the Authority's research activities, whether carried out within its own organisation or commissioned externally. We realise that when fairly substantial public expenditure is involved, adequate safeguards are necessary to ensure as far as is reasonably possible that the resources are properly employed. However, it is our view that the radical changes which we consider are essential can only be successfully implemented if the top management is of the highest calibre and if it is given the greatest possible discretion and authority.

501. It is our strongly-held opinion that the facilities to be provided by the Authority constitute an integral and vital part of the nation's total library and information resources. Consequently, the maximum benefits will result only if the development of all library-based services and related information systems can be appraised as a whole in the formulation of Government policy. We are aware that, largely because of historical accident, the responsibility for libraries is divided within the Department of Education and Science. Although we were not requested to advise on this matter, we would hope that, because it is so relevant to the effective and economical administration of a national libraries organisation, the Secretary of State would be convinced of the desirability of combining all his responsibilities for libraries and for scientific and technical information within a single branch in his department. For similar reasons, we strongly urge that the Government should examine the feasibility of establishing machinery to provide it with advice on policy concerning the development and co-ordination of national information services—whether library-based or otherwise—which are the direct or indirect responsibilities of Government departments.

Commercial Services

502. We have identified specific examples of the Authority's services which could and, we believe, should be commercially self-supporting. In this category would come the photocopying and translations services, some bibliographic aids, most publications and specialised information facilities. We see no good reason why this principle should not be extended as widely as possible, so long as it does not conflict with the fundamental philosophy governing the availability of publicly-funded library services in general. We believe that the services of the National Libraries Authority give considerable scope for applying the principles of " accountable management ", as defined in Chapter 5 of the Report of the Fulton Committee on the Civil Service, and that the administrative framework which we are recommending will facilitate the application of these principles. We mention this point particularly because we consider it to be an important concomitant to the establishment of an efficient national libraries service.

137

Staffing and Grading

503. One consequence of uniting the library units under a common administration will be that a new staff structure will be required, in order to provide uniform conditions of service for comparable grades and thereby to facilitate freer movement of staff throughout the system. The present diversity of salaries, pensions, leave, etc., between the staffs of the existing institutions undoubtedly implies that standardisation will be a task of considerable complexity and that it will not be susceptible of quick solution. Failure to appreciate this could easily result in staffing negotiations dominating the early work of the new administration, to the detriment of more urgent priorities. We, therefore, would urge that in the interim period before a new staff structure can be introduced, the acute problems of grade comparability and conditions of service—for example, those arising from staff transfers between the different library units—should be dealt with on an individual basis. We also consider that any new conditions of service should not be on balance to the disadvantage of any individual on the staff of the existing institutions.

Financial Arrangements

504. In various parts of this report we have drawn attention to the difficulty we have had in estimating realistically the costs of existing services. At least in part, this is because the traditional procedure governing the supply of public funds is aimed primarily at ensuring that Parliament has the opportunity to vote all the gross sums involved, so that none is misapplied or misappropriated, rather than the economical and efficient management of the resources and services for which they are provided. The proliferation of sources of finance, each one strictly compartmentalised and largely independent of the others, not only seriously hinders effective management, but reduces the incentive to promote efficiency. In the case of the BML, buildings are the responsibility of the Ministry of Public Building and Works, salaries of DES, book binding of the Stationery Office and publications of the Trustees themselves. One effect of this is that if a policy decision results in savings in one field, those savings cannot normally be made available for use in another. For example, savings resulting from outhousing cannot be devoted to new bibliographic services.

505. A radically different approach to funding is, we believe, essential to the administrative changes that we have recommended. Our management proposals are based on the implicit assumption that the Authority's services will be assessed on their effectiveness in relation to their costs. Indeed, we do not know how else it will be possible to take responsible management decisions and make valid policy judgements. It is, therefore, axiomatic that the systems of financing, management accountancy and public accountability for the Authority should enable its operations to be realistically costed and should give the Management Board the greatest possible discretion, as well as full responsibility, over all resources governed by its policy decisions. This we think can best be done as follows:

(i) all public finance for the Authority should be derived from a single source;

(ii) all premises, maintenance, services and equipment supplied by or through Government departments should be paid for by the Authority in terms of their current market values;

(iii) the Management Board, through its accounting officer, should be required to present the Authority's accounts in a form which indicates the cost of each part of its operations, including the realistic cost of buildings and equipment;

(iv) while special arrangements might have to be made for the largest capital expenditure, the financial arrangements should be such as to give the Management Board the greatest possible freedom to deploy the Authority's resources in the most effective way;

(v) it follows from (iv) that the Board should be allowed to apply profits from its services and savings from its administration to the further development of the Authority's services.

Timing

506. Throughout this report we have endeavoured to identify the most essential tasks associated with creating an efficient and balanced service from the existing units. Some of these—such as effecting improvements to the union catalogues—can be dealt with by the present administrations, but others, equally important, depend for their fulfilment on the establishment of a unified Authority. It is, therefore, necessary that the steps to establish the new administrative system should be taken without delay. Only if this is done with a proper sense of urgency will it be possible to avoid prejudicing seriously some of the existing services and postponing intolerably the introduction of improvements.

507. A logical implication of these arguments is that the new Authority should take over at its inception the administration of all the services and institutions envisaged for it. We would mention particularly that the Management Board should assume responsibility at the earliest opportunity for the design of the new libraries in central London. The problems associated with transferring both staff and large volumes of stock from the BML and the NLRSI into their respective new buildings are bound to be formidable. If these upheavals are to be carried out smoothly and with the minimum of disruption to library services, we consider it most desirable that the new system of administration should be well-established and running smoothly considerably in advance.

508. Since we envisage the first few years of the National Libraries Authority as a time of radical change in organisation and services, we are satisfied that a Management Board having the composition that we have outlined in paragraph 486 will be fully justified. Thereafter, however, the administrative needs of the Authority may be expected to change so that at a later date it may be desirable to reduce the total membership, or to adjust the ratio of full-time to part-time members. We accordingly recommend that the Board structure should be reviewed at the end of the first five years.

CHAPTER EIGHTEEN

FINANCIAL IMPLICATIONS

Introduction

509. Even though some of the figures are necessarily imprecise, we have attempted in the following paragraphs to estimate the real costs of providing the existing national library services and the main savings and additional costs which are likely to result from the implementation of our recommendations.

Costs of Existing Services

(a) Direct costs of services

510. In Part II we drew attention to the problems of estimating the direct costs of the services of the national libraries. This is largely because the finance for most of them is borne on the votes of several different Government departments. In the case of the BML and the NRLSI, there are further difficulties because some of the costs of both libraries are inseparable from one another and from those of the British Museum as a whole.

511. However, in Table A below, we give our best estimates of these costs and we believe that, though approximate, they are reasonably correct. The figure includes expenditure on staffing, acquisitions, printing, binding and photocopying, and credit and deficit balances for services for which charges are made. The figure for the costs of the BNB, however, is drawn from that organisation's financial statement for 1967/68 and is, therefore, much more precise.

(b) Notional costs of accommodation

512. With the exception of the Bayswater division of the NRLSI, no figures based on market values are available for the cost of accommodating the five national libraries, and the accommodation costs in Table A below are, therefore, notional. They are based on the floor areas occupied by the libraries and upon advice which we have received on the probable realistic costs per square foot of accommodation in London and in Boston Spa. Allowance has been made in the estimates for rates, heating, lighting, maintenance, first costs and amortisation of buildings and land costs, but not for developer's profit (Appendix D).

513. In the case of the BNB, the figures shown are dervied from that institution's audited accounts.

Table A—Annual Costs of Existing Services

Institution	Direct costs of services (£1,000)	Notional costs of accommodation (£1,000)	Total costs (£1,000)
BML	1,250	2,000 (1)	3,250
NRLSI	400	400 (1)	800
NLLST	500	150	650
NCL	125	300	425
SML	125	200 (2)	325
Total	2,400	3,050	5,450

The following costs for the BNB are shown separately, since they are entirely met from subscriptions and charges.

BNB	150	50	200

¹ These figures are based on the floor areas now occupied by the BML and the NRLSI. Under the Trustees' present plans for the new library buildings, the BML would occupy about 950,000 square feet in central London, and the NRLSI 450,000 square feet. Together with the Colindale outhouse, which the Trustees plan to retain, this would cost about £7,000,000 per annum for accommodation alone.

² This figure is based on the floor area of Stage I of the new SML building.

Costs of Implementing our Recommendations

514. We have had to assume a basis against which the financial implications of our recommendations could be assessed. In the case of the NCL, the BNB, and the NLLST, the existing institutions in our view form a reasonable basis, because they are operating in modern buildings constructed or converted specifically for the services provided. For the SML, we have assumed in our calculations that it is operating in the new building designed for it, although it will be a few months before this happens. However, to cost those recommendations relating to the BML and the NRLSI on the basis of existing buildings and services would, we believe, be unhelpful and unrealistic. Our investigations began from the point where it was already accepted that new accommodation for both these libraries was urgently needed, in view of the inadequacies of the existing premises. We have, therefore, calculated the cost of our recommendations for these two libraries in terms of the Trustees' proposals for accommodating them in new buildings on the Bloomsbury site.

(a) Administrative recommendations

515. The only major additional expenditure involved in the implementation of our recommendation for the establishment of a National Libraries Authority will be the salaries and office accommodation for the members of the Management Board and its secretariat. The total salaries and concomitant costs for the Board members should be about £40,000 per annum and we have allowed a further £30,000 annually for their accommodation costs and secretarial assistance.

516. We estimate, therefore, that the total cost of the Management Board will be about £70,000 per annum, which represents 1 per cent of the present annual cost of the five libraries (see Table A). We consider that this is a reasonable price to pay for the management of a national libraries service and for the close co-ordination of policies and services without which many of the savings identified below would not be realisable.

(b) Recommendations concerning the BML

517. A policy of outhousing lightly-used material from the BML should produce very substantial savings. At present, about 7 per cent of the BML's holdings are outhoused at Woolwich. We have assumed that computerised methods of stock control will enable approximately twice this proportion to be outhoused from the future National Reference Library with very little

141

inconvenience to users. This would reduce the central London closed access space requirements by about 15 per cent, i.e. by nearly 70,000 square feet compared with the BM Trustees' present plans, by providing an equivalent storage area on a low-cost site.

518. We are aware that outhousing part of the collections will almost certainly result in a slight overall increase in the costs of maintenance and staffing. However, the reduction in accommodation costs would be so great that the net annual saving resulting from the assumed level of outhousing would be about £275,000.

519. We have recommended that the national photocopying service should be provided at a realistic charge to users, and thus the expansion of the photocopying facilities at present provided by the BML should ideally recover its full cost. However, because it will probably be difficult to apportion accurately some of the overheads between the photocopying and other services of the library, and because it is legally inadmissible to make a profit on photocopying material in copyright, we feel it prudent to allow for a small loss on the increased services to be provided. This we have estimated at £10,000 per annum.

(c) Recommendations covering the NRLSI and regional reference facilities

520. Although we intend that the Central Science and Patent Collections should constitute a very large library—certainly the largest science reference library in the country—the implementation of our recommendations will enable substantial savings to be made in relation to the present proposals of the British Museum Trustees for the future of the NRLSI. We have proposed that:

> (i) comprehensive coverage of all foreign scientific material is not necessary;
>
> (ii) the lightly-used material should be outhoused, not retained beneath a new library at Bloomsbury;
>
> (iii) co-ordination between the scientific library services of the Authority should enable the Central Science and Patent Collections to economise in the cost of collecting reports and in the provision of information services.

Until further detailed studies are carried out it will not be possible to estimate with any precision the savings resulting from (i) and (iii), although we would expect them to be appreciable. It is also difficult at this stage to estimate the possible savings from outhousing, but, even if they were no more than 10 per cent of the annual accommodation costs for the proposed new NRLSI, they would amount to £225,000 per year.

521. We have also recommended that regional reference facilities should be strengthened in those areas where industry is concentrated. To estimate the expenditure involved would require further careful study for which there has been insufficient time. However, we think that it would be reasonable to expect on the basis of the real costs of services of the national libraries that

142

substantial improvements in the regional facilities would be possible if the Government were to decide that the savings that we have proposed for the NRLSI were employed for this purpose.

(d) Recommendations concerning the NCL and inter-library lending

522. We have recommended that the NCL loan stock and its staff engaged on the supply of loans from central stock should be transferred to Boston Spa in the near future. At a later date the union catalogues and the staff associated with them would also move there from central London. The transfer of these services will release the Store Street building for other purposes. In Appendix D we show that annual savings up to a maximum of about £230,000 could result if the building could be used for other activities of the National Libraries Authority which would have to be in central London and for which additional similar accommodation would otherwise be required. Although considerable new building will be required in London and elsewhere for the administrative, reference, research and other activities of the Authority, we consider it unlikely that the full theoretical saving will be achieved, either for the reasons which are discussed in Appendix D, or because for other reasons it may not be possible to use the Store Street premises to the best advantage. We think, therefore that these potential savings should be estimated conservatively and we assess them at two thirds of the theoretical maximum.

523. Improvements to the NCL's union catalogues would require extra expenditure initially to eliminate the backlog of entries awaiting insertion. The NCL currently spends about £13,000 per annum on maintaining the catalogues and, at the present rate of insertion, could probably bring them fully up to date if this expenditure were doubled for a period of three to five years.

524. The grants to the " inner circle " of large co-operating libraries, which we have recommended should be given special responsibilities for inter-library lending, will involve recurrent expenditure. Although the annual sum required will depend upon the extent of these libraries' contributions and on their present organisation, we do not think it will be necessary to budget for very large expenditure under this heading. On the basis of the present costs to the NCL of packing and despatching items loaned from central stock, we estimate a maximum of £25,000 per annum for these grants, excluding capital grants for the purchase of complex equipment necessary for library automation.

525. Although we have argued that the central loan stock in the humanities and social sciences should be selectively expanded, we cannot tell from the data available to us how much additional expenditure could be justified by the principles which are set out in Chapter 11 to govern the level of expansion. On balance, however, we doubt whether this will involve an increase of more that 100 per cent over the NCL's present acquisitions grant of £25,000.

(e) The National Reports Centre

526. The establishment of a national centre for reports at Boston Spa will clearly require some extension of the accommodation, staff and stock of the NLLST, although it will be very largely based on the NLLST's existing provision for this type of material. We have estimated the *additional* annual cost of the

Reports Centre at about £35,000 on the basis of 5 per cent of the present real cost of the NLLST's services of all types. As reports contribute only a minor activity of the NLLST, we believe that this figure should generously cover any additional expenditure involved.

(f) *Recommendations concerning the SML*

527. We have proposed that the SML should not be administered by the National Libraries Authority, but should be integrated with the Lyon Playfair Library of Imperial College. Rationalisation of the stocks, services and acquisition policies of the two libraries will certainly produce substantial savings, and we think it reasonable to assume that the total saving of direct costs will be equivalent to about one third of the SML's present direct costs, i.e. about £40,000 per annum. So far as accommodation costs are concerned, however, the saving will probably be less than one third of the SML's costs, since Imperial College will be relying on the SML for some of the library accommodation necessary for college members. We have, therefore, based our estimate of the probable economies in accommodation on one quarter of the real annual cost of the floor area in Stages I and II of the new building. On these bases, the total savings may be expected to be about £120,000 per annum. However, in suggesting this figure, we are assuming that the library space surplus to requirements as a result of the recommended amalgamation will be used by Imperial College for other purposes and that Stage II will not be built as originally planned, so that the full potential economies may be realised.

(g) *The National Bibliographic Service*

528. The financial consequences of integrating the BNB with the cataloguing departments of the BML and the NCL are very difficult to assess. However, we think it would not be too optimistic to assume that the overall reduction in expenditure will be equivalent to at least 25 per cent of the total real costs of the BML's present cataloguing operations, including an appropriate allowance for accommodation at current market prices. This saving we put at £100,000 per annum.

529. We have recommended that the production of select bibliographies and the provision of scientific abstracting services should be charged for on a properly costed basis. These facilities should, therefore, very largely recover their costs.

(h) *Research*

530. In Chapter 16, we recommended a substantial programme of applied research to be carried out or sponsored by the National Libraries Authority. Some of this would be in respect of responsibilities transferred to the Authority from OSTI and, on this account, would not involve additional expenditure of public funds. Of the research not at present covered by OSTI's responsibilities some would be paid for ultimately out of the receipts of services which would become financially self-supporting. The remainder, mostly concerning the non-revenue earning activities of the Authority, would involve additional

144

expenditure. By allowing £100,000 per year for all *additional* research expenditure, we envisage that the total research programme controlled by the Authority's Management Board would be several times this figure.

(i) Co-operative acquisition

531. In the overall national coverage of library material, the ideal should be to make available in this country at least one copy of every publication likely to be of research value. Although this ideal should be approached as closely as possible, the extent of its attainment will clearly depend on the availability of national resources. It is, therefore, not possible to estimate the annual level of grant to libraries co-operating with the NRL in the acquisition of foreign material.

(j) Automatic data processing

532. Because we were unable to estimate the cost or practicability of introducing ADP to the operations and services of the national libraries, we recommended that a detailed feasibility study should be carried out. On the basis of our general experience of the introduction of computers, we would expect improvements in services rather than savings in cost to result. Indeed, the maintenance of existing services and urgently needed improvements made possible by ADP may result in extra expenditure, at least in the early years of a National Libraries Authority. This should not, in our view, be a deterrent, so long as the additional expenditure were justified on a cost-benefit basis.

Conclusion

533. All our estimates show that it is possible to provide many necessary improvements leading to overall better services for an annual expenditure of between £¼ million and £½ million less than might otherwise have been necessary. They do not, however, include the cost of ADP on the scale which we think will be required for greatest efficiency, nor do they allow for expenditure on schemes for co-operative coverage of literature, as we have not been able to quantify these two items of expenditure with a useful degree of precision. Nevertheless, we are encouraged to believe that, with an expenditure of national resources no greater than that which would have been necessary on the national libraries had they continued their independent existences and present policies, it will be possible to develop a national library information system unequalled elsewhere, providing greatly improved services for users of every type and covering all kinds of literature. This does not imply, however, that expenditure on the services of the national libraries will not have to increase; indeed, it is inevitable in our view, that information facilities of all types are bound to become more costly as the total quantity of recorded knowledge grows and as better services are more heavily used. If the national investment on information systems is to give a worthwhile return, the principles of accountable management, to which the Fulton Committee drew attention and which we have interpreted in the context of the national libraries, will need to be rigorously applied, irrespective of whether the costs of the services are met from charges to users or directly from public funds.

LIST OF RECOMMENDATIONS

LENDING AND PHOTOCOPYING (CHAPTER 11)

The supply of scientific literature

1. The relative costs and the advantages to both the user and the supplying library of satisfying a request by loan or by photocopy should be investigated. (Paragraph 241)

2. The NLLST should continue to develop generally along its present lines, but placing greater emphasis on photocopying, if trends in demand indicate that this is desirable. (Paragraph 242)

3. The NRLSI should concentrate its photocopying resources on meeting the requirements of its personal visitors, and those of remote users, for material —such as patent literature—which is not available from Boston Spa. (Paragraph 242)

4. The SML should continue to make a small contribution to national lending and photocopying services, by helping to supply publications not available from other sources. Its assistance would be required mainly for older scientific publications, particularly the literature of the history of science and technology. (Paragraph 242)

5. The services at present provided by the NCL in assisting the location of rarely used material would still to some extent be necessary in the future. (Paragraph 242)

6. The bibliographic activities of the TIL Centre, relating to report literature, partly duplicate those of the NLLST without either or both covering all reports to a sufficient standard. The existing bibliographic resources should be co-ordinated, so as to produce as economically as possible complete bibliographic coverage of all reports. (Paragraph 245)

7. A National Reports Centre at Boston Spa should be established, with the responsibility to collect and process reports in all subjects. The services now available for reports at the NLLST should be incorporated in the new centre. (Paragraph 248)

8. The development of a National Reports Centre would make possible beneficial sharing of work with the TIL Centre at St. Mary Cray. The duplication of services for supplying reports which at present exists between the TIL Centre and the NLLST should thereby be reduced to a minimum. (Paragraphs 246 and 248)

The supply of literature for the humanities and the social sciences

9. The loan stocks of the NCL should be transferred to Boston Spa. (Paragraph 259)

10. Future additions to the loan stocks at Boston Spa should be made in cases where: (i) there is a need for the fastest possible service, (ii) the intensity of demand is likely to be sufficiently high to produce an acceptably low unit cost of issue, or (iii) the material is not available more cheaply from another source. (Paragraph 260)

Inter-library lending

11. The highest priority should be given to bringing the union catalogues fully up to date. (Paragraph 264)

12. Financial assistance should be available to enable a few large libraries to work in particularly close association with the national inter-library lending service. (Paragraph 265)

13. The university libraries of Oxford and Cambridge are particularly well fitted for such a role. The possibility of associating them in this way with the national lending service should be explored. (Paragraph 266)

14. The extensive and routine application of Telex to inter-library lending should be given detailed consideration. (Paragraph 268)

15. High priority should be given to improving and developing the photo-copying service at the BML and its outhouses. Adequate provision for photocopying should be made in any new buildings to be provided in the future. (Paragraph 272)

16. Because the supply of information should not be impeded by copyright restrictions, initiative should be taken by the Government to obtain as soon as possible an agreement to simplify the procedures and reduce the limitations imposed by copyright, whilst protecting the interests of authors and publishers. (Paragraph 273)

17. Where photocopying cannot provide a satisfactory solution and where material is not easily available from any other source, the national reference collections should lend from their stocks. (Paragraph 273)

18. Publications legally deposited, material which could not be replaced in any form from any other source, or items of high intrinsic value should, however, not be available on loan from the reference collections. (Paragraph 274)

19. Items from the stocks of the national reference collections should be loaned only for use in another library and for a short period of time. (Paragraph 275)

REFERENCE FACILITIES (CHAPTER 12)

The arts and the humanities

20. A national reference library should not carry out functions which are the responsibilities of local authorities. The design of any new building for the BML should, therefore, provide for such public reference facilities as cannot be made available, even in the long term, in other ways. (Paragraph 283)

21. Although the administration of the BML will in future require staff exceptionally well versed in library technology and in the most modern methods of library management, it will continue to need substantial numbers of subject specialists. It is essential, therefore, that the conditions of service and career prospects should continue to be attractive to scholars. (Paragraph 284)

22. The BML's future policy for the arts and humanities should be to continue to provide as complete coverage as possible in those subjects where its collections are uniquely good. In others, where large special libraries are already catering for a substantial proportion of the national demand, the BML's policy for acquisition should take into account the existing pattern of usage, so that the resources of all these libraries may be utilised most effectively. (Paragraph 285)

23. The Department of Prints and Drawings should be regarded as a library department and should be included in any consideration of national reference library services. (Paragraph 287)

24. The future administration of the British Library of Art at the V & A Museum should be the subject of further examination by the Department of Education and Science, in association with a national libraries organisation. (Paragraph 291)

The social sciences

25. The principles which should govern the acquisitions policies of the BML for the arts and humanities should also be applied to social science material. However, there should be no major change of the library's acquisitions policy for the social sciences which might prejudice its value in serving inter-disciplinary studies. (Paragraph 294)

26. The organisation which will administer the national libraries should, in collaboration with the Social Science Research Council, initiate discussions with the BLPES and other interested institutions, in order to collect and make available in the most practical and economic way the primary literature necessary for research in the social sciences. (Paragraph 297)

Science and technology

27. Regional reference facilities serving major industrial areas should be developed: (i) to provide a good standard of general coverage, for the most part relating to recent serial publications; (ii) to include specialist provision reflecting the particular characteristics and requirements of local industry; (iii) to give convenient access to all the principal bibliographic aids, in order that lightly used material not available locally may be identified and obtained through the NLLST. (Paragraph 305)

28. The coverage of the NRLSI should be adequate to satisfy needs for: (i) a comprehensive collection of British and foreign patent literature; (ii) such technical and trade literature as is associated with (i) above; (iii) other technical and scientific literature which, with (ii), would satisfy a high proportion of the south-east regional reference requirements, in association with other libraries in the region; (iv) bibliographic, information and referral services needed to support the library's other operations. (Paragraph 307)

29. The BML should continue to hold and collect scientific publications likely to be of importance to historians and other principal users of the library. This collection should differ in character from and be much smaller than that at the NRLSI. (Paragraph 310)

30. The SML should not be administered by a national libraries organisation, but should be fully integrated with the Lyon Playfair Library of Imperial College. (Paragraph 315)

31. When the two libraries are combined, the privileges and services at present available to the Science Museum staff should continue. To ensure this, the Museum should be represented on all the bodies controlling the administration and policy of the combined library and its acquisitions policy should reflect these responsibilities. (Paragraph 316)

32. The photocopying and other services at present provided by the SML for the other South Kensington museums should be maintained. (Paragraph 316)

33. Adequate funds, administratively separate from those of Imperial College, should be made available for the continued development of the special collection in the history of science and technology. Similar provision should also be made in respect of any other specialised material which is at present provided primarily for the use of the Science Museum staff. (Paragraph 316)

34. Lending and photocopying from the combined stocks through the national network should be on conditions at least as unrestricted as those of the SML's at present. (Paragraph 316)

Outhousing material from the BML and NRLSI

35. In view of the exceptionally high cost of storing library material in central London, lightly used material in the BML and NRLSI, including legal deposit publications in this category, should be outhoused to one or more stores on low cost land. (Paragraphs 309, 324, 341)

36. Outhouses should be purpose-built and, if at all possible, have facilities for readers. (Paragraph 324)

37. Lightly used material selected for outhousing should be stored where it can, if necessary, be transferred to the main reference collection within twenty-four hours. (Paragraph 324)

38. Proliferation of widely scattered outhouses should be avoided. (Paragraph 324)

149

39. The storage of newspapers and periodicals at Colindale should continue, but microform copies of the most heavily used items should be permanently available for consultation in the main reading rooms of the BML. (Paragraph 325)

The internal organisation of the BML and NRLSI

40. A new national reference library to replace the BML should consist essentially of specialised reference facilities with their own reading rooms and associated services. In this way the library would adapt its resources to the specialised information requirements of researchers in different disciplines, whilst retaining the unique advantages of its vast stocks and broad coverage for scholars engaged in inter-disciplinary studies. (Paragraph 326)

41. The new library building should be readily adaptable to changing needs, changing services and rapid developments in library technology. (Paragraph 326)

42. Because of the great difficulties associated with administering a very large open access library, only the most heavily and generally used publications—including standard reference works, indexes, abstracts and certain periodicals—should be directly accessible to readers. However, the present policy at the BML of giving selected readers access to the closed stacks in exceptional circumstances should continue and, in the new library, possibly be extended. (Paragraph 327)

43. Because the disadvantages of the open access form of organisation will be much less important in the case of the NRLSI, this library should continue to provide for some time ahead open access to a substantial proportion of its stocks. (Paragraph 328)

44. Because of the impact that automated information retrieval systems are likely to make on scientific libraries in the decades immediately ahead, it is improbable that the initial arrangements within a new scientific reference library will continue unchanged for more than a small part of the expected life of a new building. Special attention should be paid to this point when a new building to replace the existing NRLSI is designed and constructed. (Paragraph 330)

The administration of the BML and the NRLSI

45. Although it will be desirable to maintain some links between the library and antiquities departments of the British Museum, the administrative responsibilities for the library should be separated completely from those for the museum. (Paragraph 333)

46. The four library departments of the BML—Printed Books; Manuscripts; Oriental Printed Books and Manuscripts; and Prints and Drawings—should become the National Reference Library. (Paragraph 333)

47. With the establishment of a national libraries organisation, the NRLSI should be administered separately from the BML. The NRLSI should become the Central Science and Patent Collections. (Paragraph 334)

The preservation of British printed material

48. The present arrangement for legal deposit at the BML should, in principle, continue. However, the relevant provision of the 1911 Copyright Act should be amended so as to require the deposit of one copy of all British publications with a national libraries organisation. (Paragraph 337)

49. The reference division of a national libraries organisation should continue the BML's special responsibility for actively collecting and preserving important unpublished British material. (Paragraph 338)

50. Because of the continually increasing task of storing and preserving national archival material, the possibility of retaining only a proportion of legally deposited material should be examined in detail. (Paragraph 340)

51. A national libraries organisation should have the responsibility for ensuring that adequate research into methods of archival preservation is put in hand. (Paragraph 343)

52. It should also be empowered to dispose of legally deposited material where it considers that a microform or photocopy is likely to be an acceptable substitute to users. (Paragraph 343)

53. The problems of preserving material published in media other than the written word should be regularly re-appraised by the Secretary of State for Education and Science, in consultation with the national libraries organisation and other relevant bodies. (Paragraph 344)

The site for the National Reference Library

54. Geographical separation of the library departments of the British Museum from the antiquities departments would not have advantages for staff or visitors nor would it assist the creation of a national libraries service. From library considerations alone, therefore, the Bloomsbury site is the most suitable for the NRL. (Paragraph 358)

55. If, for other reasons, it is decided to make such a separation, a site for the National Reference Library should be found in central London which would be convenient to those who normally work in the institutions in both Bloomsbury and Aldwych. (Paragraph 359)

The site for the Central Science and Patent Collections

56. There is no compelling reason why the Central Science and Patent Collections should be immediately adjacent to the National Reference Library. On the other hand, there is also no compelling reason why the CSPC should be sited in the immediate vicinity of the Patent Office. They should, however, be in central London. (Paragraph 366)

151

57. The national libraries organisation should co-ordinate and encourage the application of automatic data processing to the bibliographic services now being carried out by professional bodies and research associations, so as to develop as speedily as practicable full bibliographic coverage in machine-readable form.   (Paragraph 377)

58. The feasibility of applying automatic data processing to both the internal management operations and the services of the reference, lending, bibliographic, and administrative divisions of a national libraries organisation should be studied in detail and without delay.   (Paragraph 385)

59. To ensure the closest possible co-operation between the national libraries and other libraries and information services, there should be wide consultation between these bodies during the course of the feasibility study.   (Paragraph 386)

BIBLIOGRAPHIC FACILITIES (CHAPTER 14)

The concept and functions of a National Bibliographic Service

60. Within a national libraries organisation there should be established a National Bibliographic Service, which initially would combine the bibliographic activities of the BML, the NCL, the NRLSI, the NLLST, and the BNB. Its main functions should be the compilation and publication of an index of all British publications, the production of catalogue entries, the answering of bibliographic enquiries, bibliographic research, and the co-ordination of national and international bibliographic work. (Paragraph 408)

61. In the future, the National Bibliographic Service should develop so as to meet as nearly as possible the bibliographic needs of all types of user. However, bibliographic work should in general be undertaken only where its cost is likely to be recovered or, in the case of a continuing service, where there are good prospects of its becoming self-supporting in a reasonable length of time. (Paragraph 410)

Legal Deposit

62. The 1911 Copyright Act should be amended to require publishers to effect legal deposit with the national libraries organisation on or before the date of publication. (Paragraph 412)

Abstracting and indexing services for science and technology

63. The National Bibliographic Service should be given the responsibility for co-ordinating the total national scientific bibliographic effort and for representing internationally British interests in this field. (Paragraph 415)

64. The Service should extend the effort being made by the NLLST to fill gaps in existing bibliographic coverage. (Paragraph 416)

65. The National Bibliographic Service should have sufficient resources to carry out bibliographic research necessary for the development of new techniques and of national and international bibliographic standards. (Paragraph 416)

66. The responsibilities now exercised by OSTI in these areas should be transferred to the National Bibliographic Service. (Paragraph 417)

Translations

67. The functions of Aslib in indexing translations should be incorporated into the National Bibliographic Service, together with those at present being carried out by the NLLST. (Paragraph 418)

68. The Russian Translation Service provided by the NLLST should be maintained and a similar service should be available for translating from Japanese. (Paragraph 419)

69. All translation facilities should be charged for on a properly costed basis. (Paragraph 419)

Scientific information services

70. In order to avoid undesirable duplication of effort, any information or referral services provided by the national science libraries should be developed in close co-ordination with each other and with other services provided by agencies outside the national libraries system. (Paragraph 420)

The location of the bibliographic services

71. The compilaiton of the national bibliography, most of the cataloguing work, and the main bibliographic enquiry services will have to be centred near the national reference collections and should, therefore, be situated in central London. (Paragraph 421)

72. Some of the specialised bibliographic services, particularly those associated with scientific literature, should, however, be based on Boston Spa. (Paragraph 422)

A loan locating centre

73. There should be a single centre to which loan and photocopy requests for all material in every subject should be addressed. This should be at Boston Spa. (Paragraphs 424 and 425)

74. The union catalogues should remain in central London only until such time as the relative importance of the speculative search has substantially declined and the main centre of the National Bibliographic Service is well established. (Paragraph 430)

75. Thereafter, the union catalogues should be transferred to the loan locating centre at Boston Spa. (Paragraph 430)

76. The loan locating service should be administered as an integral part of the National Bibliographic Service. (Paragraph 431)

Safeguards for existing collections

77. The administration of a national libraries organisation should be empowered to offer financial or other support to important libraries facing acute financial difficulties, in return for an undertaking that their stocks and services would be available to meet national demands. (Paragraph 433)

A policy for future acquisitions

78. Because it is not practicable for the National Reference Library itself to cover comprehensively all subjects, schemes of co-operative acquisition between the national libraries and others will be necessary if adequate provision of foreign publications for research is to be obtained. (Paragraph 440)

79. Co-operative acquisition between libraries in Britain should be based on a series of agreements of limited scope, each involving co-operation between a national library, which would usually be the NRL and, at the most, a small number of other libraries. (Paragraph 442)

80. Although ·most of the participating libraries would probably be in London, appropriate provincial collections should also be included. (Paragraph 442)

81. A national libraries organisation should have discretion in negotiating the terms of particular schemes of co-operative acquisition with the libraries concerned. (Paragraph 443)

82. Policy relating to the operation of particular schemes should be determined in consultation with panels of subject experts and users, rather than solely by librarians. (Paragraph 443)

83. A national libraries organisation should be empowered to make grants to co-operating libraries in recognition of their national responsibilities. (Paragraph 443)

84. There should be safeguards incorporated into co-operative acquisition agreements to ensure that the material acquired for the nation by any library not administered by a national libraries organisation would at all times be adequately protected; that it would be made available as freely as the holdings of the National Reference Library; and that it would not be lost to the nation through any change in the administration or location of the co-operating library. (Paragraph 443)

85. In order that the needs of users of the co-operating libraries may be met, material acquired by the National Reference Library under a co-operative acquisition scheme should be available on loan to co-operating libraries, even though it may not be among those limited categories of material available for loan through the national inter-library lending service. The conditions governing arrangements of this kind must, however, ensure that the material is not jeopardised. (Paragraph 443)

Other kinds of co-operation

86. A national libraries organisation should have the responsibility to identify situations where other forms of co-operation might prove advantageous and to negotiate suitable agreements in such circumstances. (Paragraph 446)

National Libraries of Scotland and Wales

87. A national libraries organisation should have particular responsibilities for initiating discussions with the Scottish and Welsh National Libraries where it considers co-operation desirable. (Paragraph 447)

RESEARCH AND TRAINING (CHAPTER 16)

Library Research

88. In order to improve the effectiveness of the existing services of the national libraries and to evolve new services in response to users' requirements, the following types of research relating to the national libraries should be undertaken: (i) the collection of statistical data, (ii) operational research, (iii) research related to forward planning, (iv) research concerning new applications of computers, (v) research and development on library technology. (Paragraphs 454 to 463)

89. A national libraries organisation should have adequate resources to meet such research requirements. (Paragraph 465)

90. These resources should be entirely at the disposal of the organisation's administration to deploy in the ways it considers most useful. It should establish such research facilities of its own as it considers necessary and it should be empowered to sponsor in other libraries or research institutions that research which it is unable to carry out within its own organisation. (Paragraphs 465, 466)

91. It should be encouraged to carry out or fund research projects of wide application to other library and information activities, so long as the research has some relevance to the efficient operation and potential development of the national library services. This implies that a national libraries organisation would increasingly assume many of the responsibilities now exercised by OSTI. (Paragraph 466)

92. Consideration should be given to the creation of machinery to bring together the major national interests engaged in the development of information techniques, so as to co-ordinate effectively the total research effort and to assist in the formulation of national research policies. (Paragraph 467)

Education and Training

93. A national libraries organisation should have as one of its important responsibilities the task of making the results of its research and development as widely known as possible to librarians and to others for whom the knowledge would be useful. (Paragraph 468)

94. The contribution of the national libraries to professional training should be to supplement the existing arrangements, in collaboration with those at present responsible for the training of librarians. (Paragraph 469)

95. Appropriate activities should include courses and conferences on specialist topics and research, practical training for undergraduate and non-graduate students who intend eventually to make a career in one of the national libraries, and the provision of facilities for post graduate research. (Paragraph 469)

96. Short courses of the type now organised by the NLLST and the NRLSI for their users should be continued and extended to cover other activities and services of a national libraries organisation. (Paragraph 470)

The National Libraries Authority

97. The existing administrative arrangements for the BML—including the NRLSI—the NCL, the NLLST, and the BNB should be terminated and these institutions should become the responsibility of a new statutory and independent public body, acting on behalf of the Crown, to be known as the National Libraries Authority. The Authority should assume full administrative responsibilities for those functions and services of OSTI and Aslib which should form part of the national libraries organisation. (Paragraph 482)

98. The stock and the appropriate parts of the property of the existing institutions, with the exceptions given in recommendation 117, should be vested in the Authority. (Paragraph 482)

99. The Authority should employ all the staff necessary to fulfil its functions. (Paragraph 483)

The National Libraries Management Board

100. The National Libraries Authority should be administered by a board which would exercise corporate responsibilities for management policies. (Paragraph 484)

101. This Board should consist of a Chairman, a Secretary and a maximum of three other full time members, together with up to three part-time members. (Paragraph 486)

102. All members of the Management Board should be appointed by the Secretary of State for Education and Science. (Paragraph 486)

103. The Chairman of the Management Board should be the accounting officer and, as such, be responsible to the Secretary of State for the disposition of the Authority's resources. (Paragraph 487)

104. The Authority should give careful attention to the effective formulation and presentation of proposals for the maintenance and development of its services. The Secretary should have special responsibilities for this. (Paragraph 488)

105. Formal administrative machinery should be established to enable staff and personnel matters to be adequately represented at Board level. (Paragraph 489)

106. Other members of the Management Board should have particular responsibilities in ensuring the successful implementation of different aspects of the Authority's policies. The ways in which these responsibilities are distributed should reflect the qualities and expertise of the different members. (Paragraph 490)

107. The Minister of Technology should be consulted over the appointment of one of the full-time members to the Board. (Paragraph 491)

108. The part-time members should be paid for their services. (Paragraph 492)

109. Part-time members should normally hold office for a period of three years, renewable once only. (Paragraph 492)

110. In the appointment of the part-time members account should be taken of the need to establish and maintain channels of communication between the Authority and other library and information systems and the special position of the NRL. The regular change in the composition of the part-time members should reflect developments in the Authority's services and modifications in the character of the Board's responsibilities. (Paragraph 492)

The Executive Committee

111. An Executive Committee, composed of the heads of all the major service units in the Authority and chaired by the Chairman of the Management Board should be established. (Paragraph 493)

112. There should also be a structure of standing and *ad hoc* sub-committees, on which the appropriate Management Board members and senior executives would serve together. (Paragraph 493)

Advisory Councils

113. An Advisory Council should be associated with each major library unit or service. (Paragraph 494)

114. The Head of the unit concerned should be an *ex officio* member of the relevant Advisory Council; the remaining membership should reflect, though not exclusively, the use that is made of its services. Management Board members should have a right of attendance at any meeting of an Advisory Council. (Paragraph 494)

Trustees of the National Reference Library

115. A new trustee body to be known as the Trustees of the National Reference Library should be appointed by the Government. (Paragraph 495)

116. In order to maintain the historic links between the new library and the British Museum, the Trustees of the NRL should have a minority of members who are also Trustees of the British Museum. (Paragraph 495)

117. The Trustees of the NRL should be invested with those library funds and that material to be housed in the NRL which it is possible to identify as having been privately donated or bequeathed in the past in trust to the Trustees of the British Museum. (Paragraph 496)

118. The Trustees should ensure that the expenditure of trust fund capital or income and the handling of material held in trust were in accord with the terms of the original donations or bequests. However, the determining of the particular use and disposition to which Trust material and funds might be put should rest with the Management Board of the National Libraries Authority. (Paragraph 496)

159

119. The Trustees of the NRL should have representation on that library's Advisory Council up to two fifths of the total membership. (Paragraph 497)

120. The Secretary of State should appoint one of the part-time members of the Management Board from a list of names suggested by the Trustees of the NRL. (Paragraph 498)

Relations with Central Government

121. The responsibilities of the Secretary of State for Education and Science for libraries and for scientific and technical information should be administered through a single branch in DES. (Paragraph 501)

122. The Government should examine the feasibility of establishing consultative machinery to advise it on policy concerning the development and co-ordination of national information services—whether library-based or otherwise—which are the direct or indirect responsibilities of Government departments. (Paragraph 501)

Staffing and Grading

123. New conditions of service resulting from the creation of a unified staff structure throughout the Authority should not be on balance to the disadvantage of any individual on the staff of the existing institutions. (Paragraph 503)

Financial Arrangements

124. All public finance for the Authority should be derived through a single source, which should be the Secretary of State for Education and Science. (Paragraphs 483 and 505)

125. All premises, maintenance, services and equipment supplied by or through Government departments should be paid for by the Authority in terms of their current market values. (Paragraph 505)

126. The Management Board, through its accounting officer, should be required to present the Authority's accounts in a form which indicates the cost of each part of its operations, including the realistic cost of buildings and equipment. (Paragraph 505)

127. While special arrangements might have to be made for the largest capital expenditure, the financial arrangements should be such as to give the Management Board the greatest possible freedom to deploy the Authority's resources in the most effective way. In particular, the Board should be allowed to apply profits from its services and savings from its administration to the further development of the Authority's services. (Paragraph 505)

Timing

128. The new administrative system for the national libraries should be established without delay. (Paragraph 506)

129. The National Libraries Authority should take over at its inception the administration of all the services and institutions to be under its control. (Paragraph 507).

130. The Management Board should assume responsibility at the earliest opportunity for the design of the new libraries in central London.   (Paragraph 507)

131. The structure of the Management Board should be reviewed at the end of its first five years.   (Paragraph 508)

Financial Implications

132. If the national investment in information systems is to give a worthwhile return, the principles of accountable management should be rigorously applied, irrespective of whether the costs of services are met from charges to users or directly from public funds.   (Paragraph 533)

APPENDICES TO THE REPORT OF
THE NATIONAL LIBRARIES COMMITTEE
MARCH 1969

APPENDIX A

BODIES AND INDIVIDUALS WHO SUBMITTED WRITTEN EVIDENCE

(a) Bodies which submitted Written Evidence

Advisory Committee on Scientific and Technical Information
African Studies Association of the United Kingdom
Antiquarian Booksellers' Association
Aslib
Association of Commonwealth Universities
Association of Contemporary Historians
Association of First Division Civil Servants (British Museum Branch)
Association of London Chief Librarians
Association of Municipal Corporations
Association of University Teachers
Association of University Teachers (Scotland)
U.K. Atomic Energy Authority
Berkshire Libraries Group
Bibliographical Society
Bodleian Library
Booksellers Association
British Academy
British Institute of Management
British Museum
British National Bibliography
British Nutrition Foundation Ltd.
B.P. Chemicals Ltd.
British Society for the History of Science
British Standards Institution
British Steel Corporation (Midland Group)
      ”   ”   ”   (Northern and Tubes Group)
C. A. Parsons Ltd.
Cambridge Scientific Instruments Ltd.
Chartered Institute of Patent Agents
Chemical Society
County Councils Association
Committee on Biological Information
Committee of Departmental Librarians
Committee on Latin America
Confederation of British Industry
Conference on Library Co-operation
Copyright Agency of London
Council of City Research and Information Libraries
Council of Engineering Institutions
Denis Ferranti Group
Department of Education and Science
Dr. Williams's Library
English Electric Diesels Ltd.
Geological Society of London
Geologists' Association
H.M. Stationery Office
Historical Association
I.C.I. Dyestuffs Division

Inner London Education Authority
Institute of British Geographers
Institute of Directors
Institute of Information Scientists
Institute of Physics and the Physical Society
Institution of Professional Civil Servants
John Laing Ltd.
Joint Committee on Books for Children
The Librarians of Institutes and Schools of Education
Library Advisory Council (England)
       ,,   ,,   ,,   (Wales)
Library Association
London Boroughs Association
London Library
Medical Research Council
Ministry of Technology
Modern Humanities Research Association
Monsanto Chemical Industries Ltd.
Museums Association
National Book League
National Central Library
National Committee on Regional Library Co-operation
National Institute of Economic and Social Research
National Lending Library for Science and Technology
National Library of Scotland
National Library of Wales
Patent Office
Political and Economic Planning
Pressed Steel Fisher Ltd.
Public Record Office
Publishers Association
Rolls-Royce Ltd.
Royal Commission on Historical Manuscripts
Royal Commonwealth Society
Royal Geographical Society
Royal Historical Society
Royal Institute of British Architects, Library Board
Royal Institute of International Affairs
Royal National Institute for the Deaf
Royal Society of London
Royal Society of Edinburgh
Science Museum Library
Science Research Council
Scottish Central Library
Scottish Counties of Cities Association
Scottish Education Department
Shell Research Ltd.
Social Science Research Council
Society for Theatre Research
Society of Antiquaries of London
Society of Authors
Society of County Librarians
Society of Genealogists
Society of Public Teachers of Law
St. Pancras North Liberal Association
Standing Conference on Library Materials on Africa

Standing Conference of Librarians of the Libraries of the University of London
Standing Conference of National and University Libraries
Tamworth Borough Council
Trade Marks, Patents and Designs Federation
Trades Union Congress
Treasury, Management Services (Computer) Division
Universities Council for Adult Education
Urban District Councils Association
Victoria and Albert Museum
Wellcome Museum of Medical Science
Welsh Office
West Midlands Regional Library Bureau
Workers' Educational Association

UNIVERSITIES

Aberdeen
Aston in Birmingham
Bath University of Technology
Birmingham
Bradford
Bristol
Brunel
Cambridge
City
Dundee
Durham
East Anglia
Edinburgh
Essex
Exeter
Glasgow
Heriot-Watt
Hull
Keele
Kent
Lancaster
Leeds
Leicester
Liverpool
London
Loughborough University of Technology
Manchester
Newcastle-upon-Tyne
Nottingham
Oxford
Reading
St. Andrews
Salford
Sheffield
Southampton
Stirling
Strathclyde
Surrey
Sussex
Warwick
York

Queen's, Belfast
Ulster

OTHER UNIVERSITY INSTITUTES, COLLEGES AND SCHOOLS
London
Bedford College
Chelsea College of Science and Technology
Imperial College of Science and Technology
Institute of Advanced Legal Studies
Institute of Classical Studies
Institute of Commonwealth Studies
Institute of Historical Research
King's College
London Graduate School of Business Studies
London School of Economics and Political Science
School of Oriental and African Studies
School of Slavonic and Eastern European Studies
Warburg Institute
University College

Manchester
Manchester Business School
Manchester Institute of Science and Technology

Wales
University College of Aberystwyth
University College of Bangor
University College of Cardiff
University College of Swansea
University of Wales, Institute of Science and Technology
St. David's College, Lampeter
Welsh National School of Medicine

(b) **Individuals who submitted Written Evidence**
Mr. F. B. Adams, Jnr., Director, The Pierpont Morgan Library, New York
Mr. A. Anderson, Librarian, Heriot-Watt University
Professor J. C. Anderson, Imperial College of Science and Technology
Mr. R. C. M. Arnot
Mr. K. J. Baker and Mr. R. Moss
Mr. J. Barker
Professor G. W. S. Barrow and colleagues, Department of Modern History, University
    of Newcastle-on-Tyne
Mr. R. B. Bateman, Librarian, City of Leeds College of Education
Mr. M. Belton, Librarian, Safety in Mines Research Establishment
Dr. R. K. Callow, Rothampstead Experimental Station
Mr. E. B. Ceadel, Librarian, University of Cambridge
Dr. G. Chandler, City Librarian, Liverpool
Mrs. G. Chinnick and colleagues
Professor J. L. Clifford, Department of English and Comparative Literature, Columbia
    University, New York
Professor K. de B. Codrington
Mr. H. M. Colvin, St. John's College, University of Oxford
Mr. L. Corbett, Information Officer, AWRE, Aldermaston
Mr. P. R. D. Corrigan
Lord Cranbrook
Miss V. Cromwell, University of Sussex
Mr. C. A. Crossley
Dr. E. Cruickshanks and colleagues

Professor R. W. Davies and Professor R. E. Smith, Department of Russian Language and Literature, University of Birmingham

Mr. A. J. Dickson, Tutor Librarian, Ealing Technical College

Professor R. P. Dore and colleagues, LSE and SOAS

Mr. F. Earnshaw, Librarian, University of Bradford

Professor R. W. V. Elliott, School of Language and Literature, The Flinders University of South Australia

Mr. R. D. L. Felton

Mr. N. R. Fisk

Mr. W. A. B. Gardener

Lord Gardiner

Mr. N. S. Gardiner, Services Electronics Research Laboratory, Ministry of Defence

Mr. P. Glencross

Mr. G. Grant McKenzie

Mr. W. L. Guttsman, Librarian, University of East Anglia

Mr. D. B. Hague

Mr. P. Havard-Williams, Librarian, Queen's University, Belfast

Miss B. Henrey

Mrs. T. G. G. Heywood

Dr. F. Hilton

Dr. K. W. Humphreys, Librarian, University of Birmingham

Mr. B. Hutchison

Professor R. S. Hutton

Professor R. Irwin and Mr. A. G. Watson, School of Librarianship and Archives, University of London

Mr. E. Junge

Professor J. Kenner

Mr. R. Landau and Mr. C. Price

Mr. M. B. Line, Librarian, Bath University of Technology

Mr. K. A. Mallaber, Librarian, Board of Trade

Mr. A. J. Mayne

Miss F. Millard

Mr. R. Moss

Professor J. Osburn, Associate Professor of History, Panhandle State College, Oklahoma

Dr. Thomas Parry, Vice Chancellor, University College of Wales

Mr. J. G. Pemberton, Assistant Librarian, University of Warwick

Mr. J. V. Pepper, Royal Naval College, Greenwich

Professor D. B. Quinn, School of History, University of Liverpool

Dr. F. W. Ratcliffe, Librarian, University of Manchester

Mr. D. T. Richnell, Librarian, University of London

Miss M. Rooker, Librarian, Huddersfield College of Education (Technical)

Dr. W. A. Smeaton, University College, London

Mr. P. A. Snow

Mr. P. Stockham, Dillon's University Bookshop Limited

Mr. W. C. Sturtevant, Institute of Social Anthropology, University of Oxford

Mr. S. C. Sutton, Librarian and Keeper, India Office Library

Mrs. J. Varley

Mr. R. Vosper, Librarian, University of California, Los Angeles

Mr. R. A. Wall, Deputy Librarian, Loughborough University of Technology

Mr. L. J. Wayman

Mr. J. D. Welding

Mr. T. Whitehall, Information Officer, Brooke Bond Research Laboratories

Mr. J. S. Whittingham

Mr. D. M. Wilson, Department of English, University College, London

Miss R. Wood

SUMMARY OF THE MAIN FINDINGS OF THE SURVEY OF THE BRITISH MUSEUM LIBRARY, APRIL, 1968

Survey carried out and Summary prepared by

THE ECONOMIST INTELLIGENCE UNIT LIMITED

CONTENTS

Symbols used in the Statistical Appendix

* = less than 1 per cent

– = nil

D. Questionnaire

SUMMARY OF THE MAIN FINDINGS OF THE SURVEY OF THE BRITISH MUSEUM LIBRARY

INTRODUCTION

A survey of the British Museum library was carried out over a six-week period beginning 29th March 1968 and ending 2nd May 1968. The broad objectives were to provide information on:

1. **Readers' characteristics**
   (a) Occupation and qualifications
   (b) Place of residence
   (c) Duration and frequency of visits
   (d) Reasons for visits.

2. **Readers' needs**
   (a) Usage of different departments and services
   (b) Methods of work
   (c) Use of catalogues and services.

The survey was carried out by means of a self-completed questionnaire. Questionnaires were issued to all readers using the library on six separate days during the six-week period; these days were selected randomly so that each day of the working week at the library (Monday to Saturday inclusive) was represented. Those readers who were present on more than one of the six survey days were asked to fill in a separate questionnaire during each visit.

The total number of visits sampled by this method was 3,777. This number was subsequently reduced to the 3,000 level indicated in the Economist Intelligence Unit proposal; in fact the number of questionnaires analysed was 3,059.

Attention is drawn to two points in the use of the following data. First, the figures given in the statistical appendix, as well as in the accompanying volumes of computer output, show a separate analysis for " visits " and " people ". The " visits " columns relate to the total number of visits made during the course of the survey irrespective of the number of visits made by individual readers. In the analysis by " people " readers who visited the library on more than one occasion during the survey have only been counted once. The number of these readers was 811 or 27 per cent of the total sample.

Secondly, the results refer only to a six-week period which may or may not be representative of readership patterns for the whole year. This limitation was recognised before the survey took place, but was accepted owing to the time scale necessary for the preparation of evidence for the Committee. Some check on the representative nature of the survey will be obtained from the follow-up survey carried out in the third week of the peak use month of August, but even then the true annual picture cannot be drawn with certainty.

A. Readers' Characteristics

1. *Occupation* (See Table 1)

Academics and students as a group are easily the dominant users of the library. Together they formed over two thirds of the total readership during the survey period. Half the readers in this group were postgraduate students; the majority of the rest were university staff.

Apart from academics and students, the only other significant occupational categories using the library were freelance writers and professional researchers.

169

Together, these categories formed some 15 per cent of the total readership, with freelance writers outnumbering professional researchers by a ratio of 2 : 1.

2. *Type and age of readers* (See Table 2)

The 151 readers with temporary tickets during the survey accounted for only 5 per cent of the total number of " visits " or 7 per cent of the " people " using the library.

Apart from temporary readers, over a half of all those with readers' tickets obtained their ticket within the last three years; most of these readers were postgraduate students or university staff members. Nearly another fifth of the readers' tickets were issued between 1959 and 1963, and a further tenth were issued between 1953 and 1959.

3. *Place of residence* (See Tables 3 to 6)

(*a*) *All readers* (Tables 3 and 4). Two thirds of the readers using the library during the survey period were living in the London postal area. Two thirds of these readers were living more than five miles away from the Museum, with the majority living between five and ten miles distance. Another fifth were living within two miles of the Museum. No doubt this proportion was increased by the large number (a third of all readers) of readers who had come to London especially to visit the Museum and had taken up temporary residence as near the Museum as possible to facilitate their work. This conclusion is supported by the fact that well over half of those readers who gave their place of work as within two miles of the Museum did so because they were mainly working at the Museum.

As may be expected, the distribution of the remaining third of readers living outside London declined with increasing distance from London. Well over half of this group came from places in the Home Counties or South-East Counties.

(*b*) *Origins of students and academic staff* (Table 5). A separate breakdown of the origin of students and academic staff shows a fairly even distribution between universities and academic institutions in London compared with the rest of Britain and overseas, but declining gradually in that order. Unfortunately, a relatively large number of students and academics did not specify their college of origin so the proportions shown in Table 5 may not be strictly accurate.

Nearly two thirds of the students and academic staff from the London area came from six colleges or institutes which are situated within easy distance of the Museum. In order of importance these were: University College, the School of Oriental and African Studies, King's College, London School of Economics, Birkbeck College and Bedford College.

A fifth of the students and academics from British universities and institutions outside London came from Oxford and Cambridge. A further tenth came from other universities in south-east England (Universities of Sussex, Reading, Southampton, Kent, Essex and East Anglia).

(*c*) *Origins of readers who normally live overseas* (Table 6)

Foreign readers formed a third of the total number of readers using the library during the survey. Half of the foreign readers came from the USA and Canada, with Americans outnumbering the Canadians by more than 3 : 1. Readers from northern and central Europe were next in importance, accounting for a fifth of the total number of foreign visitors.

Nearly half of the readers from overseas were spending six months or longer at a British University or higher academic institution.

170

4. Frequency and duration of visits (See Tables 7 and 8)

(a) *Frequency* (Table 7). Some two thirds of the readers claimed that they visited the library at least once a week, and half of these claimed that they visited the library daily. These claims seem to be slightly exaggerated since only a half of all readers said that they visited the library within the week prior to the survey, although nearly another fifth said that they visited the library in the period between one and four weeks before the survey.

Students and university staff used the library more frequently than other occupational categories. Nearly half the postgraduate students claimed to make daily visits to the library; another third claimed to come weekly. University staff visited the library almost as frequently as students, but a quarter of them came at intervals of a month or three weeks compared with only some 15 per cent of postgraduate students. As may be expected readers from foreign universities made more intensive use of the library than students and staff of British universities, and readers from universities in London came more frequently than readers from universities in other parts of Britain. In terms of "people" rather than "visits", three fifths of readers from foreign universities came to the library every day, compared with a third of readers from London universities and a quarter of readers from other British universities.

Frequent daily visitors among other occupational categories were freelance writers and non-university academic staff. Most people in other occupational categories visited the library at weekly or monthly intervals.

Nearly half the readers using the department of Oriental Printed Books and Manuscripts visited the library daily, compared with a third for the Printed Books (by day) and Manuscripts departments. Only a fifth of the evening users of the Printed Books department came daily, but this department had correspondingly more weekly visitors.

(b) *Duration* (Table 8). A third of all readers expected that it would take more than three months to complete their work at the library. A similar proportion were short-term visitors spending no more than a week at the library; well over a third of these short-term visitors expected to spend no more than one day at the library.

Academics and freelance writers were fairly equally divided between short and long-term visitors whereas readers in other occupations were mostly short-term visitors. Within the academic group, a greater proportion of readers from foreign universities were long-term visitors whereas readers from British universities outside London were mostly short-term visitors.

There was also a significant variation in the expected length of visit of readers using the main library departments. Half the readers in the Oriental Printed Books and Manuscripts department expected to stay for a period exceeding three months, whereas a similar proportion of readers using the Manuscripts department expected their visit to be completed within a week. Readers using the Printed Books department were fairly equally divided between short and long-term visitors.

Length of visit increased sharply with frequency of visit. Well over half of the readers who used the library every day expected their stay to last more than three months; this proportion fell to a third for readers who visited the library weekly, and was negligible for those who visited the library less frequently.

The average time spent in the library on one day by all readers was $4\frac{1}{2}$ hours. The average was 5 hours for postgraduate students and university staff but dropped to 3 hours for readers from industry/commerce, librarians, and civil servants/local government. Temporary ticket holders spent less time in the library on average than regular readers. Readers using non-scientific subjects tended to spend slightly longer in the library than those using scientific subjects. Also readers using the Printed Books department tended

171

to spend longer in the library than those using the Manuscripts and Oriental Printed Books and Manuscripts department.

5. *Reason for visit* (See Table 9)

The great majority of readers use the library solely in relation to their work, although a fifth of all readers indicated that the reason for their visit was connected with their leisure interests as well as their work.

The analysis by occupation shows that whereas academics were using the library almost entirely in relation to their work, the reasons were more varied for other occupational groups. Freelance writers and professional researchers were using the library mainly in relation to their work, but between a quarter and a third of them were combining their work with leisure interest. Well over a third of the readers in the industry/commerce and civil service/local government occupational categories were using the library purely for leisure reasons. Librarians regarded their use of the library primarily as a mixture of work and leisure interests.

Readers using the Printed Books and Manuscripts departments followed the general pattern for all readers, but the Oriental Printed Books and Manuscripts department had a significantly higher proportion of readers using it for reasons connected with work, and evening use of the Printed Books department was significantly greater for leisure activities.

It is perhaps significant that a third of all readers believed that the British Museum is the only library in the United Kingdom which could provide everything that they required. Moreover, this proportion corresponds closely to the proportion of readers who had not tried to obtain their requirements in another library before going to the British Museum. There was little variation by occupational categories in readers who believed that the British Museum alone could satisfy their requirements, but the proportion was markedly higher for the Manuscripts department (four fifths of readers using this department) than for any other of the library departments.

B. Readers' Needs

1. *Subjects being read* (See Table 10)

The use of the library was concentrated on three subject fields: history (a half of all readers), literature (a third of all readers) and bibliography/general reference (a quarter of all readers). Relatively little use was made of books or literature in the following subject fields: children's books, mathematics (pure and applied), applied science and technology, biology/agriculture/geology, foreign law, medicine/pharmacology, and natural sciences. None of these subjects was being read by more than 2 per cent of the total number of readers.

A third of all readers indicated that they were seeking literature in one subject field only. Nearly another third were seeking literature in just two subject fields.

Academic readers were proportionally represented in all subject fields except biology/agriculture/geology, applied science and technology, heraldry and genealogy (in the case of postgraduate students) and arts/entertainments/recreation (in the case of university staff). There was a slight tendency for postgraduate students to be more interested in subjects such as law, economics, politics, literature and philology/linguistics, whereas university staff were more interested in theology, literature, philology/linguistics and bibliography/general reference. Of the remaining two major occupational categories of reader, freelance writers had above average interests in applied science and technology, medicine, biography, geography/local history and heraldry/genealogy; professional researchers had above average interests in medicine and heraldry/genealogy.

Of the foreign readers, those from USA and Canada had above average interest in

172

literature and British law, and those from Germany/Austria in philology/linguistics. In most other cases the sample size in each subject category was too small to be of real significance.

2. *Average number of items used per reader* (See Table 11)

On average, readers who knew what they wanted (i.e. author/title of book) before visiting the library used 5 items during their visit. Only half the total sample indicated that they used items that were unknown to them before their visit; for these readers the average number of items used was 1.8.

University staff and librarians used more items on average than other readers. Undergraduates and readers from industry/commerce used the least number of items, but in each category the average use was more than 3 items. A similar number of items was used by readers in the Oriental Printed Books department. Regular readers used more items than readers with temporary tickets.

3. *Use of the library and other British Museum departments* (See Tables 12 to 14)

(*a*) *Main library departments* (Table 12). Four fifths of all readers used the Printed Books department during the day, and another tenth used the same department in the evenings. The remainder were mostly using the Manuscripts department.

In the Printed Books department there were notably fewer academic readers in the evening and a corresponding increase of most other occupational categories of reader. The Manuscripts and Oriental Printed Books and Manuscripts department had a particularly high proportion of academic readers both from British and foreign universities. As may be expected, readers using the Oriental Printed Books and Manuscripts department came mainly from the School of Oriental and African Studies as well as from foreign universities.

The literature, theology, and biography collections were of particular interest to readers who had come to London specially to visit the British Museum. These readers were less interested in scientific subjects, law, heraldry/genealogy and geography/local history.

Few readers who had come to Britain for six months or more to a university or other higher academic institution were interested in heraldry/genealogy, applied science/technology, medicine or arts/entertainment/recreation, but they were well represented in all other subjects.

Temporary ticket holders were particularly interested in history, literature, and bibliography/general reference.

Within the Printed Books department, 175 visits were made to the State Paper Room, 83 to the Map Room, and 40 to the Music Room; 40 visitors also said that they intended to use the Newspaper Library at Colindale.

(*b*) *Other British Museum departments* (Tables 13 and 14). Only a quarter of all readers intended to use more than one of the library or other Museum departments on the day of their visit, and only two thirds of these considered such use essential. Multi-departmental use was mostly by professional researchers, freelance writers and non-university academic staff; all three categories, together with university academic staff, were most inclined to find such multi-departmental use essential.

The main use of Museum departments outside the Printed Books department was concentrated on the Manuscripts department (a third of those readers using more than one department followed by the departments of Oriental Printed Books and Manuscripts, and Prints and Drawings (each with a tenth of these readers using more than one department). None of the other Museum departments was used by more than

173

4 per cent of the readers using more than one department or by 1 per cent of the total sample of readers.

4. *Satisfaction of readers' needs* (See Tables 15 and 16)

Two thirds of the readers received all that they required during their visit. Less than 2 per cent of them did not obtain anything they required. The main reasons given for books not being available were that they were mislaid, in use already or at the binders.

The subjects where readers' requirements were least satisfied were biology/geology/agriculture, applied science and technology, and economics, but there were no really significant differences for all other subjects either in the proportion of readers who received all they required or in the reasons why the books were not available.

The Manuscripts and Oriental Printed Books and Manuscripts departments were better able to satisfy readers' needs than the Printed Books department. In both cases more than four fifths of the readers obtained all they required.

A significantly higher proportion of those readers who obtained all they required at the British Museum had not tried to obtain their requirements at another library.

5. *Methods of work* (See Tables 17 to 24)

(a) *Use of other libraries* (Table 17). Well over half the readers tried to obtain their requirements in another library before going to the British Museum.

The proportion of academic readers who had tried other libraries was much higher than for readers in other occupational categories. As academics also form the major proportion of readers at the British Museum it is not suprising that the main type of library previously consulted was a university or college library. Readers in other occupations were more dependent on public libraries, although they also used college libraries and libraries of research institutions, professional or learned societies as their other major sources.

Proportionally more readers reading foreign law, biology/geology/agriculture, theology, philology, applied science and economics had tried to obtain their requirements in other libraries.

The Manuscripts department differed from the other library departments in that only a quarter of its readers had tried other libraries. Most of these readers had tried to obtain their requirements from university or college libraries.

(b) *Readers' knowledge of items they were seeking* (Table 18). Two thirds of the readers knew exactly what they wanted (e.g. title and/or author of the book) before going to the British Museum library. Most of the remainder were seeking both known and unknown items.

Academics, librarians, and readers employed in civil service or local government knew their requirements more precisely than readers in other occupational categories where only half of the readers were principally seeking known items of literature.

By subject, readers' knowledge of their requirements was greatest for economics, history, literature, politics and British law. Readers of science subjects and heraldry/genealogy were least knowledgeable about the books they wanted.

Within the library departments, readers using the Manuscripts department were most knowledgeable about their requirements; those using the Oriental Printed Books and Manuscripts departments were least knowledgeable.

Temporary ticket holders were less knowledgeable about their requirements than regular readers.

174

(c) *Reservations of books* (Table 19). Over half of all readers made advance reservations for books, and three quarters of these did so after using the books on a previous occasion.

Use of the reservation service was greatest among academic readers and librarians, and also by readers using the Oriental Printed Books and Manuscripts department.

By subject, reservations were proportionally highest for philosophy/psychology/anthropology, foreign law, literature, theology, medicine and natural science.

(d) *Use of catalogues* (Tables 20 and 21). Two fifths of all readers identified items that were unknown to them by using the library catalogues and indexes, and a fifth consulted other reference books. Other methods of identifying unknown items of literature, such as looking on the shelves or by asking the library staff, were relatively unimportant.

Professional researchers, freelance writers and readers from industry/commerce made proportionally greater use of the library catalogues and indexes; they were also relatively large users of references books. These same occupational categories were also the ones who knew less precisely what they wanted before coming to the library.

Use of catalogues was uniformly high for all subjects.

A quarter of all readers consulted the Enquiry or Central Desk during their visit but only a quarter of these did so because of difficulties in using the catalogues.

(e) *Delivery of books* (Tables 21 to 23). The major problem, which affected a third of those who consulted the Enquiry or Centre Desk, was difficulty with the delivery of books. This proportion corresponded to the proportion who waited more than one hour before receiving their first book (excluding reserved items). There were no significant variations in this proportion by type of reader, subject, regularity of visit or for those readers who had tried to obtain their requirements in another library. However, readers using the Manuscripts and Oriental Printed Books and Manuscripts departments received their books much more quickly than readers using the Printed Books department. In each case less than a tenth of the readers using these departments waited more than half an hour before receiving their first book.

In spite of the delays experienced in waiting for books, two thirds of all readers indicated that they would be prepared to wait longer than at present, if necessary. Half of them would have waited until the next day or at the most for two or three days; but more than a third of them would have been prepared to wait a week or more.

Readers who were prepared to wait longer consisted mainly of academics, freelance writers, and daily visitors to the library. Also readers using the specialised library departments (Manuscripts and Oriental Printed Books and Manuscripts) were more prepared to wait longer. There were no significant variations by subjects, nor were readers who had already tried other libraries less willing to wait than other readers.

(f) *Use of the photocopying service* (Table 24). A third of all readers indicated that they could have used photocopies equally as well as using the original material they used at the library during their visit. However only just over a half of these readers could have provided the information necessary to obtain a photocopy without first going to the library. This potential use of the photocopying service was further halved to take account of readers who would have been prepared to pay for photo-used at the library during their visit. However, only jsut over a half of these readers could have ordered photocopies of the material they wanted without first visiting the library and were prepared to pay for them.

Academics, temporary ticket holders, and readers using the Manuscripts and Oriental Printed Books and Manuscripts departments indicated that they were more able to use photocopies than other categories of reader. They also knew more precisely what they wanted and, with the exception of academics, were most willing to pay for photocopies.

For the fifth of the sample who could have ordered photocopies without first coming to the Museum, the average number of photocopy pages required was around 60 pages. Requirements of academics were double those of most other occupational categories.

C. Statistical Appendix

Table 1. Occupation of Readers

	Visits		People	
	Sample 3,059[1]	Per cent	Sample 2,248[1]	Per cent
Student—(i) Undergraduate	136	4	105	5
(ii) Postgraduate	1,191	39	815	36
Academic—(i) University staff	765	25	571	25
(ii) Other higher academic institutions	166	5	133	6
(iii) School teacher	131	4	97	4
Freelance writer	294	10	220	10
Professional researcher	139	5	100	4
Civil service/local government	86	3	72	3
Industry/commerce/banking	83	3	78	3
Librarian	56	2	42	2
Full time staff of research institution, professional association, trade federation, etc.	49	2	43	2
Journalist	30	1	25	1
Publisher/editor	25	1	22	1
British Museum staff	23	1	16	1
Private unpaid research	23	1	19	1
Others/no answer	56	2	44	2

[1] The breakdown exceeds the sample number because several readers ticked more than one occupational category in their answers to this question. The percentages are calculated on the sample number and therefore exceed 100 per cent.

Table 2. Type and Age of Readers

	Visits		People	
	Sample 3,059	Per cent	Sample 2,248	Per cent
1. *Type of Reader*				
Those with readers' tickets	2,659	87	1,848	82
Temporary readers	151	5	151	7
No answer	249	8	249	11

	Sample 2,659	Per cent	Sample 1,848	Per cent
2. *Age of Readers*				
Ticket issued 1920–31	132	5	105	6
„ „ 1932–38	66	2	52	3
„ „ 1939–48	96	4	73	4
„ „ 1949–52	115	4	91	5
„ „ 1953–55	128	5	86	5
„ „ 1956–58	131	5	100	5
„ „ 1959–61	205	8	139	8
„ „ 1962–63	246	9	163	9
„ „ 1964–65	386	15	271	15
„ „ 1966–67	1,100	41	720	39

177

Table 3. Residence of Readers

	Visits		People	
	Sample 3,059	Per cent	Sample 2,248	Per cent
In London postal area:				
Up to 2 miles from the Museum ..	407	13	277	12
2–5 miles from the Museum	325	11	222	10
5–10 miles from the Museum	825	27	543	24
Over 10 miles from the Museum ..	542	18	391	17
Home counties (Middlesex, Hertford, Essex, Surrey, Kent)	340	11	278	12
South-East counties (Sussex, Hants, Berks, Bucks, Oxford, Bedford, Northants, Hunts, Cambs, Suffolk, Norfolk)	194	6	172	8
Other parts of England	135	4	127	6
Wales	27	1	22	1
Scotland..	49	2	41	2
Ireland	8	*	8	*
No answer	210	7	170	8

Table 4. Readers' Place of Work

	Visits		People	
	Sample 3,059	Per cent	Sample 2,248	Per cent
In London postal area:				
Up to 2 miles from the Museum ..	1,486[1]	49	971[1]	43
2–5 miles from the Museum ..	206	7	157	7
5–10 miles from the Museum	239	8	186	8
Over 10 miles from the Museum ..	132	4	105	5
Home counties (Middlesex, Hertford, Essex, Surrey, Kent)	139	5	122	5
South-East counties (Sussex, Hants, Berks, Bucks, Oxford, Bedford, Northants, Hunts, Cambs, Suffolk, Norfolk)	162	5	146	6
Other parts of England	144	5	132	6
Wales	30	1	23	1
Scotland..	48	2	40	2
Ireland	8	*	8	*
No answer	466	15	360	16

[1] Of the 1,486 and 971 readers who gave their place of work within a two mile radius of the Museum, 857 and 516 did so because they were mainly working at the Museum. The remainder had offices or other places of work in the area.

Table 5. **Main Origins of Students or Staff of a University or other Academic Institution**

	Visits		People	
	Sample 2,189[1]	Per cent	Sample 1,571[1]	Per cent
London	769	35	534	34
Of which:				
University College	125	6	81	5
School of Oriental and African Studies	97	4	70	4
Kings College	72	3	52	3
London School of Economics	65	3	48	3
Birkbeck College	58	3	39	2
Bedford College	57	3	36	2
School of Slavonic and East European				
Studies	32	1	20	1
Warburg Institute..	24	1	15	1
British universities or academic institutions				
outside London	629	29	494	31
Of which:				
Oxford University	93	4	71	4
Cambridge University	46	2	36	2
Sussex University	22	1	20	1
Other Universities in South-East				
England†	57	3	—	—
Overseas..	533	24	351	22
No answer	258	12	192	12

[1] The sample figures for this Table differ from the total figures for students and academic staff given in Table 1 due to those readers who ticked more than one category in their answer to the question on occupation.

† Includes Universities of Reading, Southampton, Kent, Essex and East Anglia.

Table 6. **Origins of Readers who normally live Overseas**

	Visits		People	
	Sample 1,060	Per cent	Sample 741	Per cent
English-Speaking Countries:				
U.S.A.	422	40	270	36
Canada	120	11	82	11
Australia	46	4	30	4
West Indies	22	2	17	2
New Zealand	15	1	9	1
South Africa	8	1	7	1
Others/no answer	4	*	3	*
	637	59	418	56
Non English-Speaking Countries:				
Germany/Austria/Switzerland	127	12	82	11
France/Netherlands/Finland/Denmark ..	77	7	64	9
Egypt/Israel/Jordan/Ethiopia/Iraq/Sudan/				
Tunisia	57	6	32	4
Italy/Portugal/Spain	46	5	29	4
India/Pakistan	34	3	21	3
Malaysia/Japan..	22	2	16	2
Russia/Yugoslavia/Hungary/Bulgaria ..	13	1	13	2
Others/no answer	47	5	37	5
	423	41	323	44

179

Table 7. Frequency of Visit

	Visits		People	
	Sample 3,059	Per cent	Sample 2,248	Per cent
1. *Regularity of visit:*				
Every day	1,169	38	679	30
Every week	1,001	33	770	34
Every month	327	11	297	13
Every 3 months	222	7	204	9
Every year	82	3	75	3
No answer	258	8	223	11
	Sample 3,059	Per cent	Sample 2,248	Per cent
2. *Occasion of last visit:*				
Up to 1 week ago	1,511	49	1,017	45
Between 1 and 4 weeks ago	495	16	410	18
Between 1 and 3 months ago	278	9	234	10
Between 3 and 6 months ago	103	3	92	4
Between 6 and 9 months ago	59	2	49	2
Between 9 and 15 months ago	61	2	51	2
Longer than 15 months ago	175	6	116	5
Never	258	8	187	8
No answer	118	4	92	4

Table 8. Duration of Visit

	Visits		People	
	Sample 3,059	Per cent	Sample 2,248	Per cent
1. *Duration of present visit:*				
1 day or less	428	14	375	17
Between 1 day and 1 week	654	21	556	25
Between 1 week and 1 month	429	14	338	15
Between 1 and 3 months	345	11	232	10
Longer period	1,082	35	662	29
No answer	121	4	88	4
	Sample 3,059	Per cent	Sample 2,248	Per cent
2. *Time spent in Library on present visit:*				
1 hour	157	5	134	6
2 hours	283	9	218	10
3 hours	425	14	313	14
4 hours	411	13	316	14
5 hours	459	15	330	15
6 hours	518	17	354	16
7 hours	322	11	214	10
8 hours	199	7	137	6
9 hours	58	2	43	2
10 hours..	45	1	34	2
11 hours..	15	*	8	*
No waiting/no answer	128	4	118	5
Average time spent in the library=	4·6 hours		4·5 hours	

Table 9. Reason for Visit

	Visits		People	
	Sample 3,059	Per cent	Sample 2,248	Per cent
1. *Visit related:*				
To work..	2,293	75	1,659	74
To leisure interests	156	5	135	6
To work and leisure interests..	569	19	419	19
No answer	45	1	38	2
	Sample 2,040	Per cent	Sample 1,472	Per cent
2. *Is the British Museum the only library capable of supplying all your requirements?*				
Yes	1,011	50	736	50
No	387	19	281	19
Don't know	584	29	419	28
No answer	58	3	36	3

Table 10. Main Subjects being Read

	Visits		People	
	Sample 3,059[1]	Per cent	Sample 2,248[1]	Per cent
History ..	1,532	50	1,103	49
Literature	1,096	36	764	34
Bibliography/General Reference	842	28	597	27
Biography	493	16	347	15
Philosophy/Psychology/Anthropology	471	15	310	14
Arts/Entertainment/Recreation	394	13	306	14
Theology/Religions	386	13	267	12
Politics ..	375	12	255	11
Geography/Local History	369	12	272	12
Philology/Linguistics ..	264	9	185	8
Economics	210	7	152	7
Heraldry/Genealogy ..	140	5	106	5
British Law ..	120	4	80	4
Natural Sciences	73	2	57	3
Medicine/Pharmacology	69	2	49	2
Biology/Agriculture/Geology	63	2	50	2
Foreign Law ..	63	2	47	2
Applied Science/Technology	62	2	52	2
Mathematics, Pure and Applied	28	1	23	1
Children's Books	23	1	18	1
Other subjects ..	4	*	3	*
No answer	57	2	48	2

[1] As readers were asked to indicate all the subject fields they were using during their visit the numerical breakdown by subject is much greater than the sample number, and the percentages exceed 100 per cent.

Table 11.   **Average Number of items used per Reader**

	Visits	People
1. *Items that were known to the reader before his visit:*		
Known items that were supplied..	5·0	4·8
Known items that were not supplied	0·7	0·7
2. *Items that were unknown to the reader before his visit:*		
Unknown items that were supplied	1·8	1·8

Table 12.   **Use of Library Departments**

	Visits		People	
	Sample 3,059	Per cent	Sample 2,248	Per cent
1. *Readers using library departments:*				
Printed Books Department	2,854	93	2,089	93
Of which:				
Use by day	2,549	83	1,864	83
Use by evening	305	10	225	10
Manuscripts Department	159	5	130	6
Oriental Printed Books and Manuscripts				
Department	44	1	28	1
2. *Readers using one library department only:*				
Those using only one department	2,165	71	1,566	70
Those using more than one department ..	836	27	636	28
No answer	57	2	46	2

Table 13.   **Use of Museum Departments other than the Printed Books Department by Readers using more than one Library Department**

	Visits			People		
	Sample 836	Per cent	Per cent of Total Sample 3,059	Sample 636	Per cent	Per cent of Total Sample 2,248
Manuscripts	294	35	10	224	35	10
Oriental Printed Books and Manu-						
scripts	87	10	3	54	8	2
Prints and Drawings	77	9	3	61	10	3
Greek and Roman Antiquities ..	32	4	1	31	5	1
British and Mediaeval Antiquities	27	3	1	22	3	1
Western Asiatic Antiquities ..	27	3	1	23	3	1
Egyptian Antiquities	22	3	1	19	3	1
Coins and Medals	18	2	1	16	3	1
Oriental Antiquities	17	2	1	13	2	1
Ethnography	11	1	*	9	1	*
Laboratory	1	*	*	1	*	*

Table 14. Readers who found it essential to use Departments
other than the Printed Books Department

	Visits			People		
	Sample 836	Per cent	Per cent of Total Sample 3,059	Sample 636	Per cent	Per cent of Total Sample 2,248
Manuscripts	213	25	7	160	25	7
Oriental Printed Books and Manuscripts	59	7	2	54	8	2
Prints and Drawings	56	6	2	43	7	2
Greek and Roman Antiquities ..	15	2	*	14	2	1
Western Asiatic Antiquities ..	15	2	*	13	2	1
British and Mediaeval Antiquities	14	2	*	11	2	*
Coins and Medals	14	2	*	12	2	1
Egyptian Antiquities	12	1	*	9	1	*
Oriental Antiquities	8	1	*	8	1	*
Ethnography	7	1	*	6	1	*
Laboratory	—	—	—	—	—	—

Table 15. Satisfaction of Readers' Needs

	Visits		People	
	Sample 3,059	Per cent	Sample 2,248	Per cent
Readers who obtained *all* they required ..	2,040	67	1,472	65
Readers who obtained some of their requirements	869	28	647	29
Readers who obtained none of their requirements	53	2	46	2
No answer	96	3	83	4

Table 16. Reasons for the Non-availability of Books

	Visits		People	
	Sample 1,019[1]	Per cent	Sample 776[1]	Per cent
Mislaid	256	25	187	24
In use	213	21	139	18
At the binders	117	11	91	12
Book not in library	93	9	73	9
Uncertain pressmark	87	9	68	9
Destroyed	74	7	61	8
Outhoused	52	5	42	5
Book did not arrive	52	5	39	5
Unable to wait	23	2	20	3
Others	279	27	216	28
No answer	9	1	6	1

[1] The breakdown exceeds the sample number because readers were asked to tick as many categories as were applicable. The percentages are calculated on the sample number and therefore exceed 100 per cent.

Table 17. Readers who tried another Library before trying the British Museum

	Visits		People	
	Sample 3,059	Per cent	Sample 2,248	Per cent
1. Use of another library:				
Tried another library	1,764	58	1,318	59
Did not try another library	1,192	39	853	38
No answer	102	3	77	3
	Sample 1,764[1]	Per cent	Sample 1,318[1]	Per cent
2. Types of library used:				
University or college library	1,274	72	934	71
Public library	654	37	501	38
Library of research institution, professional or learned society	333	19	258	20
Government library	147	8	107	8
National Library of Scotland, National Library of Wales	64	4	51	4
National Lending Library for Science and Technology, National Central Library ..	58	3	43	3
Industrial or firm's library	20	1	14	1
Abroad	334	19	229	17

[1] The breakdown exceeds the sample number because readers were asked to tick as many categories as were applicable. The percentages are calculated on the sample number and therefore exceed 100 per cent.

Table 18. Readers' Knowledge of Books/Literature they were seeking

	Visits		People	
	Sample 3,059	Per cent	Sample 2,248	Per cent
Seeking known items	1,967	64	1,418	63
Seeking both known and unknown items ..	925	30	686	31
Seeking unknown items	74	2	65	3
Seeking professional assistance	28	1	23	1
Seeking a quiet place to read	20	1	19	1
Others	35	1	31	1
No answer	56	2	47	2

Table 19. Reservation of Books/Literature

	Visits		People	
	Sample 3,059	Per cent	Sample 2,248	Per cent
1. *Readers who reserved books before visiting the library:*				
Did reserve in advance	1,710	56	1,134	50
Did not reserve in advance	1,059	35	863	38
No answer	123	4	107	5

	Sample 1,710	Per cent	Sample 1,134	Per cent
2. *Readers who reserved books after using them on a previous occasion:*				
Used books previously	1,343	79	867	76
Did not use books previously	187	11	156	14
No answer	180	10	111	10

Table 20. Methods of Identifying unknown items of Literature

	Visits		People	
	Sample 3,059	Per cent	Sample 2,248	Per cent
By consulting the catalogues and indexes ..	1,186	39	890	40
By consulting other reference books.. ..	653	21	476	21
By looking on the shelves	180	6	146	6
By asking the staff	132	4	115	5
No answer	104	3	65	3

185

Table 21. **Readers who consulted the Enquiry Desk, Centre Desk or Member of the Reading Room Staff**

	Visits		People	
	Sample 3,059	Per cent	Sample 2,248	Per cent
1. *Consultations:*				
Readers who did	830	27	661	29
Readers who did not	1,848	60	1,305	58
No answer	375	12	277	12
	Sample 830	Per cent	Sample 661	Per cent
2. *Reasons for consultations:*				
Difficulties with delivery of books	301	36	242	37
Difficulties with the catalogues	192	23	155	23
Advice about bibliographies and reference books	164	20	125	19
To locate literature not in the British Museum	43	5	37	6
Difficulties with literature in foreign languages	20	2	14	2
Difficulties in finding a seat	13	2	12	2
Other reasons	182	22	147	22
No answer	61	7	51	8

Table 22. **Time spent awaiting Delivery of first Book (excluding reserved items)**

	Visits		People	
	Sample 2,146	Per cent	Sample 1,595	Per cent
Up to half an hour	609	28	458	29
½ to 1 hour	854	40	621	39
1 to 1½ hours	485	23	366	23
1½ to 2 hours	117	5	93	6
Over 2 hours	80	4	57	4

Table 23.   Attitude of Readers to waiting longer for Books

	Visits		People	
	Sample 3,059	Per cent	Sample 2,248	Per cent
1. *Number of readers prepared to wait longer:*				
Would wait longer	2,006	66	1,423	63
Woult not wait longer	441	14	371	17
No answer	611	20	454	20
	Sample 2,006	Per cent	Sample 1,423	Per cent
2. *How much longer?*				
Until tomorrow	604	30	446	31
2 to 3 days	408	20	296	21
4 to 6 days	131	7	93	7
More than a week	743	37	504	35
No answer	119	6	84	6

Table 24.   Potential Use of the Photocopying Service

	Visits		People	
	Sample 3,059	Per cent	Sample 2,248	Per cent
1. *Readers who could have made equal use of photocopies:*				
Those who could	967	32	738	33
Those who could not	1,741	57	1,221	54
No answer	350	11	289	13
2. *Readers who could have supplied sufficient information for photocopies without coming to the museum:*				
Those who could	537	18	409	18
Those who could not	1,778	58	1,307	58
No answer	733	24	532	24
	Sample 537	Per cent	Sample 409	Per cent
3. *Readers who would be prepared to pay for photocopies at 3d. a page:*				
Would pay	223	42	179	44
Would not pay	252	47	189	46
No answer	28	5	20	5
	Sample 497		Sample 380	
4. *Average number of pages required for photocopying*	60·6		58·3	

D. Questionnaire

PART A

1. Which *ONE* of the following occupational categories most closely applies to you?

Student   (i) Undergraduate..   ..   ..

            (ii) Postgraduate ..   ..

Academic (i) University staff   ..   ..

            (ii) Other higher academic institution staff   ..   ..

            (iii) School teacher   ..   ..

Industry/commerce/banking ..   ..

Civil service/local government   ..   ..

Full-time staff of research institution, professional association, trade federation, etc.   ..   ..

Journalist (newspapers and broadcasting media) ..   ..

Librarian   ..   ..

Self-employed (i) Professional researcher ..   ..

                    (ii) Freelance writer ..   ..

Staff of National Central Library or B.N.B.   ..   ..

British Museum staff (please state department)......................................

Other (please specify)...

2. If you are a *STUDENT* or on the *STAFF* of a university or other academic institution, please specify

If London University, please give the name of the college

....

If another university or other academic institution please give the name of the *institution*

....

3(a) Where do you live *and* work at present?   *Live*   *Work*
In London

    (i) Postal districts
        W1 ..   ..   WC1, 2 ..   ..

    (ii) Postal districts
        EC1, 2, 3, 4   ..   SE1   ..   ..   ..⎫
        N1 ..   ..   ..   SW1   ..   ..   ..⎬ ....
        NW1   ..   ..   W2   ..   ..   ..⎭

    (iii) Postal districts
        E1, 2, 3, 5, 8, 9, 14   SW2, 3, 4, 5, 6, 7, 8, 9, 10⎫
                          11   ..   ..⎪
        N4, 5, 6, 7, 8, 15, 16,   SE5, 8, 11, 14, 15, 16, 17,⎬ ....
          19   ..   ..   22, 24 ..   ..   ..⎪
        NW2, 3, 4, 5, 8, 11   N6, 8, 9, 10, 11, 12, 14 ..⎭

    (iv) All other postal districts   ....

    Home counties (Middlesex, Hertford, Essex, Surrey, Kent)   ..   ..

    South-east counties (Sussex, Hants, Berks, Bucks, Oxford, Bedford, Northants, Hunts, Cambs, Suffolk, Norfolk)   ..   ..

    Other parts of England ..   ..

    Wales ..   ..

								Live	*Work*

Scotland   ..   ..

Ireland   ..   ..

(*b*) If you gave your place of work as London postal districts W1, WC1, WC2, is this because
You are working mainly at the Museum?   ..   ..
Your office or other place of work is located in these postal districts?   ..   ..

4(*a*) If you normally live outside the British Isles, please specify the country   (i) English-speaking countries (please name country) ....
   (ii) Non-English-speaking countries (please name country) ....

(*b*) If you normally live outside London or live overseas, have you come to London especially to visit the British Museum?   YES....................
NO ....

(*c*) If you are from overseas, have you come to this country for six months or more to a university or other higher academic institution?   YES....................
NO ....

5(*a*) If you visit this library regularly, please indicate about how frequently.   Every day   ....
Every week   ....
Every month   ....
Every 3 months   ....
Every year   ....

(*b*) For how many days do you expect your *present* visit to the library to last? (If you have been using the library continuously for one or more days already as part of your present visit, include these previous days in your answer).

1 day or less   ..   ..

Between 1 day and 1 week   ..   ..

Between 1 week and 1 month   ..   ..

Between 1 month and 3 months   ..   ..

Longer period   ..   ..

---

6. Is the reason for your visit related   to your work   ....

to your leisure interests   ....
to your work and leisure interests   ....

---

7. In what subject field(s) are you seeking information or literature *to-day*? (Tick as many categories as are applicable)

Bibliography, General Reference
Theology, Religions
Philology, Linguistics
Philosophy, Psychology, Anthropology
Foreign Law
British Law
Economics
Politics
Heraldry and Genealogy
History
Geography and Local History

Mathematics, Pure and Applied
Biology, Agriculture, Geology
Applied Science, Technology
Natural Sciences
Medicine, Pharmacology
Biography
Literature
Arts, Entertainment, Recreation
Children's Books
Other (please specify)
....

189

8(*a*) Did you try to obtain what you require in **another library**   YES...................

     before coming to the British Museum?   NO ....

(*b*) If *YES*, where did you try before?

    Public library   ..   ..

    University or college library   ..   ..

    Government library   ..   ..

    Library of research institution, professional or learned

      society, etc. ..   ..

    Industrial or firm's library   ..   ..

    National Lending Library of Science and Technology,

      National Central Library   ..   ..

    National Library of Scotland, National Library of

      Wales ..   ..

    Abroad ..   ..

    Other (please specify)...

9(*a*) *Today*, have you come to use the resources of this depart-   YES...................

     ment *only?*   ..   ..   NO ....

(*b*) If you intend to use other parts of the Museum as well today, which parts of the Museum are these?   (Tick as many categories as are applicable)

Department

    Printed Books   (i) General Library ..   ..

               (ii) Map Room   ..   ..

               (iii) Music Room   ..   ..

               (iv) State Paper Room   ..   ..

               (v) National Reference Library of Science and Invention, Holborn (former Patent Office Library)   ....

               (vi) Newspaper Library (Colindale)   ....

    Manuscripts   ..   ..

    Oriental Printed Books and Manuscripts   ..   ..

    Prints and Drawings   ..   ..

    Coins and Medals   ..   ..

    Egyptian Antiquities   ..   ..

    Western Asiatic Antiquities   ..   ..

    Greek and Roman Antiquities   ..   ..

    British and Mediaeval Antiquities   ..   ..

    Oriental Antiquities   ..   ..

    Ethnography   ..   ..

    Laboratory   ..   ..

(*c*) Is it essential for you to use these other departments in   YES...................

    conjunction with your visit *today?*   ..   ..   NO ....

10. When did you last visit the library? (If you have already
    been here for one or more days continuously and today's
    visit is part of this longer visit, please refer to the last
    separate occasion when you visited the library)

    Up to 1 week ago .. ..

    Between 1 and 4 weeks ago .. ..

    Between 1 and 3 months ago .. ..

    Between 3 and 6 months ago .. ..

    Between 6 and 9 months ago .. ..

    Between 9 and 15 months ago .. ..

    Longer than 15 months ago .. ..

    Never .. ..

PART B

WE SHOULD LIKE VERY MUCH TO KNOW ABOUT YOUR EXPERIENCE AT
THE LIBRARY *TODAY*. WOULD YOU THEREFORE PLEASE COMPLETE THIS
PART OF THE QUESTIONNAIRE JUST BEFORE YOU LEAVE

1(a) Did the British Museum provide all that you required on   ALL....................

     your visit today?   SOME..................

     NONE..................

(b) If ALL, is the British Museum the only library in the   YES....................

     United Kingdom capable of providing everything you   NO ....

     required on your visit today?   DON'T KNOW..........

(c) If your answer to 1(b) is YES, would you please briefly explain why

     ....

     ....

     ....

---

2. In your visit *today*, were you principally seeking

     Items that were known to you (i.e. title and/or author)   ....

     Items that were unknown to you .. ..

     Both known and unknown items .. ..

     Professional assistance .. ..

     Other (please specify)..

3(a) If the items you were seeking *today* were known to you
      (i) Did you reserve any of them in advance .. YES....................

      NO ....

      (ii) If YES, is this because you placed them on   YES....................

      reserve after using them on a previous occasion?   NO ....

(b) Of the items you were seeking and which were known to you   ....
      (i) Please specify the number of items supplied to
        you *today* .. ..
      (ii) Please specify the number of items *NOT* supplied
        to you *today* .. ..

191

4(a) If some of the items you were using *today* were unknown to you before your visit to the library, how did you identify them? (Tick as many categories as are applicable)

By consulting the British Museum catalogues and indexes .. ..

By consulting other reference books .. ..

By looking on the shelves .. ..

By asking the staff .. ..

(b) If some of the items you are using *today* were unknown to you before your visit to the library, please specify the number of these items supplied to you today .. ..

---

5. If you have *NOT* obtained all the items requested today, was it because an item was

Mislaid .. ..

Destroyed .. ..

At the binders .. ..

In use .. ..

Outhoused .. ..

Uncertain pressmark .. ..

Other (please specify)..

6(a) Did you consult the Enquiry Desk, Centre Desk or   YES...................

Member of Staff in the Reading Room *today?*   NO ....

(b) If *YES*, was it because of

(i) difficulties with the British Museum catalogues   ....

(ii) difficulties with the delivery of books .. ..

(iii) difficulties with literature in foreign languages ..   ..

(iv) need to locate literature not in the British Museum   ....
(v) need for advice about bibliographies and reference books .. ..

(vi) other difficulties (please specify)..

---

7. Excluding reserved items, how long did you have to wait before receiving the first item you requested *today?*

Up to half-an-hour .. ..

½ to 1 hour .. ..

1 to 1½ hours .. ..

1½ to 2 hours .. ..

Over 2 hours .. ..

8(a) Would you have been prepared to wait longer if your   YES...................

requirements had not been met *today?*   NO ....

(b) If *YES*, how much longer?

Until tomorrow .. ..

2 to 3 days .. ..

4 to 6 days .. ..

more than 1 week .. ..

9(a) Could you have made equal use of photocopies of the items you consulted *today*?

YES.....................

NO ....

(b) Could you have supplied sufficient information on the items you wanted to enable photocopies to be supplied to you without your coming to the Museum?

YES.....................

NO ....

(c) If *YES*,

    (i) about how many pages would have had to be photocopied? .. .. Number of pages........

    (ii) would you be prepared to pay for this service if each page cost threepence? .. .. ..

YES.....................

NO ....

---

10. Roughly how long did you spend altogether in the library *today*? .. .. Number of hours........

---

11. What is your reader's ticket number? .. ..

If you are holding a temporary ticket please tick here .. ..

ANALYSIS OF READERS' APPLICATION SLIPS AT
THE BRITISH MUSEUM LIBRARY, APRIL, 1968
survey carried out and analysis prepared by
THE ECONOMIST INTELLIGENCE UNIT LIMITED

CONTENTS

Symbols used in the Statistical Appendix
* = less than 1 per cent
– = nil

Throughout the Tables two figures are given for each breakdown i.e. 595
13

The upper figure is the actual number of items involved; the lower figure is the percentage of the base figure shown at the top of the column.

ANALYSIS OF READERS' APPLICATION SLIPS AT THE
BRITISH MUSEUM LIBRARY

INTRODUCTION

This report contains an analysis of 4,601 readers' application slips which were selected randomly from the total number of application slips returned to the British Museum library during the six-week period 29 March–2 May 1968 on which the EIU survey of library usage took place.

From the application slips five separate pieces of information have been obtained:

1. Subject
2. Length of loan
3. Date of publication
4. Whether the book is a monograph or series
5. Whether the book is housed at Bloomsbury or Woolwich

Only one of these pieces of information—subject—was contained in the EIU survey. The figures from the two sources differ considerably, both in the order and relative importance, for the three main subjects being used. This is not surprising since the three main subjects shown by the EIU survey included History and Bibliography/General Reference. The readers' subjective interpretation of " History " in a self-filled questionnaire is likely to differ widely from the more rigid interpretation provided by the British Museum staff when classifying the application slips, especially if the reader is seeking information on the historical aspects of a particular subject. Secondly, use of Bibliography/General Reference books is likely to be highly underrated in a survey based entirely on readers' application forms.

These differences apart, there is a reasonable measure of agreement between the results obtained by the two survey methods, though it should be stressed that the two are not strictly comparable.

1. Subjects

The analysis of the readers' application slips shows that readers' requirements were concentrated in eight subject categories, of which literature was easily the most important. In order of importance the subjects were:

Subject	Per cent
Literature..	24
Theology, Religion	10
Biography	9
History	9
Geography, Local History	8
Philosophy, Psychology, Anthropology	7
Arts, Entertainment, Recreation	6
Politics	6
Economics	5
	—
	84
	—

A further eight subject categories each received only 1 per cent of the total applications. These were: Foreign Law, British Law, Heraldry and Genealogy, Mathematics (Pure and Applied), Biology/Agriculture/Geology, Applied Science and Technology, Natural Sciences, and Medicine/Pharmacology.

195

2. Length of Loan

Two thirds of all books were on loan for no more than three days. Well over half of these books were on loan for two days. Only 13 per cent of all books were on loan for more than a week (six days), and over half of these were returned within two weeks.

Short loans were above average in the following subject categories: Heraldry and Genealogy, Mathematics, Biography, Children's Books, and Geography and Local History. The period of loan was slightly longer for books on Politics and Applied Science/Technology, but even for these categories the majority of books were returned within one week.

3. Date of Publication

Over half the books used were published in the period 1800–1949, of which the single most important period was 1850–1899 (15 per cent of the total number of readers' applications).

Date of Publication	Per cent
Pre-1799	18
1800–1899	24
1900–1949	32
1950–1959	13
1960–1968	14

Use of the pre-1799 books was most notable among Law subjects, Theology, Mathematics, Biology/Agriculture/Geology, and Natural Sciences. Nineteenth century books were most notable among Law subjects, Heraldry and Genealogy, and Geography and Local History.

Of the recent books, there were above average applications for books on Applied Science/Technology, and Arts, Entertainment, Recreation.

4. Monograph/Series

Over four fifths of the applications were for monographs.

By subject, monographs were most used for Biography (99 per cent), Medicine/Pharmacology (92 per cent), British Law (92 per cent), and Theology (91 per cent). Series were most used for Bibliography/General Reference (44 per cent), Mathematics (41 per cent), and Philology/Linguistics (35 per cent).

5. Bloomsbury/Woolwich

Ninety-nine per cent of the applications were for books kept at Bloomsbury. Books kept at Woolwich were in three main subject categories: Politics (12 books), Economics (seven books), and Literature (seven books).

STATISTICAL APPENDIX

Table 1. Subject by Length of Loan

	Total	Theology, Religions	Philology, Linguistics	Philosophy, Psychology, Anthropology	Foreign Law	British Law	Economics	Politics	Heraldry and Genealogy	History	Bibliography, General Reference
Base	4,601	447	133	344	35	60	210	266	44	400	199
1 day	595	29	10	24	2	6	11	22	2	30	10
2 days	1,798	193	56	146	13	24	88	84	26	175	84
3 days	624	65	29	44	6	7	21	41	9	52	26
4 days	373	52	6	27	2	12	27	32	1	27	17
5 days	302	24	6	22	6	5	13	15	2	31	18
6 days	192	16	6	9	3	8	10	29	5	16	9
7 days	106	11	1	16	2	5	6	11	—	12	9
8 days	64	12	—	6	1	8	5	31	—	4	5
9 days	50	6	3	5	3	5	2	12	1	3	4
10 days	34	4	2	2	—	8	—	14	2	4	2
11–15 days	119	11	4	10	1	—	8	15	1	10	2
16–19 days	32	5	3	3	—	—	4	6	2	5	3
20–39 days	103	5	1	14	1	—	6	4	1	10	3
40–59 days	32	1	4	4	—	—	3	2	2	4	2
60–79 days	17	1	3	3	—	—	—	1	—	1	7
80–99 days	22	2	1	2	—	—	2	—	—	3	4
100–149 days	34	5	1	2	1	—	3	1	—	5	1
150–199 days	19	3	—	2	—	1	—	—	—	3	1
200–249 days	17	1	1	—	—	2	—	1	—	1	2
250–299 days	17	1	—	—	—	—	—	—	—	3	1
Over 300 days	12	—	—	1	—	—	—	—	—	1	1

Table 1. Subject by Length of Loan—continued

	Total	Mathematics, Pure and Applied	Biology, Agriculture, Geology	Applied Science, Technology	Natural Sciences	Medicine, Pharmacology	Biography	Literature	Arts, Entertainment, Recreation	Children's Books	Geography and Local History
Base	4,601	29	65	28	59	61	428	1,094	298	17	375
1 day	595	4	10	2	2	4	174	134	24	2	90
2 days	1,798	14	15	7	3	7	41	12	8	12	24
3 days	624	19	25	6	27	30	105	427	133	9	124
4 days	373	66	38	21	46	49	25	39	45	53	33
5 days	302	2	11	6	9	8	43	163	42	2	42
6 days	192	7	3	21	15	13	10	15	14	12	11
7 days	106	2	5	2	6	2	31	86	25	—	23
8 days	64	7	5	7	10	3	7	8	8	1	27
9 days	50	1	8	4	3	4	13	73	17	6	5
10 days	34	3	1	14	5	7	3	7	6	—	20
11–15 days	119	—	2	—	2	3	15	51	13	—	4
16–19 days	32	—	1	—	3	1	5	5	6	—	—
20–39 days	103	1	2	3	3	2	5	20	2	2	5
40–59 days	32	3	1	11	5	1	1	2	3	12	1
60–79 days	17*	—	2	4	—	2	5	16	1	—	3
80–99 days	22	—	1	14	1	3	4	11	4	—	1
100–149 days	34	—	2	—	2	—	2*	7	4	—	*
150–199 days	19	—	1	—	—	2	8	27	1	—	5
200–249 days	17*	—	2	—	—	2	2	8	9	—	1
250–299 days	17*	—	2	—	1	—	6	26	3	1	3
Over 200 days	12*	—	1	—	2	—	1	2	4	6	1

Table 2. Subject by Date of Publication

	Total	Theology, Religions	Philology, Linguistics	Philosophy, Psychology, Anthropology	Foreign Law	British Law	Economics	Politics	Heraldry and Genealogy	History	Bibliography, General Reference
Base	4,601	447	133	344	35	60	210	266	44	400	199
1400–1499	11	4	—	3	—	—	—	—	—	1	—
1500–1599	147	33	6	19	3	—	—	—	1	13	1
1600–1699	319	75	11	22	2	7	5	13	2	35	7
1700–1799	387	33	8	19	6	8	11	5	2	25	26
1800–1849	401	33	5	13	14	13	5	21	5	28	16
1850–1899	693	70	18	27	3	19	17	8	11	55	36
1900–1909	225	20	9	14	8	32	23	27	22	20	18
1910–1919	216	26	7	10	23	12	11	23	50	23	10
1920–1929	330	29	5	32	2	3	10	9	5	28	5
1930–1939	414	26	12	31	6	—	5	3	4	40	3
1940–1949	274	19	9	22	1	3	12	20	9	25	15
1950–1959	581	42	17	56	3	5	15	16	2	61	21
1960	89	5	13	1	2	5	17	21	5	9	11
1961	79	9	6	7	6	8	8	8	1	2	6
1962	76	4	17	14	3	—	19	3	2	7	3
1963	90	4	13	10	1	2	9	4	—	8	2
1964	81	3	5	11	3	1	4	2	—	7	—
1965	98	7	4	7	2	2	5	4	—	8	2
1966	55	3	2	10	6	1	2	5	—	2	5
1967	34	1	2	3	1	2	1	2	—	6	3
1968	—	—	—	—	—	—	—	—	—	—	—

Table 2. Subject by Date of Publication—continued

Date	Total	Mathematics, Pure and Applied	Biology, Agriculture, Geology	Applied Science, Technology	Natural Sciences	Medicine, Pharmacology	Biography	Literature	Arts Entertainment, Recreation	Children's Books	Geography and Local History
Base	4,601	29	65	28	59	61	428	1,094	298	17	375
1400–1499	11	—	—	—	—	—	1	2	—	—	—
1500–1599	*	—	1	—	1	—	*	*	4	—	9
1600–1699	147	6	2	—	2	5	9	42	4	—	2
1700–1799	319	21	6	4	9	8	2	4	1	—	18
1800–1849	387	4	9	3	9	9	14	74	3	—	5
1850–1899	401	14	9	1	15	15	3	7	15	2	38
1900–1909	693	1	14	1	11	6	22	120	5	12	10
1910–1919	225	3	6	4	19	10	30	11	20	2	59
1920–1929	216	3	9	3	5	5	7	108	7	12	16
1930–1939	330	10	10	1	8	8	79	10	61	3	77
1940–1949	414	—	15	11	3	10	18	154	20	18	21
1950–1959	274	3	3	2	5	16	22	14	19	3	22
1960	581	—	5	7	6	6	34	46	6	18	6
1961	89	10	8	9	10	10	54	4	15	1	14
1962	2	—	3	32	—	—	13	83	5	6	4
1963	79	—	—	7	1	1	4	8	15	1	26
1964	2	—	—	—	2	2	1	90	29	2	7
1965	76	2	4	2	3	—	7	8	10	—	5
1966	90	7	6	7	5	—	2	53	25	1	8
1967	2	—	—	—	1	1	5	5	8	6	2
1968	81	—	—	—	2	2	1	122	59	—	3

Table 3. Subject by Monograph/Series, Bloomsbury/Woolwich

	Total	Theology, Religions	Philology, Linguistics	Philosophy, Psychology, Anthropology	Foreign Law	British Law	Economics	Politics	Heraldry and Genealogy	History	Bibliography, General Reference
Base	4,601 / 100	447 / 100	133 / 100	344 / 100	35 / 100	60 / 100	210 / 100	266 / 100	44 / 100	400 / 100	199 / 100
Monograph	3,807 / 83	408 / 91	86 / 65	285 / 83	30 / 86	55 / 92	165 / 79	204 / 77	32 / 73	341 / 85	111 / 56
Series ..	790 / 17	39 / 9	47 / 35	59 / 17	5 / 14	5 / 8	44 / 21	61 / 23	12 / 27	59 / 15	88 / 44
Bloomsbury	4,564 / 99	447 / 100	133 / 100	344 / 100	34 / 97	60 / 100	203 / 97	253 / 95	44 / 100	398 / 99	199 / 100
Woolwich ..	35 / 1	— / —	— / —	— / —	1 / 3	— / —	7 / 3	12 / 5	— / —	2 / 1	— / —

	Total	Mathematics, Pure and Applied	Biology, Agriculture, Geology	Applied Science, Technology	Natural Sciences	Medicine, Pharmacology	Biography	Literature	Arts, Entertainment, Recreation	Children's Books	Geography and Local History
Base	4,601 / 100	29 / 100	65 / 100	28 / 100	59 / 100	61 / 100	428 / 100	1,094 / 100	298 / 100	17 / 100	375 / 100
Monograph	3,807 / 83	17 / 59	55 / 85	24 / 86	48 / 81	56 / 92	422 / 99	906 / 83	225 / 76	15 / 88	315 / 84
Series ..	790 / 17	12 / 41	10 / 15	3 / 11	11 / 19	5 / 8	6 / 1	188 / 17	73 / 24	2 / 12	60 / 16
Bloomsbury	4,564 / 99	29 / 100	63 / 97	27 / 96	59 / 100	61 / 100	428 / 100	1,087 / 99	297 / 100	17 / 100	373 / 99
Woolwich ..	35 / 1	— / —	2 / 3	— / —	— / —	— / —	— / —	7 / 1	1 / *	— / —	2 / 1

Table 4. Date of Publication by Length of Loan

	Total	1400–1499	1500–1599	1600–1699	1700–1799	1800–1849	1850–1899	1900–1909	1910–1919	1920–1929	1930–1939	1940–1949	1950–1959	1960	1961	1962	1963	1964	1965	1966	1967	1968
Base ..	4,601	11	147	319	387	401	693	225	216	330	414	274	581	89	79	76	90	81	98	55	34	—
1 day	595	—	14	21	52	48	102	30	29	57	65	41	79	11	10	4	9	8	9	3	3	—
2 days	1,798	5	54	119	142	153	300	84	106	132	172	110	212	35	26	31	27	29	38	13	9	—
3 days	624	4	29	60	64	62	90	27	27	41	47	27	66	10	10	11	18	11	14	7	3	—
4 days	373	—	13	32	30	36	49	16	15	24	37	24	45	9	13	8	20	14	14	7	2	—
5 days	302	1	9	21	21	30	45	25	15	11	23	14	35	8	13	11	6	9	6	5	6	—
6 days	192	—	5	7	8	7	24	11	17	13	6	5	37	3	6	4	5	9	3	9	2	—
7 days	106	—	3	7	2	4	3	11	4	10	12	6	6	3	5	1	6	5	4	4	12	—
8 days	64	1	3	11	5	4	11	5	4	3	4	9	12	2	1	5	2	2	4	2	3	—
9 days	50	—	2	3	—	2	3	3	2	2	3	3	12	—	2	—	3	—	—	1	—	—
10 days	34	—	—	1	—	—	1	1	—	—	2	1	3	—	1	—	1	—	—	—	—	—
11–15 days ..	119	—	2	5	5	9	13	6	4	6	11	8	17	6	3	6	4	2	6	1	3	—
16–19 days ..	32	—	1	2	6	3	2	3	2	3	4	3	3	—	—	—	—	—	—	—	—	—
20–39 days ..	103	—	1	3	2	1	15	1	2	8	4	7	8	2	3	1	3	2	4	2	2	—
40–59 days ..	32	—	—	1	6	2	2	—	—	2	5	2	5	2	—	—	1	—	1	—	—	—
60–79 days ..	17	—	—	1	2	4	2	1	—	5	1	—	3	—	3	—	3	3	4	2	2	—
80–99 days ..	22	—	—	—	3	2	5	1	—	1	3	1	5	—	1	—	1	—	—	—	—	—
100–149 days ..	34	—	2	2	1	4	5	2	2	3	3	2	4	1	3	—	1	—	2	—	1	—
159–199 days ..	19	—	1	1	4	1	4	—	—	2	4	2	7	—	4	—	1	—	2	2	—	—
200–249 days ..	17	—	—	1	1	—	2	—	—	3	1	1	1	2	—	—	1	—	—	2	1	—
250–299 days ..	17	—	—	1	3	1	2	1	—	2	3	1	5	2	1	—	1	—	1	—	—	—
300 and over	12	—	—	1	2	—	2	1	—	1	1	1	2	—	—	—	1	—	—	—	—	—

Table 5. Date of Publication by Subject

	Total	1400–1499	1500–1599	1600–1699	1700–1799	1800–1849	1850–1899	1900–1909	1910–1919	1920–1929	1930–1939	1940–1949	1950–1959	1960	1961	1962	1963	1964	1965	1966	1967	1968
Base	4,601	11	147	319	387	401	693	225	216	330	414	274	581	89	79	76	90	81	98	55	34	—
Theology,	447	4	33	75	33	33	70	20	26	29	26	19	42	5	9	4	4	3	7	3	2	—
Religions,	10	36	22	24	9	8	10	9	12	9	6	7	7	6	11	5	4	4	7	5	6	—
Philology,	133	—	6	11	5	5	18	9	7	12	17	8	17	5	2	3	2	2	4	1	—	—
Linguistics,	3	3	4	1	19	13	3	4	3	4	4	3	3	6	3	3	10	2	4	2	6	—
Philosophy,	344	27	19	22	19	3	27	14	10	32	31	22	56	11	7	14	10	11	7	10	18	—
Psychology,	7		13	7	5	3	4	6	5	10	7	8	10	12	9	18	11	14	7	18		—
Anthropology																						
Foreign Law	35		3	2	5	1	8	2	1	2		2	3	1	1	2	1		1	1	1	—
British Law	1		2	1	1	*	1	1	*	1	3	3	1	1	1	3	1		1	1	3	—
Economics	60			7	8	19	7	2			17	1	5	1		1	1		1	1	2	—
Politics	210			2	1	1	1	1	2	1	4	9	33	8	10	2	9	6	9	2	6	—
Heraldry and Genealogy	266			5	1	7	23	10	6	15	21	17	6	9	13	3	10	11	13	5	7	—
History	44			13	3	27	23	4	20	16	5	21	38	8	4	4	5	14	13	9	21	—
Bibliography, General Reference	400	1	1	4	21	5	3	4	9	5	1	8	7	9	5	5	6					—
	1	9	13	1	2	28	55	20	23	28	40	25	61	9		7	8	7	8	6	1	—
	199		9	11	25	7	8	9	10	11	8	10	9	10	3	9	9	9	8	11	3	—
	4		1	7	6	16	36	10	5	2	15	21	11	31	6	4		2	2	5		1	—

203

Table 5. Date of Publication by Subject—continued

Subject	Total	1400–1499	1500–1599	1600–1699	1700–1799	1800–1849	1850–1899	1900–1909	1910–1919	1920–1929	1930–1939	1940–1949	1950–1959	1960	1961	1962	1963	1964	1965	1966	1967	1968
Mathematics, Pure and Applied	29	—	—	6	4	1	3	—	3	2	3	1	3	—	—	—	—	2	—	1	—	—
Biology, Agriculture, Geology	65	—	1	6	9	6	10	3	3	5	3	5	1	2	—	—	—	2	2	—	—	—
Applied Science, Technology	28	—	—	2	—	1	—	2	—	2	1	1	2	2	—	—	—	—	2	2	—	—
Natural Sciences	59	—	1	—	11	5	3	1	1	—	6	3	9	2	1	3	1	2	4	1	3	—
Medicine, Pharmacology	61	—	5	9	3	5	10	6	—	—	4	5	5	—	—	—	—	—	—	—	—	—
Biography	428	1	9	14	22	30	79	22	23	45	62	34	54	4	7	5	6	1	3	5	2	—
Literature	1,094	2	42	74	120	108	154	46	47	83	90	53	122	18	20	19	25	26	20	17	8	—
Arts, Entertainment, Recreation	298	—	4	3	15	20	61	19	22	25	22	25	59	4	5	11	6	5	6	4	—	—
Children's Books	17	—	—	—	6	2	3	3	1	—	—	—	1	—	—	—	—	—	—	—	—	—
Geography and Local History	375	—	9	18	38	59	77	22	14	26	37	16	27	5	8	3	7	3	4	—	2	—

Table 6. Date of Publication by Monograph/Series, Bloomsbury/Woolwich

	Total	1400–1499	1500–1599	1600–1699	1700–1799	1800–1849	1850–1899	1900–1909	1910–1919	1920–1929	1930–1939	1940–1949	1950–1959	1960	1961	1962	1963	1964	1965	1966	1967	1968
Base	4,601	11	147	319	387	401	693	225	216	330	414	274	581	89	79	76	90	81	98	55	34	—
Monograph	3,807 (83)	11 (100)	147 (100)	312 (98)	349 (90)	335 (84)	544 (78)	182 (81)	176 (81)	256 (78)	340 (82)	216 (79)	464 (80)	74 (83)	65 (82)	57 (75)	72 (80)	67 (83)	79 (81)	39 (71)	21 (62)	—
Series	790 (17)	—	—	7 (2)	38 (10)	66 (16)	148 (21)	43 (19)	40 (19)	74 (22)	74 (18)	57 (21)	117 (20)	15 (17)	14 (18)	18 (24)	18 (20)	13 (16)	19 (19)	16 (29)	13 (38)	—
Bloomsbury	4,564 (99)	11 (100)	147 (100)	319 (100)	387 (100)	400 (100)	690 (100)	223 (99)	215 (100)	324 (98)	407 (98)	272 (99)	574 (99)	87 (98)	79 (100)	74 (97)	88 (98)	80 (99)	97 (99)	55 (100)	34 (100)	—
Woolwich	35 (1)	—	—	—	—	1 (*)	3 (*)	2 (1)	1 (*)	6 (2)	7 (2)	2 (1)	7 (1)	2 (2)	—	1 (1)	2 (2)	—	1 (1)	—	—	—

Table 7. Monograph/Series, Bloomsbury/Woolwich by Length of Loan

	Total	Monograph	Series	Bloomsbury	Woolwich
Base	4,601	3,807	790	4,564	35
1 day..	595	551	44	595	—
	13	14	6	13	—
2 days	1,798	1,430	367	1,798	—
	39	38	46	39	—
3 days	624	503	120	623	—
	14	13	15	14	—
4 days	373	321	52	371	2
	8	8	7	8	6
5 days	302	248	53	298	3
	7	7	7	7	9
6 days	192	152	40	190	2
	4	4	5	4	6
7 days	106	87	19	103	3
	2	2	2	2	9
8 days	64	56	8	59	5
	1	1	1	1	14
9 days	50	47	3	49	1
	1	1	*	1	3
10 days	34	33	1	34	—
	1	1	*	1	—
11–15 days	119	94	25	109	10
	3	2	3	2	29
16–19 days	32	27	4	28	4
	1	1	1	1	11
20–39 days	103	80	23	101	2
	2	2	3	2	6
40–59 days	32	29	3	31	1
	1	1	*	1	3
60–79 days	17	14	3	17	—
	*	*	*	*	—
80–99 days	22	21	1	21	1
	*	1	*	*	3
100–149 days ..	34	29	5	34	—
	1	1	1	1	—
150–199 days ..	19	17	2	19	—
	*	*	*	*	—
200–249 days ..	17	15	2	17	—
	*	*	*	*	—
250–299 days ..	17	10	7	17	—
	*	*	1	*	—
Over 300 days ..	12	11	1	12	—
	*	*	*	*	—

Table 8. Monograph/Series, Bloomsbury/Woolwich by Date of Publication

	Total	Monograph	Series	Bloomsbury	Woolwich
Base	4,601	3,807	790	4,564	35
1400–1499	11 *	11 *	— —	11 *	— —
1500–1599	147 3	147 4	— —	147 3	— —
1600–1699	319 7	312 8	7 1	319 7	— —
1700–1799	387 8	349 9	38 5	387 8	— —
1800–1849	401 9	335 9	66 8	400 9	1 3
1850–1899	693 15	544 14	148 19	690 15	3 9
1900–1909	225 3	182 5	43 5	223 5	2 6
1910–1919	216 5	176 5	40 5	215 5	1 3
1920–1929	330 7	256 7	74 9	324 7	6 17
1930–1939	414 9	340 9	74 9	407 9	7 20
1940–1949	274 6	216 6	57 7	272 6	2 6
1950–1959	581 13	464 12	117 15	574 13	7 20
1960	89 2	74 2	15 2	87 2	2 6
1961	79 2	65 2	14 2	79 2	— —
1962	76 2	57 1	18 2	74 2	1 3
1963	90 2	72 2	18 2	88 2	2 6
1964	81 2	67 2	13 2	80 2	— —
1965	98 2	79 2	19 2	97 2	1 3
1966	55 1	39 1	16 2	55 1	— —
1967	34 1	21 *	13 2	34 1	— —
1968	— —	— —	— —	— —	— —

Table 9.   Monograph/Series, Bloomsbury/Woolwich by Subject

	Total	Monograph	Series	Bloomsbury	Woolwich
Base	4,601	3,807	790	4,564	35
Theology, Religions	447	408	39	447	—
	10	11	5	10	—
Philology, Linguistics	133	86	47	133	—
	3	2	6	3	—
Philosophy, Psychology, Anthropology	344	285	59	344	—
	7	7	7	8	—
Foreign Law ..	35	30	5	34	1
	1	1	1	1	3
British Law	60	55	5	60	—
	1	1	1	1	—
Economics	210	165	44	203	7
	5	4	6	4	20
Politics	266	204	61	253	12
	6	5	8	1	34
Heraldry and Genealogy	44	32	12	44	—
	1	1	2	1	—
History	400	341	59	398	2
	9	9	7	9	6
Bibliography, General Reference	199	111	88	199	—
	4	3	11	4	—
Mathematics, Pure and Applied	29	17	12	29	—
	1	*	2	1	—
Biology, Agriculture, Geology	65	55	10	63	2
	1	1	1	1	6
Applied Science, Technology	28	24	3	27	—
	1	1	*	1	—
Natural Sciences ..	59	48	11	59	—
	1	1	1	1	—
Medicine, Pharmacology	61	56	5	61	—
	1	1	1	1	—
Biography	428	422	6	428	—
	9	11	1	9	—
Literature	1,094	906	188	1,087	7
	24	24	24	24	20
Arts, Entertainment, Recreation	298	225	73	297	1
	6	6	9	7	3
Children's Books ..	17	15	2	17	—
	*	*	*	*	—
Geography and Local History	375	315	60	373	2
	8	8	8	8	6

FOLLOW-UP SURVEY OF READERS
USING THE BRITISH MUSEUM LIBRARY, AUGUST, 1968

survey carried out and report prepared by

THE ECONOMIST INTELLIGENCE UNIT LIMITED

CONTENTS

Symbols used in the Statistical Appendix

* = less than 1 per cent
– = nil

E Questionnaire—See Appendix B (i)

FOLLOW-UP SURVEY OF READERS USING THE BRITISH MUSEUM LIBRARY

INTRODUCTION

A short follow-up survey of readers using the British Museum library was carried out in the third week of August 1968. Essentially its purpose was to find out if there were any differences in readership characteristics and needs in the peak period of use in the year compared with the earlier survey carried out in April, and particularly to measure any changes due to the large number of foreign visitors who were known to use the library during the summer months. The questionnaire and method of sampling used were identical in both surveys, but whereas all six days of the working week at the library were covered in the April survey, only two days—21st and 22nd August—were covered in the August survey. A total of 1,469 visits, representing 1,188 different people, were sampled during the two days. These figures are approximately half the sample analysed for the April survey.

The present report and accompanying tables of computer output follow the same layout as the report and results of the first survey. However, the commentary in the tables is confined to pointing out the main differences between the two surveys rather than repeating all the details of the analysis contained in the previous report. A short section of conclusions on the two surveys is given at the end of the commentary on the tables.

A. Readers' Characteristics

1. *Occupation* (See Table 1)

The main difference in occupational category shown by the two surveys is confined to the academic group of readers. If anything, there was a slight increase in the use of the library by academics in August compared with April, but within this group the relative importance of postgraduate students and university staff was reversed. In April, postgraduate students were one and a half times as numerous as university staff; in August, university staff exceeded the number of postgraduate students, though by a much smaller margin.

2. *Type and Age of Readers* (See Table 2)

The proportion of readers with temporary tickets rose in August, though this group still did not exceed a tenth of the total readership.

The year base 1966/67 has been extended to include tickets issued in 1968. Consequently the percentage of readers in this group has increased slightly. Otherwise there are no significant changes.

3. *Place of Residence* (See Tables 3 to 6)

(a) *All Readers* (*Tables 3 and 4*). Although the proportion of readers who claimed to have come to London especially to visit the British Museum library rose from a third in April to a half in August, their distribution by place of residence and work was almost identical in both surveys.

(b) *Origins of Students and Academic Staff* (*Tables 5 and 6*). One of the major changes shown by the August survey was the substantial increase in the proportion of academic readers from overseas. In April these readers formed a quarter of all academic readers; in August they formed well over a half. Also the overseas contingent of readers increased from a third to a half of the total sample of readers. Nearly all the new overseas readers come from Europe, and particularly from two groups

210

of countries—France/Netherlands/Finland/Denmark and Italy/Portugal/Spain. Even so, the U.S.A. (the origin of a third of all overseas readers) remained the largest single origin in spite of a relative decline in its proportion of the total.

The proportion of readers from universities and institutions in London fell from a third to a fifth of the academic category. Among the individual colleges the falls were most marked for University College and Birkbeck College; in August no readers were recorded from Birkbeck College.

The proportion of readers from universities and institutions outside London fell even more sharply than from those in London—from a third to a tenth. However, this change had no effect on the proportion of readers originating from Oxford, Cambridge, or other universities in south-east England.

4. Frequency and Duration of Visits (See Tables 7 and 8)

(a) Frequency (Table 7). In line with the increase in the number of overseas academic readers there was an increase in the proportion of annual visitors and a decline in the proportion of short-term visitors, particularly the weekly visitor. Annual visitors formed 9 per cent of the sample in August compared with 3 per cent in April.

(b) Duration (Table 8). The influx of overseas academic readers was also reflected in the duration of visits. In August a half of all readers expected their visit to last between one week and three months compared with a quarter who fell in this category in April. The corresponding decline in other categories was split fairly evenly between short and long term visitors.

On average, readers spent half an hour longer in the library in August than in April. The comparative figures were respectively 5 hours and 4½ hours.

5. Reason for Visit (See Table 9)

The basic reasons for visiting the British Museum library were identical in both surveys.

B. Readers' Needs

1. Subjects Being Read (See Table 10)

In spite of the changes within the academic category the basic subject requirements of readers were essentially the same in August as in April, but with an increase in emphasis for books on Literature. Certainly this subject was a major attraction for the influx of readers from Europe since, among other subjects, about three quarters of them were reading Literature.

Table 11 indicates that readers were using the library more intensively in August than in April, since there was a slight increase in the average number of known and unknown items supplied to each reader.

2. Use of the Library and other British Museum Departments (see Tables 12 to 14)

(a) Main Library Departments (Table 12). The proportion of readers using the main library departments was the same in both surveys. If anything there was marginally greater use of the Manuscripts department and marginally less use of the Oriental Printed Books and Manuscripts department. Again readers from foreign universities, and particularly from the U.S.A., made greatest use of the Manuscripts department.

Within the Printed Books department there was proportionately less use of the Map Room in August than in April, but greater use of the Newspaper Library at Colindale. However, in both cases, the number of readers involved was small.

(*b*) *Other British Museum Departments* (*Tables* 13 *and* 14). Although the proportion of readers who indicated that they intended using more than one library department rose between the two surveys from a quarter to a third, there was no corresponding increase in the use of the various British Museum departments. Indeed, the usage of each of the three most used departments—Manuscripts, Oriental Printed Books and Manuscripts, Prints and Drawings—was lower in August than in April. Use of the other departments was unchanged.

3. *Satisfaction of Readers' Needs* (See Tables 15 and 16)

The main changes in the satisfaction of readers' needs were confined to slight increases in the proportion of books already in use, at the binder or not in the library. These differences may be attributed to the greater number of readers using the library during the peak month of August, and also to the special requirements of the increased number of foreign readers. Even so the proportion of readers who obtained all, some, or more of their requirements remained unchanged.

4. *Methods of Work* (See Tables 17 to 24)

(*a*) *Use of Other Libraries* (*Table* 17). With the increase in the number of foreign visitors there was an increase in the proportion of readers who had tried to obtain their requirements in another library before trying the British Museum, and particularly those who had tried in libraries abroad. With fewer British academics using the library in August there was also a decline in the proportion of those readers who had tried university or college libraries first.

(*b*) *Readers' Knowledge of Items they were Seeking* (*Table* 18). There were no changes in the proportions of readers who were seeking known as opposed to unknown items of literature.

(*c*) *Reservation of Books* (*Table* 19). More readers reserved books in advance in August than in April, no doubt due to the increase in the number of annual readers who only had a limited amount of time to carry out their research. There was no increased use of the reservation service by readers who had used the same book on a previous occasion.

(*d*) *Use of Catalogues* (*Tables* 20 *and* 21). There was little change in the methods of identifying unknown items of literature, except for marginally greater use of the catalogues and reference books. There was a slight increase in the proportion of readers who experienced difficulties in using the catalogues, but they remained well below a tenth of the total sample.

(*e*) *Delivery of Books* (Tables 22 and 23). The greater use of the library in August was reflected in the lengthening of the time spent waiting for books to be delivered. On average, the delay experienced by readers who had not reserved books in advance was nearer one hour than half an hour as recorded in April.

With the increase in medium-term visitors, particularly those from abroad, it is not suprising that there was a decline in the willingness of readers to wait longer than necessary to obtain books, although the proportion who were prepared to wait, largely because they had no alternative, was still nearly two thirds of the total sample.

(*f*) *Use of the Photocopying Service* (Table 24). While there were no changes in the proportions of readers who could have made equal use of photocopies and could have ordered them without first coming to the library, there was a significant increase in the proportion who would be prepared to pay for this service at a rate of 3d. a page.

C. Conclusions

The main feature of the two readership surveys is the striking similarity they show in the broad pattern of usage of the British Museum library. In spite of significant changes in the composition of the academic group of readers, their requirements and methods of work do not differ widely, though restrictions on time, particularly for the overseas readers, cause certain variation in the frequency and duration of visits.

Basically the British Museum is catering for academic readers whose interests are concentrated in what might be termed pure arts subjects, and especially in literature and history. Few of these readers require to use the general Museum departments in conjunction with their work in the Printed Books department, and even fewer find the use of other departments essential to their work. As regards methods of work, the majority of readers are sophisticated researchers in that they know in advance precisely what they are looking for, make extensive use of the reservation service, and are sufficiently familiar with the use of catalogues and other library services to locate unknown items with only a moderate amount of assistance.

While there is general satisfaction with the service currently offered by the British Museum library, the surveys reveal two areas where there is scope for some improvement. First, a sizeable minority of readers (a quarter) do not obtain all their requirements and a major reason for this is that the books required have been mislaid. Secondly it would be useful if delivery times for books could be shortened. Long delays in obtaining books were certainly the major source of irritation for the several readers who made complaints in person to the survey team, and the results of the questionnaire showed that a significant number of readers were affected in this way.

D. Statistical Appendix

Table 1. Occupation of Readers

	Visits		People	
	Sample 1,469[1]	Per cent	Sample 1,188[1]	Per cent
Student (i) Undergraduate	111	8	95	8
(ii) Postgraduate	458	31	372	31
Academic (i) University staff..	503	34	392	33
(ii) Other higher academic institutions ..	88	6	66	6
(iii) School teacher ..	84	6	65	5
Freelance writer	124	8	106	9
Professional researcher	55	4	48	4
Civil Service/local government	42	3	36	3
Industry/commerce/banking ..	40	3	33	3
Full time staff of research institution, professional association, trade federation, etc.	36	2	29	2
British Museum staff ..	32	2	26	2
Journalist	24	2	22	2
Librarian	19	1	16	1
Private unpaid research	18	1	15	1
Publisher/editor	5	*	5	*
Others/no answer	41	3	32	3

[1] The breakdown exceeds the sample number because several readers ticked more than one occupational category in their answers to this question. The percentages are calculated on the sample number and therefore exceed 100 per cent.

Table 2. Type and Age of Readers

	Visits		People	
	Sample 1,469	Per cent	Sample 1,188	Per cent
1. *Type of Reader:*				
Those with readers' tickets	1,178	80	897	76
Temporary readers	116	8	114	10
No answer	175	12	175	14
	Sample 1,178	Per cent	Sample 897	Per cent
2. *Age of Readers:*				
Ticket issued 1920–31 ..	29	2	24	3
,, ,, 1932–38 ..	40	3	32	4
,, ,, 1939–48 ..	33	3	26	3
,, ,, 1949–52 ..	56	5	42	5
,, ,, 1953–55 ..	51	4	39	4
,, ,, 1956–58 ..	94	8	70	8
,, ,, 1959–61 ..	82	7	62	7
,, ,, 1962–63 ..	118	10	87	10
,, ,, 1964–65 ..	164	14	120	13
,, ,, 1966–68 ..	511	44	395	43

214

Table 3. Residence of Readers

	Visits		People	
	Sample 1,469	Per cent	Sample 1,188	Per cent
In London postal area:				
Up to 2 miles from the Museum ..	209	14	161	14
2–5 miles from the Museum	158	11	119	10
5–10 miles from the Museum	347	24	279	23
Over 10 miles from the Museum ..	227	15	189	16
Home counties (Middlesex, Hertford, Essex, Surrey, Kent)	126	9	114	10
South-East counties (Sussex, Hants, Berks, Bucks, Oxford, Bedford, Northants, Hunts, Cambs, Suffolk, Norfolk)	92	6	79	7
Other parts of England	70	5	55	5
Wales	11	1	5	*
Scotland..	21	1	18	2
Ireland	6	*	5	*
No answer	202	14	164	14

Table 4. Readers' Place of Work

	Visits		People	
	Sample 1,469	Per cent	Sample 1,188	Per cent
In London postal area:				
Up to 2 miles from the Museum ..	633[1]	43	507[1]	43
2–5 miles from the Museum	95	6	78	7
5–10 miles from the Museum	84	6	71	6
Over 10 miles from the Museum ..	55	4	47	4
Home counties (Middlesex, Hertford, Essex, Surrey, Kent)	46	3	41	3
South-East counties (Sussex, Hants, Berks, Bucks, Oxford, Bedford, Northants, Hunts, Cambs, Suffolk, Norfolk)	71	5	61	5
Other parts of England	68	5	54	5
Wales	10	1	5	*
Scotland..	23	2	21	2
Ireland	9	1	8	1
No answer	375	26	295	25

[1] Of the 633 and 507 readers who gave their place of work within a two mile radius of the Museum, 386 and 301 did so because they were mainly working at the Museum. The remainder had offices or other places of work in the area.

Table 5. Main Origins of Students or Staff of a University or other Academic Institution

	Visits		People	
	Sample 965[1]	Per cent	Sample 767[1]	Per cent
London	217	22	180	23
Of which:				
School of Oriental and African Studies	39	4	32	4
University College	32	3	27	4
Kings College	27	3	23	3
Bedford College	18	2	15	2
London School of Economics	17	2	16	2
Warburg Institute	6	1	4	1
School of Slavonic and East European Studies	2	*	1	*
British Universities or Academic Institutions outside London	97	10	77	10
Of which:				
Oxford University	37	4	28	4
Cambridge University	24	2	18	2
Sussex University..	12	1	11	1
Other Universities in South-East England†	24	2	20	3
Overseas..	544	56	419	55
No answer	107	11	91	12

[1] The sample figures for this Table differ from the total figures for students and academic staff given in Table 1 due to those readers who ticked more than one category in their answer to the question on occupation.

† Includes Universities of Reading, Southampton, Kent, Essex and East Anglia.

Table 6.   Origins of Readers who normally live Overseas

	Visits		People	
	Sample 711	Per cent	Sample 552	Per cent
English Speaking Countries:				
USA	241	34	195	35
Canada	67	9	50	9
Australia	15	2	13	2
West Indies	7	1	5	1
New Zealand	7	1	7	1
South Africa	1	*	1	*
Others/no answer	8	1	5	1
	346	49	276	50
Non English-Speaking Countries:				
France/Netherlands/Finland/Denmark	124	17	92	17
Italy/Portugal/Spain	79	11	61	11
Germany/Austria/Switzerland	64	9	49	9
Egypt/Israel/Jordan/Ethiopia/Iraq/Sudan/ Tunisia	34	5	25	5
India/Pakistan	27	4	17	3
Malaysia/Japan	7	1	5	1
Russia/Yugoslavia/Hungary/Bulgaria	3	*	2	*
Others/no answer	27	4	25	5
	365	51	276	50

Table 7.   Frequency of Visit

	Visits		People	
	Sample 1,469	Per cent	Sample 1,188	Per cent
1. *Regularity of Visit:*				
Every day	589	40	450	38
Every week	340	23	286	24
Every month	108	7	101	9
Every 3 months	104	7	85	7
Every year	133	9	104	9
No answer	195	14	162	13
2. *Occasion of Last Visit:*				
Up to 1 week ago	561	38	454	38
Between 1 and 4 weeks ago	186	13	157	13
Between 1 and 3 months ago	119	8	100	8
Between 3 and 6 months ago	73	5	58	5
Between 6 and 9 months ago	32	2	21	2
Between 9 and 15 months ago	141	10	109	9
Longer than 15 months ago	139	9	109	9
Never	163	11	128	11
No answer	55	4	52	4

Table 8. Duration of Visit

	Visits		People	
	Sample 1,469	Per cent	Sample 1,188	Per cent
1. Duration of Present Visit:				
1 day or less	127	9	123	10
Between 1 day and 1 week	263	18	224	19
Between 1 week and 1 month	345	23	279	23
Between 1 month and 3 months	369	25	279	23
Longer period	321	22	246	21
No answer	44	3	37	3
2. Time spent in Library on Present Visit:				
1 hour	62	4	54	5
2 hours	113	8	97	8
3 hours	169	12	139	12
4 hours	180	12	152	13
5 hours	152	10	126	11
6 hours	190	13	147	12
7 hours	182	12	144	12
8 hours	156	11	121	10
9 hours	77	5	59	5
10 hours	70	5	44	4
11 hours	20	1	14	1
No waiting/no answer	88	6	84	7
Average time spent in Library	5·2 hours		5·0 hours	

Table 9. Reason for Visit

	Visits		People	
	Sample 1,469	Per cent	Sample 1,188	Per cent
1. Visit Related:				
To work	1,094	74	877	74
To leisure interests	76	5	66	6
To work and leisure interests	279	19	228	19
No answer	20	1	17	1
	Sample 1,007	Per cent	Sample 800	Per cent
2. Is the British Museum the only Library Capable of Supplying all Your Requirements?				
Yes	519	52	414	52
No	155	15	120	15
Don't know	307	30	244	31
No answer	27	3	23	3

218

Table 10. Main Subjects being Read

	Visits		People	
	Sample 1,469[1]	Per cent	Sample 1,188[1]	Per cent
History	685	47	541	46
Literature	610	42	478	40
Bibliography/General Reference	356	24	279	23
Arts/Entertainment/Recreation	216	15	181	15
Biography	205	14	164	14
Theology/Religions	204	14	162	14
Philosophy/Psychology/Anthropology ..	185	13	148	12
Philology/Linguistics	147	10	115	10
Politics	146	10	110	9
Geography/Local History	144	10	118	10
Economics	94	6	72	6
Heraldry/Genealogy	68	5	59	5
Natural Sciences	45	3	38	3
Medicine/Pharmacology	35	2	26	2
British Law	34	2	25	2
Biology/Agriculture/Geology	29	2	23	2
Foreign Law	23	2	18	2
Applied Science/Technology	23	2	21	2
Mathematics, Pure and Applied	21	1	16	1
Children's Books	15	1	12	1
Other subjects	—	—	—	—
No answer	12	1	10	1

[1] As readers were asked to indicate all the subject fields they were using during their visit the numerical breakdown by subject is much greater than the sample number, and the percentages exceed 100 per cent.

Table 11. Average number of Items used per Reader

	Visits	People
1. *Items that were known to the reader before his visit:*		
Known items that were supplied	5·5	5·3
Known items that were not supplied	0·7	0·7
2. *Items that were unknown to the reader before his visit:*		
Unknown items that were supplied	2·3	2·1

Table 12. Use of Library Departments

	Visits		People	
	Sample 1,469	Per cent	Sample 1,188	Per cent
1. *Readers using any Library Department:*				
Printed Books Department	1,381	94	1,112	94
Of which:				
Use by day	1,208	82	966	81
Use by evening	173	12	146	13
Manuscripts Department	65	4	56	5
Oriental Printed Books and Manuscripts				
Department	23	2	20	2
2. *Readers using one Library Department only:*				
Those using only one department	937	64	748	63
Those using more than one department ..	516	35	425	36
No answer	16	1	15	1

Table 13. Use of Museum Departments other than the Printed Books Department by Readers using more than one Library Department

	Visits			People		
	Sample 516	Per cent	Per cent of total sample 1,469	Sample 425	Per cent	Per cent of total sample 1,188
Manuscripts	116	22	8	92	22	8
Oriental Printed Books and Manuscripts	38	7	3	32	8	3
Prints and Drawings	28	5	2	26	6	2
Greek and Roman Antiquities ..	19	4	1	17	4	1
British and Mediaeval Antiquities	16	3	1	15	4	1
Oriental Antiquities	13	2	1	12	3	1
Western Asiatic Antiquities ..	11	2	1	10	2	1
Egyptian Antiquities	8	2	1	7	2	1
Coins and Medals	6	1	*	5	1	*
Ethnography	5	1	*	4	1	*
Laboratory	—	—	—	—	—	—

Table 14. Readers who found it essential to Use Departments other than the Printed Books Department

	Visits			People		
	Sample 516	Per cent	Per cent of total sample 1,469	Sample 425	Per cent	Per cent of total sample 1,188
Manuscripts　　..　　..　　..	89	17	6	67	16	6
Oriental Printed Books and Manu- scripts　　..　　..　　..　　..	24	5	2	21	5	2
Prints and Drawings　　..　　..	19	4	1	18	4	2
Greek and Roman Antiquities　..	11	2	1	9	2	1
British and Mediaeval Antiquities	10	2	1	9	2	1
Oriental Antiquities　　..　　..	8	2	1	7	2	1
Western Asiatic Antiquities　..	7	1	*	6	1	1
Coins and Medals ..　　..　　..	4	1	*	3	1	*
Egyptian Antiquities　　..　　..	4	1	*	3	1	*
Ethnography　　..　　..　　..	3	1	*	2	1	*
Laboratory ..　　..　　..　　..	—	—	—	—	—	—

Table 15. Satisfaction of Readers' Needs

	Visits		People	
	Sample 1,469	Per cent	Sample 1,188	Per cent
Readers who obtained *all* they required　..	1,007	69	800	67
Readers who obtained some of their require- ments　　..　　..　　..　　..　　..	398	27	328	28
Readers who obtained none of their require- ments ..　　..　　..　　..　　..　　..	13	1	11	1
No answer　　..　　..　　..　　..　　..	51	3	49	4

221

Table 16.   Reasons for the non-availability of Books

	Visits		People	
	Sample 462[1]	Per cent	Sample 388[1]	Per cent
In use	117	25	92	24
Mislaid	109	24	89	23
At the binders	78	17	62	16
Book not in library	67	15	51	13
Destroyed	44	10	30	8
Outhoused	33	7	24	6
Book did not arrive	30	6	25	6
Uncertain pressmark	21	5	19	5
Unable to wait	17	4	15	4
Others	31	7	24	6
No answer	3	1	3	1

[1] The breakdown exceeds the sample number because readers were asked to tick as many categories as were applicable.   The percentages are calculated on the sample number and therefore exceed 100 per cent.

**Table 17.   Readers who tried another Library before trying
The British Museum**

	Visits		People	
	Sample 1,469	Per cent	Sample 1,188	Per cent
1. Use of Another Library:				
Tried another library	920	63	734	62
Did not try another library	516	35	426	36
No answer	33	2	28	2
	Sample 920[1]	Per cent	Sample 734[1]	Per cent
2. Types of Library Used:				
University or college library	586	64	462	63
Public library	296	32	247	34
Library of research institution, professional or learned society	153	17	120	16
Government library	61	7	51	7
National Library of Scotland, National Library of Wales	31	3	24	3
National Lending Library for Science and Technology, National Central Library ..	25	3	22	3
Industrial or firm's library	8	1	8	1
Abroad	323	35	247	34

[1] The breakdown exceeds the sample number because readers were asked to tick as many categories as were applicable.   The percentages are calculated on the sample number and therefore exceed 100 per cent.

222

Table 18. Readers' knowledge of Books/Literature they were seeking

	Visits		People	
	Sample 1,469[1]	Per cent	Sample 1,188[1]	Per cent
Seeking known items	938	64	746	63
Seeking both known and unknown items ..	470	32	389	33
Seeking unknown items	50	3	42	4
Seeking professional assistance	25	2	19	2
Seeking a quiet place to read	4	*	4	*
Others	13	1	10	1
No answer	29	2	28	2

[1] The breakdown exceeds the sample number because readers were asked to tick as many categories as were applicable. The percentages are calculated on the sample number and therefore exceed 100 per cent.

Table 19. Reservation of Books/Literature

	Visits		People	
	Sample 1,469	Per cent	Sample 1,188	Per cent
1. *Readers who Reserved Books before Visiting the Library:*				
Did reserve in advance	943	64	725	61
Did not reserve in advance	383	26	339	29
No answer	68	5	58	5
	Sample 943	Per cent	Sample 725	Per cent
2. *Readers who Reserved Books after using them on a previous occasion:*				
Used books previously	735	78	556	77
Did not use books previously	120	13	98	14
No answer	89	9	72	10

Table 20. Methods of identifying unknown items of Literature

	Visits		People	
	Sample 1,469	Per cent[1]	Sample 1,188	Per cent[1]
By consulting the catalogues and index ..	615	42	499	42
By consulting other reference books.. ..	341	23	271	23
By looking on the shelves	81	6	70	6
By asking the staff	68	5	65	5
No answer	24	2	21	2

[1] The percentages are based on the total sample since it is not known from the questionnaire how many readers were looking for unknown items of literature only.

Table 21. Readers who consulted the Enquiry Desk, Centre Desk or Member of the Reading Room Staff

	Visits		People	
	Sample 1,469	Per cent	Sample 1,188	Per cent
1. *Consultations:*				
Readers who did	423	29	352	30
Readers who did not	838	57	660	56
No answer	208	14	176	15
	Sample 423[1]	Per cent	Sample 352[1]	Per cent
2. *Reasons for Consultations:*				
Difficulties with delivery of books	159	38	130	37
Difficulties with the catalogues	124	29	103	29
Advice about bibliographies and reference books	72	17	66	19
To locate literature not in the British Museum	34	8	25	7
Difficulties with literature in foreign languages	5	1	4	1
Difficulties in finding a seat	5	1	5	1
Other reasons	89	21	76	22
No answer	7	2	6	2

[1] The breakdown exceeds the sample number because readers were asked to tick as many categories as were applicable. The percentages are calculated on the sample number and therefore exceed 100 per cent.

Table 22. Time spent awaiting Delivery of first Book (excluding reserved items)

	Visits		People	
	Sample 996	Per cent	Sample 810	Per cent
Up to half an hour	252	25	212	26
½ to 1 hour	335	34	260	32
1 to 1½ hours	297	30	243	30
1½ to 2 hours	64	6	58	7
Over 2 hours	48	5	37	5

Table 23. Attitude of Readers to waiting longer for Books

	Visits		People	
	Sample 1,469	Per cent	Sample 1,188	Per cent
1. *Number of Readers Prepared to Wait Longer:*				
Would wait longer	913	62	722	61
Would not wait longer	190	13	162	14
No answer	366	25	304	26
	Sample 913	Per cent	Sample 722	Per cent
2. *How much Longer?*				
Until tomorrow	334	37	268	37
2 to 3 days	180	20	138	19
4 to 6 days	66	7	52	7
More than a week	291	32	233	32
No answer	47	5	36	5

Table 24. Potential use of the Photocopying Service

	Visits		People	
	Sample 1,469	Per cent	Sample 1,188	Per cent
1. *Readers who could have made equal use of Photocopies:*				
Those who could	476	32	395	33
Those who could not	799	54	621	52
No answer	194	13	172	14
2. *Readers who could have Supplied Sufffcient Information for Photocopies without coming to the Museum:*				
Those who could	275	19	229	19
Those who could not	839	57	669	56
No answer	355	24	290	24
	Sample 275	Per cent	Sample 229	Per cent
3. *Readers who would be Prepared to Pay for Photocopies at 3d. a page:*				
Would pay	143	52	122	53
Would not pay	104	38	81	35
No answer	7	3	7	3
	Sample 275		Sample 229	
4. *Average Number of Pages Required for Photocopying*	63·6		64·5	

REPORT OF SURVEY OF LOAN REQUESTS
AT THE NATIONAL CENTRAL LIBRARY

MARCH—APRIL, 1968

survey carried out and report prepared by

THE STAFF OF THE NCL.

1. Introduction

In 1964, the NCL undertook a six months' survey of loan requests at the invitation of the Parry Committee. The more significant results of this survey, together with conclusions drawn from them, were embodied in a report submitted to the Parry Committee, copies of which have been made available to the present National Libraries Committee. A briefer description of the results was given in an article in the Library Association Record, August 1966, vol. 68, no. 8, pp. 289–294, 305 by S.P.L. Filon and I. P. Gibb. The present survey has been undertaken in order to see firstly whether any significant changes have taken place since 1964 in the loan demand made on the NCL or in its ability to satisfy this demand, and secondly whether any such changes would indicate any further support to or modification of the conclusions given on pp. 19–23 of the 1964 Survey.

2. Methods

The present shorter survey covered the period 11th March–5th April 1968. As in 1964 a survey form (generally similar to that used in 1964) was coded for each application dealt with; a specimen form is attached. In 1964 most of the tabulation of results was done by the DES computer; this was not available in 1968, and the tables have been produced by means of the Library's punched-card sorter. Because of the comparative slowness of this latter method, the analysis is in some cases less detailed than in 1964, and does not cover all the aspects of the 1964 survey. Analysis of these data is however continuing and further results would be available at a later date.

3. General notes on tables

In order to simplify presentation, the breakdown by language has been restricted to three groups: English-language books published in Great Britain, English-language books published abroad (of which the great majority are American), and foreign language books. These are referred to as British, American, and foreign, respectively.

Categories of libraries have been restricted to the following:

NCL
Other (British) National libraries
University libraries
Public libraries
Special libraries (divided into A—libraries of learned societies and other research libraries, and B—other special libraries, e.g. training colleges, commercial and industrial libraries)
Overseas libraries

In the case of the source of supply a figure is given for applications satisfied by Regional Library Systems in those cases where the name of the actual supplying libraries was not notified to NCL.

In several tables a figure is given against the heading " Unknown "; this usually indicates mis-coding or mis-punching.

Table I. Basic Statistics

	1968	1964
(a) Applications received during survey period	10,868	53,902
Applications satisfied	8,462	42,526
Percentage satisfied	77·9	78·9

	1968			1964		
	No.	% of total	% satisfied	No.	% of total	% satisfied
(b) Analysis of requests by subject groups						
Humanities	5,646	51·9	78·8	24,829	46·1	78·4
Social Sciences	2,314	21·3	80·7	8,880	16·5	81·2
Science and Technology	2,905	26·8	73·9	20,173	37·4	78·5
Total	10,868	100·0	77·9	53,902	100·0	78·9
(c) Analysis of requests by type of publication						
Books	8,676	79·8	80·4	41,762	77·5	79·6
Periodicals	2,192	20·2	67·7	12,140	22·5	76·6
Total	10,868	100·0	77·9	53,902	100·0	78·9
(d) Analysis of requests by language groups						
British	4,516	41·6	87·0	22,593	41·9	89·3
American	4,061	37·3	73·7	20,852	38·7	72·9
Foreign	2,291	21·1	67·1	10,457	19·4	68·4
Total	10,868	100·0	77·9	53,902	100·0	78·9

Comments

4. The overall success rate has declined from 78·9% to 77·9%. This rate does however fluctuate from year to year by a small percentage, probably depending more on the quantity and quality of staff available at any particular time than on any other factor.

5. It will however be noted (from Table I(c)) that there has been a slight increase in the success rate for books, while there has been a significant decline in the success rate for periodicals. (See also Tables III(a) and III(b)). There has been a decline in the success rate for science and technology as compared with other subjects (see Table I(b)). The success rate for scientific periodicals has dropped from 77·2% to 65·5%. These decreases are likely to be mainly due to the following causes:

    (i) The NLLST has considerably expanded its collections since 1964.

    (ii) Libraries now mainly apply first to the NLLST for scientific periodicals (70% of those in the 1968 survey who stated whether they had tried NLLST, as compared with 30% for books). In 1964 the NCL more often requested items from NLLST on behalf of other libraries (see also comments to Table II). The NCL satisfies 80% of scientific requests which have not first been to NLLST, and 61% of those which have.

    (iii) The NCL has published supplements to BUCOP since 1964; libraries therefore apply direct to other libraries for those periodicals listed in BUCOP rather than applying to NCL. The requests for periodicals are therefore more and more for the scarce and obscure titles.   This is supported by the fact that a quarter of the satisfied requests for foreign periodicals were supplied by overseas libraries.

The drop in the proportion of NCL requests which are for science and technology is no doubt accounted for by (i) and (ii) above.

6. There is little difference in the distribution of applications by languages.   The increase in foreign language requests would be accounted for by the higher proportion of requests in the humanities, as about two thirds of foreign language requests are for the humanities.

Table II.   Sources of Applications and Supply

Type of Library	Applications received from		Applications satisfied by	
	No.	%*	No.	%*
NCL ..	22 (23)	0·2 (0·0)	1,709 (7,780)	20·2 (18·3)
University	4,213 (15,054)	38·8 (28·0)	3,371 (12,623)	39·9 (29·7)
Public..	3,957 (24,729)	36·5 (45·9)	1,475 (7,835)	17·5 (18·5)
Special—A	337 (2,329)	3·1 (4·3)	679 (3,632)	8·0 (8·6)
B	1,644 (8,968)	15·1 (16·7)	528 (3,666)	6·3 (8·6)
Other National	35 (99)	0·3 (0·2)	100 (1,354)	1·2 (3·2)
Overseas	646 (2,647)	6·0 (4·9)	367 (2,162)	4·3 (5·1)
Regions†	— (—)	— (—)	223 (3,404)	2·6 (8·0)
Unknown	14 (57)	— (—)	10 (70)	— (—)
Total	10,868 (53,902)	100·0 (100·0)	8,462 (42,526)	100·0 (100·0)

1964 results in brackets.
* Excluding " unknown."
† Library unknown.

Comments

7. The annual number of applications received has increased by over 30% since 1964. The smaller proportion of requests from public and special libraries in 1968 does not therefore represent an actual decline in number.   There has however been a very considerable increase in the number of requests received from university libraries, partly explained by the increase in the number of such libraries.   There has also been a smaller, but significant, increase in the number of requests from overseas libraries.

8. The proportion of requests satisfied by university libraries has increased *pari passu* with their applications; in general requests from university libraries are more likely to be satisfied from the NCL stock or from other university libraries than from other sources.   The proportion satisfied from NCL stock has also increased and is now larger than the public libraries' share; the actual annual number of books lent from NCL stock has increased by about 60% over the 4 years.   The most significant decrease (apart from the source of supply given as Regions-library unknown, where the decrease represents a better standard of reporting information to NCL) is in the case of other national libraries.   The reason for this is that in 1964, the NCL was still applying to the NLLST on behalf of other libraries; this is now done comparatively rarely, as these other libraries are encouraged to apply direct to NLLST.

Table III. Applications Analysed by Date and Language

Date	British		American		Foreign		Total	
	No.	% satisfied	No.	% satisfied	No.	% satisfied	No.	% satisfied
-1899	990 (4,198)	84·0 (83·6)	104 (514)	51·9 (59·1)	327 (1,337)	63·3 (64·2)	1,422 (6,049)	76·9 (77·2)
1900-1949	1,921 (10,388)	87·0 (89·3)	1,089 (6,921)	73·7 (73·3)	918 (3,999)	67·1 (68·5)	3,928 (21,308)	78·7 (80·2)
1950-1959	698 (4,362)	91·8 (94·6)	996 (6,731)	78·0 (78·5)	404 (2,543)	67·6 (71·5)	2,098 (13,636)	80·6 (82·3)
1960-	824 (2,954)	87·7 (91·8)	1,822 (6,264)	72·8 (69·0)	570 (2,140)	70·8 (68·3)	3,216 (11,358)	76·3 (74·8)
No date	83 (691)	—	50 (422)	—	72 (438)	—	205 (1,551)	—
Total	4,516 (22,593)	87·0 (89·3)	4,061 (20,852)	73·7 (72·9)	2,291 (10,457)	67·1 (68·4)	10,868 (53,902)	77·9 (78·9)

1964 figures in brackets.

Table III (a). Applications for Books

Date of Publication	British No.	% satisfied	American No.	% satisfied	Foreign No.	% satisfied	Total No.	% satisfied
−1899 ..	939	84·6	95	52·6	268	61·2	1,302	77·4
1900–1949 ..	1,697	88·9	908	74·1	674	68·7	3,279	80·7
1950–1959 ..	563	94·0	786	80·5	265	70·2	1,614	83·5
1960–	593	91·4	1,426	76·6	319	80·3	2,338	80·8
No date	64		26		53		143	
Total ..	3,856	88·7	3,241	75·9	1,579	69·4	8,676	80·4
1964 Total ..	19,285	89·5	15,593	72·1	6,884	68·6	41,762	79·6

Table III (b). Applications for Periodicals

Date of publication	British No.	% satisfied	American No.	% satisfied	Foreign No.	% satisfied	Total No.	% satisfied
−1899 ..	51	74·5	9	44·4	59	72·9	119	71·4
1900–1949 ..	224	72·3	181	71·8	244	62·7	649	68·6
1950–1959 ..	135	83·0	210	68·6	139	62·6	484	70·9
1960–	231	78·4	396	59·3	251	59·0	878	64·2
No date	19		24		19		62	
Total ..	660	77·3	820	65·0	712	62·1	2,192	67·7
1964 Total ..	3,308	87·8	5,259	75·4	3,573	68·0	12,140	76·6

Table IV. Source of Supply According to Language Groups Divided into Current Material (post-1950) and Older Material (pre-1950)

	1950 onwards			Pre-1950			Total
	British	American	Foreign	British	American	Foreign	
NCL ..	274 (20·1)	412 (19·7)	87 (12·9)	737 (28·8)	167 (18·7)	32 (3·7)	1,709 (20·2)
University	457 (33·6)	1,032 (49·2)	335 (49·7)	658 (25·6)	414 (46·3)	465 (54·1)	3,371 (39·9)
Public	372 (27·4)	212 (10·1)	17 (2·5)	715 (27·8)	112 (12·5)	47 (5·5)	1,475 (17·5)
Special—A	85 (6·3)	166 (7·9)	69 (10·2)	186 (7·2)	87 (9·8)	86 (10·0)	679 (8·0)
B	118 (8·7)	195 (9·3)	26 (3·9)	114 (4·4)	53 (5·9)	22 (2·6)	528 (6·3)
Other National	16 (1·2)	12 (0·6)	20 (3·0)	21 (0·8)	7 (0·8)	24 (2·8)	100 (1·2)
Overseas	2 (0·1)	51 (2·4)	116 (17·2)	4 (0·2)	29 (3·2)	175 (20·3)	367 (4·3)
Regions	36 (2·6)	16 (0·8)	4 (0·6)	133 (5·2)	25 (2·8)	9 (1·0)	223 (2·6)
Unknown	— (—)	3 (—)	— (—)	3 (—)	— (—)	4 (—)	10 (—)
Total ..	1,360	2,099	674	2,571	894	864	8,462
		4,133			4,329		

Figures in brackets indicate percentage of total supplied by each source (excluding "unknown").

Comments

9. The figures in Tables III and IV are for both books and periodicals in all subjects. Table III (a) and III (b) give a breakdown of the figures in Table III into books and periodicals. The NCL stock is shown to be a particularly important source of supply for older British books. It also makes a substantial contribution towards the supply of American books of all dates. It should, however, be noted that it consists mainly of *books* in the humanities and social sciences, and the proportion lent in these categories would be much higher. For example, the growing acquisition of American non-scientific books by the NCL has led to an increased success rate for these (78 per cent as against 72 per cent in 1964), the NCL share increasing from 17 per cent to 22 per cent. The additional book fund available in 1968/69 will help to increase this percentage further, although funds still fall far short of what is needed to tackle this problem thoroughly. It should also be noted that the NCL has bought few British books published since 1958 (except for the Adult Class service, which this survey does not include), as the Regional Library Systems have between them agreed to acquire all such books appearing in the BNB. The NCL stock is now the largest source of loans of older British books; this no doubt reflects the NCL's role in acting as a recipient of books other libraries no longer wish to retain.

10. The date distribution of requests differs in the three subject groups. Half the applications in the humanities are for items more than 30 years old; the comparable figure for the social sciences is 14 years, and for science and technology 12 years. In the case of the last, it must be noted that this is a residual demand, as the NLLST has the principal responsibility for the supply of scientific literature. It is understood that half their requests are for items less than four years old.

Table V. Search Methods

	NCL stock		Catalogue				Speculative approaches		Overseas libraries		Unknown	Total supplied	Total Applications	% Found in catalogue †‡	% Supplied from Catalogue locations †§
			1st locations		Other locations										
	No.	%*	No.	%*	No.	%*	No.	%*	No.	%*	No.	No.	No.	%	%
1964 :: :: ::	7,780	18·3	19,079	44·9	6,556	15·4	6,849	16·3	2,162	5·1	100	42,526	53,902	70·1	60·6
1968 :: :: ::	1,709	20·6	4,064	48·9	1,342	16·1	830	10·0	367	4·4	150	8,462	10,868	74·5	66·0

* Of total *supplied*, excluding " unknown " search method.
† Including items in NCL stock at time of application, but excluding those purchased as a result of the application.
‡ Of total applications (including those items not supplied for which locations are in the catalogue).
§ Of total applications.

Table V (a). Locations Traced Through NCL Union Catalogues According to Language Groups

	Items located*	% traced in catalogue of applications received*	% supplied from catalogue locations*
British	3,925 (18,762)	86·9 (83·0)	78·1 (74·4)
American	2,879 (13,735)	70·9 (65·9)	62·9 (55·6)
Foreign	1,252 (5,310)	54·6 (50·8)	46·9 (40·8)
Total	8,056 (37,807)	74·5 (70·1)	66·0 (60·6)

1964 figures in brackets.

* Including those in NCL stock at time of application but excluding those purchased as a result of the application.

Table VI. Failures of Locations

Survey	Total locations found (other than NLC stock)	First location failures	
		No.	%
1964	30,780	11,701	38·0
1968	6,389	2,325	36·4

Comments

11. Table V gives comparative figures (1964 and 1968) for the methods of search. Analysis by language groups of locations traced is given in Table V (a). It is very encouraging to note that, apart from the increased percentage supplied from the NCL stock, there has been a marked increase in the percentage of satisfied requests supplied from catalogue locations (from 60·3 per cent to 65 per cent), particularly in those supplied by the first catalogue locations. Since these two methods of supply are normally by far the quickest, this will have increased the speed of supply. The NCL has had comments from a number of libraries to this effect in the last year or two.

12. The increase in the effectiveness of the union catalogues has probably been due to two main causes:

(i) the refiling of the catalogues according to the simplified (Berghoeffer) rules, which allows a much greater rate of insertion per man-hour;

(ii) a management study by senior library staff of the organisation of the union catalogue work, which led to the employment of more part-time staff for this work. With suitable full-time supervisory staff, this has led to increased productivity.

13. The need to rely less on " speculative approaches " will not only help to speed up the service, but will reduce the burden on co-operating libraries, which are asked to check requests for items which they may or may not have.

14. It is also encouraging to note (Table VI) that despite the large increase in the use of catalogue locations, there has been a slight increase in the percentage of first

235

location failures. Since these latter are of a significantly different nature for books as compared with periodicals, the following comment (which includes some further analysis) is made.

15. Books

The first location failures total 1,596 (33·6 per cent) out of 4,753 items located outside NCL stock. By far the largest percentage of these were temporarily unavailable (77 per cent made up of 54 per cent on loan, binding or in use, and 23 per cent " decline to lend ", normally because of local demand). Only 6·7 per cent had been withdrawn. This suggests that the more books which can be added to the central loan collection the better, as local use often restricts availability on inter-library loan.

16. Periodicals

The first location failures total 729 (49·5 per cent) out of 1,636 items located outside NCL stock. The majority (51 per cent) were reported as " not held ", normally meaning " part not held " rather than " title not held ". 12 per cent were on loan when requested, and libraries declined to lend a further 29 per cent. (In many cases the holding library would offer a photocopy to the applying library, but the NCL would not necessarily be notified of these.) No titles were reported " withdrawn ". This shows a growing reluctance on the part of libraries to lend periodicals, suggesting that the NCL function in relation to periodicals is tending to become more one of providing locations, either published in BUCOP or given in response to applications. (See also paragraph 18.)

Conclusions

17. While the results of the 1968 survey have revealed certain marked differences from those of the 1964 survey, these strengthened the conclusions reached on pp. 19–23 of the 1964 survey. In these, the NCL claimed its main field of activity was that of the provision of books in the humanities and social sciences, in particular current American and foreign language books and older books in all languages (but especially British). It was then considered desirable that the current books should be acquired for the NCL's loan stock; the older books should also be acquired by the NCL when this was possible, but the union catalogues should be developed particularly in relation to these older books. In all these areas the NCL is now more successful than in 1964, although the book fund needed to develop the Library's loan stock is nothing like as large as it should be.

The proportions of failures which could be dealt with by an expansion of this loan stock remain about the same as quoted on pp. 19–20 of the 1964 survey. The annual book production of the U.S.A. has, however increased, and therefore the number of books needing to be purchased has increased (probably from about 5,000 a year to 7,000 a year). However, the number of requests for American non-scientific books published in the current decade has increased more than threefold since 1964, although the length of the period since the beginning of 1960 has less than doubled. The union catalogues have dealt more effectively than in 1964 with a higher annual intake of requests but again more money is needed for their development.

18. Those areas where the proportion of requests has declined, or where the NCL is less able to satisfy requests are those where other sources have been developed; scientific literature (provided by the NLLST) and periodicals in non-scientific subjects, where the publication of the union catalogue (BUCOP) has increased the amount of direct lending. It is, however, still felt that there should be greater central provision of non-scientific periodicals in order to relieve the burden on other libraries for the supply of these; it would be desirable to obtain more information from other libraries about excessive demands on their periodical holdings.

Column	Punch	Coding details	Column	Punch	Coding details
		DETAILS OF ITEM REQUESTED			**RESULT OF APPLICATION**
9–11		DATE	27		SUPPLY POSITION
				0	Supplied on loan
				1	Supplied as p/c
12–13		SUBJECT		2	All copies on loan
				3	Ref. in appl. lib.
				4	Lib. decl. to lend
14		TYPE		5	Lib. is non-lending
	–	Unknown		6	Ref. at BM only
	0	Others		7	No copy in UK
	1	Ordinary monograph	28		SUPPLY POSITION—OVERSEAS
	2	Part of mono. series			
	3	Multi-vol. work		x	Resubmitted appl.
	4	Conf. procs.		0	No copy overseas
	5	Govt. publn.		1	Not loanable overseas
	6	Musical score			
	7	Thesis	29		SUPPLYING LIBRARY (Code as 25)
			30		TIME TAKEN
	8	Newspaper		0	Unknown
	9	Periodical		1	1 day
				2	2–5 days
				3	6–10 days
				4	11–15 days
15–17		LANGUAGE		5	16–20 days
				6	21–30 days
				7	31 days–2 months
				8	2–3 months
				9	Over 3 months
		ROUTE OF APPLICATION			**METHOD OF SEARCH**
24		NLLST tried?			CATALOGUE
	0	No	35		1st location
	1	Yes			
	2	Not stated	36		2nd location
25		APPLYING LIBRARY	37		3rd location
	0	NCL			
	1	National	38		4th location
	2	University			
	3	New university	39		5th or later location
	4	Other college			
	5	Public	40		NEGATIVE RESULT
	6	Government		0	No entry
	7	Learned soc. etc.		1	Pos. entry–not avail.
	8	Commercial		2	Negative entry
	9	Overseas			SPECULATIVE APPROACHES
			41		1st attempt
			42		2nd attempt
			43		3rd attempt
			44		4th attempt
			45		5th or later attempt
			46		NEGATIVE RESULT
				0	No approaches made
				1	Locn. found–not available
				2	Purchased by NCL
				3	No locns. found

ADDITIONAL COMMENTS AND SURVEY DATA FROM THE NATIONAL CENTRAL LIBRARY

A tabulation for the time taken to supply the satisfied requests in the 1968 Survey has been produced. (Table attached.)

This shows that the median time of supply from British sources is 6·5 working days (i.e. time within which 50 per cent of items are supplied) and that 80 per cent are supplied after 15·5 working days. The mean time of supply from British sources is about 11 working days.

Overseas loans clearly take considerably longer, only slightly more than one-quarter being supplied within the first two months. (Those which appear as being supplied within the first week are probably wrongly coded punched cards.)

It is unfortunately difficult to make any valid comparison with the results of the 1964 Survey. The main reason for this is the very large number of satisfied requests in the 1964 Survey for which the time taken to supply was unknown. These amounted to 7,635, or 18 per cent of all satisfied applications. The much smaller number of " unknown " (3·8 per cent) in the 1968 Survey can mainly be ascribed to mispunching or miscoding, and in any case this small proportion would not make the 1968 results significantly different.

The reason for the very large reduction in " unknowns " is probably mainly due to the improved follow-up procedures which have been possible in the last two years with the increase in staff which has been granted. Such reminders as were made in 1964 took place after a much longer period, and in most cases libraries did not (or could not) give the date of supply. However, it would seem likely that many of these items were not supplied until reminders were sent, and therefore quite a large proportion of the " unknowns " would come in the periods four weeks to two months, or over two months. If this hypothesis is correct, then the 1968 results would show a considerable improvement on 1964. However, this evidence is not concrete enough to form any reliable conclusions, and it is perhaps better to ignore the 1964 results. The 1968 results do, however, provide a reliable basis for assessing the present situation and for comparison with any future results.

1968 SURVEY

Time taken to satisfy requests

	British Sources			Overseas Sources			Un-known No.	Total		
	No.	%	Cumu-lative %	No.	%	Cumu-lative %		No.	%	Cumu-lative %
By return	930	11·9	11·9	1	0·3	0·3		931	11·4	11·4
Up to 1 week	2,248	28·9	40·9	3	0·8	1·1		2,251	27·7	39·1
1–2 weeks	1,969	25·2	66·0	1	0·3	1·4		1,970	24·2	63·3
2–3 weeks	1,037	13·3	79·3	1	0·3	1·7		1,038	12·8	76·1
3–4 weeks	622	8·0	87·3	4	1·1	2·8		626	7·7	83·8
4 weeks–2 months	776	10·0	97·3	91	25·7	28·5		867	10·6	94·4
Over 2 months	203	2·7	100·0	253	71·5	100·0		456	5·6	100·0
Sub-Total	7,785			354			—	8,139		
Time unknown	160			13			150	323		
Total	7,945			367			150	8,462		

238

Tables V, V (a) and VI of the 1968 Survey gave some figures relating to the efficiency of the NCL union catalogues; paragraphs 11–16 commented on these figures. Since that report was submitted some further analysis of this aspect of the Library's work has been made and the more important results from this are noted in this paper.

It has also been possible in the course of this further analysis to allocate to their appropriate place the 150 requests shown in Table V of the Survey as search method— Unknown. This makes a very slight difference to the percentages shown in the first five columns. Table A (appended to this note) gives a comparative analysis for 1964 and 1968 of (i) the results of catalogue checking and (ii) the method of supply. This Table shows both the greater usefulness of the NCL stock and the Catalogue in providing locations for items requested, and the greater effectiveness of these in actually supplying these items, thus reducing the dependence on the lengthier methods of supplying books (by speculative searches and by international loans).

Table B gives some additional figures for two groups of material in which the NCL has been particularly concerned, (i) American books in the humanities and social sciences published since 1950, and (ii) British books in the same subjects published up to 1950. Table B shows that the higher than average success rate is entirely due to the greater efficiency of the NCL bookstock in these fields, and emphasizes the points made in paragraph 9 of the 1968 Survey Report. This is not, however, at the expense of other catalogue locations, as the percentage supplied from these remains around the average.

It has been suggested by those who question the value of union catalogues that, while much material may be included in them, the chances of actually obtaining this material on loan is not high. Analysis shows, however, that if there are one or more locations in the NCL catalogue the probability of the item being supplied from one of these locations is 88 per cent; in the case of books (as opposed to periodicals) this figure is 91 per cent. These are comparable with the actual availability of material from the NLLST.

The other point that has been argued in this connection relates to the non-availability of first locations tried and to the lower availability of material at subsequent locations. It is true that local use may conflict with national use, and that therefore the more that can be supplied from the NCL stock, the more certain (and quicker) the service will be. However, much material in the humanities and social sciences can no longer be acquired for this central loan collection. One function of union catalogues must be therefore to provide alternative locations for material not available at the first location and it appears that the NCL catalogues are successful in providing these. Moreover, although an anlysis (by the NLLST) of requests to the N.W. Region shows a drop in availability from 65·8 per cent at 1st location to 43·5 per cent at 3rd location, the NCL catalogue shows a much smaller drop. This varies slightly by subject and by date of publication, but for the humanities is only from 69 per cent to 62 per cent, and for pre-1950 books in the humanities there is no drop (69 per cent in both cases). Also, availability is higher than average for foreign language books (75 per cent), and again there is no decline at subsequent locations. As other analysis shows that on loan is the most significant reason for the non-availability of books, and that the percentage on loan tends to increase slightly at later locations, it seems that any drop in availability is mainly due to requests for books in comparatively heavy demand. Because this drop is more marked in the case of recent books, it could be offset by more money being available to the NCL for the purchase of current books.

There are some additional points of interest arising from this analysis, and these are briefly noted below.

Books

1. There is no significant variation in the overall performance of the union catalogue (as opposed to the NCL stock) by subject group. The higher success rate in the humanities and social sciences is a result of the greater strength of the NCL stock in these fields.

2. A lower proportion of foreign language books is found in the catalogue, although this proportion found has increased by about 4 per cent since 1964. However, the availability of such books from first locations is comparatively high (75 per cent). Since about 15 per cent of foreign language books supplied come from overseas libraries, this suggests that it is a national deficiency in acquisition, rather than catalogue inadequacy, which is responsible.

3. Only about 2 per cent of catalogue failures are because the book has been withdrawn. This is a much less significant factor than in the case of regional catalogues, and is presumably due (at least in part) to the greater inclusion of university library holdings in the NCL catalogue.

4. " On loan " is a more important reason for first location failure in science and technology and the social sciences (15 per cent) than in the humanities (8 per cent). This is partly because of the greater demand for more recent books in the former, and partly because the duplication of requests for a particular book is lower in the humanities.

5. However, " on loan " is a very important reason for location failures (over 20 per cent) for post-1950 American books in the humanities and social sciences. This emphasizes again the importance of building up the NCL stock of these books.

6. The figures for books found by speculative approaches (see Table B) are artificially inflated by the non-incorporation in the NCL catalogue of regional locations for post-1959 British books. Since these are known to be held under subject specialization schemes, the approaches are not strictly " speculative " when the NCL needs to arrange a loan for a current British book (e.g. to an overseas library). If these were excluded from " speculative approaches ", the overall percentage found by this method would drop by between 1 per cent and 2 per cent.

Periodicals

1. The overall success rate of the catalogue is comparable to that for books, *except* in the case of science and technology. This is due to the NLLST's dealing with a high percentage of the demand, leaving the NCL with a residue of difficult and obscure material to handle. This is confirmed by the relatively higher proportion of scientific periodicals which are not found in the catalogue, and the fact that a lower proportion is not available when it is found (suggesting that there is little local demand for these titles).

2. A higher proportion of periodical requests than of book requests is found in the catalogue, presumably because a more concerted effort has been made over the last 40 years to produce union catalogues of periodicals (Union Catalogue of Periodicals in University Libraries, BUCOP and the World List of Scientific Periodicals).

3. However, availability from locations is lower than for books. Although " on loan " is an insignificant factor for periodicals, " decline to lend " is a much more important reason for non-availability. This reflects a growing trend among university libraries towards restricting periodicals to the library (for internal users as well). Moreover, in many cases the particular part requested is not held, although the title is; libraries in reporting to a union catalogue do not in general report minor gaps in holdings, or minor additions to them.

240

4. About 25 per cent of foreign language periodicals supplied come from overseas libraries. (Cf. Books, paragraph 2)

Two further factors should be borne in mind about catalogue efficiency:

(1) More loans could be arranged from overseas libraries, but in many cases the reader does not wish the request pursued. This may be for reasons of time, cost or comparative lack of importance attached to the item concerned.

(2) This success rate does not include locations (of non-loanable copies) provided to the enquiring library. These locations may suffice in many cases as

    (a) the reader may visit the holding library;

    (b) a photocopy (particularly of a periodical article) may be obtained by the enquirer from the holding library.

Table A: Catalogue Efficiency (General)

	1964		1968	
(i) *Catalogue information*	%	%	%	%
(a) In NCL stock	13		16	
(b) Other locations in catalogue	57		59	
(c) Total items with positive location in catalogue		70		75
(d) Negative entries (items previously searched for, but not located)		7		6
(e) No entries in catalogue		23		19
TOTAL		100		100

	1964		1968	
(ii) *Results of requests*	%	%	%	%
Supplied:				
(a) From NCL stock*	13		16	
(b) From other catalogue locations	48		50	
(c) Total from catalogue locations		61		66
(d) By speculative searches		13		9
(e) By international loan		4		3
(f) Purchased by NCL		1		–**
(g) TOTAL SUPPLIED		79		78
Not supplied		21		22
TOTAL		100		100

  * excluding those purchased after search has failed to trace a loanable copy (see (f))

  ** less than 1%

Table B: Catalogue Efficiency (Humanities and Social Sciences)

(i) *American books published from 1950 onwards*

Supplied		1968	
		%	%
(a) From NCL stock	.. ..	22	
(b) From other catalogue locations	.. ..	48	
(c) Total from catalogue locations	.. ..		70
(d) By speculative searches	.. ..		12
(e) By international loan	.. ..		_*
(f) Purchased by NCL	.. ..		1
(g) TOTAL SUPPLIED	.. ..		83
Not supplied	.. ..		17
	TOTAL		100

* less than 1%

(ii) *British books published before 1950*

Supplied		1968	
		%	%
(a) From NCL stock	.. ..	28	
(b) From other catalogue locations	.. ..	51	
(c) Total from catalogue locations	.. ..		79
(d) By speculative searches	.. ..		8
(e) By international loan	.. ..		_*
(f) Purchased by NCL	.. ..		_*
(g) TOTAL SUPPLIED	.. ..		87
Not supplied	.. ..		13
	TOTAL		100

* less than 1%

NB—The tabulations available of the 1964 Survey do not give the breakdown needed to provide comparisons with the 1968 figures in these tables.

REPORT OF SURVEY OF USERS' REQUIREMENTS
AT THE NATIONAL CENTRAL LIBRARY, 1968

survey carried out and report prepared by
THE STAFF OF THE NCL

1. 372 copies of a questionnaire were sent to a selection of public, university and special libraries, together with copies of recent requests submitted by these libraries. Information was sought on the category of reader, the purpose and importance of the request, and the importance attached to the speed with which the request could be satisfied.

2. The results to some extent were predictable; for example, the majority of requests received from special libraries were on behalf of persons doing formal research work as part of their employment, that the largest group of readers within public libraries required works of general interest, and that within universities the majority of requests were connected with formal and private research and made on behalf of academic staff and postgraduate students.

3. Certain interesting facts do however emerge, and can be summarised as follows:

Special libraries

Approximately a third of the requests received from special libraries were on behalf of persons not directly connected with the applying library, which suggests the considerable use made of them by outside users.

Public libraries

Apart from the large number of readers falling into the " general public " group, the next biggest group consists of professional people, followed by students or apprentices. In this sample a higher proportion of undergraduates used the interlending system via public libraries than through the universities. Approximately 7% of the requests were made on behalf of writers.

Importance attached to a request

The degree of importance attributed to requests tended to vary in emphasis as between the three main types of library. In special libraries the peak occurs in the category " important ", the majority of the remaining requests being " essential " or " very important ". In public libraries there is a more even spread in the degree of importance: roughly the same number of readers considered the material essential for their purposes as of those who professed a " minor interest " in the works required. In university libraries the concentration occurs in the first three categories of importance —nearly half the requests being " essential " or " very important " and a third being " important ".

Time factor

Speed in satisfying applications must obviously be arrived at as a general principle. However, it is important to observe priorities in doing so and to devote most effort to requests marked urgent, or for which a time limit is given. The cost of providing material not located by simple means such as the central loan stock or union catalogue, increases the more quickly one tries to obtain it; expensive follow-up procedures have to be used. Therefore it is important to investigate the needs of various categories of reader in regard to the speed of supply of material requested.

Contrary to the general belief that it is nearly always essential to satisfy a request by return of post, the results show that many readers are prepared to accept reasonable delays, although the delay which is considered acceptable varies between types of library. In special libraries the largest group of readers required material within 2 weeks and considered a delay of more than one month intolerable. In public libraries two thirds of all the readers state that they would be prepared to accept delays of between two weeks and two months, whilst in university libraries only 9 out of 124 readers felt that a delay of more than one month was reasonable.

Categorisation of applications

It is apparent from the summary of replies that the demand on, and the expectations from, the interlending service varies considerably, both from within the same type of library and between the various types of library. This suggests that apart from the present coding of requests to indicate the type of search required, it may be thought desirable to introduce a coding to indicate a time element for each category of search. Whilst very urgent requests would continue to receive priority treatment, the further coding could result in a more ecomonic planning of the work.

General

In addition to the questionnaire relating to individual requests, libraries were asked to indicate by precentages the categories of all readers using the interlending system. The replies received resembled very closely the proportions shown by the replies to the individual questionnaires.

SPECIAL LIBRARIES

1. **Category of reader**

A—University academic staff	3
B—Lecturers in non-university colleges	17
C—Postgraduate student	5
D—Undergraduate student	2
E—Other student, apprentice, etc.	5
F—Member of firm, research association or society to which your library is attached	36
G—Member of a profession	6
H—Author	—
I—General public	—
J—Other	4
K—Unknown	—
	78

2. **Purpose of request**

A—Formal research work	45
B—Private research	6
C—Use in connection with profession	9
D—For teaching purposes	9
E—Study for degree	1
F—Study for other qualification	5
G—Use in connection with non-vocational education	—
H—General interest	1
J—Other	—
K—Unknown	2
	78

3. Importance (work)

A—Essential	.. ..	11
B—Very important	.. ..	11
C—Important	.. ..	33
D—Useful	.. ..	16
E—Minor interest	.. ..	—
F—Unknown	.. ..	7
		78

4. Importance (speed)—(1) Reasonable delay

A—By return	.. ..	4
B—Within 1 week	.. ..	13
C—Within 2 weeks	.. ..	26
D—Within 3 weeks	.. ..	12
E—Within 1 month	.. ..	13
F—Within 2 months	.. ..	5
G—Longer than 2 months	.. ..	1
H—No reply	.. ..	4
		78

Importance (speed)—(2) Intolerable delay

A—By return	.. ..	—
B—Within 1 week	.. ..	—
C—Within 2 weeks	.. ..	7
D—Within 3 weeks	.. ..	2
E—Within 1 month	.. ..	5
F—Within 2 months	.. ..	22
G—Longer than 2 months	.. ..	34
H—No reply	.. ..	8
		78

UNIVERSITY LIBRARIES   PUBLIC LIBRARIES

1. Category of reader

University		Public	
A	67	A	3
B	2	B	2
C	44	C	3
D	4	D	14
E	—	E	12
F	1	F	5
G	5	G	37
H	1	H	16
I	—	I	61
J	3	J	12
K	2	K	—
	— 129		— 165

2. Purpose of request

University		Public	
A	85	A	14
B	22	B	36
C	4	C	11
D	7	D	9
E	3	E	12
F	3	F	16
G	—	G	6
H	3	H	50
J	1	J	9
K	1	K	2
	— 129		— 165

3. Importance (work)

A	..	..	..	20
B	..	..	..	36
C	..	..	..	44
D	..	..	..	19
E	..	..	..	2
F	..	..	..	8
			—	129

3. Importance (work)

A	..	..	..	22
B	..	..	..	34
C	..	..	..	43
D	..	..	..	37
E	..	..	..	20
F	..	..	..	9
			—	165

4. Importance (speed)—
   (1) Reasonable delay

A				3
B	..	..	..	10
C	..	..	..	35
D	..	..	..	35
E	..	..	..	32
F	..	..	..	7
G	..	..	..	2
H	..	..	..	5
			—	129

4. Importance (speed)—
   (1) Reasonable delay

A	..	..	..	—
B	..	..	..	13
C	..	..	..	34
D	..	..	..	34
E	..	..	..	48
F	..	..	..	19
G	..	..	..	3
H	..	..	..	14
			—	165

Importance (speed)—
   (2) Intolerable delay

A	..	..	..	—
B	..	..	..	—
C	..	..	..	3
D	..	..	..	8
E	..	..	..	17
F	..	..	..	45
G	..	..	..	42
H	..	..	..	14
			—	129

Importance (speed)—
   (2) Intolerable delay

A	..	..	..	—
B	..	..	..	—
C	..	..	..	1
D	..	..	..	2
E	..	..	..	20
F	..	..	..	36
G	..	..	..	77

(longer time specified,
e.g. 6 months–7)

H	..	..	..	22
			—	165

QUESTIONNAIRE

NATIONAL CENTRAL LIBRARY READER SURVEY
PLEASE ENCIRCLE THE APPROPRIATE LETTERS

Name of Library...

I. Category of Reader
- A. University academic staff
- B. Lecturers in other colleges
- C. Postgraduate student
- D. Undergraduate student
- E. Other student, apprentice, etc.
- F. Member of firm, research association or society to which your library is attached
- G. Member of a profession
- H. Author
- I. General public
- J. Other (please specify)
- K. Unknown

II. Purpose of Request
- A. Formal research work (i.e. as part of reader's employment)
- B. Private research (e.g. for writing a book)
- C. Use in connection with profession
- D. For teaching purposes
- E. Study for degree (N.B. research for higher degree to be put under A)
- F. Study for other qualifications
- G. Use in connection with non-vocational education
- H. General interest
- J. Other (please specify)
- K. Unknown

III. Importance attached to work requested
(N.B. It is assumed that all requests are of importance, but that the degree of importance may vary.)
- A. Essential
- B. Very important
- C. Important
- D. Useful
- E. Minor interest
- F. Unknown

IV. Importance attached to speed with which request is satisfied
(N.B. It is assumed that all readers would like the material they request more or less immediately. There may, however, be some variation. Please indicate in Column 1 what is regarded as a reasonable delay, and in Column 2 what would be regarded as an intolerable delay.)

	1	2
A. By return		
B. Within 1 week		
C. Within 2 weeks		
D. Within 3 weeks		
E. Within 1 month		
F. Within 2 months		
G. Longer than 2 months		

Signature of Librarian.............................
247

REPORT OF SURVEY OF DUPLICATION OF REQUESTS
AT THE NATIONAL CENTRAL LIBRARY, JANUARY–MAY 1968

survey carried out and report prepared by

THE STAFF OF THE N.C.L.

1. A survey was undertaken during the period from 15th January–29th May 1968, in order to investigate the incidence of duplication of requests for the same book. Periodicals were excluded from the survey.

Method

2. The sample used consisted of all requests for books for which the catalogue headings began with A, C, L, P or W. This gave a 21 per cent sample of all book requests received in this period. Copies of the request forms were filed, each day's intake being checked for duplication against the cumulative file in each main subject division (humanities, social sciences, and science and technology).

Results

3. Table I gives figures for the cumulative totals, at weekly intervals, of titles requested in each main subject field, and of the number of titles for which more than one request had been received, together with the percentage of such duplication.

4. Table II analyses the duplicate requests received within each subject field by date of publication and by language groups (British; American and other English-language books published abroad; foreign languages).

Comments

6. It should be noted that the service in science and technology provided by the NLLST affects the results in this subject field. The demand on the NCL is mainly a residual one for older books, and for current books outside the language coverage, or below the specialist level, of the NLLST. The rate of duplication in scientific requests to the NCL is therefore considerably below that which would arise from an examination of all inter-library loan requests in this field. To some extent requests for the most frequently required books in all subjects may be filtered off by the Regional Library Systems before they reach NCL; this applies mainly to requests for the more recent British books.

7. In all cases, of course, time and the growing total of titles against which new requests can be matched for duplication produce a growing percentage of duplication. However, the duplication rate in the humanities grows more slowly than that in the other subjects. (Table I.)

A similar comparison can be made between the number of duplicates after approximately 1,700 requests in each subject group, as follows:—

Humanities	45
Social Sciences	117
Science and Technology	137

8. Table II shows that the greatest incidence of duplication in the humanities occurs with current American books, and with older (and presumably out-of-print) British books. In the social sciences the duplicate demand is predominantly for current American books. These results support the NCL's acquisition policy of purchasing as many current American books in the humanities and social sciences as funds permit, and of collecting by donation, and (where desirable and possible) by purchase in the second-hand market, older British books.

9. An attempt has been made to assess very roughly the comparative size of the pools of active literature required to meet this demand in the three subject groups.

Clearly, if no duplication arose at all, then this pool would consist of the cumulative total of requests received to infinity. Conversely, if after one month no requests for fresh books were received, the pool would consist of the total requests received in the first month. The true figure must lie somewhere between these two extremes.

This crude model is based on the technique for estimating the population of, say, fish in a lake. To do this, a sample of fish is caught and marked, and then replaced in the lake. After an interval to allow for the fish to be randomly mixed, a second sample is taken. The proportion of marked fish in the second example to the total of the second sample should (with random fluctuations) be the same as the proportion of all the fish that were marked to the total population of the lake. That is, if the first sample $=n_1$, the second sample $=n_2$, the number of marked fish in the second sample $=r$, and the total population of fish $=P$, then

$$\frac{n_1}{P} = \frac{r}{n_2} \text{ or } P = \frac{n_1 \, n_2}{r}$$

The same technique could have been followed by forming the first sample (n_1) from those requests received in, say, the first month, and forming the second sample (n_2) from those requests received in the second month, then checking the second sample against the first for duplication (r). However, a continuous sampling method was chosen in order to give a bigger sample in the time available. This means that each incoming request was checked against all its predecessors, so that on each occasion the cumulative first sample (of titles requested) against which a request is checked is one less than the cumulative second sample (of requests checked), so that $n_1+1=n_2$, or $n_1 \approx n_2 =$ (say) n. The formula then becomes

$$P = \frac{n_1 \, (n_1+1)}{r}, \text{ or } P \approx \frac{n^2}{r}$$

Applying this to the figures for 28th February, 10th April and 27th May the following results are produced:

Date	Humanities		Social Sciences		Science and Technology*	
February 28th ..	n 1,980 r 53	P 74,000 5P 370,000	n 688 r 22	P 21,500 5P 107,500	n 822 r 28	P 24,000 5P 120,000
April 10th	n 3,578 r 146	P 88,000 5P 440,000	n 1,195 r 66	P 22,000 5P 110,000	n 1,340 r 84	P 21,500 5P 107,500
May 27th	n 5,101 r 282	P 92,500 5P 462,500	n 1,852 r 157	P 22,000 5P 110,000	n 1,852 r 157	P 21,000 5P 105,000

* But see paragraph 6.

P relates to an approximate 20 per cent sample (see paragraph 2), and values of 5P are therefore given as well.

This indicates that a very much larger pool of literature is needed to deal with requests in the humanities. In all cases this pool will grow by the addition of new publications, which in theory should be balanced by the removal of books no longer wanted. However, these results do not of course indicate what particular books

249

are required.   Further analysis based on the type of results given in Table II may assist in determining at least the categories of books most, and least, required.   It will be considerably easier to determine which new books are most likely to be wanted than to determine which older books are no longer wanted.   It is unlikely therefore that in practice books will be discarded from a national loan collection, which will therefore contain a growing number of books for which demand is improbable.   Because of the greater concentration of demand in science and technology for more recent books, this may be more of a problem in that field than in the humanities where the average life of the literature is longer.

Table I

Date	Social Sciences			Science and Technology			Humanities		
	Cumulative total of titles requested	Duplication of titles	% Duplication	Cumulative total of titles requested	Duplication of titles	% Duplication	Cumulative total of titles requested	Duplication of titles	% Duplication
January 17	25	0	—	32	0	—	73	0	—
24	142	1	0·7	191	0	—	355	5	1·4
31	259	3	1·2	340	6	1·7	775	10	1·3
February 7	361	8	2·2	475	12	2·5	1,086	21	1·9
14	464	11	2·4	595	17	2·9	1,363	31	2·3
21	574	13	2·3	726	21	2·9	1,686	44	2·6
28	688	22	3·2	822	28	3·4	1,980	53	2·7
March 6	781	30	3·8	923	35	3·8	2,294	67	2·9
13	876	42	4·8	1,030	47	4·6	2,601	81	3·1
20	962	52	5·4	1,110	56	5·0	2,853	95	3·3
27	1,047	60	5·7	1,203	63	5·2	3,123	106	3·4
April 3	1,130	61	5·4	1,276	72	5·6	3,357	128	3·8
10	1,195	66	5·5	1,340	84	6·3	3,578	146	4·1
22	1,274	70	5·5	1,428	98	6·9	3,840	168	4·3
29	1,369	79	5·8	1,520	106	7·0	4,108	189	4·6
May 6	1,471	90	6·1	1,607	119	7·4	4,412	212	4·8
13	1,545	103	6·7	1,680	135	8·0	4,621	230	5·0
20	1,628	112	6·9	1,759	145	8·2	4,895	253	5·2
27	1,702	117	6·9	1,852	157	8·5	5,101	282	5·5

251

Table II—Analysis of Duplicated Requests

	Science and Technology	Social Sciences	Humanities
BRITISH			
Pre-1900	5	1	29
1900–1909	—	1	10
1910–1919	1	3	9
1920–1929	1	3	24
1930–1939	7	2	37
1940–1949	8	5	17
1950–1959	17	7	18
1960–	18	14	9
No date	—	2	2
AMERICAN			
Pre-1900	1	2	3
1900–1909	1	—	1
1910–1919	1	—	3
1920–1929	1	3	5
1930–1939	4	1	13
1940–1949	6	8	11
1950–1959	15	23	21
1960–	50	48	42
FOREIGN			
Pre-1900	—	—	5
1900–1909	1	—	1
1910–1919	1	—	1
1920–1929	—	—	2
1930–1939	3	—	3
1940–1949	2	1	9
1950–1959	—	—	5
1960–	3	3	7

REPORT OF SURVEY OF UNSATISFIED LOAN REQUESTS AT THE NATIONAL LENDING LIBRARY FOR SCIENCE AND TECHNOLOGY, JULY 1968

survey carried out and report prepared by

THE STAFF OF THE NLLST

During the week commencing 17th July 1968 the NLL carried out a survey of its unsatisfied loan requests. There were 1,052 of these and this represents 9·1 per cent of the requests which were accepted that week. The satisfied requests account for 86·6 per cent of the total, and the remaining 4·3 per cent were passed to the Science Museum and the London School of Economics to see if they could satisfy these particular items.* No data are included in the report about the requests which these two libraries were not able to satisfy. Previous surveys have shown, however, that the Science Museum Library requests have a satisfaction rate of about 40 per cent and that the rate at LSE is about 70 per cent.

The analysis of the sample of failures gave the following results:

	%
1. Serial title not held at all (excludes 4)	13·6
2. Other serials (excludes 4)	47·6
3. Books (excludes 4)	31·6
4. Conference reports	7·2
	100·0

With regard to the action which the NLL will take as a result of these unsatisfied requests, the position is as follows:

	%
(a) Items which were found after a special search at the NLL ..	3·2
(b) Items which are known to be on order when the request was received	8·3
(c) Items we would expect to purchase (mainly very recent books)	10·6
(d) Items for which an order will be placed as a result of the request	4·0
(e) Items which come up for review in survey of serial holdings ..	32·7
(f) Items where there is insufficient information to place an order..	36·5
(g) Items which are out of scope	4·8
	100·1

The above figures show that out of the total number of requests the NLL receives, there are 0·3 per cent of the items which it holds but fails to find. Some of these required much searching for this survey, in order to locate the items concerned.

The largest category in the above list is the one where insufficient information is

---

* Other requests were received by the library, but were not included in the above totals which are used in calculating the satisfaction rate. They are items which were returned to the borrower for later reapplication. This happens when the reference supplied is obviously inadequate, or when the request has obviously arrived well in advance of the date of receipt. A number of requests for English translations of Russian articles fall into this latter category.

supplied. The borrower may have requested a perfectly genuine item, but he has not supplied sufficient information. It may be that we hold the item under an alternative title or that the title given is correct but we are unable to locate the correct publisher.

The details of the survey are as follows:

BOOKS

English Language

	Found	On order	Expect to purchase	Will order from request	Will be reviewed in serial survey	Insufficient informa-tion to order	Out of scope	Total
Pre 1962	—	—	—	—	—	12	—	12
1962–1966	—	1	1	14	—	21	—	37
1967–1968	—	—	98	—	—	—	—	98
Undated	—	—	3	19	—	88	—	110
Other	12	9	—	—	—	—	29	50
Total ..	12	10	102	33	—	121	29	307

All Languages

	Found	On order	Expect to purchase	Will order from request	Will be reviewed in serial survey	Insufficient informa-tion to order	Out of scope	Total
English	12	10	102	33	—	121	29	307
Russian	—	—	—	—	—	15	—	15
Other	—	—	4	—	—	3	—	7
Theses	—	—	—	—	—	3	—	3
All books ..	12	10	106	33	—	142	29	332

Steps were taken as a result of a previous survey to acquire English language books upon publication. When these books are being received upon publication, there should be far fewer unsatisfied requests in this category, though it will never be possible to completely eliminate it. It will also be noted that there were a large number of undated book requests. These were checked in " Books in Print " and none are at present available for purchase for the NLL stock. A further check was made against the British Museum catalogue (and its supplement, i.e. up to 1965). Only 10 out of the eighty-eight were located.

SERIALS

Part not held

	Found	On order	Expect to purchase	Will order from request	Will be reviewed in serial survey	Insufficient informa-tion to order	Out of scope	Total
Science	—	4	—	—	181	—	—	185
Medical	—	5	—	—	117	—	—	122
Social Science ..	—	47	—	—	46	—	—	93
Reports	—	—	—	—	—	90	—	90
Other	11	—	—	—	—	—	—	11
Part not held ..	11	56	—	—	344	90	—	501

Title not held

Title not held ..	11	21	—	7	—	82	22	143

The situation for back issues of social science periodicals should be much improved in the near future when the parts which have already been ordered arrive in the library. The choice of further items for secondhand purchase will (as in the past) be based on surveys of requests for the periodical parts which we do not hold. (The previous surveys were conducted 1963/4 and 1966/7) Some two thirds of these requests are for parts which precede our holding, and the other one third are for parts where we have a gap in our holding.

CONFERENCES

	Found	On order	Expect to purchase	Will order from request	Will be reviewed in serial survey	Insufficient informa-tion to order	Out of scope	Total
Conferences	—	—	6	2	—	68	—	76

These figures reflect the difficulty, of borrowers and the NLL alike, in obtaining complete details of the publications of conferences. Out of these seventy-six items which were checked, it was only possible to locate eight of the items in the bibliographies. It also seems likely that some of these requests are for papers which were delivered at conferences but for which no proceedings were ever published.

REPORT OF
SURVEY OF LOAN AND PHOTOCOPY ISSUES
AT THE
NATIONAL LENDING LIBRARY FOR SCIENCE AND TECHNOLOGY
DECEMBER 1968
survey carried out and report prepared by
THE STAFF OF THE NLLST

SURVEY OF NLL ISSUES

This survey was requested by the National Libraries Committee and carried out during the week beginning 9th December. The period of the survey may not give quite typical results, because most university terms finished during the survey week and the postal services were beginning to slow up under the Christmas pressure. However, as the purpose of the survey was to provide a general description of the NLL issues, any variation between the actual figures and the average appeared to be of secondary importance.

The sample used in the survey was every third item received in the packing bay for despatch. To avoid interfering with the normal operations of the library, the data recorded had to be limited to the information available at the despatch points. This was as follows:

(a) Information which could be obtained from the address label, i.e.
   (i) location of consignee
   (ii) type of organisation
   (iii) whether a loan or photocopy request.

(b) Information which could be obtained from the item to be despatched, i.e.
   (i) Date of publication
   (ii) Subject of item—if a borrower required only a particular article, this was not known at the despatch point
   (iii) Language or languages of the item
   (iv) Whether a book, a serial, or a report
   (v) Whether a translation into English or not.

A copy of the coding form and the coding schedules used is attached in the Appendix.

Results

In all, the sample consisted of 4,348 items. 120 of these were for abroad and the remainder for the United Kingdom. The output during the survey week was about 8 per cent down on that of the average for November.

Overseas Requests

These were divided up as follows:

Eire	21
Europe, excluding the British Isles	50
Outside Europe	49

Overseas requests now account for about 3 per cent of the requests received by the NLL. A year ago the figure was about 2 per cent.

United Kingdom Requests

Type of Borrower. The general results are given in Table 1. It will be noted that Government departments (which do not pay for loan or photocopy forms) make a relatively greater use of the photocopying service (29 per cent of requests are for photocopies, compared with an average of 3·6 per cent from other organisations).

Table 1

Type of organisation	Type of request			Total	(%)
	Loan	Photocopy	Not known		
Industrial	1,472	48	—	1,520	(36)
Government	268	111	—	379	(9)
Research Association	56	1	1	58	(1)
Nationalised industry (excluding steel)	140	3	—	143	(3)
Atomic Energy Authority	98	—	—	98	(2)
Research Council	76	5	—	81	(2)
Hospital	103	6	—	109	(3)
Local Government	8	—	—	8	—
Other government-aided research institutes	31	1	—	32	(1)
C.A.B.	17	—	—	17	—
University	1,050	38	—	1,088	(26)
Other educational	382	15	—	397	(9)
Other non-profit making organisations	109	12	1	122	(3)
Public Library	146	1	—	147	(3)
Aslib	16	—	—	16	—
Other	2	2	—	4	—
Not known	9	—	—	9	—
Total	3,983	243	2	4,228	(98)

The largest group of requests (40 per cent) came from industry (private and nationalised). About a quarter of the requests came from universities.

The figures obtained show a higher proportion of requests from universities and other educational establishments than a previous survey. For subsequent analyses the types of organisation were divided into " industrial ", " university " and " others ".

Location. The general results are given in Table 2. The particular results for universities by areas are given in Table 3. There is a relatively low use in Oxford and Cambridge which, no doubt, is mainly due to the better library facilities in those universities. It may, however, be partly due to the difficulty of identifying some university institutes at Oxford and Cambridge as part of the universities.

Table 2

Geographical location	Type of organisation				Total	%
	Industrial	University	Other	Not known		
Area within 20 miles of NLL ..	33	108	35	—	176	4
Rest of Yorkshire	52	59	51	—	162	4
London postal districts	198	252	374	—	824	19
Home Counties	429	58	298	—	785	19
S.E. Counties	229	115	318	1	663	16
S.W. Counties..	52	50	113	—	215	5
Midlands	193	113	159	1	466	11
N.W. Counties	156	102	109	—	367	9
North Counties	62	39	43	—	144	3
Wales	41	45	10	—	96	2
Scotland	67	123	99	—	289	7
Northern Ireland	7	23	3	—	33	1
Not known	1	1	6	—	8	—
Total	1,520	1,088	1,618	2	4,228	100

Table 3

	Number of requests from universities	Number of academic staff in universities	Number of requests per 1,000 staff
London	252	4,700	53·4
Berkshire	16	613	26·0
Cambridge	8	1,067	7·5
Devon	13	277	46·9
Durham	27	382	70·4
Essex	2	130	15·3
Gloucestershire	18	771	23·3
Hampshire	31	438	70·4
Kent	23	220	104·0
Lancashire	101	3,104	32·6
Leicestershire	27	621	43·5
Norfolk	11	191	55·0
Northumberland	12	925	13·0
Nottinghamshire	25	512	48·8
Oxford	5	1,339	3·7
Somerset	19	251	75·8
Staffordshire	13	228	56·8
Surrey	27	267	101·0
Sussex	43	426	101·0
Warwickshire..	46	1,433	31·8
Yorkshire <20	108	1,791	60·2
Yorkshire >20	59	1,172	50·3
Wales	45	1,529	29·4
Scotland	123	3,897	31·7
Northern Ireland	23	626	36·8
Total	1,077	26,910	40·0
Total for counties with < 500 academic staff	209	2,810	74·4
Oxbridge	13	2,406	5·4

The relatively high use by the smaller universities is indicated in Table 3. The issues (excluding issues to universities) per million population are given in Table 4. The figures suggest that the location of the NLL has little effect on the demand. For instance, the issues to Scotland and Yorkshire, which have similar populations, are approximately the same. The relatively low issues in Northern Ireland and Wales are possibly a reflection on the nature and magnitude of the industrial activities in these regions. The figures for London and for the Home Counties (which together received 38 per cent of the issues) indicate that the library facilities in Central London have not made the NLL less necessary in these areas.

258

Table 4

Geographical location	Population of region in 1966	Number of requests in survey excluding universities	Requests/ million population
Yorkshire	4,900,000	171	35
London	5,700,000	572	100
Home Counties	6,600,000	727	110
S.E. Counties..	6,600,000	548	83
S.W. Counties	3,800,000	165	43
Midlands	8,400,000	353	42
N.W. Counties	6,700,000	265	40
Northern Counties	2,800,000	105	38
Wales	2,700,000	51	19
Scotland	5,200,000	166	32
Northern Ireland	1,500,000	10	7
Total	54,900,000	3,133	57

Date of Publication. Data showing the issues by date of publication and subject, date of publication and type of publication, and date of publication by type of organisation are given in Tables 5, 6 and 7. The results here confirm those of previous surveys which indicated that about half the items issued by the library were published in the last forty months. It will be noted that there is a slightly heavier demand for recent material from industrial organisations than from other organisations. Nearly 90 per cent of the items despatched were dated 1950 or later. However, it should be appreciated that, in addition to issues shown, some of the pre–1960 requests are supplied by the Science Museum at the request of the NLL.

Table 5

Subject	Date of publication								Total
	1966–1968	1960–1965	1950–1959	1940–1949	1930–1939	1910–1929	Pre 1909	Not known	
General	51	29	13	4	3	1	1	1	103
Pure and Applied Science	1,479	764	493	143	87	56	25	30	3,077
Medicine	334	210	87	35	14	4	2	5	691
Agriculture	45	26	24	7	3	1	—	—	106
Social Science	100	67	38	7	4	—	1	—	217
Other	18	11	4	—	—	—	—	—	33
Not known	—	1	—	—	—	—	—	—	1
Total	2,027	1,108	659	196	111	62	29	36	4,228
Percentage of total ..	48	26	16	5	3	1	1	1	(101)

Table 6

Type of publication	Date of publication								Total
	1966–1968	1960–1965	1950–1959	1940–1949	1930–1939	1910–1929	Pre 1909	Not known	
Serial	1,726	921	602	180	103	59	27	24	3,642
Book	145	138	43	10	4	2	2	4	348
Report	154	49	14	6	4	1	—	8	236
Not known	2	—	—	—	—	—	—	—	2
Total	2,027	1,108	659	196	111	62	29	36	4,228

There was no significant difference between the data distribution for serials and for books.

Table 7

Type of organisation	Date of publication								Total
	1966–1968	1960–1965	1950–1959	1940–1949	1930–1939	1910–1929	Pre 1909	Not known	
Industrial	(58%) 876	319	209	60	29	10	9	8	1,520
University	(35%) 378	352	210	59	36	25	11	17	1,088
Other	(48%) 772	437	239	77	46	27	9	11	1,618
Not known	1	—	1	—	—	—	—	—	2
Total	2,027	1,108	659	196	111	62	29	36	4,228

Industry uses significantly more 1966/68 material than universities (58 per cent *cf* 35 per cent).

Other Results. Other results of the survey are indicated as follows:

Table 8—Type of organisation and type of publication
Table 9—Type of publication and subject
Table 10—Type of organisation and subject
Table 11—Type of publication and language
Table 12—Type of organisation and language
Table 13—Whether a translation or not

Table 8

Type of publication	Type of organisation				Total
	Industrial	University	Other	Not known	
Serial	1,334	946	1,360	2	3,642
Book	107	77	164	—	348
Report	78	64	94	—	236
Not known	1	1	—	—	2
Total	1,520	1,088	1,618	2	4,228

Table 9

Subject	Type of publication				Total
	Serial	Book	Report	Not known	
General	98	1	4	—	103
Pure and Applied Science ..	2,600	271	205	1	3,077
Medicine	646	38	6	1	691
Agriculture	96	8	2	—	106
Social Science	179	22	16	—	217
Other	22	8	3	—	33
Not known	1	—	—	—	1
Total	3,642	348	236	2	4,228

Table 10

Subject	Type of organisation				Total
	Industrial	University	Other	Not known	
General (covering more than one of the following groups) ..	35	26	42	—	103
Pure and Applied Science ..	1,209	684	1,183	1	3,077
Medicine	190	252	248	1	691
Agriculture	32	38	36	—	106
Social Science	44	79	94	—	217
Other	10	8	15	—	33
Not known	—	1	—	—	1
Total	1,520	1,088	1,618	2	4,228

Table 11

Language	Type of publication				Total
	Serial	Book	Report	Not known	
English	2,926	328	232	1	3,487
French	102	3	2	—	107
German	221	2	1	—	224
Cyrillic	91	8	—	—	99
Oriental	31	—	—	—	31
Multilingual	205	7	—	1	213
Other	66	—	1	—	67
Total	3,642	348	236	2	4,228

Table 12

Language	Type of organisation			Not known	Total
	Industrial	University	Other		
English	1,247	865	1,373	2	3,487
French	41	38	28	—	107
German	88	62	74	—	224
Cyrillic	39	22	38	—	99
Oriental	12	9	10	—	31
Multilingual	68	73	72	—	213
Other	25	19	23	—	67
Not known	—	—	—	—	—
Total	1,520	1,088	1,618	2	4,228

Table 13

Translation	No	4,095
	Yes	128
	Not known	5
Total		4,228

Consideration of Results

The low use of the NLL in Wales and Northern Ireland has been known for some time, but particular efforts to increase the relative use in these areas have had little result.

The relatively low percentage of requests for photocopies, except from Government departments, suggest that the latter are possibly taking the right actions for the wrong reasons. In some libraries photocopies are very expensive, because even when they are of small articles, they are treated as acquisitions to the library and special records are made of them. Efforts are being made to persuade librarians to take a new approach to this problem.

NLL.
January 1969

APPENDIX

SURVEY 9–13th DECEMBER 1968

Type of request	Loan	1
	Photocopy	2

Type of organisation

Geographical location

Date

Type of publication

Translation	NO	1
(into English)	YES	2

Language

Subject

COUNTY CODING FOR NLL LIST OF OFFICIAL BORROWERS

London 01
Wales 02
Scotland 03
N. Ireland 04
Channel Islands 05
Eire 06
Europe excluding British Isles 07
Outside Europe 08

WEST REGION	Cornwall 10	Bedfordshire 20
	Devon 11	Berkshire 21
	Dorset 12	Buckinghamshire .. 22
	Somerset 13	Cambridgeshire 50
		Cheshire 60
SOUTH REGION	Bedfordshire 20	Cornwall.. 10
	Berkshire 21	Cumberland 61
	Buckinghamshire .. 22	Derbyshire 51
	Gloucestershire .. 23	Devonshire 11
	Hampshire and the	Dorsetshire 12
	Isle of Wight .. 24	Durham 70
	Hertfordshire 25	Essex 30
	Oxfordshire 26	Gloucestershire 23
	Sussex 27	Hampshire 24
	Wiltshire 28	Herefordshire 40
		Hertfordshire 25
HOME COUNTIES	Essex 30	Huntingdonshire .. 52
	Kent 31	Isle of Man 64
	Middlesex 32	Kent 31
	Surrey 33	Lancashire 62
		Leicestershire 53
WEST MIDLAND REGION	Herefordshire 40	Lincolnshire 54
	Monmouthshire .. 41	Middlesex 32
	Shropshire 42	Monmouthshire.. .. 41
	Staffordshire 43	Norfolk 55
	Warwickshire 44	Northamptonshire .. 56
	Worcestershire .. 45	Northumberland .. 71
		Nottinghamshire .. 57
EAST MIDLAND REGION	Cambridgeshire .. 50	Oxfordshire 26
	Derbyshire 51	Rutlandshire 58
	Huntingdonshire .. 52	Shropshire 42
	Leicestershire 53	Somersetshire 13
	Lincolnshire 54	Staffordshire 43
	Norfolk.. 55	Suffolk 59
	Northamptonshire .. 56	Surrey 33
	Nottinghamshire .. 57	Sussex 27
	Rutland 58	Warwickshire 44
	Suffolk 59	Westmorland 63
		Wiltshire 28
NORTH WEST REGION	Cheshire 60	Worcestershire 45
	Cumberland 61	Yorkshire 72
	Lancashire 62	Yorkshire 73
	Westmorland 63	
	Isle of Man 64	

NORTH EAST REGION	Durham	..	..	70
	Northumberland		..	71
	Yorkshire—less than 20 miles	..	..	72
	Yorkshire—more than 20 miles	..	..	73

TYPE OF ORGANIZATION

10 Industrial organization (including steel industry)
20 Government establishment
30 Research Association
31 Nationalized industry (excluding steel)
32 Atomic Energy Authority
33 Research Council
34 Hospital
35 Local Government
36 Other government-aided research institutes
37 C.A.B.
40 University/C.A.T.
50 Other educational establishment
60 Other non-profit making organizations (professional and learned societies, trade and development organizations, research institutes)
70 Public Library
80 Aslib
00 Other

TYPE OF PUBLICATION

1. Serial (excluding report)
2. Book
3. Report

LANGUAGE

1. English
2. French
3. German
4. Cyrillic
5. Oriental
6. Multilingual
7. Other

SUBJECT

0 GENERAL (covering more than one of the following groups)
1 PURE AND APPLIED SCIENCE, except agriculture and medicine (but including physical geography, parts of architecture, photography)
2 MEDICINE
3 AGRICULTURE
4 SOCIAL SCIENCE (including normal psychology, town planning, social and economic geography, parts of architecture)
5 OTHER

DECEMBER SURVEY

Type of request   The type of request form, not what was actually supplied.
Type of organization   See coding sheet.
                       Any hospital address which indicated that it was a medical school was coded as a university. MRC units in hospitals were coded as research councils.

Geographical location	Location to which the item was actually sent, though it was possible for the request to originate elsewhere.
Date	Date of publication of the item.
Type of publication	*Book*—an item which would be identified by an individual title rather than a serial title.

Report—The term " Report Literature " as used within the NLL relates to material which is somewhat difficult to define, but is fairly easy to recognise. It is concerned with documents which " are not published in the normal way ". Often the reports are prepared on typewriters and duplicated. As a rule, the number of copies prepared is limited and the circulation of the reports may be restricted because they are " confidential " in the security or in the commercial sense. The material is not available in general through normal publishing channels and, as a rule, it is not covered by the normal abstracting and indexing publications. Each report is a separate entity. It may be the basis of a future article in a normal periodical or it may remain for ever hidden by its " confidential " status. Unlike the ordinary scientific paper, a report is not referred before it is issued.

The greater part of the report literature of the world originates in the U.S.A. It is mainly a by-product of the research contract system used by the U.S. Federal Agencies. Many of these contracts are concerned with defence work and the security classification of the documents at first issued may be anything from " Open " to " Top Secret ". The NLL is only concerned with the " Open " material and has a fairly comprehensive collection of the U.S. reports in this category. The majority of these reports are now received on microfiche and they are covered by special bibliographical tools prepared in the U.S.A.

Serial—any other item which can be obtained on a serial order.

Translation	Any item translated from another language into English. This includes cover-to-cover translations of periodicals, but not English editions of foreign language periodicals which differ from the original.
Language	Since it was not known which parts of the publication were required by the borrower, this had to be taken as the language of the whole publication. Some publications contain articles in various languages.
Subject	This was the subject of the whole publication, rather than the individual article. Publications covering more than one subject category were placed in the general category.

SUMMARY OF THE MAIN FINDINGS OF THE READERSHIP SURVEY AT THE NATIONAL REFERENCE LIBRARY OF SCIENCE AND INVENTION (HOLBORN DIVISION) JULY 1968
survey carried out and summary prepared by
THE ECONOMIST INTELLIGENCE UNIT LIMITED

Contents

SUMMARY OF THE MAIN FINDINGS OF THE READERSHIP SURVEY AT THE NATIONAL REFERENCE LIBRARY OF SCIENCE AND INVENTION (HOLBORN DIVISION)

Introduction

A survey of readers using the National Reference Library of Science and Invention (NRLSI) was carried out over a two-week period beginning 12 July 1968 and ending 27 July 1968. The broad objectives were to provide information on:

1. Readers' Characteristics

(a) Occupation and parent organisation.

(b) Place of residence/work.

(c) Frequency and duration of visits.

(d) Reasons for visits.

2. Use of the Library

(a) Subject fields in which readers were seeking information, measuring as far as possible the amount of inter-disciplinary use of material.

(b) Methods of search to establish the amount of use that is made of catalogues, indexes and other bibliographic tools.

(c) The volume and type of material used.

The survey was carried out by means of a self-completed questionnaire. Questionnaires were issued to all readers using the library on six separate days during the survey period; these days were selected randomly so that each day of the working week at the library (Monday to Saturday inclusive) was represented. No reader was asked to fill in more than one questionnaire, but repeat visits were recorded separately by allocating each reader a number at the time of his first visit and recording his subsequent visits against this number. This enabled an independent check to be made on readers' frequency of visit, although for practical reasons repeat visits were only recorded once for each day so that the maximum number of repeat visits obtainable was five (one for each of the last five survey days).

The total number of readers sampled was 1,178, which was lower than expected judging from a previous readership survey carried out in 1963 when more than 1,300 readers were sampled over a survey period of less than four days. The most likely reason for the smaller sample obtained in the present survey is that it took place at the end of July when the number of readers is lower due to the beginning of the summer holiday period. No doubt this reason can be checked by reference to the NRLSI figures of attendance obtained from the signatures in the visitors' books. However, one point should be made about the use of figures based on the signatures. It became apparent during the course of the survey that many readers sign both the visitors' book at the entrance to the main library as well as the book at the entrance to the Chancery House section of the library if they use both sections of the library during the course of a single visit or even if they make separate visits to both sections on a single day. A small proportion may even sign one, or both, books more than once on a single day. Thus while the NRLSI figures record to some extent the number of visits made to each section of the library during the day (remembering that readers are required to sign the visitors' book once only each day irrespective of the number of separate visits they make) the survey figures record a reader once only for each day, irrespective of the number of times he signed the visitors' book. The two sets of figures are therefore not comparable in absolute terms.

A. Readers' Characteristics

1. Occupation and Parent Organisations
(See Tables 1 and 2)

Patent workers as a group were the main users of the library. Together they formed well over one third of the total readership during the survey period. Over half the patent workers were patent agents or technical assistants.

A second major group of users were research workers, forming one third of total readership. Within this group the largest single categories of readers were research and development workers and academics.

The final main group, under a quarter of total readership, can be categorised roughly as librarians and writers with these two occupations dominating the group.

The main parent organisational groups were firms of patent agents, responsible for a quarter of all readers; industry and commerce, responsible for a third of all readers; and academic institutions, responsible for over a tenth of all readers. Two thirds of the patent workers came from patent firms; most of the rest were employed in industry and commerce. Research workers came predominantly either from commerce and industry (research and development workers and technical consultants) or academic institutions (academic staff and postgraduates). From the librarian/writer group librarians mainly came from industry and commerce, while writers mostly worked for publishers or were self employed. As a single category self employed persons accounted for a tenth of all readers.

2. Place of Residence/Work
(See Tables 3, 4 and 5.)

(a) Residence (Table 4). Little under half of all readers lived in the London postal area, mainly over three miles from the library, while a similar proportion lived in the Home Counties. A tenth of all readers lived in other parts of the U.K., especially the South Eastern Counties. The major occupational groups fitted more or less into this overall pattern.

(b) Work (Table 5). Three quarters of all readers worked in the London postal area, while half of all readers worked within one mile of the library. Those not working in London worked mainly in the Home Counties or South Eastern Counties. Only a few readers gave their place of work as abroad.

Readers in the major occupational groups fitted into the overall pattern; however, as might be expected, most patent workers, especially those from patent agencies, had offices within a mile of the library; non-patent workers tended to have their work places more evenly spread throughout London. They also accounted for the bulk of readers working outside London.

Of those who said they worked within a mile of the library almost all said they did so because their place of work was in that area. Only patent searchers differed from this pattern; a fifth of this occupational group gave their place of work as within a mile of the library because they mainly worked in the library.

(c) Origins of Academic Readers. (Table 3) Half of the academic readers were attached to London colleges while a third of them did not indicate their academic institution. No individual London colleges predominated. Readers from foreign colleges were rare unless they accounted for the large numbers not giving their college of origin.

3. Frequency and Duration of Visit
(Tables 6, 7 and 8)

(a) Frequency (Table 6). Three quarters of all readers claimed to come at least once a month, over half claimed to come at least weekly while a third claimed to come at least several days a week.

Patent workers were the most frequent visitors to the library. Three quarters or more of all patent workers claimed to come at least weekly, while from among them two thirds of workers from patent agencies claimed to come at least several days a week. Half the patent searchers claimed at least a daily visit. Non-patent workers came less frequently than patent workers, and accounted for the bulk of the monthly visitors. Half of all non-patent major occupational groups came either weekly or monthly except postgraduate and technical consultants. Both of these groups had a large proportion of readers coming several days a week.

Over three quarters of those readers who claimed at least a weekly visit and just under three quarters of those claiming a monthly visit, worked in London. These two groups of regular visitors accounted for the bulk of the total readership. Over half of the less frequent visitors also lived in London except for those coming less frequently than every six months (a small category) nearly two thirds of whom lived outside London.

(b) *Duration* (Table 7). Two fifths of all readers spent under one hour on their visit, a fifth spent 1–2 hours while a tenth spent 2–3 hours. A further tenth spent over 5 hours.

Patent workers spent a shorter time in the library than non-patent workers. Over four fifths of patent agents/technical assistants and other patent workers spent less than two hours in the library, and two thirds of this group spent less than one hour. Three quarters of all readers from patent agencies spent less than one hour in the library. Patent searchers were the only group of patent workers to spend a long period in the library, a third of them coming for over five hours.

Whereas most patent workers came to the library for less than one hour or one to two hours, two thirds of non-patent workers were spread fairly evenly over the three shortest periods shown in the table. A third of librarians came for over five hours.

On average, regular visitors spent less time in the library than other categories of reader. Nearly half of those who claimed to use the library weekly or several days a week stayed for less than one hour. The comparable proportion for other groups of readers was about a third.

4. Reasons for Visit
(See Tables 9, 10 and 11)

(a) *General Reasons* (Table 9). The great majority of readers, over four fifths, used the library solely for work purposes. A tenth of all readers indicated that their visit was related to both work and leisure interests.

Analysis by occupation shows that most patent workers came exclusively for work purposes with the exception of " other " patent workers, a fifth of whom came at least partly for leisure reasons. Under a fifth of research and development workers came for leisure or work and leisure reasons, as did a quarter of writers/editors and technical consultants.

(b) *Specific Reasons* (Table 10). The largest single reason for visiting the library was to make use of the patent section, a reason given by little under a half of all readers. A third came to consult non-patent literature for which they had specific references while a further third came to search for non-patent material which was unknown to them before their visit. A tenth of all readers said they had come to browse.

Most patent workers came to use the patent section (Group 1) though only half the category " other " patent workers gave this as a reason. However a quarter of all patent workers also gave each of the non-patent reasons listed in the table under Group 4.

Between a third and a half of all non-patent occupations came for each one of the reasons listed in Group 4, and especially to consult material for which they already had known references. Though smaller proportions of non-patent workers came to consult other recent material (Group 2) or made abstracts from journals (Group 3) most readers giving these two reasons were non-patent workers. Among non-patent occupations a third or more of librarians, technical consultants and research and development workers also intended to use the patent section during their visit.

269

An unduplicated analysis of the four groups of reasons listed in Table 10 shows that nearly half of librarians, technical consultants and research and development workers came for patent reasons while over half of all patent workers gave non-patent reasons (Group 4). A fifth of patent agents and technical assistants and a half " other " patent workers did not come for patent reasons at all.

(c) *Reasons why NRLSI was chosen first before other Libraries* (Table 11). Three quarters of all readers did not try another library before visiting the NRLSI. Of these the largest proportion, two fifths, gave the comprehensive patent stock as their reasons, while its convenient location and its comprehensive general stock were each cited as reasons by a quarter of the readers. Forty readers gave the open access facilities as a reason for choosing the NRLSI before other libraries.

Few patent workers had tried other libraries; over half of them gave the comprehensive patent stock as their reasons for using the NRLSI. A quarter of patent workers gave the convenient location as a reason.

Smaller proportions of non-patent occupations had come first to the NRLSI. Among those who had done so the main reason given was the comprehensive general stock, though a quarter of librarians and research and development workers also gave the comprehensive patent stock as a reason.

B. Use of Library

1. Subjects Used
(See Table 12)

An analysis of subjects used shows that readers' interests cover a wide range of subjects, and that interest in technological aspects exceeds that in scientific aspects by a ratio of at least 2:1 for most subjects.

Subjects in which greatest interest was shown were manufacturing processes and products, used by a quarter of all readers, mechanical engineering and polymer industries, each used by a fifth of all readers, chemical science, other chemical industries and electronics, each used by under a fifth of all readers. Subjects in which relatively little interest was shown were nuclear technologies, mathematics, earth sciences, agriculture, medicine and bibliography.

Patent agents and patent searchers were most interested in the technological application of manufacturing processes and products, and mechanical engineering; both subjects were used by a fifth of these occupational groups. Librarians also showed interest in these two subjects as well as chemical science and the technological application of polymer industries and other chemical industries. Academics showed most interest in physical science. Technical consultants and research and development workers were mainly interested in the technological application of mechanical engineering, manufacturing processes and products, electronics, polymer industries and also chemical science. However, the breadth of subjects used gives little opportunity for establishing any significant relationships between occupational groups and subjects.

Subjects Grouped by Scientific Aspect and Technological Application (Table 12). As indicated above, the technological application of a subject was of far greater interest to most readers than the scientific aspect. Two fifths of all readers were interested in only the technological application of subjects while a fifth of all readers were interested in the scientific aspect only. These proportions applied to all major occupational groups except for academics and postgraduates; half of these groups were interested only in scientific aspects. A third of librarians and research and development workers were interested only in technological aspects.

A fifth of all readers consulted (a) both aspects of the same subject and (b) both aspects of different subjects. In each case the occupational groups librarian, technical consultant and research and development workers showed above average interest in consulting both aspects of either the same subject or unrelated subjects.

270

2. Type of Material Used
(See Tables 13, 14 and 15.)

(a) *Use of Patent Literature by Occupational Groups Patent Agent/Technical Assistant and Patent Searchers* (Table 13). One hundred readers either did not answer this section of the questionnaire or did not use patent material. Of those who did answer, over half used only U.K. patents and a fifth used only foreign patents. A third of patent searchers used both U.K. and foreign patents as opposed to a sixth of patent agents/technical assistants.

(i) *U.K. Patents.*
By far the largest volume of all items required were specifications published in the last 25 years. Specifications from earlier periods formed only a sixth of the total requirements. Over half the usage of recent specifications was by patent agents/technical assistants. Most of the specifications published in earlier periods were used by patent searchers.

The average use of specifications was much higher than for any of the other categories of patent material. On average each patent worker who consulted patent material used 34 specifications. The average for all patent workers visiting the library was 24.

The usage of abridgements was only a quarter that of specifications. Again the main requirement was for abridgements published in the last 25 years. Patent searchers were the main users of abridgements, with non-agency patent workers predominating over the agency workers. The average use of abridgements by all patent workers consulting patent material was nine. The average use of abridgements by all patent workers visiting the library was six.

(ii) *Foreign Patents*
The pattern of use for foreign patents was similar to that for U.K. abridgements. Most items required were published in the last 25 years and patent searchers were the predominant users. The average use of foreign patents for all patent workers consulting patent material was seven, while the average use for all patent workers visiting the library was five.

The volume of " other " patent literature required was about a quarter of all U.K. specifications required. Most of the usage was by patent agents/technical assistants. The average use of " other " patent items for patent workers consulting " other " patent items was 11. The average for all patent workers was five.

(b) *Use of Non-Patent Items by Patent and Non-Patent Workers* (Table 15). Periodicals were easily the most used item of non-patent literature, especially periodicals published in 1966–68. Those published in 1960–65 were also heavily used in relation to other items. There was a steady decline in use of earlier periodicals. There was a similar fall off in use of abstracts, books and " other " items by date of publication, although there was a relatively high usage of abstracts published between 1960–1965 and pre–1910.

Average use of all non-patent items was twice as high for non-patent workers as for patent workers. This was also true for individual categories of items. Over two thirds of total periodical usage was by non-patent readers. The only significant group of patent workers to use periodicals were patent searchers, particularly for periodicals published between 1940 and 1960. On average readers of periodicals used 13 items.

Three quarters of the total usage of abstracts was by non-patent workers. Main users of material published between 1960 and 1968 were patent searchers, librarians, research/development workers and postgraduates. Little use was made of items published between 1910 and 1949. The pre-1910 items were mainly used by librarians/information officers.

Average use of abstracts by those actually consulting abstracts was 13 items per worker.

Three quarters of the usage of books was by non-patent workers. Research/development workers were significant users of books in all the time periods analysed

271

separately. Patent agents/technical assistants were large users of books published post-1940. Average use of books per reader consulting books was six per reader.

" Other " items were mostly used by non-patent workers except for items published in 1966–68 where patent workers were of equal importance. Academics and writers/editors showed most interest in " other " items. Average use of " other " items was similar to that for books at five items per reader who was using this category of literature.

3. Use of the Photocopy Service
(See Tables 16 to 20)

(a) *As Shown in Questionnaire* (Table 16). One fifth of all sectors used the photocopy service. Patent agents were the main group of users (nearly a fifth), while patent searchers and research/development workers each accounted for an eighth of total users. As a group patent workers were a third of all users of the photocopy service.

The main demand for photocopies was divided between patent specifications/abridgements and periodicals, in nearly equal amounts. Demand for monographs and trade literature was small. Two fifths of patent items were used by patent workers. Non-patent users accounted for three quarters of the periodical photocopies. A third of these items were needed by librarians/information officers. Other major users were research/development workers and writers/editors.

(b) *Analysis of Photocopy Application Slips* (see Tables 17–20). A separate analysis was made of actual photocopy application slips dealt with at the library on the same full working days as the questionnaire survey took place. This analysis was undertaken to give a more complete picture of the use of the photocopying service since it was believed that the greater part of the usage was by postal rather than personal application, so that an analysis based solely on the questionnaire would be misleading. In fact the number of actual photocopy orders dealt with during the survey was 1,278, whereas only 229 readers made personal applications at the library. Even allowing for an average of more than one order per reader, it is clear that non-readers are the major users of the photocopying service. The results of the separate analysis are as follows:

(i) *Patents.* Patent items accounted for three quarters of all items photocopied. Four fifths were delivered by post and paid for by deposit account. Half of these orders originated from London postal districts; the Home Counties accounted for another eighth. The average number of items ordered on each form was three.

(ii) *Periodicals.* Under one quarter of items photocopied were periodicals. Half of them were delivered to waiting readers, half were sent by post. Half were paid for by cash and half by deposit account. Again London postal districts and the Home Counties accounted for the bulk of the orders, but the Southern region was also of some significance with a tenth of the orders. Nearly a half were published in 1966–68, a fifth in 1960–65 and under a third in 1950–59. The average number of items per periodical order form was two.

(iii) *Books.* Very few books were photocopied—239 in all. Half of these were delivered to the waiting reader and half were sent by post. Half were paid for by cash and half by deposit account. Most orders originated from London postal districts. Demand was mainly for books published since 1950. Each book order form averaged one item.

4. Origin of Enquiries from Outside London
(See Table 21)

A third of all readers were seeking information for clients outside London. Two thirds of these enquiries were handled by patent workers, and especially by those from firms of patent agents. Within the non-patent occupational categories a half of the librarians and technical consultants were seeking information for clients outside London.

Over half of all enquiries from outside London came from the UK while two fifths came from abroad.

The UK enquiries were well dispersed geographically, with major origins in the Home Counties, South East Counties and North West. A quarter of all readers in the sample had enquiries from clients in the Home Counties.

Enquiries from outside the UK came from 35 countries though the only significant ones were the USA, Japan and West Germany. A sixth of readers had enquiries from clients in the USA.

5. Methods of Identifying Specific Items
(See Tables 22 and 23)

(a) *Methods Used in the Library* (Table 22). The two main methods used for identifying material were by consulting the periodicals index and by only looking on the shelves. Each of these methods was used by a third of all readers. There was also substantial usage of all other methods with the exception of published bibliographic tools and asking the staff.

Patent workers were heavy users of the open access facilities and " other " indexes; half of all non-patent occupational categories used the periodicals index. In general however, no significant trend emerged by occupational group.

(b) *Use of Other Libraries prior to using the NRLSI* (Table 23). Only a fifth of all readers had tried other libraries prior to visiting the NRLSI. They were almost all non-patent workers, over a fifth of each main occupational category, though over half of academics and postgraduates had tried elsewhere first. A third of new visitors had tried elsewhere. Three quarters of those readers who had tried elsewhere worked in London; the rest worked in the Home Counties.

Of the readers who had tried other libraries first just under a half had tried university libraries, and a quarter had tried both public libraries and industrial or firms' libraries. The other significant type of library tried was that belonging to a research or professional association.

Half the academic and postgraduate readers had tried University libraries but otherwise there was no significant difference between the other occupation groups.

6. Readers Needing a Further Visit to Complete their Enquiry
(See Table 24)

Two fifths of all readers said they would need a further visit to complete their enquiry while two fifths said they would not. A fifth gave no answer.

With the exception of patent agents/technical assistants, " other " patent workers and academic staff, over two fifths of each major occupational group said they would need a further visit to complete their enquiry.

STATISTICAL APPENDIX

Table 1.   Occupation of Readers

	Sample 1,158	Per cent
Patent agent/technical assistant	259	22
Patent searcher	103	9
Patent examiner	36	3
Trade-mark searcher	25	2
Librarian/information officer	86	7
Abstractor	36	3
Writer/editor	64	6
Market researcher	37	3
Translator	26	2
Engineer	13	1
Technical consultant	62	5
Research and development worker	135	12
Academic or research staff of university	36	3
Staff of other academic institution	20	2
Postgraduate student	74	6
Freelance inventor	40	3
Technical occupation	12	1
Other	94	8

Table 2.   Parent Organisation of Readers

	Sample* 1,158	Per cent
Firm of patent agents/trade-mark agents	285	25
University	117	10
Other academic institution	44	4
Research association, professional or learned society	47	4
Industry/commerce	375	32
Nationalised industry	16	1
Civil service/local government	75	6
Publisher	54	5
Self-employed	94	8
Retired/unemployed	15	1
Others	61	5

* The breakdown exceeds the sample number because several readers ticked more than one category in their answer to this question.   The percentages are based on the sample of 1,158 and therefore exceed 100 per cent.

Table 3.   Origins of Academic Readers

	Sample 164	Per cent
Imperial College	4	2
University College	16	10
King's College	7	4
Other London colleges	62	38
Colleges in UK but outside London	23	14
USA	1	0
Scandinavia	1	0
Japan	1	0
No answer	49	30

Table 4.   Area of Residence

	Sample 1,158	Per cent
In London Postal Area:		
Within 1 mile of Library	25	2
1–3 miles from Library	69	6
3–10 miles from Library	219	19
Over 10 miles from Library	179	15
Home Counties	498	43
South East Counties	88	8
Other parts of England	30	3
Wales	2	0
Scotland	4	0
Ireland	2	0
Abroad	8	0
No answer	29	3

Table 5.   Area of Work

	Sample 1,158	Per cent
In London Postal Area		
Within 1 mile of Library	544*	47
1–3 miles from Library	175	15
3–10 miles from Library	76	7
Over 10 miles from Library	60	5
Home Counties	152	13
South East Counties	48	4
Other parts of England	27	2
Wales	1	0
Scotland	3	0
Ireland	1	0
Abroad	8	0
No answer	59	5

* Of the 544 readers who gave their place of work within one mile of the library, 477 did so because their office was located in the area and 42 because they were working mainly at the NRLSI.

Additional Analysis Produced from Data Supplied by the Economist Intelligence Unit

Analysis of Area of Work by Total Number of Visits

	Total visits 1,829	Per cent
In London Postal Area:		
Within 1 mile of Library	1,008	55
1–3 miles from Library	261	14
3–10 miles from Library	102	5
Over 10 miles from Library	86	5
Home Counties	195	11
South East Counties	52	3
Other parts of England	26	1
Wales	1	0
Scotland	4	0
Ireland	1	0
Abroad	9	0
No answer	84	5

Table 6. Frequency of Visit

	Sample 1,158	Per cent
Several times a day	45	4
Daily	71	6
Several days a week	231	20
Weekly..	315	27
Monthly	203	18
Every 3 months	60	5
Every 6 months	24	2
Less frequently than every 6 months	26	2
Infrequently but for short periods	95	8
Never before	84	7
No answer	3	0

Table 7. Length of Time Spent in Library

	Sample 1,158	Per cent
Up to 1 hour	477	41
1–2 hours	244	21
2–3 hours	170	15
3–4 hours	73	6
4–5 hours	35	3
Over 5 hours	101	9
No answer	57	5

Table 8. Numbers of Visits Actually Made

	Sample 1,158	Per cent
One visit	793	68
Two visits	193	17
Three visits	77	7
Four visits	49	4
Five visits	40	3
Six visits	1	0

Table 9. General Reasons for Visit

	Sample 1,158	Per cent
For work reasons	977	84
For leisure reasons	62	5
For both reasons	110	9

276

Table 10. Specific Reasons for Visit

	Sample* 1,158	Per cent
Group 1		
To consult new patents specifications	205	19
To use the patents section	503	43
Group 2		
To consult other recent material	189	16
Group 3		
To make abstracts from journals	203	18
Group 4		
To consult periodical articles or literature for which readers had specific references	407	35
To classify or consult partially known references..	318	27
To search for references or material which were unknown before visit	395	34
To browse	103	9
Other reasons	82	—

* The breakdown exceeds the sample number because many readers ticked more than one category. The percentages are calculated on the sample number and therefore exceed 100 per cent.

Table 11. Reasons Why Readers Visited the NRLSI Before Trying Other Libraries

	Sample 801	Per cent
Open access	41	5
Convenient location	182	23
Comprehensive patent stock	354	44
Comprehensive general stock	224	28

277

Table 12. Subjects Used

	Scientific Aspects		Technological Application	
	Sample 1,158*	Per cent	Sample 1,158*	Per cent
1. *All Subjects*				
Manufacturing processes	77	7	206	18
Mechanical engineering	71	6	169	15
Polymer industries	88	8	151	13
Other chemical industries	62	5	110	9
Electronics	64	6	110	9
Transportation	34	3	104	9
Electronical and magnetic engineering ..	41	4	86	7
Metallurgy	45	4	83	7
Storage, handling, packaging	29	3	72	6
Life technologies	31	3	64	6
Computers	34	3	59	5
Optical instruments, photography	31	3	58	5
Civil engineering	24	2	50	4
Nuclear technologies	18	2	26	2
Agriculture	10	1	18	2
Scientific aspects only				
Chemical science	183	16		
Physical science	73	6		
Life sciences	61	5		
Earth sciences	40	3		
Mathematics	23	2		
Non-scientific, non-technological				
Non-scientific topics	84	7		
Medicine	49	4		
Bibliography	37	3		
Patents/trade-marks	22	2		
Translations/dictionaries	6	1		
Other	13	1		
No answer	104	9		
2. *Proportion of sample using one aspect of subject only (i.e. scientific or technological aspect)*				
Scientific aspect only	212	18		
Technological aspect only	465	40		
3. *Proportion of sample consulting both scientific and technological aspect of subjects*				
Same subject	263	23		
Unrelated subjects	243	21		

* As readers were asked to indicate all the subject fields they were using during their visit the numerical breakdown by subject is much greater than the sample number, and the percentages exceed 100 per cent.

Table 13. Use of Patent Material by Patent Agents, Technical Assistants, Patent Searchers

	Sample 360	Per cent
1. *All patent readers*		
Only UK patents	139	39
Only foreign patents	48	13
Both UK and foreign patents	59	16
No answer	108	30

2. *Total number of items used*	UK Patents		Foreign Patents	Other Patent Material
Date/age of publication	Specifica-tions	Abridge-ments		
Last 25 years	7,256	1,577	1,215	⎫
26–50 years	956	600	431	⎬ 1,977
Over 50 years	317	86	30	⎭
3. *Average number of items used*				
Average for all patent workers visiting the library	24	6	5	5
Average for all patent workers consulting specifications, abridgements or foreign patents	34	9	7	—
Average for all patent workers consulting other patent literature	—	—	—	11

Table 14. Number of Items of Non-Patent Literature Used by all Readers

Published Between	1966–68	1960–65	1950–59	1940–49	1930–39	1910–29	Pre 1910
Periodicals	3,761	1,449	791	367	221	99	19
Abstracts	665	730	224	68	31	74	106
Books	654	544	261	101	49	36	25
Other	101	75	46	9	11	8	5

Table 15. Average Number of Non-Patent Items Used

	All Readers	Patent Workers	Non-Patent Workers
Periodicals			
Average for all readers	6	3	7
Average for all readers consulting non-patent material	7	4	9
Average for all readers consulting periodicals ..	13	—	—
Abstracts			
Average for all readers	2	1	2
Average for all readers consulting non-patent material	2	1	3
Average for all readers consulting abstracts ..	13	—	—
Books			
Average for all readers	1·4	1	1·8
Average for all readers consulting non-patent material	1·8	1·2	2·2
Average for all readers consulting books	6	—	—
Others			
Average for all readers	0·22	0·19	0·24
Average for all readers consulting non-patent material	0·28	0·24	0·30
Average for all readers consulting other items ..	5	—	—
Overall average of non-patent items consulted			
Average for all people visiting the library.. ..	9	5	12
Average for all people consulting non-patent material	11	7	14

Table 16. Use of the Photocopy Service

	Sample 1,158	Per cent
1. *All readers*		
Those who used the photocopy service	229	20
Those who did not use the photocopy service	821	71
No answer	107	9

	Items	Pages
2. *Number of Photocopies made*		
Patent specification or abridgement	583	2,362
Periodicals	454	1,699
Monographs	44	75
Trade literature	24	60

Table 17. Photocopy Analysis of Items—By Method of Delivery/Payment

	All orders	Patents	Periodicals	Books	Others
Total	1,278	2,558	692	39	9
(a) *Method of Delivery*					
While you wait	386	459	309	20	1
Postal delivery	891	2,096	383	19	8
(b) *Method of payment*					
Cash	309	300	331	19	—
Deposit	928	2,209	305	19	9
Free	41	49	55	1	—

Table 18. Photocopy Analysis of Items—By Region of Origin

	All orders	Patents	Periodicals	Books	Others
Total	1,278	2,558	692	39	9
London Postal District ..	641	1,242	308	26	6
Home Counties	230	323	181	5	3
North	22	41	11	—	—
Yorks and Humberside	25	80	1	—	—
North West	62	162	3	1	—
East Midlands	10	34	1	—	—
West Midlands	60	198	1	1	—
South	100	164	70	6	—
South West	24	53	10	—	—
Wales	17	64	1	—	—
Scotland	14	41	1	—	—
Ireland	5	12	36	—	—
Abroad	46	130	31	—	—

Table 19. Photocopy Analysis of Items—By Publication Date

	All orders	Patents	Periodicals	Books	Others
Total	1,278	2,558	692	39	9
1966–68	179	24	284	5	—
1960–65	107	—	138	12	4
1950–59	83	3	214	7	—
1940–49	30	50	1	—	—
1930–39	25	—	36	—	—
1910–29	18	—	15	4	—
Pre 1910	6	—	7	—	—

Table 20. Analysis of Photocopy Orders

1. Average Number of Items per Order

Patents	3
Periodicals	2
Books	1
Other material	2

2. Number of Items and Pages Photo-copied

Total numbers of orders	1,278
Total pages copied	22,517
Average number of pages per order ..	18
Total number of items copied ..	3,314
Average number of items copied per order	2·6

Table 21. Whether Information Sought for Enquiry Originating Outside London

	Sample 1,158	Per cent
1. All readers		
Yes	426	37
No	728	63

	Sample 426	Per cent
2. Origin of Enquiry		
Home Counties	98	23
South East Counties	63	15
South West	19	4
West Midlands	18	4
North West	35	8
Scotland	11	3
France	12	3
Japan	18	4
USA	76	18
West Germany	31	7
Other Countries	72	17

Table 22. Methods of Identifying Specific Items

	Sample 1,158*	Per cent
By using the periodicals index	374	32
By only looking on the shelves	346	30
By using the classified subject indexes	234	20
By using the author/name catalogues	208	18
By using other indexes	191	16
By using published bibliographic tools	151	13
By asking the staff	147	13
No answer	101	9

* As readers were asked to indicate as many methods as were applicable, the breakdown exceeds the sample number and the percentages total more than 100 per cent.

Table 23. Readers who tried Another Library before trying the NRLSI

	Sample 1,158*	Per cent
1. *Use of another library*		
Yes	217	19
No	918	79
No answer	20	2
	Sample 217	Per cent
2. *Types of other library used*		
University/college library	86	40
Public library	58	28
Industrial or firm's library	54	25
Library of research association, professional or learned society	37	17
Science Museum library	18	8
Government library	12	6
National Lending Library for Science and Technology	6	3
British Museum library	6	3
National Central Library	4	2
Abroad	6	3
Other libraries	9	4
No answer	3	1

* The breakdown exceeds the sample number because readers were asked to tick as many categories as were applicable. The percentages are calculated on the sample number and therefore exceed 100 per cent.

Table 24. Need of a Future Visit to Complete Enquiry

	Sample 1,158	Per cent
Yes	449	39
No	480	41
No answer	228	30

QUESTIONNAIRE

N.B. *Please answer all questions by placing a tick in the appropriate box unless specifically asked to do otherwise.*

1. Please state the type of organisation with which you are associated. (Tick one category only)

Card 1 (16)

Firm of Patent Agents/Trade-mark Agents	☐	1
University	☐	2
Other academic institution	☐	3
Research association, professional or learned society, etc.	☐	4
Industry/Commerce	☐	5
Nationalised Industry	☐	6
Civil Service/Local government	☐	7
Publisher	☐	8
Self-employed	☐	9
Retired/unemployed	☐	0
Other (please specify)...		(17)

What is the nature of your occupation? (Tick one category only)

2(a)

Patent Agent/Technical Assistant	☐	(18) 1	Technical consultant	☐	0
Patent searcher	☐	2	Market researcher	☐	x
Patent examiner	☐	3	Research/Development	☐	y
Trade-mark searcher	☐	4	Abstractor	☐	1(19)
Librarian/Information officer	☐	5	Writer or editor	☐	2
Academic or research staff of university	☐	6	Translator	☐	3
Staff of other academic institution	☐	7	Freelance inventor	☐	4
Postgraduate student	☐	8	Other (please specify)		(20)
Undergraduate student	☐	9			

284

2(b) If you are a STUDENT or on the STAFF of a university or other academic institution, please give the name of the college/institution

In London ....(21)

Rest of UK outside London...(22)

Overseas ....(23)

3(a) Where do you live *and* work at present?

In London			Live		Work	
(i) Postal districts						
WC1, 2 ..	..	EC1, 4	☐	1 (24)	☐	1 (25)
(ii) Postal districts						
EC2, 3 ..	..	SE1				
N1 ..	..	SW1	☐	2	☐	2
NW1 ..	..	W1, 2				
(iii) Postal districts						
E1, 2, 3, 5, 8, 9, 14		SW2, 3, 4, 5, 6, 7, 8, 9, 10, 11 ..				
N4, 5, 6, 7, 8, 15, 16, 19		SE5, 8, 11, 14, 15, 16, 17, 22, 24 ..	☐	3	☐	3
NW2, 3, 4, 5, 8, 11		W6, 8, 9, 10, 11, 12, 14 ..				
(iv) Any other postal district	..	..	☐	4	☐	4
Home Counties (Middlesex, Hertford, Essex, Surrey, Kent)			☐	5	☐	5
South East Counties (Sussex, Hants, Berks, Bucks, Oxford, Bedford, Northants, Hunts, Cambs, Suffolk, Norfolk)			☐	6	☐	6
Other parts of England ..	..	.. ..	☐	7	☐	7
Wales ..	.. ..	.. .. ..	☐	8	☐	8
Scotland ..	.. ..	.. .. ..	☐	9	☐	9
Ireland ..	.. ..	.. .. ..	☐	0	☐	0
Other (please specify).....................			☐		☐	(26)
						(27)

(b) If you gave your place of work as London postal districts WC1, 2; EC1, 4, is this because

You are working mainly at this library .. ☐ 1 (28)

Your office or other place of work is located in these postal districts ☐ 2

4(a) Is any of the information you are seeking today for an enquirer or client outside London? (29)

Yes .. ☐ 1

No .. ☐ 2

(b) If *YES*, please indicate the place of origin of the enquiry (if the place of origin is in the UK please give the name of the town or, alternatively, the county; if the place of origin is abroad please give the name of the country).

UK: Town................. County.................... (30)

Abroad: (Country) .... (31)

(32)

5. About how frequently do you visit this library? (33)

Several times a day .. .. ☐	1
Daily.. .. .. ☐	2
Several days a week .. .. ☐	3
Weekly .. .. ☐	4
Monthly .. .. ☐	5
Every 3 months .. .. ☐	6
Every 6 months .. .. ☐	7
Less frequently than every 6 months .. .. .. ☐	8
Infrequently, but for short periods .. .. .. ☐	9
Never before .. .. ☐	0

6. Is the reason for your visit today related (34)

To your work? .. .. ☐	1
To your leisure interests? .. .. ☐	2
To your work and leisure interests? .. .. .. ☐	3

7. Why have you come to this library today? (35)
(Tick as many categories as are applicable)

To consult new patent specifications .. .. .. ☐	1
To use the patents section.. .. .. ☐	2
To consult other recent material .. .. ☐	3

286

To make abstracts from journals..	☐	4
To consult periodical articles or literature for which you already had specific references	☐	5
To clarify or consult partially known references	☐	6
To search for references or material which were unknown to you before your visit	☐	7
To browse	☐	8
Other reasons (please specify).....................................		(36)
		(37)

8(a) Did you try to obtain what you require in another library before coming here? (38)

	Yes ..	☐	1
	No ..	☐	2

(b) If *YES* where did you try before? (39)

Public library	☐	1
University or college library	☐	2
Government library	☐	3
Library of a research association, professional or learned society	☐	4
Industrial or firm's library	☐	5
British Museum library, Bloomsbury	☐	6
Science Museum library	☐	7
National Lending Library for Science and Technology ..	☐	8
National Central Library	☐	9
Abroad	☐	0
Other (please specify)...		(40)

(c) If *NO*, why did you come here? (41)

....

....

....

9. Please tick the subject or subjects in which you are seeking information or literature TODAY.

N.B. The following list is divided into two columns—Scientific Aspects and Technological Applications—to differentiate between those who are interested in the pure or theoretical aspects of a subject and those who are interested in the practical aspects of a subject, although it is recognised that in many cases the reader may be interested in both. Please put a tick in one or both columns next to the subject as appropriate. For example if you are seeking information on the Aerodynamics of Propellers put a tick in the column headed " Scientific Aspects " next to the subject category "Transportation and Vehicles "; but if your interest is Propellor Manufacture put a tick in the column headed " Technological Applications " next to the same subject category.

	Scientific Aspects	Technological Applications	(42)
Physical science (e.g. relativity, radiation, etc.)	☐ 1		
Nuclear technologies	☐ 2	☐	3
Mechanical Engineering, Heat technologies (including machinery, engines, refrigeration)	☐ 4	☐	5
Manufacturing processes and products (including production engineering, workshop practice, assembly, metal products, timber products, fabrics, printing, glassware, etc.)	☐ 6	☐	7
Storage; Handling; Packaging	☐ 8	☐	9
Transportation; Vehicles..	☐ 0	☐	x
Civil engineering (including architecture, building bridges, docks, reservoirs, etc.)	☐ 1	☐	(43) 2
Electronics; Telecommunications ..	☐ 3	☐	4
Electrical and magnetic engineering ..	☐ 5	☐	6
Optical instruments; photography ..	☐ 7	☐	8
Computers; instrumentation	☐ 9	☐	0
Mathematics	☐ x		
Earth sciences; Mining industries (including geology, mineralogy, astronomy, etc.)	☐ y		
Chemical science (e.g. inorganic chemistry, physical chemistry)	☐ 1		(44)
Metallurgy	☐ 2	☐	3
Polymer industries (including plastics, synthetic fibres, pulp, paper, etc.) ..	☐ 4	☐	5

288

Other chemical industries (including explosives, detergents, fertilisers, dyes, etc.) .. .. ☐ 6 ☐ 7

Life sciences (e.g. botany, zoology, physiology, bacteriology) .. .. .. ☐ 8

Life technologies (including foods, fermentation, sewage disposal, etc.) .. ☐ 9 ☐ 0

Agriculture; Forestry; Fisheries.. .. ☐ x y

Medicine; Public Health .. .. .. ☐ 1

(45)

Non-scientific topics (including law, librarianship, information, methodology, heraldry, commerce, management, etc.) ☐ 2

Bibliography .. .. ☐ 3

Other (please specify and state whether scientific or technical).......... (46)

.... (47)

.... (48)

10. How did you identify the specific items you required today?.. .. (49)
(Tick as many categories as are applicable)

By consulting the author and name catalogue .. .. .. ☐ 1

By consulting the classified subject catalogue .. .. .. ☐ 2

By consulting the periodicals index .. .. ☐ 3

By consulting other indexes of this library .. .. .. ☐ 4

By consulting published bibliographic tools (e.g. abstracts, bibliographies, etc.) .. .. ☐ 5

By asking the staff .. .. ☐ 6

By ONLY looking on the shelves .. .. ☐ 7

11(a) How long did you spend in the library on this occasion?

(50)

Up to 1 hour .. ☐ 1 Between 3 and 4 hrs. ☐ 4

Between 1 and 2 hrs. ☐ 2 Between 4 and 5 hrs. ☐ 5

Between 2 and 3 hrs. ☐ 3 Over 5 hours .. ☐ 6

(b) Will another visit be necessary to enable you to complete your present enquiry? .. .. .. Yes .. ☐ | (51) 1

No .. ☐ | 2

12(a) Did you make use of the photocopy service? .. Yes .. ☐ | (52) 1

No .. ☐ | 2

(b) If YES, how many *items* did you have photo-copied? Please fill in the grid according to the type of material you had photocopied. For example if you had extracts photo-copied from 20 period-icals fill in the grid as	Patent speci-fication or abridgement		Periodicals		Mono-graphs		Trade Literature	
	(52)	(53)	(54)	(55)	(56)	(57)	(58)	(59)

Periodicals

(54)	(55)
2	0

(c) If you used the photo-copy service today, approximately how many *pages* did you have photocopied? Again, please fill in the grid as in 12(b) using one square for each digit of the num-ber stated.	Patent speci-fication or abridgement			Periodicals			Mono-graphs			Trade Literature		
	(60)	(61)	(62)	(63)	(64)	(65)	(66)	(67)	(68)	(69)	(70)	(71)

To be completed by Patent Agents, Technical Assistants and Patent Searchers only

13(a) Excluding this week's new specifications, how many items of patent literature have you looked at during your visit today? Please put the total number for each category specified in the appropriate spaces provided below. (For UK Patent specifications give the *number of specifications;* for UK Patent abridgements and Foreign Patents give the *number of volumes.*) For example, if you used 125 specifications published in the last 25 years fill in grid as:

Specifications

(13)	(14)	(15)
1	2	5

Date/age of Publications	UK Patents						Foreign Patents		
	Specifications			Abridgements					
Last 25 years	(13)	(14)	(15)	(16)	(17)	(18)	(19)	(20)	(21)
26–50 years	(22)	(23)	(24)	(25)	(26)	(27)	(28)	(29)	(30)
Over 50 years	(31)	(32)	(33)	(34)	(35)	(36)	(37)	(38)	(39)

(*b*) If you have also used any other Patent literature (e.g. indexes, bulletins, official gazettes, patent law books, etc.) please give the *number* of items looked at.

Write in number   ..

40/41/42

To be completed by Patent Agents, Technical Assistants and Patent Searchers only

14. Please list the *titles* and tick dates of publication of any periodicals which you have consulted during your visit today.

Card 3

Title of Publication	(13)	Date of Publication					
	1966–1968	1960–1965	1950–1959	1940–1949	1930–1939	1910–1929	Pre-1910

To be completed by all readers (including Patent Agents, Technical Assistants and Patent Searchers)

15. How many NON-PATENT items have you used on this occasion? (Please put the total for each of the categories listed in the appropriate box according to date of publication). For example, if you used 35 periodicals published in the period 1966–68 fill in grid as:—

1966–68

	(13)	(14)
Periodicals ..	3	5

Card 4

Published between	1966–68		1960–65		1950–59		1940–49		1930–39		1910–29		Pre-1910	
Periodicals	(13)	(14)	(15)	(16)	(17)	(18)	(19)	(20)	(21)	(22)	(23)	(24)	(25)	(26)
Abstracts, etc. ..	(27)	(28)	(29)	(30)	(31)	(32)	(33)	(34)	(35)	(36)	(37)	(38)	(39)	(40)
Books	(41)	(42)	(43)	(44)	(45)	(46)	(47)	(48)	(49)	(50)	(51)	(52)	(53)	(54)
Other	(55)	(56)	(57)	(58)	(59)	(60)	(61)	(62)	(63)	(64)	(65)	(66)	(67)	(68)

N.B. It is known that the use of this Library involves considerably more than the study of that literature which is found to be wholly appropriate for the purpose in hand. Sometimes a large number of volumes has to be quickly evaluated and rejected before the right references can be selected. This is an important and wholly valid use of the Library. It is, in fact, one of the greatest assets of an open-access reference library. If the use of this Library is to be accurately surveyed, it is essential that every item of literature taken from the shelf and opened be counted in this analysis; if two or more items come within a single bound volume, they should be counted separately. If this is not done, the resources of this Library may be undervalued, and your future needs may not be fully assessed.

Your co-operation in filling in this chart is therefore earnestly requested as being in your own interests.

A spare copy is provided on the next page for rough working during the course of your visit.

16. **Rough Working Chart**

Published between	1966–68	1960–65	1950–59	1940–49	1930–39	1910–29	Pre-1910
Periodicals							
Abstracts, etc.							
Books							
Other							

RESULTS OF SURVEY
AT THE
SCIENCE MUSEUM LIBRARY, MARCH–APRIL, 1968

survey carried out by

THE STAFF OF THE SML

CONTENTS

Symbols used in the tables

   * less than 1%

   — Nil

Table 1 (relates to Question 1). **Organisation with which readers were associated** (All readers)

Categories	Sample 1,412	Per cent
(i) Science Museum..	65	5
British Museum (Natural History)	12	*
Institute of Geological Sciences	6	*
Victoria and Albert Museum ..	1	*
Other Museum ..	1	*
(ii) Imperial College of Science and Technology..	860	61
Other college or institute of London University	102	7
University (excluding London University)	100	7
Other higher academic institution	51	4
School	30	2
(iii) Industry/commerce	83	6
Civil Service/Local Government	13	*
Nationalised industry	7	*
Research Council	5	*
Research association, professional or learned society, etc...	24	2
Self-employed	27	2
Other	23	2
No answer	2	*

Table 2 (relates to Questions 1 and 2). **Readers from ICST**

Categories	Sample 860	Per cent
Academic staff	181	21
Postgraduate students	439	51
Undergraduate students	193	22
Other staff	12	1
No answer	35	4

Table 3 (relates to Question 2). **Nature of Occupation of Readers**

Categories	Sample 1,412	Per cent
Academic staff of university..	193	14
Staff of other higher academic institution ..	25	2
Staff of school	6	*
Postgraduate student..	475	34
Undergraduate student	300	21
Other type of student	73	5
Research/development	111	8
Consultant	12	*
Inventor	2	*
Patent agent or lawyer	3	*
Engineer	43	3
Librarian	35	3
Information officer	24	2
Professional writer	10	*
Translator	3	*
Retired..	10	*
Other	78	6
No answer	9	*

Table 4 (relates to Question 3(*a*)).   **Frequency of Use of the SML**
(All readers)

Categories								Sample 1,412	Per cent
Daily	..	..	..	..	..		..	90	6
More than once a week	..	..	..	..	..		..	264	19
About once a week ..	..	..	..	..		· ..	..	260	18
1 to 3 times a month	..	..	..	..	..		..	356	25
About once a quarter	..	..	..	..	..		..	147	10
About once a year ..	..	..	..	..	..		..	37	3
Rarely	..	..	..	..	..		..	238	17
No answer	..	..	..	..	..		..	20	1

Table 5 (relates to Question 3(*a*)).   **Frequency of Use of the SML**
(Non-ICST readers)

Categories								Sample 552	Per cent
Daily	..	..	..	..	..		..	36	7
More than once a week	..	..	..	..	..		..	64	12
About once a week ..	..	..	..	..	..		..	57	10
1 to 3 times per month	..	..	..	..	..		..	94	17
About once a quarter	..	..	..	..	..		..	74	13
About once a year ..	..	..	..	..	..		..	27	5
Rarely	..	..	..	..	..		..	189	34
No answer	..	..	..	..	..		..	11	2

Table 6 (relates to Question 3(*a*)).   **Frequency of Use of the SML**
(ICST academic and non-academic staff, postgraduate and undergraduate students)

Categories								Sample 860	Per cent
Daily	..	..	..	..	..		..	54	6
More than once a week	..	..	..	..	..		..	200	23
About once a week ..	..	..	..	..	..		..	203	24
1 to 3 times per month	..	..	..	..	..		..	262	30
About once a quarter	..	..	..	..	..		..	73	9
About once a year ..	..	..	..	..	..		..	10	1
Rarely	..	..	..	..	..		..	49	6
No answer	..	..	..	..	..		..	9	1

Table 7 (relates to Questions 1, 2 and 3(*a*)).   **Frequency of Use of the SML**
(ICST readers: academic staff)

Categories								Sample 181	Per cent
Daily	..	..	..	..	..		..	17	9
More than once a week	..	..	..	..	..		..	40	22
About once a week ..	..	..	..	..	..		..	44	24
1 to 3 times per month	..	..	..	..	..		..	54	30
About once a quarter	..	..	..	..	..		..	19	11
About once a year ..	..	..	..	..	..		..	1	*
Rarely	..	..	..	..	..		..	5	3
No answer	..	..	..	..	..		..	1	*

Table 8 (relates to Questions 1, 2 and 3(a)).   **Frequency of use of the SML**
(ICST readers: Postgraduates)

Categories							Sample 439	Per cent
Daily	..	..	..	..	..	..	19	4
More than once a week	..	..	..	..	..	..	76	17
About once a week ..	..	..	..	..	..	..	112	26
1 to 3 times per month	..	..	..	..	..	..	167	38
About once a quarter	..	..	..	..	..	..	38	9
About once a year ..	..	..	..	..	..	..	4	*
Rarely	..	..	..	..	..	..	18	4
No answer	..	..	..	..	..	..	5	1

Table 9 (relates to Questions 1, 2 and 3(a)).   **Frequency of use of the SML**
(ICST readers: Undergraduates)

Categories							Sample 193	Per cent
Daily	..	..	..	..	..	..	13	7
More than once a week	..	..	..	..	..	..	65	34
About once a week ..	..	..	..	..	..	..	42	22
1 to 3 times per month	..	..	..	..	..	..	32	17
About once a quarter	..	..	..	..	..	..	14	7
About once a year ..	..	..	..	..	..	..	5	3
Rarely	..	..	..	..	..	..	20	10
No answer ..	..	..	..	..	..	..	2	1

Table 10 (relates to Question 3(b)).   **Average duration of each visit to the SML**

Categories							Sample 1,412	Per cent
Up to 1 hour ..	..	..	..	..	..	..	659	47
Up to half a day ..	..	..	..	..	..	..	393	28
Up to 1 day	..	..	..	..	..	..	87	6
Longer	..	..	..	..	..	..	12	*
No answer	..	..	..	..	..	..	261	19

Table 11 (relates to Question 4(a)).   **Distance travelled by readers to make visit to the SML**

Categories							Sample 1,412	Per cent
Less than 1 mile ..	..	..	..	..	..	..	907	64
1 to 2 miles ..	..	..	..	..	..	..	114	8
2 to 5 miles ..	..	..	..	..	..	..	137	10
5 to 10 miles ..	..	..	..	..	..	..	99	7
10 to 20 miles ..	..	..	..	..	..	..	80	6
20 to 50 miles ..	..	..	..	..	..	..	32	2
Over 50 miles ..	..	..	..	..	..	..	25	2
No answer ..	..	..	..	..	..	..	18	1

Table 12 (relates to Question 4(b)(i)).   **Distance from the SML to the readers' normal place of residence**

Categories							Sample 1,412	Per cent
Less than 1 mile	..	..	..	..	..	..	293	21
1 to 2 miles	..	..	..	..	..	..	169	12
2 to 5 miles	..	..	..	..	..	..	252	18
5 to 10 miles	..	..	..	..	..	..	239	17
10 to 20 miles	..	..	..	..	..	..	192	14
20 to 50 miles	..	..	..	..	..	..	93	7
Over 50 miles	..	..	..	..	..	..	160	11
No answer	..	..	..	..	..	..	14	1

Table 13 (relates to Question 4(b)(ii)).   **Distance from the SML to the readers' normal place of work**

Categories							Sample 1,412	Per cent
Less than 1 mile	..	..	..	..	..	..	904	64
1 to 2 miles	..	..	..	..	..	..	71	5
2 to 5 miles	..	..	..	..	..	..	119	8
5 to 10 miles	..	..	..	..	..	..	58	4
10 to 20 miles	..	..	..	..	..	..	38	3
20 to 50 miles	..	..	..	..	..	..	25	2
Over 50 miles	..	..	..	..	..	..	107	8
No answer	..	..	..	..	..	..	90	6

Table 14 (relates to Question 4(c)).   **Country of Residence**

Categories						Sample 1,412	Per cent
Outside Great Britain	..	..	..	..	..	204	15
No answer	..	..	..	..	..	1,208	85

Table 15 (relates to Question 5).   **Reason for Visit**

Categories							Sample 1,412	Per cent
Work	..	..	..	..	..	..	1,139	81
Leisure interests	..	..	..	..	..	..	76	5
Both work and leisure interests	..	..	..	..	..	159	11
No answer	..	..	..	..	..	..	38	3

Table 16 (relates to Question 6).   **Method of use of the SML**

Categories	Sample 1,412	Per cent
Consulting items of literature for which specific reference known	793	56
Consulting less precisely known, or unknown, items of literature	163	12
Consulting items in both the above categories	146	10
Searching for literature in a particular field	320	23
Seeking items of information	127	9
Ordering a photocopy	63	5
Using the SML micro-reading equipment	—	—
Using the SML as a place in which to study	291	21
Using the SML for other purposes	57	4
No answer	23	2

Table 17 (relates to Question 7(*a*)).   **Previous search in other libraries**

Categories	Sample 1,412	Per cent
SML not the first library of search	640	45
SML the first library of search	635	45
No answer	137	10

Table 18 (relates to Question 7(*b*)).   **Other libraries previously consulted**

Categories	Sample 640	Per cent
University or college library..	449	70
BML, NLLST, NRLSI, NCL	71	11
Government library	13	2
Library of a research association, professional or learned society, etc.	59	9
Industrial or firm's library	31	5
Public library	73	11
Abroad	7	1
Other	48	8
No answer	6	*

Table 19 (relates to Question 8).   **Ability to read literature in foreign languages**

Categories	Sample 1,412	Per cent
French	817	58
German	636	45
Russian	93	7
Italian	119	8
Spanish	120	8
Polish	26	2
Chinese	15	1
Japanese	12	*
Other	109	8
No answer	400	28

298

Table 20 (relates to Question 9). **Subject fields in which information or literature was sought**
(All readers)

UDC	Subject	Sample 1,412	Per cent
001/09, 413..	Miscellaneous subjects (e.g. bibliography, dictionaries) ..	14	1
02 ..	Librarianship	9	*
1 ..	Philosophy and Psychology	9	*
3 ..	Social sciences	15	1
5 ..	General science	33	2
51 ..	Mathematics	123	9
52/529 ..	Astronomy, including Surveying ..	16	1
53 ..	Physics	241	17
54/548 ..	Chemistry ..	337	24
549, 55/553..	Geology and Geophysics ..	73	5
56 ..	Palaeontology	3	*
57/59 ..	Biology, including Biochemistry ..	162	12
6 ..	General technology..	6	*
61 ..	Medical sciences, public health and safety	50	4
62 ..	Engineering, including Mechanical engineering, Nuclear energy, Electrical engineering, Mining, Civil engineering (with building), Transport engineering, Space science	225	16
63 ..	Agriculture ..	8	*
65 ..	Business management and techniques ..	13	*
66/67 ..	Chemical and allied industries (including Metallurgy) ..	85	6
7 ..	Arts ..	9	*
77 ..	Photography	41	3
91 ..	Geography ..	4	*
92/93 ..	History of science and technology (with Biography) ..	53	4
No answer ...	..	205	15

Table 21 (relates to Question 9). **Subject fields in which information or literature was sought**
(ICST readers)

UDC	Subject	Sample 860	Per cent
001/09, 413..	Miscellaneous subjects (e.g. bibliography, dictionaries) ..	6	*
02	Librarianship	—	—
1	Philosophy and Psychology	6	*
3	Social sciences	6	*
5	General science	26	3
51	Mathematics	73	9
52/529 ..	Astronomy, including Surveying	6	*
53	Physics	181	21
54/548 ..	Chemistry	283	33
549, 55/553..	Geology and Geophysics	40	5
56	Palaeontology	1	*
57/59 ..	Biology, including Biochemistry	48	6
6	General technology..	1	*
61	Medical sciences, public health and safety ..	19	2
62	Engineering, including Mechanical engineering, Nuclear energy, Electrical engineering, Mining, Civil engineering (with building), Transport engineering, Space science	106	12
63	Agriculture	4	*
65	Business management and techniques	6	*
66/67 ..	Chemical and allied industries (including Metallurgy)	45	5
7	Arts	5	*
77	Photography	22	3
91	Geography	—	—
92/93 ..	History of science and technology (with Biography)	12	1
No answer	.. ..	142	17

Table 22 (relates to Question 10). **Methods of search in the SML**

Categories	Sample 1,412	Per cent
Author or subject catalogue consulted	602	43
Other bibliographic tools consulted	205	15
Library staff asked for help	338	24
Shelves only consulted	211	15
No answer	317	22

Table 23 (relates to Question 11). **Results of search in the SML**

Categories	Sample 1,412	Per cent
Wholly successful	731	52
Partially successful	186	13
Unsuccessful	264	19
No answer	231	16

Table 24 (relates to Question 12). **Time spent in the SML on this occasion**

Categories								Sample 1,412	Per cent
Up to 1 hour	..	..	..	..	..	..	..	817	58
1 to 2 hours	..	..	..	..	..	..	..	204	15
2 to 3 hours	..	..	..	..	..	..	..	120	9
Over 3 hours	..	..	..	..	..	..	..	154	11
No answer	..	..	..	..	..	..	..	117	8

QUESTIONNAIRE

SCIENCE MUSEUM LIBRARY SURVEY

1. Please state the type of organisation with which you are associated.
(Tick only ONE alternative)

Science Museum		
British Museum (Natural History) ..		
Institute of Geological Sciences ..		
Victoria and Albert Museum		
Other museum		

Imperial College of Science and Technology		
Other college or institute of London University		
University (excluding London University)		
Other higher academic institution ..		
School		

Industry/commerce		
Civil service/local government		
Nationalised industry		
Research Council		
Research association, professional or learned society, etc.		
Self-employed		
Other (please specify)		

2. What is the nature of your occupation?
(Tick only ONE alternative)

Academic staff of university		
Staff of other higher academic institution		
Staff of school		
Postgraduate student		
Undergraduate student		

302

Any other type of student		
Research/development		
Consultant		
Inventor		
Patent agent or lawyer		
Engineer		
Librarian		
Information officer		
Professional writer		
Translator..		
Retired		
Other (please specify)		

3(a) Do you generally use this library?

Daily		
More than once a week		
About once a week		
1 to 3 times a month		
About once a quarter		
About once a year		
Rarely		

3(b) If you visit this library regularly, how long, *on average*, does each visit last?

Up to 1 hour		
Up to half a day		
Up to one day		
Longer		

4(a) How far have you travelled today to visit this library?

0 to 1 mile	Over 1 to 2 miles	Over 2 to 5 miles	Over 5 to 10 miles	Over 10 to 20 miles	Over 20 to 50 miles	Over 50 miles

303

4(b) How far from this library is:—

Miles	Your normal place of residence in Britain	Your normal place of work
Up to 1 mile		
Over 1 to 2		
Over 2 to 5		
Over 5 to 10		
Over 10 to 20		
Over 20 to 50		
Over 50 miles		

4(c) If you normally live outside Great Britain, please tick here   ..

5. Is the reason for your visit today related

To your work		
To your leisure interests..		
To both your work and leisure interests		

6. In your visit today, do you intend to (More than one category can be ticked)

Consult items of literature for which you have specific references		
Consult less precisely known or unknown items of literature		
Consult items of literature covering BOTH the above categories		
Search for literature in a particular field		
Seek item(s) of information		
Order a photocopy (perhaps after first consulting a literature item)		
Use the library's micro-reading equipment		
Use the library as a place in which to study		
Use the library for other purposes ..		

7(a) Have you tried to obtain what you require in another library before coming to the Science Museum?   ..

Yes ..		
No ..		

304

7(b) If YES, where did you try before?

University or college library		

The British Museum Library   ..   ..
The National Lending Library for
  Science and Technology   ..   ..
The National Reference Library of
  Science and Invention (Patent Office
  Library)..   ..   ..   ..
The National Central Library		

Government library		
Library of a research association, professional or learned society, etc...		
Industrial or firm's library		
Public library		
Abroad		
Other (please specify)		

8. In which foreign languages are you prepared to read literature?

French		
German		
Russian		
Italian		
Spanish		
Polish		
Chinese		
Japanese		
Other (please specify)		

9. Please state the subject field(s), (NOT exceeding three), in which you are seeking information or literature today.

1	
2	
3	

10. In trying to find the publications required, did you

Consult author or subject catalogues ..		
Consult any other bibliographic tools, e.g. abstracts, bibliographies, etc. ..		
Ask the library staff for help		
Look only on the shelves		

305

11. Did you get what you wanted?

Yes	..	..		
No	..	..		
Some of it		..		

12. How long did you spend in the library on this occasion?

Up to 1 hour	..	..	..	..	
Over 1 to 2 hours		..	..	..	
Over 2 to 3 hours		..	..	..	
Over 3 hours	..	..	..	..	

13. Please supply the following information for all publications seriously consulted.

Name of Publication	Author (where appropriate)	Date of Publication

NOTES ON THE IMPLICATIONS OF OPEN ACCESS IN LARGE REFERENCE LIBRARIES BY Mr. E. B. CEADEL, LIBRARIAN, CAMBRIDGE UNIVERSITY LIBRARY

1. Preliminary considerations

No large research library can be wholly open-access. Certain volumes must always be locked away because they are too valuable, rare, fragile, large or small to risk being exposed upon open shelves. (Books that are very large are liable to suffer damage by falling sideways or forwards when adjoining volumes are moved by readers in an open access area, and small volumes are too easily pocketed or misplaced.)

Of the approximately three million volumes in Cambridge University Library, about 40 per cent are on open access, and many of those that are on open access at present are at serious risk. When the extension building now in progress is completed it is likely to be general policy to have the majority of books published in the last hundred years or so on open access, and most earlier books in reserved shelves, which will mean that only about a third of the total book-stock will be on open access. Insofar as it is possible to generalise, it might be said that no more than a third of the book-stock of a large national reference library could be safely placed on open access.

2. Advantages of open access

It is unquestionable that in the average university, professional or technical library there is no substitute for letting readers have browsing contact with the books at the shelves. Even a casual glance at the books on adjoining shelves may have an electrifying effect upon a research worker who suddenly finds a volume that provides a new approach to his subject, or a new source which the inevitably second-hand tools of catalogues and bibliographies have failed to mention. Scientists are known to gain a high proportion of their literature references from conversations with fellow-scientists, whereas in the Humanities the research worker often picks up his most valuable leads from wandering around the shelves of his library.

Open access consultation is also, in the case of a reader fully familiar with the library he is using, by far the most rapid method of working. He can walk to the shelf containing the book he needs in two or three minutes at the most: if he finds that it does not provide the information he expected, he escapes the annoyance that he would have felt had he waited for it to be fetched.

However effective bibliographies and subject-catalogues are, they must very often fail to include books that would be relevant to a researcher's needs, and they equally often quote books which turn out to be irrelevant. For someone taking up a new field of research who wants to find his way in to the material, a day in an open access collection will usually be more beneficial than a fortnight in a completely closed collection where all items have to be fetched to a reading room.

3. The need for an open access collection to be effectively subject-classified

In a library that consists entirely of closed stacks there is no inherent need for a subject-classification scheme, (and in fact subject-classification, except in the broadest sense, is a wasteful luxury in a closed stack library). Provided that each volume is given a distinctive shelf-mark, and that the library's catalogues indicate the volume's shelf-mark to enable it to be fetched to a reading room, it does not in the least matter how the books are arranged in the shelves—by successive date of publication, by size, or by any other simple and rapid method.

But open access can only be effective with an effective subject-classification scheme. The provision of such subject-classification is in itself an expensive undertaking, since the classification of each volume, to be properly carried out, needs not only expert knowledge of each subject-field but also an examination of existing book-stock to

307

ensure consistency with previous practice. In addition, in the case of a large library which combines open and closed stacks, even the reaching of a decision whether a volume should be placed in the open or closed collection is often a time-consuming activity if it is to be done efficiently (and where millions of books are involved, a large library that does not operate efficiently will soon degenerate into chaos). For example, if a large library of this kind is given a book published in 1850, it may take a specialist two or three hours of search of booksellers' catalogues to determine whether it is easily replaceable if placed on open access, or whether it is a rare edition worth £100 which should be kept locked up.

Even though great and expensive effort may be put into subject-classification for an open access library, users of open access libraries are always liable to think that a minutely classified open access library makes a subject-catalogue unnecessary. This is not so. For example, a book on the actors' masks used in the No-drama of Japan would appear in a subject catalogue in three places, under Fine Arts, Drama and Japanese literature, but on the shelves it could appear in only one of these places, and would therefore be missing from two other places where it might reasonably be expected to be found. Books in series, also, are normally kept together, so readers expecting to find them in the appropriate subject-classification will usually be disappointed. For these reasons, a reader relying entirely on subject-classification in an open access library may miss as much as a quarter of the books on his subject.

Subject-classification schemes are liable to become out of date as academic subjects change and their boundaries and terminologies alter. The scheme in use in Cambridge University Library, started in 1900, is now woefully inadequate in some parts: books on computers come under a heading devised for calculating machines. Yet re-classification is prohibitively expensive in man-power. To introduce open access into a national reference library which was not already equipped with good subject-classification would be a Sisyphean undertaking.

One further point may be added. Above a certain size of library, subject-classification tends to lose its effectiveness. One can work one's way through two hundred books on General Economics in a small library, or among two thousand in a larger library: twenty thousand books on General Economics in a big library are liable to be too large an assignment for browsing.

4. Miscellaneous consequences of open access for a library's economy

It is obvious that there are many differences between the way an open access collection and a closed collection are handled and housed. These differences are, however, far more far-reaching than library trustees and architects often realise: some are listed here:—

(a) *Layout.* In a reserved collection the gangways can be narrow and there is no need for windows to give natural light and ventilation as the only users are staff fetching books: indeed, the wastage of gangway spaces can now be almost entirely eliminated by the use of modern mechanically-propelled mobile shelving. There is no need for tables and chairs to be provided in the bookstack, since these are provided in the reading rooms. In an open access collection, however, wide gangways and corridors are inevitable, and natural light and natural ventilation are very desirable to give pleasant working conditions. In addition, tables and chairs among the shelves are certain to be expected by readers. In a large building, the provision of natural light and natural ventilation demands internal courts as well as external fenestration. It would be no exaggeration to say that a properly-planned open access collection would occupy from two and a half times to three times the area of a properly-planned closed collection of the same number of volumes.

(b) *Allowance for expansion.* The above statement makes no allowance for another factor. A closed stack collection which shelves books not by subject but by a simple method such as size or year of publication will accept books on to the shelves at only a limited number of positions and can continue to do so until it is 99·9 per cent full. But an open access collection will need, according to the minuteness of its system of subject-classification, to have five, ten, twenty or even fifty thousand different vacant spaces into which new books may, when received, be correctly placed, according to their subject-classification numbers. When an open access library has become more than 80 per cent full, a large amount of staff time is wasted in moving books to the left or to the right to accommodate new accessions in their correct positions. In order to accommodate a newly acquired hundred-volume set in its right place according to its subject-classification, it may be necessary to move five thousand volumes in adjoining shelves while at the same time maintaining appropriate expansion points between them. The difference between 100 per cent usage of shelves and 80 per cent usage, in terms of capital and maintenance costs in a collection of millions of volumes, is great.

(c) *Binding costs.* It is standard practice, quite rightly, in open access libraries for all volumes to have been bound, to give added protection against heavy or careless use. A closed stack collection can economise greatly in binding, and only such items as are seen to need binding are bound. At a time when most books cost almost £2 to bind, the saving is considerable; there is also the problem of delays in book-binding, owing to the excess of demand over supply. An unbound volume in a closed stack collection can be produced in a supervised reading-room immediately it has been catalogued, whereas a delay of up to a year in waiting for a book to be bound for the open shelves is not uncommon.

(d) *Need to provide for selective retirement to closed access.* No open access book can remain on open access for ever. It may become rare and valuable: its physical condition may deteriorate so much that it needs the protection of closed stacks: alternatively it may become obsolete and therefore may not justify its space on the open shelves. In a small library which is not a reference library the problems are relatively simple. The obsolete books are thrown away and the rare ones picked out and locked up. But in a large reference library the difficulties of selective retirement are considerable, since in a com-bined open-access and closed-access library the only guide in the catalogue to the reader as to whether a book is in an open-access or closed-access area is the shelf-mark (thus in Cambridge University Library the reader soon learns that a book with a shelf-mark starting 220 is on open access, while one with a shelf-marking starting S220 is in the closed stacks). It is therefore inevitable that in a large reference library arranged on open access by a subject-classification scheme, the transfer of each volume to closed shelves means the alteration of its class-mark, with considerable consequential alteration of labels, shelf-lists, catalogue entries and so on. The total labour involved in transferring hundreds of thousands of volumes is enormous.

5. Problems of allowing shelf-access to readers

(a) *Lack of control over book-stock.* In a large reference collection entirely in closed stacks, it is always possible for the staff to maintain absolute control over the contents of the library. Whenever a book is removed from its proper position to be sent to a reading room, or to be repaired in the bindery, or to be consulted by a member of staff, a slip of paper is left as a matter of routine in the gap giving exact details of where the book has been taken. Thus whenever a reader asks for a volume it can be either found in its place in the shelves or its whereabouts can be immediately traced. In an open access library it is hardly possible to compel readers to submit to the discipline of leaving slips behind when they take a volume from the shelves, and readers are free to take volumes to any reading room or open area of the library they please. There is in consequence a constant degree of frustration among readers at finding that books that they wish to see are not to be found on the shelves, even though they call day after day to look for them. The larger the open access collection is, the greater is the problem. The staff can do little to help in such circumstances. The book needed may be accidentally misplaced in the wrong position: it may even be deliberately misplaced by a reader who does not want his continued use of it to be interrupted by someone else finding it in its correct place. In Cambridge University Library there are at any one time thousands of books, many of them in heavy demand, which are virtually unfindable somewhere on the premises. This would probably not be a satisfactory state of affairs in a national reference library.

(b) *The need for regular shelf-checks.* In a closed stack library it can be assumed that as all books are handled by trained staff, they will always be correctly placed in their right positions on the shelves. In an open access library where readers handle the books the disorder of the books on the shelves steadily increases: in a large open access library where the subject-classification scheme is minute and in consequence more complicated, the disorder grows more rapidly. The only way of dealing with this is to close the library to the public for a week or a fortnight each year, and in that time to turn most of the staff on to checking the shelf-order. Although the use of open access means a reduction in the number of staff used for book-fetching, the saving is to a certain degree offset by the time taken in putting the books back in order.

(c) *Dangers of mutilation and theft.* In a closed stack library where material is supplied to readers in reading rooms affording close invigilation, there is little chance of mutilation or theft. In a large open access collection, without invigilation, the most serious mutilations and thefts can and do take place. A major national research library presumably has the duty of preserving important research material in as perfect a condition as possible. However close may be the check upon the credentials of those admitted to a library, most serious damage is sometimes done by readers who would be expected to be beyond reproach. The danger of mutilation or theft naturally increases in proportion to the rarity of the material consulted.

(d) *The implied relationship between open access and borrowing.* A reader who has a volume issued to him in a reading room after having signed an order for it and then sits studying it under the eye of an invigilator has little chance of thinking that he has any claim upon it. A reader who can take a book freely out of open access shelves and can use it freely day after day in the library is liable to feel that he has certain rights over it—such as the right of borrowing it for home use. In most libraries open access and the right of borrowing for home reading are linked almost automatically. Cambridge University Library grants borrowing rights to senior members of the University, and consequently there is no particular difficulty in respect of this matter for the majority of users. There is evidence, however, to suggest that many of our mutilations and thefts are due to categories of readers who are allowed into the library but are forbidden to borrow. It may be added, of course, that the fact that borrowing, as well as open access, is permitted at Cambridge makes it difficult to maintain the library as an effective reference library. There is a constant tug of war between irreconcilable interests, the interests of those who come here and expect to find every single item in place on the shelves and the interests of those who wish to borrow items for their use in their studies or laboratories. If anything can be said confidently, it is that it is absolutely impossible to run a really efficient large reference library consisting of only one copy of each book unless all the books are at all times under the complete control of the library staff.

6. **Applicability of the above comments to the use of open access in national reference libraries**

Two assumptions may perhaps be made, firstly, that university staff and professional people in general will only go to a national reference library for special and rare

310

material not contained in local university or professional libraries normally available to them, and, secondly, that a national reference library will only think it proper to put on open access material that is not special and rare. If these assumptions are correct, there is little to be gained from providing such open access facilities.

Another assumption that may reasonably be made is that most university and professional people will have done their preliminary browsing in their normal libraries and will have come to a national reference library to track down specific items not available in their normal libraries. If this is so, there is no call for an open access " browsing " approach, since only named works will be needed.

A further consideration is that an open access collection of any size has to be used fairly frequently by a reader before its layout and contents are easily understood. It may be doubted whether the open access area of a national reference library would be used regularly by a sufficient number of persons to make the open access system an attraction to them.

A final point worth considering is the difference in the function of a shelf-mark, depending on whether a large library consists of entirely closed stacks or of mixed open access and closed stack. In the former case the reader has no decision to take. He merely copies the shelf-mark from the catalogue, hands it in at the reading room desk, and waits for the volume to arrive. In a mixed library, the reader, after copying the shelf-mark, has then to reach a decision on whether the volume is on open access or not. He reaches this decision by consulting a finding list on which all possible shelf-marks are listed, together with an indication of whether they are on open access or not, and, if they are, where in the library they may be found. Unless the list of shelf-marks is clear and simple, the reader is involved in difficulties and complications. Such difficulties and complications diminish with experience of the building, but it is doubtful whether infrequent visitors to a national reference library would benefit from such arrangements.

7. Conclusion

Many people assume that the time spent in fetching books to the reading room of a very large closed-stack library inevitably involves a wait of an hour or more, and it is thought that a quicker service is impossible. This is not necessarily so. With adequate staffing (this is essential—libraries are too often under-staffed) and efficient organisation any book should normally be fetched in fifteen minutes or less. In Cambridge University Library the time spent in fetching any of the million and a half books in the closed stacks is normally well under ten minutes, and after the completion of our extension building in which the relative positions of the bookstacks and the reading rooms have been carefully planned, the time should be much less than five minutes.

There may be a case for permitting limited access to closed-stack areas for specially approved persons, either alone or escorted by a member of staff. This may be particularly time-saving both for the staff and the reader if, for example, it is desired to check a series of references in a succession of volumes of a periodical.

NOTES ON COSTINGS

A. Accommodation Costs

In Chapters 11, 12, 14 and 18 reference is made to the necessity of including realistic assessments of the costs of accommodation in costing library services. With few exceptions, the present methods of accounting for building costs for the national libraries do not reflect current market values. Attempts have, therefore, been made to arrive at more realistic figures for annual costs which would cover land charges, first cost and amortisation of buildings, maintenance, rates, heating and similar recurrent expenditure. Inevitably, it is not possible to be exact, partly because judgement is involved, but also because the estimates depend on interest rates and market variables. Except where otherwise stated, the figures quoted below are based on professional valuations for purpose-built library accommodation. In all cases they should be regarded as the minimum costs, as the lowest figure has been taken where the estimate covered a range of values.

Central London (including Bloomsbury, Holborn and Aldwych)
Accommodation for books, readers and comprehensive
services, including inter-library lending .. .. £5 per sq. ft. per year

South Kensington
Accommodation for books, readers and library services £4 per sq. ft. per year

Colindale
Accommodation mainly for book storage; some reader
accommodation and library services .. .. £2 per sq. ft. per year

Bayswater*
Accommodation for books, readers and library services £1·5 per sq. ft. per year

Woolwich
Storage only .. .. £1·25 per sq. ft. per year

Boston Spa
Accommodation mainly for storage, photo-copying and
despatch services; some reader accommodation .. £1·1 per sq. ft. per year

* The estimate for the Bayswater accommodation is based on current rental, plus an allowance for rates and conversion costs. This figure almost certainly under-estimates the cost of a specially constructed building for similar purposes.

B. Book Storage Costs

The cost of storing publications is a function of the cost of the accommodation and the method of stacking. For open access, it is artificial to separate book storage area from readers' accommodation and this will not, therefore, be attempted. In libraries like the BML where most of the books are stored separately from the reading rooms, there are two main methods of book storage:

    (i) conventional book stacks or presses; and
    (ii) high-density compact storage.

In both cases, the number of items accommodated per unit area of flooring obviously varies with the number of shelves in the stack, the average size of the books, the fraction of floor area not occupied by the stacks, and the proportion of stack area not occupied by books. A commonly achieved storage density for conventional closed stacks is 14 to 17 books per sq. ft. of floor. In the case of compact storage a substantial increase in density of storage is possible; an approximate figure for comparison would be 22 to 27 books per sq. ft. of floor.

If the cost of the shelving is neglected as being slight in comparison with building and related expenditure, the cost of book storage in central London is between 6s.

and 7s. per volume per year if conventional stacking is employed, whilst the corresponding figures for compact storage are between 3s. 9d. and 4s. 6d.

In the existing national libraries, including the new NCL building in Store Street, virtually all storage is in conventional stacks. However, the closed access book store in the new SML will have compact storage shelving, and the Trustees' plans for a new building to replace the existing BML provide for compact storage ultimately to replace an initial installation of conventional book presses.

In Chapter 12, paragraph 321, the figure of 5s. per year is quoted for the cost of storing one volume in central London. This is derived by assuming a storage density of 20 volumes per sq. ft., the mean of the values for conventional and compact storage quoted above. Storage costs in other locations would be approximately in the ratio of the accommodation costs listed in Section A above. Also in paragraph 321, it is suggested that outhousing even a small proportion of the book-stock would result in substantial savings. This can be shown as follows:

Total book storage for new building to replace existing
    BML (Appendix 6 to the Trustees' evidence) ..   ..   650,000 sq. ft.
Cost of accommodation in central London   ..   ..   £5 per sq. ft. per year
Cost of accommodation on low-cost site (e.g. Boston Spa)   £1·1 per sq. ft. per year

Thus potential saving per unit area per annum in providing storage on a low cost site, rather than in central London, is £3·9.

If the effects of scale are neglected, each per cent of the total required storage area which is provided on a low cost site gives rise to a potential annually recurrent saving of about £25,000.

C. Costs of Lending

I. The National Lending Library for Science and Technology

1. Direct costs of lending and photocopying

The total direct expenditure for 1967/1968, less receipts, was £458,186, excluding receipts and expenditure on translation services. (See NLLST evidence.)

As 536,132 issues were made by NLLST during the same period, the direct costs per issue amounted to about £0·85.

2. Accommodation

New buildings at Boston Spa constructed to serve a similar function as the existing structures would have a nominal rent of about £0·85 per sq. ft. With rates, heating, light, etc., accommodation costs would total about £1·1 per sq. ft. per year.

Since NLLST occupies about 150,000 sq. ft. (NLLST evidence), the annual cost of accommodation would total £165,000, equivalent to a cost per issue lof £0·3.

3. Total cost of the service

The direct and accommodation costs together total £623,000, equivalent to a total cost per issue of £1·15.

II. The National Central Library

1. Direct Costs

The major part, amounting to £110,000,* of the NCL's direct costs, is associated with its lending services and can be divided into costs incurred in (i) lending from its central stock (21,000 loans in year 1967/1968) and (ii) operating the inter-library loan locating service (78,000 loans in 1967/1968). Although the following apportionments are of necessity approximations, they have been made with care and after consultation with the staff of the NCL.

313

NCL Total Expenditure* £					Central Stock £	Inter-Library Lending £
	Salary Costs					
12,600	Acquisitions	..	..	..	9,000	3,600
4,000	Loans from stock ..	..	..	..	4,000	—
33,900	Inter-library loans..	..	..	..	—	33,900
9,000	Bibliographic work	..	..	..	1,000	8,000
12,900	Union catalogues ..	..	..	..	1,300	11,600
2,400	Research ..	..	..	..	500	1,900
21,000	General Administration	..	..	..	2,600	18,400
95,800					18,400	77,400
	Other Direct Costs					
300	Library van ..	..	..		—	300
9,800	Book fund—general loan stock ..		..		9,800	—
2,700	reference books		..		500	2,200
1,200	binding	..	..	..	1,000	200
14,000					11,300	2,700
109,800	TOTAL DIRECT COSTS ..		..	..	29,700	80,100
	Direct costs per unit loan		..	..	£1·42	£1·03

* In certain cases, the figures used in the calculations differ slightly from those quoted in the NCL evidence, because allowance has been made for the library's services which are not directly associated with its lending activities.

2. *Accommodation*

Working area

From the plans of the Store Street building, the total floor area of about 60,000 sq. ft. is divided amost equally between book store and other accommodation. The 30,000 sq. ft. which are not used for book storage are largely working space associated with the NCL's lending functions. For costing purposes, this has been apportioned between central stock lending and inter-library lending in the ratio of the respective salary costs, i.e. 18 : 77.

The small space occupied by BUCOP has been neglected.

	Central Stock £	Inter-Library Lending £
Working area—30,000 sq. ft., £5 per sq. ft.	28,000	122,000

Book storage

At present there are about 30,000 sq. ft. of book storage space in Store Street of which about 18,000 sq. ft. are occupied. However, a further 9,000 sq. ft. at Woolwich is occupied by books. For costing purposes, it is realistic to provide for some unoccupied space, as adequate accommodation has to be secured and paid for in advance of requirements. The whole of the NCL's present stock could be accommodated in the existing Store Street premises, but there would be scarcely any space remaining for future acquisitions. For costing calculations, therefore, it has been assumed that the NCL requires the Store Street bookstore, plus the area at Woolwich currently occupied. This probably underestimates the reserve required for future expansion and, in fact, the NCL already has available unoccupied storage at Woolwich.

Storage area

	Central Stock	Inter-Library Lending
	£	£
30,000 sq. ft. in Store Street, £5 per sq. ft. ..	150,000	—
9,000 sq. ft. in Woolwich, £1·25 per sq. ft.	11,000	—
TOTAL ACCOMMODATION COSTS	189,000	122,000
Accommodation costs per unit loan ..	£9·00	£1·57

3. *Total costs of services*

	Central Stock	Inter-Library Lending
DIRECT AND ACCOMMODATION COSTS TOGETHER	219,000	202,000
These are equivalent to the following total costs per unit loan	£10·42	£2·59

4. *Changes in costs which could result from cheaper accommodation*

If the NCL's direct loan service from stock were located at Boston Spa, the costs of comparable accommodation there would be:

Working area—£1·1 per sq. ft.	£6,200
Book storage—£1·1 per sq. ft.	£42,900
	£49,100

Assuming no change in direct costs of £29,700	
the total cost of the service would be about	£79,000
and the cost per unit loan would be	£3·76

Similarly, if the NCL's inter-library loan locating service were also at Boston Spa, accommodation for this would be:

Working area—£1·1 per sq. ft.	£26,800
Assuming no change in direct costs of £80,100	
the total cost of the service would be about	£107,000
and the cost per unit loan would be	£1·37

It would, therefore, appear that if NCL's lending services were operating at Boston Spa the annual costs would be £186,000 annually, compared with present £421,000. In theory, therefore, savings of £235,000 per year could be made by transferring the NCL from London to a low cost site. However, savings of this magnitude are unlikely to be realised because the Store Street premises, designed specifically for the NCL's activities, would have to be employed for other purposes. In particular, the full theoretical saving may not be achieved if other services of the National Libraries Authority were accommodated there, because:

(i) it would be unlikely that Store Street would be the exact size for a self-contained unit and, hence, some wastage would be inevitable;

(ii) it would be unlikely for the existing accommodation to be ideal without some conversion;

(iii) if comparable accommodation were provided as part of a much larger unit (e.g. a new National Reference Library) it might be cheaper to provide.

INDEX

INDEX

Printed in Great Britain under the authority of HER MAJESTY'S STATIONERY OFFICE
By HARRISON AND SONS, LTD., London.

(SO 9/1887) Dd. 136647 K24 5/69 H & S Ltd. Gp. 3336/1 SBN.